DEPARTMENT OF PUBLIC INFORMATION

# BASIC FACTS

## ABOUT THE UNITED NATIONS

**UNITED NATIONS**
New York, 2000

Published by the News and Media Division
United Nation Department of Public Information
New York, NY 10017
www.un.org

Note: Data current as of December 2000, unless otherwise stated

ISBN: 92-1-100850-6
United Nations Publication
Sales No. E.00.I.21

# CONTENTS

## Chapter 5: Humanitarian Action      245

## Chapter 6: International Law      259

## PART THREE

## *APPENDICES*

## *BOXES*

## CHARTS AND MAPS

# UNITED NATIONS WEB SITES

United Nations: www.un.org

United Nations system: www.unsystem.org

## United Nations Programmes and Offices:

United Nations Development Programme (UNDP): www.undp.org

United Nations Volunteers (UNV): www.unv.org

United Nations Conference on Trade and Development (UNCTAD): www.unctad.org

United Nations Environment Programme (UNEP): www.unep.org

United Nations Human Settlements Programme (UN-Habitat): www.unhsp.org

United Nations International Research and Training Institute for the Advancement of Women (INSTRAW): www.un-instraw.org

United Nations Childrenís Fund (UNICEF): www.unicef.org

World Food Programme (WFP): www.wfp.org

United Nations Population Fund (UNFPA): www.unfpa.org

United Nations International Drug Control Programme (UNDCP): www.undcp.org

United Nations High Commissioner for Human Rights: www.unhchr.ch

United Nations High Commissioner for Refugees (UNHCR): www.unhcr.ch

United Nations Relief and Works Agency for Palestine Refugees (UNRWA): www.unrwa.org

United Nations University (UNU): www.unu.edu

United Nations Institute for Training and Research (UNITAR): www.unitar.org

United Nations Research Institute for Social Development (UNRISD): www.unrisd.org

Joint United Nations Programme on HIV/AIDS: www.unaids.org

## United Nations Regional Commissions

Economic Commission for Africa (ECA): www.uneca.org

Economic Commission for Europe (ECE): www.unece.org

Economic Commission for Latin America and the Caribbean (ECLAC): www.eclac.org

Economic Commission for Asia and the Pacific (ESCAP): www.unescap.org

Economic Commission for Western Asia (ESCWA): www.escwa.org.lb

**United Nations Specialized Agencies:**

International Labour Organization (ILO): www.ilo.org

Food and Agriculture Organization of the United Nations (FAO): www.fao.org.

United Nations Educational, Scientific and Cultural Organization (UNESCO): www.unesco.org

World Health Organization (WHO): www.who.int

World Bank: www.worldbank.org

International Monetary Fund (IMF): www.imf.org

International Civil Aviation Organization (ICAO): www.icao.org

Universal Postal Union (UPU): www.upu.int

International Telecommunication Union (ITU): www.itu.int

World Meteorological Organization (WMO): www.wmo.ch

International Maritime Organization (IMO): www.imo.org

World Intellectual Property Organization (WIPO): www.wipo.int

International Fund for Agricultural Development (IFAD): www.ifad.org

United Nations Industrial Development Organization (UNIDO): www.unido.org

International Atomic Energy Agency (IAEA): www.iaea.org

# LIST OF ACRONYMS

| | |
|---|---|
| DDA | Department of Disarmament Affairs |
| DESA | Department of Economic and Social Affairs |
| DPA | Department of Political Affairs |
| DPI | Department of Public Information |
| ECA | Economic Commission for Africa |
| ECE | Economic Commission for Europe |
| ECLAC | Economic Commission for Latin America and the Caribbean |
| ECOSOC | Economic and Social Council |
| ESCAP | Economic and Social Commission for Asia and the Pacific |
| ESCWA | Economic and Social Commission for Western Asia |
| FAO | Food and Agriculture Organization of the United Nations |
| IAEA | International Atomic Energy Agency |
| IBRD | International Bank for Reconstruction and Development (World Bank) |
| ICAO | International Civil Aviation Organization |
| ICJ | International Court of Justice |
| ICRC | International Committee of the Red Cross |
| IDA | International Development Association (World Bank) |
| IFAD | International Fund for Agricultural Development |
| IFC | International Finance Corporation (World Bank) |
| ILO | International Labour Organization |
| IMF | International Monetary Fund |
| IMO | International Maritime Organization |
| INSTRAW | International Research and Training Institute for the Advancement of Women |
| ITC | International Trade Centre UNCTAD/WTO |
| ITU | International Telecommunication Union |
| MIGA | Multilateral Investment Guarantee Agency (World Bank) |
| NGOs | Non-governmental organizations |
| OCHA | Office for the Coordination of Humanitarian Affairs |
| ODC | Office on Drugs and Crime |
| OHCHR | Office of the United Nations High Commissioner for Human Rights |
| OLA | Office of Legal Affairs |
| UNCTAD | United Nations Conference on Trade and Development |
| UNDCP | United Nations International Drug Control Programme |

| UNDP | United Nations Development Programme |
| UNEP | United Nations Environment Programme |
| UNESCO | United Nations Educational, Scientific and Cultural Organization |
| UNFPA | United Nations Population Fund |
| UNHCR | Office of the United Nations High Commissioner for Refugees |
| UNHSP (UN-Habitat) | United Nations Human Settlements Programme |
| UNICEF | United Nations Children's Fund |
| UNICRI | United Nations Interregional Crime and Justice Research Institute |
| UNIDIR | United Nations Institute for Disarmament Research |
| UNIDO | United Nations Industrial Development Organization |
| UNIFEM | United Nations Development Fund for Women |
| UNITAR | United Nations Institute for Training and Research |
| UNRISD | United Nations Research Institute for Social Development |
| UNRWA | United Nations Relief and Works Agency for Palestine Refugees in the Near East |
| UNU | United Nations University |
| UNV | United Nations Volunteers |
| UPU | Universal Postal Union |
| WFP | World Food Programme |
| WHO | World Health Organization |
| WIPO | World Intellectual Property Organization |
| WMO | World Meteorological Organization |
| WTO | World Trade Organization |

# FOREWORD

With the dawn of a new century, the United Nations continues to undergo profound changes, reflecting the momentous transitions and changes of our era.

Globalization is transforming the world. While it brings great benefits to some countries and individuals — faster growth, higher living standards, new opportunities — a backlash has arisen because these benefits are distributed so unequally and because the global market is not yet underpinned by values and rules that address key social concerns such as the protection of human rights, labour standards and the environment. Globalization has also, unwittingly, made it easier for what I have called "uncivil society" — crime, disease, terrorism, drug- and arms-trafficking — to move across borders. Our challenge today is to make globalization an engine that lifts people out of hardship and misery, not a force that holds them down.

The past half century has brought unprecedented economic gains. Most people today can expect to live longer than their parents. They are better nourished, enjoy better health, are better educated, and on the whole face more favourable economic prospects. But there is also widespread deprivation and despair. More than 1 billion people must survive on less than $1 a day. Striking inequality persists within and among countries. Diseases such as AIDS and malaria threaten to undo years of progress. Worsening the poverty gap is the "digital divide" between the technology-rich and the technology-poor. At a time when information and knowledge have become the main source of wealth and power, half the developing world's people have never made or received a telephone call, much less used a computer. Bringing these people into the mainstream is one of our biggest projects. In my Millennium Report, *We the Peoples,* I announced several major initiatives aimed at harnessing the potential of information technology to the quest for development.

Poverty and inequality are fertile ground for conflict. Wars between states have become less frequent, but in the last decade brutal internal wars have claimed more than 5 million lives, and driven many times that number of people from their homes. Weapons of mass destruction continue to cast their shadow of fear. We must think of security less as defending territory, and more in terms of protecting people. And whether we are talking of conflict prevention, peacekeeping, post-conflict peace-building or other peacemaking tools at the disposal of the international community, we must be sure that when the United Nations is called upon to act, it is given the mandate and resources to do the job.

The United Nations has no independent military capability, and very modest funds. Its influence derives from the force of the values it represents, its role in helping to set and sustain global norms and international law, its ability to stimulate global concern and action, and the trust inspired by its practical work on the ground to improve people's lives. The effectiveness of the United Nations in all of these endeavours depends on partnerships: among governments, civil society groups and the private sector, and most of all among people, reaching across the lines that might otherwise divide. It relies on high-level political support, such as that voiced in September 2000 at the Millennium Summit, the largest gathering of world leaders in history. And it depends on informed public opinion. I hope this new edition of *Basic Facts about the United Nations* will help promote understanding about the United Nations and its presence in people's lives.

Kofi A. Annan
Secretary-General

# PART ONE

## Chapter 1

**The United Nations: Organization**

# THE UNITED NATIONS: ORGANIZATION

The name "United Nations", coined by United States President Franklin D. Roosevelt, was first used in the "Declaration by United Nations" of 1 January 1942, during the Second World War, when representatives of 26 nations pledged their governments to continue fighting together against the Axis Powers.

States first established international organizations to cooperate on specific matters. The International Telecommunication Union was founded in 1865 as the International Telegraph Union, and the Universal Postal Union was established in 1874. Both are now United Nations specialized agencies.

In 1899, the first International Peace Conference was held in The Hague to elaborate instruments for settling crises peacefully, preventing wars and codifying rules of warfare. It adopted the Convention for the Pacific Settlement of International Disputes and established the Permanent Court of Arbitration, which began work in 1902.

The forerunner of the United Nations was the League of Nations, an organization conceived in similar circumstances during the First World War, and established in 1919 under the Treaty of Versailles "to promote international cooperation and to achieve peace and security." The International Labour Organization was also created under the Treaty of Versailles as an affiliated agency of the League. The League of Nations ceased its activities after failing to prevent the Second World War.

In 1945, representatives of 50 countries met in San Francisco at the United Nations Conference on International Organization to draw up the United Nations Charter. Those delegates deliberated on the basis of proposals worked out by the representatives of China, the Soviet Union, the United Kingdom and the United States at Dumbarton Oaks, United States, in August-October 1944. The Charter was signed on 26 June 1945 by the representatives of the 50 countries. Poland, which was not represented at the Conference, signed it later and became one of the original 51 Member States.

The United Nations officially came into existence on 24 October 1945, when the Charter had been ratified by China, France, the Soviet Union, the United Kingdom, the United States and a majority of other signatories. **United Nations Day** is celebrated on 24 October each year.

# United Nations Charter

The Charter is the constituting instrument of the Organization, setting out the rights and obligations of Member States, and establishing the United Nations organs and procedures. An international treaty, the Charter codifies the major principles of international relations — from the sovereign equality of States to the prohibition of the use of force in international relations.

## Preamble to the Charter

The Preamble to the Charter expresses the ideals and common aims of all the peoples whose governments joined together to form the United Nations:

> "WE THE PEOPLES OF THE UNITED NATIONS DETERMINED to save succeeding generations from the scourge of war, which twice in our lifetime has brought untold sorrow to mankind, and to reaffirm faith in fundamental human rights, in the dignity and worth of the human person, in the equal rights of men and women and of nations large and small, and to establish conditions under which justice and respect for the obligations arising from treaties and other sources of international law can be maintained, and to promote social progress and better standards of life in larger freedom,
>
> "AND FOR THESE ENDS to practice tolerance and live together in peace with one another as good neighbours, and to unite our strength to maintain international peace and security, and to ensure, by the acceptance of principles and the institution of methods, that armed force shall not be used, save in the common interest, and to employ international machinery for the promotion of the economic and social advancement of all peoples,
>
> "HAVE RESOLVED TO COMBINE OUR EFFORTS TO ACCOMPLISH THESE AIMS. Accordingly, our respective Governments, through representatives assembled in the city of San Francisco, who have exhibited their full powers found to be in good and due form, have agreed to the present Charter of the United Nations and do hereby establish an international organization to be known as the United Nations."

## Purposes and principles

The **purposes** of the United Nations, as set forth in the Charter, are:

- to maintain international peace and security;
- to develop friendly relations among nations based on respect for the principle of equal rights and self-determination of peoples;

## Amendments to the United Nations Charter

The Charter may be amended by a vote of two thirds of the Members of the General Assembly and ratification by two thirds of the Members of the United Nations, including the five permanent members of the Security Council. So far, four Charter Articles have been amended, one of them twice:

- in 1965, the membership of the Security Council was increased from 11 to 15 (Article 23) and the number of affirmative votes needed for a decision was increased from seven to nine, including the concurring vote of the five permanent members for all matters of substance rather than procedure (Article 27);
- in 1965, the membership of the Economic and Social Council was increased from 18 to 27, and in 1973, was increased to 54 (Article 61);
- in 1968, the number of votes required in the Security Council to convene a General Conference to review the Charter was increased from seven to nine (Article 109).

- to cooperate in solving international economic, social, cultural and humanitarian problems and in promoting respect for human rights and fundamental freedoms;
- to be a centre for harmonizing the actions of nations in attaining these common ends.

The United Nations acts in accordance with the following *principles:*

- it is based on the sovereign equality of all its Members;
- all Members are to fulfil in good faith their Charter obligations;
- they are to settle their international disputes by peaceful means and without endangering international peace and security, and justice;
- they are to refrain from the threat or use of force against any other state;
- they are to give the United Nations every assistance in any action it takes in accordance with the Charter;
- nothing in the Charter is to authorize the United Nations to intervene in matters which are essentially within the domestic jurisdiction of any state.

## Membership

Membership of the United Nations is open to all peace-loving nations which accept the obligations of the Charter and are willing and able to carry out these obligations *(for list of Member States, see page 289).*

The General Assembly admits new Member States on the recommendation of the Security Council. The Charter provides for the suspension or expulsion of a Member for violation of the principles of the Charter, but no such action has ever been taken.

## Official languages

Under the Charter, the official languages of the United Nations are Chinese, English, French, Russian and Spanish. Arabic has been added as an official language of the General Assembly, the Security Council and the Economic and Social Council.

# Structure of the Organization

The Charter established six principal organs of the United Nations, which are the: General Assembly, Security Council, Economic and Social Council, Trusteeship Council, International Court of Justice and Secretariat. The United Nations family, however, is much larger, encompassing 15 agencies and several programmes and bodies (*see page 36, and the chart on pages 22-23*).

## General Assembly

The General Assembly is the main deliberative organ. It is composed of representatives of all Member States, each of which has one vote. Decisions on important questions, such as those on peace and security, admission of new Members and budgetary matters, require a two-thirds majority. Decisions on other questions are by simple majority.

### Functions and powers

Under the Charter, the functions and powers of the General Assembly include:

- to consider and make recommendations on the principles of cooperation in the maintenance of international peace and security, including the principles governing disarmament and arms regulation;
- to discuss any question relating to international peace and security and, except where a dispute or situation is being discussed by the Security Council, to make recommendations on it;[1]
- to discuss and, with the same exception, make recommendations on any question within the scope of the Charter or affecting the powers and functions of any organ of the United Nations;

---

[1] Under the "Uniting for peace" resolution adopted by the General Assembly in November 1950, the Assembly may take action if the Security Council, because of lack of unanimity of its permanent members, fails to act where there appears to be a threat to international peace, breach of the peace or act of aggression. The Assembly is empowered to consider the matter immediately with a view to making recommendations to Members for collective measures, including, in case of a breach of the peace or act of aggression, the use of armed forces when necessary to maintain or restore international peace and security.

- to initiate studies and make recommendations to promote international political cooperation, the development and codification of international law, the realization of human rights and fundamental freedoms for all, and international collaboration in economic, social, cultural, educational and health fields;
- to make recommendations for the peaceful settlement of any situation, regardless of origin, which might impair friendly relations among nations;
- to receive and consider reports from the Security Council and other United Nations organs;
- to consider and approve the United Nations budget and to apportion the contributions among Members;
- to elect the non-permanent members of the Security Council, the members of the Economic and Social Council and those members of the Trusteeship Council that are elected; to elect jointly with the Security Council the Judges of the International Court of Justice; and, on the recommendation of the Security Council, to appoint the Secretary-General.

## Sessions

The General Assembly's regular session usually begins each year in September. The 2000-2001 session, for example, is the fifty-fifth regular session of the General Assembly. At the start of each regular session, the Assembly elects a new President, 21 Vice-Presidents and the Chairpersons of the Assembly's six Main Committees. To ensure equitable geographical representation, the presidency of the Assembly rotates each year among five groups of states: African, Asian, Eastern European, Latin American and the Caribbean, and Western European and other states.

In addition, the Assembly may meet in special sessions at the request of the Security Council, of a majority of Member States, or of one Member if the majority of Members concur. Emergency special sessions may be called within 24 hours of a request by the Security Council on the vote of any nine Council members, or by a majority of the United Nations Members, or by one Member if the majority of Members concur.

At the beginning of each regular session, the Assembly holds a general debate, often addressed by heads of state and government, in which Member States express their views on the most pressing international issues. Most questions are then discussed in its six Main Committees:

- **First Committee** (Disarmament and International Security);
- **Second Committee** (Economic and Financial);
- **Third Committee** (Social, Humanitarian and Cultural);
- **Fourth Committee** (Special Political and Decolonization);
- **Fifth Committee** (Administrative and Budgetary);
- **Sixth Committee** (Legal).

Some issues are considered only in plenary meetings, rather than in one of the Main Committees. All issues are voted on through resolutions passed in plenary meetings, usually towards the end of the regular session, after the committees have completed their consideration of them and submitted draft resolutions to the plenary Assembly.

Voting in committees is by a simple majority. In plenary meetings, resolutions may be adopted by acclamation, without objection or without a vote, or the vote may be recorded or taken by roll-call.

While the decisions of the Assembly have no legally binding force for governments, they carry the weight of world opinion, as well as the moral authority of the world community.

The work of the United Nations year-round derives largely from the decisions of the General Assembly — that is to say, the will of the majority of the Members as expressed in resolutions adopted by the Assembly. That work is carried out:
- by committees and other bodies established by the Assembly to study and report on specific issues, such as disarmament, peace-keeping, development and human rights;
- in international conferences called for by the Assembly; and
- by the Secretariat of the United Nations — the Secretary-General and his staff of international civil servants.

## Security Council

The Security Council has primary responsibility, under the Charter, for the maintenance of international peace and security.

The Council has 15 members: 5 permanent members — China, France, the Russian Federation, the United Kingdom and the United States — and 10 elected by the General Assembly for two-year terms.

Each member has one vote. Decisions on procedural matters are made by an affirmative vote of at least 9 of the 15 members. Decisions on substantive matters require nine votes, including the concurring votes of all five permanent members. This is the rule of "great Power unanimity", often referred to as the "veto" power. If a permanent member does not agree with a decision, it can cast a negative vote, and this act has power of veto. All five permanent members have exercised the right of veto at one time or another. If a permanent member does not fully agree with a decision but does not wish to cast its veto, it may abstain.

Under the Charter, all Members of the United Nations agree to accept and carry out the decisions of the Security Council. While other organs of the United Nations make recommendations to governments, the Council alone has the power to take decisions which Member States are obligated under the Charter to carry out.

## Functions and powers

Under the Charter, the functions and powers of the Security Council are:

- to maintain international peace and security in accordance with the principles and purposes of the United Nations;
- to investigate any dispute or situation which might lead to international friction;
- to recommend methods of adjusting such disputes or the terms of settlement;
- to formulate plans for establishing a system to regulate armaments;
- to determine the existence of a threat to the peace or act of aggression and to recommend what action should be taken;
- to call on Members to apply economic sanctions and other measures not involving the use of force to prevent or stop aggression;
- to take military action against an aggressor;
- to recommend the admission of new Members;
- to exercise the trusteeship functions of the United Nations in "strategic areas";
- to recommend to the General Assembly the appointment of the Secretary-General and, together with the Assembly, to elect the Judges of the International Court of Justice.

The Security Council is so organized as to be able to function continuously, and a representative of each of its members must be present at all times at United Nations Headquarters. The Council may meet elsewhere: in 1972, it held a session in Addis Ababa, Ethiopia; in 1973 it met in Panama City, Panama; and in 1990 it meet in Geneva, Switzerland.

When a complaint concerning a threat to peace is brought before it, the Council's first action is usually to recommend that the parties try to reach agreement by peaceful means. The Council may set forth principles for a peaceful settlement. In some cases, the Council itself undertakes investigation and mediation. It may dispatch a mission, appoint special representatives or request the Secretary-General to use his good offices.

When a dispute leads to fighting, the Council's first concern is to bring it to an end as soon as possible. The Council may issue ceasefire directives that can be instrumental in preventing wider hostilities.

The Council may also dispatch military observers or a peacekeeping force to help reduce tensions, keep opposing forces apart and create conditions of calm in which peaceful settlements may be sought. Under Chapter VII of the Charter, the Council may decide on enforcement measures, including economic sanctions (such as trade embargoes), arms embargoes or collective military action (*see Chapter 2*).

The Council has established two International Criminal Tribunals to prosecute crimes against humanity in the former Yugoslavia and in Rwanda (*see page 35*). The Tribunals are subsidiary organs of the Council.

After the Gulf war, to verify the elimination of Iraq's weapons of mass destruction, the Council established the United Nations Special Commission (UNSCOM). Its responsibilities have been taken over by the United Nations Monitoring, Verification and Inspection Commission (UNMOVIC), which the Council established in 2000 (*see Chapter 2, page101*).

A working group of the General Assembly has been considering Council reform since 1993, including equitable representation and expansion of membership.

## Economic and Social Council

The Charter established the Economic and Social Council as the principal organ to coordinate the economic, social, and related work of the United Nations and the specialized agencies and institutions — known as the United Nations family of organizations (*see page 49*). The Council has 54 members, who serve for three-year terms. Voting in the Council is by simple majority; each member has one vote.

### Functions and powers

The functions and powers of the Economic and Social Council are:

- to serve as the central forum for discussing international economic and social issues, and for formulating policy recommendations addressed to Member States and the United Nations system;

- to make or initiate studies and reports and make recommendations on international economic, social, cultural, educational, health and related matters;
- to promote respect for, and observance of, human rights and fundamental freedoms;
- to assist in preparing and organizing major international conferences in the economic, social and related fields and promote a coordinated follow-up to these conferences;
- to coordinate the activities of the specialized agencies, through consultations with and recommendations to them, and through recommendations to the General Assembly.

Through its discussion of international economic and social issues and its policy recommendations, ECOSOC plays a key role in fostering international cooperation for development and in setting the priorities for action.

## Sessions

The Council generally holds several short sessions throughout the year to deal with the organization of its work, as well as one four-week substantive session in July, alternating between New York and Geneva. The session includes a high-level segment, attended by Ministers and other high officials, to discuss major economic, social and humanitarian issues. The year-round work of the Council is carried out in its subsidiary and related bodies.

## Subsidiary and related bodies

The Council's subsidiary machinery includes:
- nine functional commissions, which are deliberative bodies whose role is to consider and make recommendations on issues in their areas of responsibility and expertise: Statistical Commission (*see Chapter 3, page 155*), Commission on Population and Development (*see Chapter 3, page 176*), Commission for Social Development (*see Chapter 3, page 159*), Commission on Human Rights (*see Chapter 4, page 223*), Commission on the Status of Women (*see Chapter 3, page 179, and Chapter 4, page 234*), Commission on Narcotic Drugs (*see page 187*), Commission on Crime Prevention and Criminal Justice (*see Chapter 3, page 189*), Commission on Science and Technology for Development (*see Chapter 3, page 156*) and Commission on Sustainable Development (*see Chapter 3, page 196*);
- five Regional Commissions: Economic Commission for Africa (Addis Ababa, Ethiopia), Economic and Social Commission for Asia and the Pacific (Bangkok, Thailand), Economic Commission

for Europe (Geneva, Switzerland), Economic Commission for Latin America and the Caribbean (Santiago, Chile) and Economic and Social Commission for Western Asia (Beirut, Lebanon) (*see below, page 32*).

- five standing committees and expert bodies: Committee for Programme and Coordination, Commission on Human Settlements, Committee on Non-Governmental Organizations, Committee on Negotiations with Intergovernmental Agencies and Committee on Energy and Natural Resources;

- a number of expert bodies on subjects such as development planning, natural resources, and economic, social and cultural rights.

The Council also cooperates with and to a certain extent coordinates the work of United Nations programmes (such as UNDP, UNEP, UNICEF and UNFPA) and the specialized agencies (such as FAO, WHO, ILO and UNESCO), all of which report to the Council and make recommendations for its substantive sessions.

### Relations with non-governmental organizations

Under the Charter, the Economic and Social Council consults with non-governmental organizations (NGOs) concerned with matters within its competence. Over 1,600 NGOs have consultative status with the Council. The Council recognizes that these organizations should have the opportunity to express their views, and that they possess special experience or technical knowledge of value to its work.

The Council classifies NGOs into three categories: category I organizations are those concerned with most of the Council's activities; category II organizations have special competence in specific areas; and organizations that can occasionally contribute to the Council are placed on a roster for ad hoc consultations.

NGOs with consultative status may send observers to meetings of the Council and its subsidiary bodies and may submit written statements relevant to its work. They may also consult with the United Nations Secretariat on matters of mutual concern.

Over the years, the relationship between the United Nations and affiliated NGOs has developed significantly. Increasingly, NGOs are seen as partners who are consulted on policy and programme matters and seen as valuable links to civil society. NGOs around the world, in increasing numbers, are working daily with the United Nations community to help achieve the objectives of the Charter.

## Trusteeship Council

The Trusteeship Council (*see also Chapter 7, page 276*) was established by the Charter in 1945 to provide international supervision for 11 Trust Territories placed under the administration of 7 Member States, and ensure that adequate steps were taken to prepare the Territories for self-government or independence. The Charter authorized the Trusteeship Council to examine and discuss reports from the Administering Authority on the political, economic, social and educational advancement of the peoples of Trust Territories; to examine petitions from the Territories; and to undertake special missions to the Territories.

By 1994, all Trust Territories had attained self-government or independence, either as separate States or by joining neighbouring independent countries. The last to do so was the Trust Territory of the Pacific Islands (Palau), which became the 185$^{th}$ Member State.

Its work completed, the Trusteeship Council—consisting of the five permanent members of the Security Council, China, France, the Russian Federation, the United Kingdom and the United States— has amended its rules of procedure to meet as and where occasion may require.

## International Court of Justice

Located at The Hague, the Netherlands, the International Court of Justice (*see also Chapter 6, page 259*) is the principal judicial organ of the United Nations. It settles legal disputes between states and gives advisory opinions to the United Nations and its specialized agencies. Its Statute is an integral part of the United Nations Charter.

The Court is open to all states that are parties to its Statute, which include all Members of the United Nations and Switzerland. Only states may be parties in contentious cases before the Court and submit disputes to it. The Court is not open to private persons and entities or international organizations.

The General Assembly and the Security Council can ask the Court for an advisory opinion on any legal question. Other organs of the United Nations and the specialized agencies, when authorized by the Assembly, can ask for advisory opinions on legal questions within the scope of their activities.

### Jurisdiction

The Court's jurisdiction covers all questions that states refer to it, and all matters provided for in the United Nations Charter, or in international treaties and conventions. States may bind themselves in advance to accept the jurisdiction of the Court, either by signing a treaty or convention that provides for referral to the Court or by making a declaration to that effect. Such declarations accepting compulsory jurisdiction often contain reservations excluding certain classes of disputes.

In accordance with its Statute, the Court decides disputes by applying:

- international conventions establishing rules expressly recognized by the contesting states;
- international custom as evidence of a general practice accepted as law;
- the general principles of law recognized by nations; and
- judicial decisions and the teachings of the most qualified scholars of the various nations.

## Membership

The Court is comprised of 15 Judges elected by the General Assembly and the Security Council, voting independently. They are chosen on the basis of their qualifications, and care is taken to ensure that the principal legal systems of the world are represented in the Court. No two Judges may be from the same country. The Judges serve for a nine-year term and may be re-elected. They cannot engage in any other occupation during their term of office.

The Court normally sits in plenary session, but may form smaller units called chambers if the parties so request. Judgments given by chambers are considered as rendered by the full Court. The Court also has a Chamber for Environmental Matters and forms annually a Chamber of Summary Procedure.

## Secretariat

The Secretariat — an international staff working in duty stations around the world — carries out the diverse day-to-day work of the Organization. It services the other principal organs of the United Nations and administers the programmes and policies laid down by them. At its head is the Secretary-General, who is appointed by the General Assembly on the recommendation of the Security Council for a five-year, renewable term.

The duties carried out by the Secretariat are as varied as the problems dealt with by the United Nations. These range from administering peacekeeping operations to mediating international disputes, from surveying economic and social trends to preparing studies on human rights and sustainable development. Secretariat staff also inform the world's communications media about the work of the United Nations; organize international conferences on issues of worldwide concern; and interpret speeches and translate documents into the Organization's official languages.

The Secretariat has a staff of about 8,900 under the regular budget, drawn from some 160 countries. As international civil servants, staff members and the Secretary-General answer to the United Nations alone for their activities, and take an oath not to seek or receive instructions from any government or outside authority. Under the Charter, each Member State undertakes to respect the exclusively international character of the responsibilities of the Secretary-General and the staff, and to refrain from seeking to influence them improperly.

The United Nations, while headquartered in New York, maintains a significant presence in Addis Ababa, Bangkok, Beirut, Geneva, Nairobi, Santiago and Vienna, and has offices all over the world.

### Secretary-General

Equal parts diplomat and advocate, civil servant and CEO, the Secretary-General is a symbol of United Nations ideals and a spokesman for the interests of the world's peoples, in particular the poor and vulnerable. The current Secretary-General, and the seventh occupant of the post, is Mr. Kofi Annan, of Ghana, who took office on 1 January 1997.

The Charter describes the Secretary-General as "chief administrative officer" of the Organization, who shall act in that capacity and perform "such other functions as are entrusted" to him or her by the Security Council, General Assembly, Economic and Social Council and other United Nations organs. The Charter also empowers the Secretary-General to "bring to the attention of the Security Council any matter which in his opinion may threaten the maintenance of international peace and security". These guidelines both define the powers of the office and grant it considerable scope for action. The Secretary-General would fail if he did not take careful account of the concerns of Member States, but he must also uphold the values and moral authority of the United Nations, and speak and act for peace, even at the risk, from time to time, of challenging or disagreeing with those same Member States.

This creative tension accompanies the Secretary-General through day-to-day work, which includes attendance at sessions of United Nations bodies; consultations with world leaders, government officials and others; and worldwide travel intended to keep him in touch with the peoples of Member States and informed about the vast array of is-

## Previous Secretaries-General

Under the Charter, the Secretary-General is appointed by the General Assembly upon the recommendation of the Security Council. Mr. Annan's predecessors were: Boutros Boutros-Ghali (Egypt), who held office from January 1992 to December 1996; Javier Pérez de Cuéllar (Peru), who served from January 1982 to December 1991; Kurt Waldheim (Austria), who held office from January 1972 to December 1981; U Thant (Burma, now Myanmar), who served from November 1961, when he was appointed acting Secretary-General (he was formally appointed Secretary-General in November 1962) to December 1971; Dag Hammarskjöld (Sweden), who served from April 1953 until his death in a plane crash in Africa in September 1961; and Trygve Lie (Norway), who held office from February 1946 to his resignation in November 1952.

sues of international concern that are on the Organization's agenda. Each year, the Secretary-General issues a report on the work of the Organization that appraises its activities and outlines future priorities.

One of the most vital roles played by the Secretary-General is the use of his "good offices" — steps taken publicly and in private, drawing upon his independence, impartiality and integrity, to prevent international disputes from arising, escalating or spreading. Since becoming Secretary-General, Mr. Annan has made use of his good offices in a range of situations, including Cyprus, East Timor, Iraq, Libya, the Middle East, Nigeria and Western Sahara.

Each Secretary-General also defines his role within the context of his particular time in office. Mr. Annan's efforts have focused on:

**Reform**. Shortly after taking office, Mr. Annan presented a sweeping reform package aimed at helping the United Nations to change with the times and adapt to a new era of global affairs.

Reform measures falling under the authority of the Secretary-General have been largely implemented or set in motion. They have been both administrative — such as a zero-growth budget and rigorous efforts to upgrade management practices — as well as organizational, with the emphasis on enabling the United Nations to respond more effectively to the growing demands placed on it, particularly in the areas of development and peacekeeping.

A new post of **Deputy Secretary-General** was created to assist the Secretary-General in the array of responsibilities assigned to his office. The first holder of this position is Ms. Louise Fréchette, who was Canada's Deputy Minister of National Defence before her appointment in 1998.

The General Assembly, meanwhile, has continued to consider several questions of institutional change that fall under its authority, including the size and composition of the Security Council, methods of financing the Organization and bringing greater coherence to the wider United Nations system of specialized agencies.

**Africa**. The Secretary-General has sought to maintain a focus on Africa and to mobilize international support for its efforts to chart a path to peace and higher levels of development. His approach is encapsulated in a 1998 report, *The causes of conflict and the promotion of durable peace and sustainable development in Africa,* which contains a comprehensive set of "realistic and achievable" measures designed to reduce political tension and violence within and between African states, and to address such key questions of development as debt, governance and the spread of diseases such as AIDS.

**Peace operations**. The 1990s saw an upsurge in United Nations peacekeeping and peacemaking activities and dramatic changes in the nature of conflict itself — primarily a decline in conflicts between states and a rise in the frequency and brutality of conflicts within states. Difficult experiences in responding to these complex humanitarian emergencies have led the Secretary-General to place great emphasis on ensuring that the United Nations, when asked to undertake a peace operation, is fully equipped to do so — militarily, financially, and politically.

In addition to measures contained in the reform plan, three key reports have contributed to this effort. The first, requested by the General Assembly and submitted by the Secretary-General in 1999, was a report of the Secretary-General that examined the atrocities committed against the Bosnian Muslim population in 1995 in the United Nations-designated "safe area" of Srebrenica. The second, commissioned by the Secretary-General and released in 1999, was an independent inquiry, led by former Swedish Prime Minister Ingvar Carlsson, into the actions of the United Nations during the 1994 genocide in Rwanda. The third, released in 2000, was a comprehensive review of United Nations peace and security activities by a high-level panel appointed by the Secretary-General and chaired by former Algerian Foreign Minister Lakhdar Brahimi (*see also Chapter 2, page 76*). This report, intended to draw conclusions for the future from the other two, contains wide-ranging recommendations for the Secretariat and the Member States, particularly those serving on the Security Council. The Secretary-General has begun implement-

# The United Nations as a catalyst for change

Today's actors on the global stage are not only states, says Secretary-General Kofi Annan in his "Millennium Report" *We the peoples: the role of the United Nations in the 21st century*\*: the private sector, NGOs and multilateral agencies increasingly work with governments to find consensus solutions to global problems.

Its own resources tightly constrained, the United Nations must strive not to usurp the role of those global actors, but to become a more effective catalyst for change and coordination among them, stimulating collective action at the global level. The Secretary-General recommends action in these areas:

- *Identifying the United Nations core strengths.* The Organization's influence derives not from power but from the values it represents, its role in helping to set and sustain global norms, its ability to stimulate global concern and action, and the trust inspired by its practical work to improve people's lives. The United Nations must build on those strengths and at the same time adapt, notably by reforming the Security Council so it can both work effectively and enjoy unquestioned legitimacy. And it must expand its relationship with civil society organizations and the private sector.

- *Networking for change.* The United Nations must supplement formal institutions with informal policy networks, bringing together international institutions, civil society, the private sector and governments in pursuit of common goals.

- *Making digital connections.* The United Nations must fully exploit the new information technology to become more efficient and to improve its interaction with the rest of the world.

- *Advancing the quiet revolution.* The United Nations needs structural reform and clearer consensus on priorities among Member States. Decisions are needed from the General Assembly — for instance to include "sunset provisions" (time limits) in new mandates and to introduce results-based budgeting. To better serve states and people alike, the United Nations "must become more effective, efficient, and accessible to the world's peoples".

The Millennium Report was issued in preparation for the Millennium Summit — the largest-ever gathering of heads of state or government. At the Summit, held at UN Headquarters from 6 to 8 September 2000, world leaders established clear directions for the Organization in the new century.The Millennium Declaration, adopted unanimously, set a series of concrete goals and specific targets for the international community to meet the central challenge of ensuring that globalization becomes a positive force for all (*see also page 128*).

---

\*"Millennium Report" *We the peoples: the role of the United Nations in the 21st century*. United Nations, 2000, ISBN 92-1-100844-1, E.00.I.16. Also available at www.un/org/millennium/sg/report.

ing those that fall within his purview, while others need the approval and support of the legislative bodies of the United Nations.

**Global Compact**. In 1999, at the World Economic Forum in Davos, Switzerland, the Secretary-General proposed a "Global Compact" between the United Nations and the world business community. The Compact is aimed at enabling all the world's people to share the benefits of globalization and embedding the global market in values and practices that are fundamental to meeting socio-economic needs. The Compact is based on nine key principles drawn from the Universal Declaration of Human Rights, the International Labour Organization fundamental principles on rights at work, and the Rio Principles on environment and development, which enjoy universal consensus among the world's governments.

The Secretary-General has asked private-sector enterprises to embrace these principles and translate them into corporate practice. He is also encouraging leaders of labour and civil society organizations to participate in the Compact and use it as a forum for dialogue on various contentious issues linked to globalization and development. The first meeting, attended by leaders from all three sectors, was held in 2000.

## Budget of the United Nations

The regular budget of the United Nations is approved by the General Assembly for a two-year period. The budget is initially submitted by the Secretary-General and reviewed by the **Advisory Committee on Administrative and Budgetary Questions**, made up of 16 experts who are nominated by their governments and elected by the General Assembly but who serve in their personal capacity. The programmatic aspects are reviewed by the Committee for Programme and Coordination, made up of 34 experts who are elected by the General Assembly and who represent the views of their governments.

The budget approved for the two years 2000-2001 is $2,535 million, $2 million higher than the 1998-1999 budget. The budget covers the costs of the United Nations programmes in areas such as political affairs, international justice and law, international cooperation for development, public information, human rights and humanitarian affairs (*see Part Three, page 308*).

The main source of funds for the budget is the contributions of Member States. These are assessed on a scale approved by the Assembly on the recommendation of the **Committee on Contributions**, made up of 18 experts who serve in their personal capacity and are selected by the General Assembly on the recommendation of its Administrative and Budgetary (Fifth) Committee (*for the scale of assessments, see Part Three, pages 289-293*).

The fundamental criterion on which the scale of assessments is based is the capacity of countries to pay. This is determined by considering their relative shares of total gross national product, adjusted to take into account a number of factors, including their per capita incomes. The Committee completely reviews the scale of assessments every three years, on the basis of the latest national income statistics, to ensure that assessments are fair and accurate. In 2000, the Assembly fixed a maximum of 22 per cent of the budget for any one contributor.

The overall financial situation of the United Nations has been precarious for several years because of the continuing failure of many Member States to pay, in full and on time, their assessed contributions. The United Nations has managed to continue to operate thanks to voluntary contributions from some countries and to its Working Capital Fund (to which Member States advance sums in proportion to their assessed contributions), and by borrowing from peacekeeping operations.

For 2000, Member States' unpaid contributions to the regular budget totalled $222 million at 31 December 2000. Out of this amount, Member States owed $200 million for 2000 and $22 million for previous years. Out of 187 assessed Member States, 142 had paid their assessments in full, while the remaining 45 had failed to meet their statutory financial obligations to the Organization.

In addition to the regular budget, Member States are assessed for the costs of the International Tribunals (*see below, page 35*), and, in accordance with a modified version of the basic scale, for the costs of peacekeeping operations (*for a list of operations, see Chapter 2, page74*).

Peacekeeping costs peaked at $3 billion in 1995, reflecting in particular the expense of operations in Somalia and the former Yugoslavia. These costs stood at around $1 billion in 1998 and at some $889 million in 1999. For 2000, costs were expected to total at least $2 billion in view of major new missions approved for Kosovo, East Timor, Sierra Leone, the Democratic Republic of the Congo, and Eritrea and Ethiopia.

At 31 December 2000, outstanding contributions for ongoing and previous peacekeeping operations totalled nearly $2 billion. Shortfalls in the receipt of assessed contributions were met by delaying reimbursements to states that had contributed troops, equipment and logistical support, thus placing an unfair burden on them.

United Nations funds and programmes — such as the United Nations Children's Fund (UNICEF), the United Nations Development Programme (UNDP) and the High Commissioner for Refugees — have separate budgets. The bulk of their resources is provided on a voluntary basis by governments, and also by individuals, as in the case of UNICEF.

The United Nations specialized agencies also have separate budgets. In 1999, the approved regular budget of the specialized agencies (except the World Bank, the International Monetary Fund and the International Fund for Agricultural Development) amounted to $1.987 billion. States also provide voluntary contributions, whose amounts have averaged around $5.5 billion.

## The United Nations family of organizations

The United Nations family of organizations (the "United Nations system") is made up of the **United Nations Secretariat**, the United Nations **programmes and funds** (such as UNICEF and UNDP) and the **specialized agencies**. The programmes and funds are subsidiary bodies of the General Assembly. The specialized agencies, linked to the United Nations through special agreements, report to the Economic and Social Council and/or the General Assembly. They have their own governing bodies and budgets, and set their own standards and guidelines. Together they provide technical assistance and other forms of practical help in virtually all areas of economic and social endeavour (*see below*).

**Administrative Committee on Coordination (ACC)**. The 26 funds, programmes and specialized agencies are members of the ACC, whose main function is facilitating increased coordination of the programmes approved by the governing bodies of the various organizations of the United Nations system. Chaired by the Secretary-General, the ACC meets twice a year to consider the substantive and management issues facing the system. ACC's work is carried out, in part, by its subsidiary bodies, each of which focuses on a particular aspect of coordination within the system.

UNITED NATIONS

# The UNITED

## INTERNATIONAL COURT OF JUSTICE

## SECURITY COUNCIL

## GENERAL ASSEMBLY

Military Staff Committee

Standing Committee and ad hoc bodies

International Criminal Tribunal for the Former Yugoslavia

International Criminal Tribunal for Rwanda

UN Monitoring, Verification and Inspection Commission (Iraq)

United Nations Compensation Commission

Peacekeeping Operations and Missions

Main Committees

Other sessional committees.

Standing committees and ad hoc bodies

Other subsidiary organs

## PROGRAMMES AND FUNDS

**UNCTAD**
United Nations Conference on Trade and Development

**ITC**
International Trade Centre (UNCTAD/WTO)

**UNDCP**
United Nations Drug Control Programme

**UNEP**
United Nations Environment Programme

**UNHSP**
United Nations Human Settlements Programme (UN-Habitat)

**UNDP**
United Nations Development Programme

**UNIFEM**
United Nations Development Fund for Women

**UNV**
United Nations Volunteers

**UNFPA**
United Nations Population Fund

**UNHCR**
Office of the United Nations High Commissioner for Refugees

**UNICEF**
United Nations Children's Fund

**WFP**
World Food Programme

**UNRWA\*\***
United Nations Relief and Works Agency for Palestine Refugees in the Near East

## OTHER UN ENTITIES

**OHCHR**
Office of the United Nations High Commissioner for Human Rights

**UNOPS**
United Nations Office for Project Services

**UNU**
United Nations University

**UNSSC**
United Nations System Staff College

## RESEARCH AND TRAINING INSTITUTES

**INSTRAW**
International Research and Training Institute for the Advancement of Women

**UNICRI**
United Nations Interregional Crime and Justice Research Institute

**UNITAR**
United Nations Institute for Training and Research

**UNRISD**
United Nations Research Institute for Social Development

**UNIDIR\*\***
United Nations Institute for Disarmament Research

\*Autonomous organizations working with the United Nations and each other through the coordinating machinery of the Economic and Social Council.
\*\*Report only to the General Assembly.

# NATIONS system

OF THE UNITED NATIONS

| ECONOMIC AND SOCIAL COUNCIL | TRUSTEESHIP COUNCIL | SECRETARIAT |
|---|---|---|

## FUNCTIONAL COMMISSIONS

Commission for Social Development
Commission on Human Rights
Commission on Narcotic Drugs
Commission on Crime Prevention
and Criminal Justice
Commission on Science and Technology
for Development
Commission on Sustainable Development
Commission on the Status of Women
Commission on Population and
Development
Statistical Commission

## REGIONAL COMMISSIONS

Economic Commission for Africa (ECA)
Economic Commission for Europe (ECE)
Economic Commission for Latin America
and the Caribbean (ECLAC)
Economic and Social Commission for Asia
and the Pacific (ESCAP)
Economic and Social Commission
for Western Asia (ESCWA)

United Nations Forum on Forests

Sessional and Standing Committees
Expert, ad hoc and related bodies

## RELATED ORGANIZATIONS

**IAEA**
International Atomic Energy Agency

**WTO (trade)**
World Trade Organization

**WTO (tourism)**
World Tourism Organization

**CTBTO Prep.com**
PrepCom for the Nuclear-Test-Ban-Treaty
Organization

**OPCW**
Organization for the Prohibition of
Chemical Weapons

## SPECIALIZED AGENCIES*

**ILO**
International Labour Organization

**FAO**
Food and Agriculture Organization
of the United Nations

**UNESCO**
United Nations Educational, Scientific
and Cultural Organization

**WHO**
World Health Organization

**WORLD BANK GROUP**

| | |
|---|---|
| **IBRD** | International Bank for Reconstruction and Development |
| **IDA** | International Development Association |
| **IFC** | International Finance Corporation |
| **MIGA** | Multilateral Investment Guarantee Agency |
| **ICSID** | International Centre for Settlement of Investment Disputes |

**IMF**
International Monetary Fund

**ICAO**
International Civil Aviation Organization

**IMO**
International Maritime Organization

**ITU**
International Telecommunication Union

**UPU**
Universal Postal Union

**WMO**
World Meteorological Organization

**WIPO**
World Intellectual Property Organization

**IFAD**
International Fund for Agricultural Development

**UNIDO**
United Nations Industrial Development
Organization

## SECRETARIAT

**OSG**
Office of the Secretary-General

**OIOS**
Office of Internal Oversight Services

**OLA**
Office of Legal Affairs

**DPA**
Department of Political Affairs

**DDA**
Department for Disarmament Affairs

**DPKO**
Department of Peacekeeping Operations

**OCHA**
Office for the Coordination
of Humanitarian Affairs

**DESA**
Department of Economic
and Social Affairs

**DGACM**
Department of General Assembly
and Conference Management

**DPI**
Department of Public Information

**DM**
Department of Management

**OIP**
Office of the Iraq Programme

**UNSECOORD**
Office of the United Nations
Security Coordinator

**OHRLLS**
Office of the High Representative
for the Least Developed Countries,
Landlocked Developing Countries
and Small Island Developing States

**ODC**
Office on Drugs and Crime

**UNOG**
UN Office at Geneva

**UNOV**
UN Office at Vienna

**UNON**
UN Office at Nairobi

# Principal United Nations Offices
## around the world

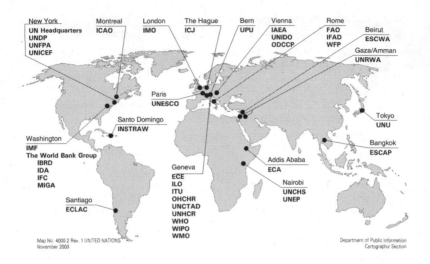

New York
**UN Headquarters**
**UNDP**
**UNFPA**
**UNICEF**

Montreal
**ICAO**

London
**IMO**

The Hague
**ICJ**

Bern
**UPU**

Vienna
**IAEA**
**UNIDO**
**ODCCP**

Rome
**FAO**
**IFAD**
**WFP**

Beirut
**ESCWA**

Gaza/Amman
**UNRWA**

Paris
**UNESCO**

Santo Domingo
**INSTRAW**

Washington
**IMF**
**The World Bank Group**
**IBRD**
**IDA**
**IFC**
**MIGA**

Santiago
**ECLAC**

Geneva
**ECE**
**ILO**
**ITU**
**OHCHR**
**UNCTAD**
**UNHCR**
**WHO**
**WIPO**
**WMO**

Addis Ababa
**ECA**

Nairobi
**UNCHS**
**UNEP**

Tokyo
**UNU**

Bangkok
**ESCAP**

Map No. 4000.2 Rev. 1 UNITED NATIONS
November 2000

Department of Public Information
Cartographic Section

## United Nations Secretariat

The United Nations Secretariat consists of departments and offices, described below. The **Executive Office of the Secretary-General**, composed of the Secretary-General and his senior advisers, establishes general policies and provides overall guidance to the Organization. The Secretariat has its headquarters in New York and offices in all regions of the world.

Three main centres of activities are in Geneva, Vienna and Nairobi. **The United Nations Office at Geneva (UNOG)**, headed by Under-Secretary-General Vladimir Petrovsky (Russian Federation), is a centre for conference diplomacy and a forum for disarmament and human rights. The **United Nations Office at Vienna (UNOV)**, headed by Under-Secretary-General Pino Arlacchi (Italy), is the headquarters for activities in the fields of international drug-abuse control, crime prevention and criminal justice, peaceful uses of outer space and international trade law. The **United Nations Office at Nairobi (UNON)**, headed by Under-Secretary-General Klaus Topfer (Germany), is the headquarters for activities in the fields of environment and human settlements.

# Office of Internal Oversight Services (OIOS)

Under-Secretary-General          Mr. Dileep Nair (Singapore)

The Office of Internal Oversight Services was created to establish a credible, effective and permanent system of oversight of United Nations operations. The Office:
- monitors and evaluates the efficiency and effectiveness of the implementation of programmes and mandates;
- conducts comprehensive internal audits;
- conducts ad hoc inspections of programmes and organizational units;
- investigates reports of mismanagement and misconduct;
- monitors the implementation of recommendations emanating from audits, evaluations, inspections and investigations;
- advises programme managers on the effective discharge of their responsibilities.

OIOS covers the Secretariat, the operational programmes and funds, major peacekeeping operations, and various other programmes. It has a staff of about 120 and a budget of some $22 million — less than the amount it earns every year by identifying irregular spending.

The Under-Secretary-General for Internal Oversight Services is appointed by the Secretary-General and approved by the General Assembly for one five-year term without possibility of renewal.

## Office of Legal Affairs (OLA)

Under-Secretary-General. The Legal Counsel    Mr. Hans Corell (Sweden)

The Office of Legal Affairs is the central legal service of the Organization. It provides legal advice to the Secretary-General, Secretariat departments and offices and principal and subsidiary organs of the United Nations in the field of public and private international law; performs substantive and secretariat functions for legal organs involved in public international law, the law of the sea and international trade law; and performs the functions conferred on the Secretary-General in Article 102 of the Charter of the United Nations and the Statute of the International Court of Justice.

OLA deals with legal questions relating to international peace and security; to the status, privileges and immunities of the United Nations; and to the credentials and representations of Member States. It prepares drafts of international conventions, agreements, rules of procedure of United Nations organs and conferences and other legal instruments; provides legal services and advice on issues of international private and administrative law and on United Nations resolutions and regulations; provides secretariat services for the General Assembly's Sixth Committee, the International Law Commission, the Commission of International Trade Law, the organs established by the United Nations Convention of the Law of the Sea, the United Nations Administrative Tribunal and other legal bodies; discharges the Secretary-General's responsibilities regarding the registration and publication of treaties and the depositary of multilateral conventions.

The head of the Office — the Legal Counsel — represents the Secretary-General at meetings and conferences of a legal nature, as well as in judicial and arbitral proceedings; certifies legal instruments issued on behalf of the United Nations; and convenes meetings of the Legal Advisers of the United Nations System and represents the United Nations at such meetings.

## Department of Political Affairs (DPA)

Under-Secretary-General    Mr. Kieran Prendergast (United Kingdom)

The Department of Political Affairs provides advice and support on all political matters to the Secretary-General in the exercise of his global responsibilities under the Charter related to the maintenance and restoration of peace and security. DPA accordingly:

- monitors, analyses and assesses political developments throughout the world;
- identifies potential or actual conflicts in whose control and resolution the United Nations could play a useful role;
- recommends to the Secretary-General appropriate action in such cases and executes the approved policy;
- assists the Secretary-General in carrying out political activities, decided by him, the General Assembly and the Security Council, in the areas of preventive diplomacy, peacemaking, peacekeeping and peace-building;
- advises the Secretary-General on requests for electoral assistance received from Member States and coordinates programmes established in response to such requests;
- advises and supports the Secretary-General in the political aspects of his relations with Member States;
- services the Security Council and its subsidiary bodies, as well as the Committee on the Exercise of the Inalienable Rights of the Pal-

estinian People and the Special Committee of 24 on Decolonization.

The head of the Department — the Under-Secretary-General for Political Affairs — among other things undertakes consultations and negotiations relating to peaceful settlement of disputes, and is the focal point for United Nations peace-building, preventive and electoral assistance activities.

## Department for Disarmament Affairs (DDA)

Under-Secretary-General        Mr. Jayantha Dhanapala (Sri Lanka)

The Department for Disarmament Affairs promotes the goal of nuclear disarmament and non-proliferation and the strengthening of the disarmament regimes in respect to other weapons of mass destruction, chemical and biological weapons. It also promotes disarmament efforts in the area of conventional weapons, especially landmines and small arms, which are the weapons of choice in contemporary conflicts.

DDA provides substantive and organizational support for norm-setting in the area of disarmament through the work of the General Assembly and its First Committee, the Disarmament Commission, the Conference on Disarmament and other bodies. It fosters preventive disarmament measures, such as dialogue, transparency and confidence-building on military matters, and encourages regional disarmament efforts; these include the United Nations Register of Conventional Arms (*see Chapter 2, page 118*) and regional forums. It also provides information on United Nations disarmament efforts.

DDA supports the development and implementation of practical measures after a conflict, such as disarming and demobilizing former combatants and helping them to reintegrate into civil society.

## Department of Peacekeeping Operations (DPKO)

Under-Secretary-General        Mr. Jean-Marie Guéhenno (France)

DPKO is the operational arm for all United Nations peacekeeping operations, and is responsible for the conduct, management, direction, planning and preparation of those operations. It develops plans and methodologies for peacekeeping operations; secures, through negotiations with governments, the personnel and equipment required for operations; provides logistical and administrative support for operations and political or humanitarian missions; proposes resource requirements, and monitors and controls funds related to peacekeeping activities; maintains contacts with parties to conflicts and members of the Security Council on the implementation of Council decisions; undertakes contingency planning for possible new operations; carries out analysis of emerging policy questions, and formulates policies and procedures in this regard. It also coordinates all United Nations activities related to landmines, and develops and supports mine action programmes in peacekeeping and emergency situations.

The head of the department — the Under-Secretary-General for Peacekeeping Operations — directs peacekeeping operations on behalf of the Secretary-General; formulates policies and guidelines for operations; and advises the Secretary-General on all related matters.

## Office for the Coordination of Humanitarian Affairs (OCHA)

Under-Secretary-General for Humanitarian Affairs
Emergency Relief Coordinator                    Mr. Kenzo Oshima (Japan)

The mandate of the Office for the Coordination of Humanitarian Affairs is to strengthen coordination among the United Nations bodies that provide assistance in response to emergencies. The Office works to secure agreement among the organizations of the Inter-Agency Standing Committee (*see Chapter 5, page 248*) on the division of responsibilities, such as establishing coordination mechanisms, mounting need-assessment missions, preparing consolidated appeals and mobilizing resources.

The core functions of the Emergency Relief Coordinator are:

- policy development and coordination, ensuring that all humanitarian issues, including those which fall between gaps in the mandates of agencies, are addressed;

- advocacy of humanitarian issues with political organs, notably the Security Council; and

- coordination of humanitarian emergency response, by ensuring that an appropriate response mechanism is established on the ground; this is done through the Inter-Agency Standing Committee, which is chaired by the Emergency Relief Coordinator.

OCHA has a staff of 439 worldwide and a core budget of $45 million for 2000-2001.

# Department of Economic and Social Affairs (DESA)

Under-Secretary-General                    Mr. Nitin Desai (India)

The Department of Economic and Social Affairs has three broad, interlinked areas of work.

First, DESA compiles, generates and analyses a broad range of social, economic and environmental data and information on relevant issues and trends. This enables Member States to carry out informed discussions and take stock of policy options. Second, it facilitates negotiations in many intergovernmental bodies that meet on economic, social and environmental matters in the United Nations, providing support to Member States as they negotiate common courses of action to address ongoing or emerging global challenges. Finally, at the request of interested governments, DESA advises them on the ways and means of translating the policy frameworks agreed at the recent series of global economic, social and environmental conferences into programmes at the country level. Through technical assistance, it also helps them build national capacities in these fields.

DESA's work includes the promotion of sustainable development, gender issues and the advancement of women, Africa and the least developed countries, development policy analysis, population, statistics, public economics and public administration, and social policy and development. It collaborates closely with NGOs and other representatives of civil society, in recognition of their contribution to the policy and operational aspects of development.

## Department of General Assembly and Conference Management (DGACM)

Under-Secretary-General                    Mr. Chen Jian (China)

The Department of General Assembly Affairs and Conference Services provides technical and secretariat support services to the General Assembly, its Main Committees and subsidiary organs, to the Economic and Social Council and most of its subsidiary bodies, and to meetings and conferences dealing with economic and social matters. It also provides meeting and documentation services to all intergovernmental bodies and expert bodies meeting in New York and in other locations, as well as translation and publishing services.

The head of the Department — the Under-Secretary-General for General Assembly Affairs and Conference Services — represents the Secretary-General in meetings related to the functions of the Department and develops conference-servicing policies and practices for the United Nations worldwide.

## Department of Public Information (DPI)

Under-Secretary-General          Mr. Shashi Tharoor (India)

DPI informs a global audience about the activities and purposes of the United Nations. It communicates the complex work of the United Nations system through a multiplicity of outreach efforts and campaigns, including the United Nations web site, radio and television, press releases, publications, documentary videos, special events, public tours and library facilities, with the assistance of its 70 information centres and services and eight United Nations Offices with information components around the world.

The head of DPI is responsible for United Nations communications policy, ensuring a coordinated and transparent flow of information on the work of the United Nations and developing a cohesive culture of communications throughout the Organization.

The Public Affairs Division conducts promotional information campaigns on global priority issues, organizes special events and exhibits, arranges issue-oriented press activities, manages workshops and special programmes for journalists, educators and other re-disseminators, provides partnerships with civil society, in particular NGOs, serves as an information resource about the United Nations for the general public, and organizes other outreach activities, including the guided tour of the United Nations Headquarters.

The News and Media Division facilitates the access of news organizations and media worldwide to news and information about the United Nations and its activities. It puts out daily news via radio and on the Internet, produces other radio and video programming, provides live TV feeds and photo coverage of United Nations meetings and events, and provides press accreditation.

The Library and Information Resources Division facilitates access to United Nations documents and publications through the products and services of the Dag Hammarskjöld Library, both directly and through its Internet site and its network of more than 350 depository libraries around the world. It also provides cartographic services and manages the publications and sales programmes (*for a list of DPI publications, see page 327*).

The Office of the Spokesman of the Secretary-General, administered by DPI, is responsible for planning the Secretary-General's media-related activities. The Spokesman, who reports directly to the Secretary-General, briefs journalists on a daily basis.

## Department of Management (DM)

Under-Secretary-General          Mr. Joseph E. Connor* (United States)

The Department of Management provides strategic policy guidance and management support to all entities of the Secretariat in three management areas: finance, human resources and support services. These fall under the purview of the Offices of Programme Planning, Budget and Accounts; Human Resources Management; and Central Support Services.

The Department is responsible for formulating and implementing improved management policies in the Secretariat; the management and training of staff; programme planning, budgetary, financial and human resources management; and technological innovations. It also provides the technical servicing for the General Assembly's Fifth Committee (Administrative and Budgetary), as well as the servicing of the Committee for Programme and Coordination.

The head of the Department — the Under-Secretary-General for Management — provides policy guidance, coordination and direction for preparing the Organization's medium-term plan and biennial budgets. He represents the Secretary-General on matters relating to management, monitors emerging management issues throughout the Secretariat and has the overall supervision of the internal system of the administration of justice.

---

*Catherine Bertini (United States) was appointed to replace Mr. Connor as Under-Secretary-General, with effect from 1 January 2003.

## Office of the Iraq Programme

Under-Secretary-General
Executive Director                    Mr. Benon Sevan (Cyprus)

The Office of the Iraq Programme manages the "oil-for-food" programme, established by the Security Council in 1995 to provide for the humanitarian needs of the Iraqi people, affected by the comprehensive sanctions imposed by the Council in 1990 following the invasion of Kuwait (*see Chapter 2, page 101*). The first oil under the programme was exported in December 1996 and the first food shipments arrived three months later. Since then, more than 10 million tonnes of foodstuff worth $4 billion, and medicine and health supplies worth $720 million, have been delivered to Iraq under the programme. In addition, humanitarian supplies for water and sanitation, agriculture, education, infrastructure and demining, worth $800 million, have arrived in Iraq.

## Office of the United Nations Security Coordinator (UNSECOORD)

Assistant Secretary-General
United Nations Security Coordinator      Mr. Tun Myat (Myanmar)

The Office of the United Nations Security Coordinator acts on behalf of the Secretary-General and the heads of United Nations agencies, programmes and funds, to ensure a coherent response by the United Nations system to any emergency situation. It is responsible for all policy and procedural matters related to security, and, on behalf of the Secretary-General, takes decisions relating to all aspects of evacuation.

The Office formulates detailed recommendations to ensure the safety and security of staff members and eligible family members of the entire United Nations system; coordinates, plans and implements inter-agency security and safety programmes; and acts as the focal point for inter-agency cooperation.

The Office is funded on an inter-agency basis by all the participants in the Administrative Committee on Coordination.

## Office of the High Representative for the Least Developed Countries, Landlocked Developing Countries and Small Island Developing States (OHRLLS)

Under-Secretary-General High Representative
for the Least Developed Countries,
Landlocked Developing Countries      Mr. Anwarul K. Chowdhury
and Small Island Developing States      (Bangladesh)

The Office of the High Representative for the Least Developed Countries (LDCs), Landlocked Developing Countries (LLDCs) and Small Island Developing States (SIDS) was established by the General Assembly in its resolution 56/227 of 24 December 2001. It aims at enhancing the mobilization and galvanization of international support for the implementation of the *Brussels Declaration and Programme of Action* adopted by the least developed countries and their development partners at the United Nations Conference held in Brussels in May 2001, and to ensure effective coordination, monitoring and review of their implementation.

The key functions of the Office include assisting the Secretary-General in ensuring the full mobilization and coordination of all parts of the United Nations system for implementation, follow-up and monitoring of the Programme of Action at country, regional and global levels; providing support to the Economic and Social Council and the General Assembly in assessing progress, as well as in the annual review of implementation of the Programme; and supporting, as appropriate, the coordinated follow-up of the implementation of the *Global Framework for Transit Transport Cooperation between Landlocked and Transit Developing Countries and the Donor Community*, as well as the *Barbados Programme of Action for the Sustainable Development of Small Island Developing States.*

Its key functions also include undertaking appropriate advocacy work in favour of least developed countries, landlocked developing countries and small island developing States in partnership with the relevant UN bodies, civil society, the media, academia and foundations; and helping to mobilize international support and resources for the implementation of the Programme of Action for Least Developed Countries, as well as for other programmes and initiatives in former landlocked developing countries and small island developing States.

## Regional Commissions

The United Nations Regional Commissions report to ECOSOC and operate under the authority of the Secretary-General. Their mandate is to initiate measures that promote the economic development of each region and strengthen the economic relations of the countries in that region, both among themselves and with other countries of the world. They are funded under the regular United Nations budget.

### Economic Commission for Africa (ECA)

Set up in 1958, ECA carries out activities encouraging the growth of the economic and social sectors of the continent. It promotes policies and strategies to increase economic cooperation and integration among its 53 member countries, particularly in the production, trade, monetary, infrastructure and institutional fields. ECA focuses on producing information and analysis on economic and social issues; promoting food security and sustainable development; strengthening development management; harnessing the information revolution for development; and promoting regional cooperation and integration. Special attention is paid to improving the condition of women, enhancing their involvement and decision-making in development, and ensuring that women and gender equity are key elements in national development.

Executive Secretary: Mr. K. Y. Amoako (Ghana)
Address: Africa Hall, P.O. Box 3001, Addis Ababa, Ethiopia
Telephone: (251 1) 51 72 00; Fax: (251 1) 51 44 16
E-mail: ecainfo@uneca.org
Internet: www.uneca.org

### Economic Commission for Europe (ECE)

Created in 1947, ECE is the forum at which the countries of North America, Europe and central Asia come together to forge the tools of their economic cooperation. ECE, which has 55 member countries, includes Israel as well. Priority areas of work include environment, transport, statistics, trade facilitation, industry, agriculture and forestry, as well as housing, building and planning. ECE is the forum where agreements are negotiated and assistance activities prepared. Its main purpose is to harmonize the policies and practices of its member countries. Such harmonization not only facilitates economic exchanges, investments and the integration of transport networks, but also makes environmental procedures more effective.

Executive Secretary: Ms. Brigita Schmognerova (Slovakia)
Address: Palais des Nations, 1211 Geneva 10, Switzerland
Telephone: (41 22) 917 44 44; Fax: (41 22) 917 05 05
E-mail: info.ece@unece.org
Internet: www.unece.org

## Economic Commission for Latin America and the Caribbean (ECLAC)

Established in 1948, ECLAC works to coordinate policies for promoting economic and social development in the region. It collaborates with its 41 member states and 7 associate members in the research and analysis of regional and national development processes. Its mission includes proposing, evaluating and following up on public policy measures as well as providing assistance in areas of specialised information.

ECLAC cooperates with national, regional and international organizations on subjects such as: agricultural development; economic and social planning; industrial, technological and entrepreneurial development; international trade, regional integration and cooperation; investment and financing; social development and equity; integration of women in development; natural resources and infrastructure; environment and human settlements; statistics; administrative management; demography and population policies.

The ECLAC system includes the Latin American and Caribbean Institute for Economic and Social Planning (ILPES), which undertakes research, provides training and furthers cooperation among the planning services of the region. There are also two subregional headquarters for Mexico and Central America (Mexico) and the Caribbean (Trinidad and Tobago), and five National Offices (Argentina, Brazil, Colombia, Uruguay and the United States).

Executive Secretary: Mr. José Antonio Ocampo (Colombia)
Address: Edificio Naciones Unidas, Avenida Dag Hammarskjöld s/n,
Casilla 179-D, Santiago, Chile
Telephone:(56 2) 210 2000/206 1519; Fax: (56 2) 208 0252/228 1947
E-mail: dpisantiago@eclac.cl
Internet: www.eclac.cl, www.eclac.org

## Economic and Social Commission for Asia and the Pacific (ESCAP)

ESCAP, established in 1947, has a mandate to address the economic and social issues of the region. It plays a unique role as the only inter-governmental forum for all the countries of Asia and the Pacific. Its 51 member states and 9 associate member states represent some 60 per cent of the world population. ESCAP gives technical support to governments for social and economic development. The assistance comes through direct advisory services to governments, training and sharing of regional experience, and information through meetings, publications and inter-country networks. ESCAP executes programmes and projects to stimulate growth, improve socio-economic conditions and help build the foundations of modern society. Three regional research and training institutions in agricultural development, statistics and technology transfer operate under its auspices. Current priority areas include promotion of inter-regional trade and investment, technology transfer, privatization and entrepreneurship, environment, urbanization, poverty alleviation, drug abuse control, population, social development and labour migration.

Executive Secretary: Mr. Kim Hak-Su (Republic of Korea)
Address: United Nations Building, Rajadamnern Avenue, Bangkok,Thailand
Telephone: (662) 288 1234; Fax: (662) 288 1000
E-mail: [surname].unescap@un.org
Internet: www.unescap.org

## Economic and Social Commission for Western Asia (ESCWA)

Established in 1973, ESCWA facilitates concerted action for the economic and social development of the countries of Western Asia by promoting economic cooperation and integration in the region. Comprised of 13 member states, ESCWA serves as the main general economic and social development forum for the region within the United Nations system. Its programmes address areas such as economic development, social development, agriculture, industry, natural resources, the environment, transport, communications and statistics.

Executive Secretary: Ms. Merwat M. Tallawy (Egypt)
Address: P.O. Box 11-8575, Riad el-Solh Square, Beirut, Lebanon
Telephone: (961) 198 1301; Fax: (961) 198 1516
E-mail: unescwa@escwa.org.lb
Internet: www.escwa.org.lb

# International Tribunals

## International Criminal Tribunal for the Former Yugoslavia (ICTY)

Established by the Security Council in 1993, the Tribunal is mandated to prosecute persons responsible for serious violations of international humanitarian law committed in the former Yugoslavia since 1991. It has 14 judges and a staff of 1,011. Its 2000 budget was $96 million.

Since its inception, 94 people have been publicly indicted. As of July 2000, 38 accused were in proceedings before the Tribunal and 26 were at large. Of those sentenced, two pleaded guilty, 13 were found guilty in first instance, four were found guilty after appeal and two were acquitted. Nine sentences had been appealed.

President: Judge Claude Jorda (France)
Chief Prosecutor: Mrs. Carla Del Ponte (Switzerland)
Registrar: Mr. Henry Hans Holthuis (Netherlands)
Headquarters: Churchillplein 1, 2517 JW, The Hague, the Netherlands
Tel.: (31 70) 416 5233; Fax: (31 70) 512 5355
Internet: www.un.org/icty

## International Criminal Tribunal for Rwanda (ICTR)

Created by the Security Council in 1994, the Tribunal has the mandate to prosecute persons responsible for genocide and other serious violations of international humanitarian law committed in Rwanda during 1994. It has three Trial Chambers made up of three judges each, and an Appeals Chamber made up of five judges. It has a staff of 729; its 2000 budget was $79 million. By 2000, it had secured the arrest of over 40 individuals and convicted several of those arrested.

President: Judge Ms. Navanethem Pillay (South Africa)
Chief Prosecutor: Mrs. Carla Del Ponte (Switzerland)
Registrar: Adama Dieng (Senegal)
P.O. Box 6016, Arusha, Tanzania
Tel. (212) 963 2850 or (255) 27 50 43 69/72
Fax (212) 963 2848 or (255) 27 50 40 00 or 50 43 73
Internet: www.ictr.un.org

# United Nations Programmes and other bodies

## United Nations Conference on Trade and Development (UNCTAD)

Established in 1964 as a permanent intergovernmental body, the United Nations Conference on Trade and Development is the principal organ of the General Assembly in the field of trade and development. Its mandate is to accelerate trade and economic development, particularly of developing countries.

UNCTAD is the focal point within the United Nations system for the integrated treatment of development and related issues in the areas of trade, finance, technology, investment and sustainable development. Its main goals are to maximize the trade, investment and development opportunities of developing countries, and to help them face challenges arising from globalization and integrate into the world economy on an equitable basis. UNCTAD pursues such goals through research and policy analysis, intergovernmental deliberations, technical cooperation, and interaction with civil society and the business sector.

UNCTAD's Conference, the highest policy-making body, is composed of the 190 member states and meets every four years. The tenth Conference was held in 2000 in Bangkok. The executive body is the Trade and Development Board, responsible for ensuring the overall consistency of UNCTAD's activities with agreed priorities.

The annual operational budget is about $50 million, drawn from the United Nations regular budget. Technical cooperation activities, financed from extrabudgetary resources, amount to about $24 million. UNCTAD has a staff of some 394.

Secretary-General: Mr. Rubens Ricupero (Brazil)
Headquarters: Palais des Nations, CH-1211 Geneva 10, Switzerland
Tel.: (41 22) 907 1234; Fax: (41 22) 907 0043
E-mail: ers@unctad.org
Internet: www.unctad.org

## International Trade Centre UNCTAD/WTO (ITC)

The International Trade Centre UNCTAD/WTO is the technical cooperation agency of UNCTAD and the World Trade Organization (WTO) for operational and enterprise-oriented aspects of international trade development. As the United Nations focal point for technical cooperation in trade promotion, ITC works with developing countries and countries with economies in transition to set up effective trade promotion programmes to expand their exports and improve their import operations.

ITC is a joint subsidiary organ of WTO and the United Nations, the latter acting through UNCTAD. Headquarters operations are financed by the United Nations and WTO. Technical cooperation programmes are funded by UNDP and voluntary contributions. The annual budget is about $33 million. ITC has a staff of about 180.

Executive Director: Mr. J. Denis Bélisle (Canada)
Headquarters: Palais des Nations, CH-1211 Geneva 10, Switzerland
Tel.: (41 22) 730 01 11; Fax: (41 22) 733 44 39
E-mail: itcreg@intracen.org
Internet: www.intracen.org

## Office on Drugs and Crime (ODC)

The Office on Drugs and Crime—formerly the Office for Drug Control and Crime Prevention (ODCCP)—was established in 1997 to enable the United Nations to enhance its capacity to address the interrelated issues of drug control, crime prevention and international terrorism. It consists of:

- the United Nations International Drug Control Programme (UNDCP); and
- the Centre for International Crime Prevention (CICP).

UNDCP is the central entity responsible for coordinating and leading all United Nations drug control activities. It serves as the repository of technical expertise in this field and provides technical advice to Member States on drug control matters. It carries out its mandate at the national, regional and global levels through a network of field offices.

CICP is the central entity responsible for activities in the field of crime prevention and criminal justice. It pays special attention to combating transnational organized crime, illicit trafficking in human beings, financial crimes and terrorism.

The budget for 2000-2001 was $166.2 million, out of which $154.9 million was for UNDCP and $11.3 million for CICP. Ninety per cent of UNDCP's and 49 per cent of CICP's resources came from voluntary contributions; the remainder came from the United Nations regular budget.

Executive Director: Mr. Antonio Maria Costa (Italy)
Headquarters: Vienna International Centre, Wagramerstrasse 5,
PO Box 500, A-1400 Vienna, Austria
Tel.: (43 1) 26060 0; Fax: (43 1) 26060 5866
E-mail: odccp@odccp.org
Internet: www.odccp.org

## United Nations Environment Programme (UNEP)

The United Nations Environment Programme was founded in 1972. Its mission is to provide leadership and encourage partnerships in caring for the environment by enabling nations and peoples to improve their quality of life without compromising that of future generations.

As the principal United Nations body in the field of the environment, UNEP sets the global environmental agenda, promotes implementation of the environmental dimension of sustainable development in the United Nations system, and serves as an authoritative advocate of the global environment.

UNEP's governing body — the Governing Council — made up of 58 countries, meets annually. Programmes are financed by the Environment Fund, made up of voluntary contributions from governments and supplemented by trust funds and a small allocation from the United Nations regular budget. The Fund's budget for 2000-2001 was $120 million. UNEP has a staff of 680.

Executive Director: Mr. Klaus Toepfer (Germany)
Headquarters: United Nations Avenue, Gigiri, Nairobi, Kenya
Tel.: (254 2) 621 234, 520 602; Fax: (254 2) 226 886 or 226 895
E-mail: cpiinfo@unep.org
Internet: www.unep.org

## United Nations Development Programme (UNDP)

The United Nations Development Programme is the main body for coordinating the United Nations development work. Its global reach and management of $2.3 billion in financial resources annually makes it the largest provider of development grant assistance in the United Nations system.

UNDP provides sound policy advice and helps build institutional and human capacity that generates equitable economic growth. It works with public and private-sector partners to make the best possible use of aid resources in confronting the challenges and opportunities offered by globalization. It is committed to promoting accountable government at all levels of society and building coalitions for action on issues critical to sustainable human development.

UNDP administers special funds and programmes, including the:
• United Nations Development Fund for Women (UNIFEM);
• United Nations Volunteer Programme (UNV);
• United Nations Capital Development Fund (UNCDF).

UNDP is governed by a 36-member Executive Board, representing both developing and developed countries. Among its major publications is the annual *Human Development Report.*

Administrator: Mr. Mark Malloch Brown (United Kingdom)
Headquarters: 1 UN Plaza, New York, NY 10017, USA
Tel.: (1 212) 906 5000; Fax: (1 212) 906 5001
E-mail: mark.malloch.brown@undp.org
Internet: www.undp.org

## United Nations Development Fund for Women (UNIFEM)

The United Nations Development Fund for Women promotes women's empowerment and gender equality. It works to ensure the participation of women in all levels of development planning and practice. It also acts as a catalyst within the United Nations system for efforts to link the needs and concerns of women to all critical issues on the national, regional and global agendas.

Since its creation in 1976, UNIFEM has supported projects and initiatives throughout the developing world that promote the political, economic and social empowerment of women. These have ranged from small grass-roots enterprises improving women's working conditions to public education campaigns and the design of new gender-sensitive laws.

UNIFEM works in autonomous association with UNDP. It reports to a Consultative Committee consisting of representatives from all regions and to UNDP's Executive Board. UNIFEM is represented at the regional and country levels by its 12 Regional Programme Advisors. The annual budget is about $20 million.

Director: Ms. Noeleen Heyzer (Singapore)
Headquarters: 304 East 45th Street, 6th floor, New York, NY 10017, USA
Tel.: (1 212) 906 6400; Fax: (1 212) 906 6705
E-mail: unifem@undp.org
Internet: www.unifem.undp.org

## United Nations Volunteers (UNV)

United Nations Volunteers was created by the General Assembly in 1970 as a subsidiary organ of the United Nations to be an operational programme in development cooperation. As a volunteer-based programme, UNV is both unique within the United Nations family and in its scale as an international undertaking. It assigns mid-career women and men to sectoral and community-based development projects, humanitarian aid and the promotion of human rights and democracy. UNV reports to the Executive Board of UNDP/UNFPA and works through UNDP's country offices around the world.

In any given year, some 4,000 UNV specialists, field workers and national UNVs, short-term business/industry consultants and returning expatriate advisers, comprising more than 140 nationalities, are at work in a similar number of countries. Two thirds are themselves citizens of developing countries and one third come from industrialized countries. More than 20,000 persons have served as UNVs since 1971.

Graduate qualifications and several years' working experience are preconditions for recruitment. Contracts are normally for two years, with shorter assignments for humanitarian, electoral and other missions. UNVs receive a modest monthly living allowance. Funding comes from UNDP, partner United Nations agencies and donor contributions to the UNV Special Voluntary Fund.

The General Assembly has designated UNV as the focal point for the **International Year of Volunteers, 2001** (E-mail: team@iyv2001.org; Internet: www.iyv2001.org).

Executive Coordinator: Dr. Sharon Capeling-Alakija (Canada)
Headquarters: Postfach 260 111, D-53153 Bonn, Germany
Tel.: (49 228) 815 2000; Fax: (49 228) 815 2001
E-mail: enquiry@unv.org
Internet: www.unv.org

## United Nations Population Fund (UNFPA)

Established operationally in 1969 at the initiative of the General Assembly, the United Nations Population Fund is the largest internationally funded source of population assistance to developing countries and countries with economies in transition. It assists countries, at their request, to improve reproductive health and family planning services on the basis of individual choice, and to formulate population policies in support of efforts towards sustainable development. The UNFPA is a subsidiary organ of the General Assembly. It has the same Executive Board as UNDP.

The UNFPA is wholly funded by voluntary contributions, which amount to some $250 million per year. Nearly two thirds of its assistance is used for reproductive health, including family planning and sexual health, to refine approaches to adolescent reproductive health, reduce maternal mortality, address HIV/AIDS and provide assistance in emergencies. Close to one third is for population and development strategies to ensure a balance between development and population dynamics by providing information, influencing policy and building national capacity in population programming. The rest is used for advocacy to mobilize resources and political commitment for population activities. UNFPA has a staff of 905.

Executive Director: Ms. Thoraya Obaid (Saudi Arabia)
Headquarters: 220 East 42nd Street, New York, NY 10017, USA
Tel.: (1 212) 297 5000; Fax: (1 212) 370 0201
E-mail: hq@unfpa.org
Internet: www.unfpa.org

## Office of the United Nations High Commissioner for Refugees (UNHCR)

Created by the General Assembly in 1950, the Office of the United Nations High Commissioner for Refugees is mandated to lead and coordinate international action for the worldwide protection of refugees and the resolution of refugee problems. Since its creation, UNHCR has helped around 50 million refugees, earning two Nobel Peace Prizes in 1954 and in 1981.

UNHCR's most important responsibility, known as "international protection", is to ensure respect for refugees' basic human rights, including their ability to seek asylum and to ensure that no one is returned involuntarily to a country where he or she has reason to fear persecution. UNHCR also promotes international refugee agreements, monitors government compliance with international law and provides material assistance such as food, water, shelter and medical care to fleeing civilians.

Today, with a staff of more than 5,000 working in 281 offices in 121 countries, the agency is looking after 21.6 million people, including refugees, returnees and people displaced within their own countries. A total of 544 NGOs work as UNHCR's operational partners.

The High Commissioner's programmes are approved and supervised by UNHCR's Executive Committee, composed of 57 member countries. Programmes are financed by voluntary contributions, mainly from governments, but also from other groups including private citizens and organizations. UNHCR receives a limited subsidy—less than 2 per cent of the total—from the United Nations regular budget, which is used exclusively for administrative costs. The 2000 budget totalled $965.2 million.

*The State of the World's Refugees*, a comprehensive analysis of problems and policies related to refugees and other displaced people, is issued every two years.

High Commissioner: Mr. Ruud Lubbers (The Netherlands)
Headquarters: 94 Rue Montbrillant, Geneva, Switzerland
Tel.: (41 22) 739 85 02; Fax: (41 22) 739 73 14
E-mail: hqpi00@unhcr.ch
Internet: www.unhcr.ch

## United Nations Children's Fund (UNICEF)

Founded in 1946, the United Nations Children's Fund helps governments, communities and families make the world a better place for children. The only United Nations organization dedicated exclusively to children and women, UNICEF is mandated to advocate for the rights of children — a child being anyone below the age of 18. Its work is guided by the Convention on the Rights of the Child, which has been ratified by almost all countries.

UNICEF works in 161 countries, areas and territories. Its activities are as varied as the challenges it faces, and include encouraging the care and stimulation that offer the best possible start in life for children, helping prevent childhood illnesses and death, making pregnancy and childbirth safe, combating discrimination, cooperating with communities to ensure that girls as well as boys attend school, helping adolescents acquire skills they need to survive and involving them in community activities. UNICEF also provides emergency response in times of crisis, helping to recreate a sense of stability, reopening schools and establishing safe spaces for children.

UNICEF is governed by a 36-member Executive Board that establishes policies, reviews programmes and approves budgets. It had a staff of some 5,600 in 1999, 86 per cent of whom were in the field. UNICEF relies entirely on voluntary governmental and non-governmental contributions; about 36 per cent of its $1.1 billion income in 1999 came from non-governmental and private sector sources.

UNICEF assigned 91 per cent of its budget to programmes on health, education, nutrition and water and sanitation.

Major publications include *The State of the World's Children* and *The Progress of Nations*.

UNICEF was awarded the Nobel Peace Prize in 1965.

Executive Director: Ms. Carol Bellamy (USA)
Headquarters: UNICEF House, United Nations, New York, NY 10017, USA
Tel.: (1 212) 326 7000; Fax: (1 212) 888 7465
E-mail: webmaster@unicef.org
Internet: www.unicef.org

## World Food Programme (WFP)

As the food-aid arm of the United Nations system, the World Food Programme is the world's largest international food-aid organization, responsible for handling annually around 3 million metric tons of food aid. Established in 1963, WFP's mandate is to help poor people in developing countries by combating world hunger and poverty. It uses food aid to promote economic and social development. In emergencies, WFP provides fast, life-sustaining relief to victims of wars and of natural and man-made disasters. Eighty per cent of its resources are used for emergency relief.

WFP has a staff of more than 5,000, over half of whom are employed on a temporary basis. In 1999, 3.4 million tons of food was delivered to 89 million people in 82 countries. Total expenditures amounted to $1.5 billion.

While a large portion of WFP's food supplies are pledged in kind by donor countries, over $300 million is bought by WFP using multilateral and bilateral cash resources. It buys more goods and services from developing countries than any other United Nations agency — $122 million in 1999 alone.

WFP is governed by the 42-member Committee on Food Aid Policies and Programmes, half of whom are appointed by ECOSOC and half by FAO. The Committee meets twice a year.

Executive Director: Mr. James T. Morris (USA);
Headquarters: Via Cesare Giulio Viola, 68/70, 00148 Rome, Italy
Tel.: (39 06) 6513-1; Fax: (39 06) 6590-632 / 637
E-mail: wpinfo@wfp.org
Internet: www.wfp.org

## United Nations Relief and Works Agency for Palestine Refugees in the Near East (UNRWA)

The United Nations Relief and Works Agency for Palestine Refugees in the Near East was established by the General Assembly in 1949 to carry out relief work for Palestine refugees. In the absence of a solution to the Palestine refugee problem, its mandate has been periodically renewed, most recently until 30 June 2002.

UNRWA initially provided emergency relief to some 750,000 Palestine refugees who had lost their homes and livelihoods as a result of the 1948 Arab-Israeli conflict. By 2000, UNRWA was providing essential health, education, relief and social services to more that 3.7 million registered Palestine refugees. Of this number, some 1.2 million lived in 59 refugee camps served by the Agency in Jordan, Lebanon, the Syrian Arab Republic, the Gaza Strip and the West Bank.

UNRWA's operations are supervised and supported by its Headquarters in Gaza and in Amman, Jordan. The Commissioner-General, who reports directly to the General Assembly, is assisted by an Advisory Commission comprised of Belgium, Egypt, France, Japan, Jordan, Lebanon, Syria, Turkey, the United Kingdom and the United States.

UNRWA employs over 22,000 area staff, mainly Palestine refugees; the United Nations covers the costs of 98 international staff posts. UNRWA depends almost entirely on voluntary contributions for its regular and emergency operations. Most contributions are in cash, although 7 per cent of income is in kind, mainly as food donations for distribution to needy refugees. The regular budget for 2000 was $360 million; over 74 per cent of it was devoted to education, health and relief and social services.

Commissioner-General: Mr. Peter Hansen (Denmark)
Headquarters (Gaza): Gamal Abdul Nasser Street, Gaza City
Tel.: (972 7) 677 7333; Fax: (972 7) 677 7555
Headquarters (Amman, Jordan):
Bayader Wadi Seer, PO Box 140157, Amman 11814, Jordan
Tel.: (962 6) 582 6171/6; Fax: (962 6) 582 6177
Internet: www.unrwa.org

## Office of the United Nations High Commissioner for Human Rights (OHCHR)

The General Assembly in 1993 established the post of United Nations High Commissioner for Human Rights as the official with principal responsibility for United Nations human rights activities. The High Commissioner is charged with promoting and protecting the enjoyment by all of civil, cultural, economic, political and social rights. The mandate is carried out through the Office of the High Commissioner for Human Rights (OHCHR).

OHCHR acts as the focal point for all human rights activities of the United Nations. It prepares reports and undertakes research at the request of the General Assembly and other policy-making bodies. It co-operates with governments and international, regional and non-governmental organizations for the promotion and protection of human rights. It acts as the secretariat for the meetings of United Nations human rights bodies.

The Office, which has a staff of some 200, is organized into three branches:

- the Research and Right to Development Branch does research and analysis on human rights issues; develops and oversees the implementation of a strategy for the realization of the right to development;
- the Activities and Programme Branch carries out an extensive programme of technical assistance to countries, provides support to fact-finding bodies (Special Rapporteurs, Working Groups, etc.) that look into alleged violations, and plays a support and training role for human rights field activities;
- the Support Services Branch ensures support for United Nations human rights bodies, like the Commission on Human Rights and the treaty bodies.

High Commissioner: Mr. Sergio Vieira de Mello (Brazil)
Headquarters: Palais Wilson, 1211 Geneva 10, Switzerland
Tel.: (41 22) 917 31 34; Fax: (41 22) 917 02 45
E-mail: Secrt.hchr@unog.ch
Internet: www.unhchr.ch

## United Nations Human Settlements Programme (UN–Habitat)

The United Nations Human Settlements Programme (UN–Habitat)—formerly known as the United Nations Centre for Human Settlements—promotes sustainable human settlements development through advocacy, policy formulation, capacity-building, knowledge creation and the strengthening of partnerships between governments and civil society.

UN–Habitat, established in 1978, is the lead agency for coordinating human settlements development activities within the United Nations family, focusing on two priority areas: adequate shelter for all, and sustainable urban development.

The Human Settlements Programme supports and works in partnership with governments, local authorities, NGOs and the private sector. Its technical programmes and projects focus on a wide range of issues, including the urban environment, urban poverty reduction, post-disaster reconstruction and water management. Most of these programmes are implemented in partnership with other bilateral support agencies.

A flagship publication is the *Global Report on Human Settlements*, a complete review of human settlements conditions worldwide.

UN–Habitat is governed by the 58-member Governing Council—formerly the Commission on Human Settlements—which meets every two years.

Executive Director: Ms. Anna Kajumulo Tibaijuka (Tanzania)
Headquarters: P.O. Box 30030, Nairobi, Kenya
Tel.: (254-2) 621-234; Fax: (254-2) 624-266/7
E-mail: habitat@unhabitat.org
Internet: www.unhabitat.org

## United Nations Office for Project Services (UNOPS)

The United Nations Office for Project Services manages project resources to help developing countries and countries with economies in transition in their quest for peace, social stability, economic growth and sustainable development.

UNOPS offers the international community a broad range of services, from overall project management to the provision of single inputs. In responding flexibly to its clients' demands, UNOPS tailors management services to their particular needs, applies methods for attaining cost-effective results, and mobilizes diverse implementing partners.

UNOPS works in partnership with dozens of United Nations organizations, developing and donor country governments, the private sector and local and international NGOs. It is entirely funded by fees earned for services rendered. It has a staff of 1,100, including project personnel.

Executive Director: Mr. Reinhart Helmke (Germany)
Headquarters: 405 Lexington Avenue, New York, NY 10174, USA
Tel.: (1 212) 457 4000; Fax: (1 212) 457 4001
E-mail: unops.newyork@unops.org
Internet: www.unops.org

## United Nations University (UNU)

The United Nations University is an international community of scholars engaged in research, postgraduate training and the dissemination of knowledge to further the United Nations aims of peace and progress. The Charter of the University was adopted in 1973; it commenced operations in 1975.

The University has 13 Research and Training Centres and Programmes around the world (*see Chapter 3, page 174*).

UNU is financed entirely by voluntary contributions from governments, agencies, foundations and individual donors. It receives no funds from the United Nations budget: its basic annual income for operating expenses comes from investment income derived from its Endowment Fund. UNU's budget for 2000 was $35.9 million. It has a staff of 211.

UNU is governed by a 24-member Council that meets annually.

Rector: Prof. Hans van Ginkel (The Netherlands)
Headquarters: 53-70 Jingumae 5-Chome, Shibuka-Ku, Tokyo
150-8925, Japan
Tel.: (81-3) 3499-2811; Fax: (81-3) 3499-2828
E-mail: mbox@hq.unu.edu
Internet: www.unu.edu

## International Research and Training Institute for the Advancement of Women (INSTRAW)

The International Research and Training Institute for the Advancement of Women was established in 1976 on the recommendation of the first World Conference on Women. It has the unique mandate to promote and undertake policy research and training programmes at the international level to contribute to the advancement of women; to enhance their active and equal participation in the development process; to raise awareness of gender issues; and to create networks worldwide for the attainment of gender equality.

An autonomous body of the United Nations, INSTRAW is governed by an 11-member Board of Trustees appointed by ECOSOC. It is funded solely from voluntary contributions made by Member States, intergovernmental bodies, NGOs and private sources.

INSTRAW's expenditure for the 1998-1999 biennium was $4.01 million.

Interim Manager/Director: Ms. Savitri Butchey (Guyana)
Headquarters: César Nicolás Penson 02-A, Santo Domingo, Dominican Republic
Tel: (1 809) 685-2111; Fax: (1 809) 685-2117
E-mail: comments@un-instraw.org
Internet: www.un-instraw.org

## United Nations Interregional Crime and Justice Research Institute (UNICRI)

The United Nations Interregional Crime and Justice Research Institute, established in 1968, carries out research, training and information activities. UNICRI:

- promotes and supports research, in collaboration with the countries concerned, to establish a reliable base of knowledge and information on organized crime; to identify strategies for crime prevention and control so as to contribute to socio-economic development and human rights protection; and to design practical systems aimed at providing support for policy formulation, implementation and evaluation;
- designs and carries out training activities at the interregional and national levels;
- promotes the exchange of information through its international documentation centre on criminology.

The Institute is funded by voluntary contributions from Member States, governmental and non-governmental organizations, and academic institutions.

Director: Mr. Alberto Bradanini (Italy)
Headquarters: Viale Maestri del Lavoro 10, 10127 Turin, Italy
Tel.: (39 011) 653 7111; Fax: (39 011) 631 3368
E-mail: unicri@unicri.it
Internet: www.unicri.it

## United Nations Institute for Training and Research (UNITAR)

An autonomous United Nations body established in 1965, the United Nations Institute for Training and Research has the mandate to enhance the effectiveness of the United Nations through training and research. UNITAR provides training to assist countries in meeting the challenges of the 21$^{st}$ century; conducts research to explore innovative training and capacity building approaches; and forms partnerships with other United Nations agencies, governments and NGOs for developing and organizing training and capacity-building programmes that meet countries' needs.

UNITAR is governed by a Board of Trustees. It is fully self-funded and is sponsored by voluntary contributions from governments, intergovernmental organizations, foundations and other non-governmental sources. Its biennial budget is about $12.5 million. UNITAR's activities are conducted out of its Headquarters in Geneva, as well as through its New York Office. It has a staff of 45.

Executive Director: Mr. Marcel Boisard (Switzerland)
Headquarters: International Environment House, Chemin des Anémones 11-13
1219 Châtelaine-Geneva, Switzerland
Tel.: (41 22) 917 1234; Fax: (41 22) 917 8047
E-mail: info@unitar.org
Internet: www.unitar.org

## United Nations Research Institute for Social Development (UNRISD)

An autonomous United Nations body founded in 1963, the United Nations Research Institute for Social Development engages in research on the social dimensions of problems affecting development. UNRISD provides governments, development agencies, grass-roots organizations and scholars with a better understanding of how development policies and processes of economic, social and environmental change affect different social groups.

UNRISD relies wholly on voluntary contributions for financing its activities. In 1999, it received contributions for about $2 million from Denmark, Finland, Mexico, the Netherlands, Norway, Sweden, Switzerland and the United Kingdom. Additional funding for specific projects was received from a variety of other bodies, bilateral donors and United Nations agencies. An 11-member Board approves the budget and the research programme.

Director: Mr. Thandika Mkandawire (Sweden)
Headquarters: Palais des Nations, CH-1211 Geneva 10, Switzerland
Tel.: (41 22) 917 3020; Fax: (41 22) 917 0650
E-mail: info@unrisd.org
Internet: www.unrisd.org

## United Nations Institute for Disarmament Research (UNIDIR)

Established in 1980, the United Nations Institute for Disarmament Research undertakes independent research on disarmament and related international security issues. Current areas of research include: peace-keeping in Africa; peace-building and small arms issues in West Africa; small arms in Latin America; seminars series on small arms; small arms in Central Asia; nuclear tactical weapons; fissile materials; handbook on arms control.

UNIDIR has a small core staff. It relies heavily on project-related, short-term contracts to implement its research programme.

The Institute is financed by voluntary contributions from states and public or private organizations. The budget is around $1.1 million.

Director: Dr. Patricia Lewis (United Kingdom)
Headquarters: Palais des Nations, CH-1211 Geneva 10, Switzerland
Tel.: (41 22) 917 3186 or 917 4263; Fax: (41 22) 917 0176
E-mail: plewis@unog.ch
Internet: www.unog.ch/unidir

# Specialized Agencies and other Organizations
## International Labour Organization (ILO)

The International Labour Organization is the specialized agency that seeks the promotion of social justice and internationally recognized human and labour rights. Established in 1919, it became the first specialized agency of the United Nations in 1946.

ILO formulates international policies and programmes to help improve working and living conditions; creates international labour standards to serve as guidelines for national authorities in putting these policies into action; carries out an extensive programme of technical cooperation to help governments in making these policies effective; and engages in training, education and research to help advance these efforts.

ILO is unique among world organizations in that workers' and employers' representatives have an equal voice with those of governments in formulating its policies. It is composed of three bodies:

- The International Labour Conference brings together governmental, employer and worker delegates from member countries every year. It sets international labour standards and acts as a forum where social and labour questions of importance to the entire world are discussed;

- The Governing Body meets twice a year and directs ILO operations, prepares the programme and budget and examines cases of non-observance of ILO standards;
- The International Labour Office is the permanent secretariat of the Organization.

Opportunities for study and training are offered at the International Training Centre in Turin, Italy. ILO's International Institute for Labour Studies' means of action include research networks; social policy forums; courses and seminars; visiting scholar and internship programmes; and publications.

On its fiftieth anniversary in 1969, ILO was awarded the Nobel Peace Prize.

ILO has a staff of about 2,250, serving at headquarters and in 40 field offices around the world. Its budget for 2000-2001 was about $467 million.

Director-General: Mr. Juan Somavía (Chile)
Headquarters: 4, route des Morillons, CH-1211 Geneva 22, Switzerland
Tel.: (41 22) 799 61 11; Fax: (41 22) 798 86 85
E-mail: webinfo@hql.ilo.ch
Internet: www.ilo.org

## Food and Agriculture Organization of the United Nations (FAO)

The Food and Agriculture Organization of the United Nations is the lead agency for rural development in the United Nations system. It works to alleviate poverty and hunger by promoting agricultural development, improved nutrition and the pursuit of food security — the access of all people at all times to the food they need for an active and healthy life. FAO was founded at a conference in Québec City on 16 October 1945, a date observed annually as World Food Day.

FAO offers development assistance, provides policy and planning advice to governments, collects, analyses and disseminates information, and acts as an international forum for debate on food and agriculture issues. Special programmes help countries prepare for emergency food crisis and provide relief assistance. On average, FAO has some 1,800 field projects operating at any one time. FAO-assisted projects attract more than $300 million per year from donor agencies and governments.

FAO is governed by the Conference of member nations, which meets biennially. The Conference elects a 49-member Council that serves as the governing body between sessions of the Conference.

The budget for 2000-2001 was $650 million. FAO has a staff of 4,034, working at headquarters and in the field around the world.

Director-General: Dr. Jacques Diouf (Senegal)
Headquarters: Viale delle Terme di Caracalla, 00100 Rome, Italy
Tel.: (39 06) 57051; Fax: (39 06) 5705 3152
E-mail: gii-registry@fao.org
Internet: www.fao.org

## United Nations Educational, Scientific and Cultural Organization (UNESCO)

UNESCO was created in 1946 to build lasting world peace founded upon the intellectual and moral solidarity of humankind. Its areas of work are education, natural sciences, social and human sciences, culture and communication.

UNESCO's programmes aim at promoting a culture of peace and human and sustainable development. They focus on: achieving education for all; promoting environmental research through international scientific programmes; supporting the expression of cultural identities; protecting and enhancing the world's natural and cultural heritage; and promoting the free flow of information and press freedom, as well as strengthening the communication capacities of developing countries.

UNESCO is supported by 178 National Commissions and some 5,000 UNESCO Associations, Centres and Clubs. It cooperates with more than 588 NGOs and foundations, as well as international and regional networks.

UNESCO's governing body — the General Conference — is made up of all member states and meets every two years. The Executive Board, consisting of 58 members elected by the Conference, is responsible for supervising the programme adopted by the Conference.

UNESCO has a staff of 2,000. The regular budget for 2000-2001 was $544 million.

Director-General: Mr. Koichiro Matsuura (Japan)
Headquarters: 7 Place de Fontenoy, 75352 Paris 07-SP, France
Tel.: (33 1) 4568-1000; Fax: (33 1) 4567-1690
E-mail: info@unesco.org
Internet: www.unesco.org

## World Health Organization (WHO)

Established in 1948, the World Health Organization promotes technical cooperation for health among nations, carries out programmes to control and eradicate disease, and strives to improve the quality of life. Its objective is the attainment by all people of the highest possible level of health.

Its strategic directions are:

- reducing excess mortality, morbidity and disability, especially in poor and marginalized populations;
- promoting healthy lifestyles and reducing health risks that arise from environmental, economic, social and behavioural causes;
- developing health systems that are more equitable and effective, respond to people's legitimate demands and are financially fair;
- developing appropriate health policies and institutional environments, and promoting the health dimension of social, economic, environmental and development policies.

WHO's governing body is the World Health Assembly: composed of 191 member states, it meets every year. Its decisions and policies are given effect by the Executive Board: composed of 32 government-appointed health experts, it meets twice a year.

WHO has Regional Offices in Brazzaville, Congo (temporarily based in Harare, Zimbabwe); Washington, D.C., USA; Cairo, Egypt; Copenhagen, Denmark; New Delhi, India; and Manila, Philippines.

WHO has a staff of about 3,800. Its regular budget for 2000-2001 was $842 million.

Director-General: Dr. Gro Harlem Brundtland (Norway)
Headquarters: 20 Avenue Appia, CH-1211 Geneva 27, Switzerland
Tel.: (41 22) 791 2111; Fax: (41 22) 791 3111
E-mail: inf@who.int
Internet: www.who.int

## World Bank Group

The World Bank is a group of five institutions: the International Bank for Reconstruction and Development (established in 1945); the International Finance Corporation (1956); the International Development Association (1960); the Multilateral Investment Guarantee Agency (1988); and the International Centre for Settlement of Investment Disputes (1966).

The common goal of all institutions is to reduce poverty around the world by strengthening the economies of poor nations. Their aim is to improve people's living standards by promoting economic growth and development.

The Bank's governing body is the Board of Governors, in which all member states are represented. General operations are delegated to a smaller group, the Board of Executive Directors, with the President of the Bank serving as Chairman of the Board.

The World Bank Group has a staff of some 11,000 and an administrative annual budget of about $1.4 billion.

Among its major publications is the annual *World Development Report*.

President: Mr. James D. Wolfensohn (USA)
Headquarters: 1818 H Street NW, Washington, D.C. 20433, USA
Tel.: (1 202) 477 1234; Fax: (1 202) 477 6391
E-mail: feedback@worldbank.org
Internet: www.worldbank.org

## International Bank for Reconstruction and Development (IBRD)

The Articles of IBRD were drawn up in 1944 at the Bretton Woods Conference, and the Bank began operations in 1946. The Bank provides loans and development assistance to middle-income countries and creditworthy poorer countries. Voting power is linked to member countries' capital subscriptions, which in turn are based on each country's relative economic strength.

The Bank obtains 90 per cent of its funds through sale of bonds in international capital markets. Over its 54-year history, only $11 billion of capital has been paid in to the Bank by its shareholders, but that amount has leveraged into more than $280 billion in loans.

In fiscal 1999 the Bank's commitments amounted to $29 billion. Adjustment lending, which includes institution-building, governance, economic policy and social protection, amounted to $15.3 billion; more than half was poverty-focused, with strong support to social sectors. Assistance for human development — education, health, nutrition and social protection — totalled $7.3 billion, or 25 per cent of lending. Loans were invested in sectors such as power, oil and gas, industry and mining, transport, urban development, water and sanitation and the financial sector.

## International Development Association (IDA)

IDA provides financing on highly concessional terms for the world's poorest countries, those that are not able to service loans from the IBRD. IBRD is responsible for its administration.

IDA loans, known as "credits", are extended mainly to countries with annual per capita incomes of less than $895. IDA "credits" are for a period of 35 to 40 years, without interest, except for a small charge to cover administrative costs. Repayment of principal does not begin until after a 10-year grace period.

The bulk of IDA's resources come from donor government contributions. These contributions come mainly from richer IDA members, but donor countries also include some countries that are current recipients of IBRD loans. Donors are asked every three years to "replenish" IDA funds. There have been 12 replenishments since IDA was established.

IDA lends on average about \$5-\$6 billion a year, especially for development projects that address people's basic needs, such as primary education, basic health services, and clean water and sanitation. IDA also funds projects that protect the environment, improve conditions for private business, build infrastructure and support reforms aimed at liberalizing countries' economies.

### International Finance Corporation (IFC)

IFC is the largest multilateral source of loan and equity financing for private-sector projects in the developing world. It finances and provides advice for private-sector ventures and projects in developing countries in partnership with private investors and, through its advisory work, helps governments create conditions that stimulate the flow of both domestic and foreign private savings and investment.

Its focus is to promote economic development by encouraging the growth of productive enterprise and efficient capital markets in its member countries. IFC participates in an investment only when it can make a special contribution that complements the role of market investors. It also plays a catalytic role, stimulating and mobilizing private investment in the developing world by demonstrating that investments there can be profitable.

IFC is a separate entity within the World Bank Group and its funds are distinct from those of IBRD. In fiscal 1999, IFC's Board of Directors approved 255 new projects amounting to \$5.3 billion.

### Multilateral Investment Guarantee Agency (MIGA)

MIGA helps to encourage foreign investment in developing countries by providing insurance (guarantees) to foreign private investors against loss caused by non-commercial (i.e. political) risks, such as currency transfer, expropriation, and war and civil disturbance. It also provides technical assistance to help countries disseminate information on investment opportunities.

MIGA's subscribed capital from its 151 member countries exceeds \$1 billion. Its Council of Governors in 1999 approved a capital increase of some \$850 million. The World Bank has transferred another \$150 million as operating capital.

MIGA has successfully promoted the flow of capital to developing countries. To date, MIGA guarantees have facilitated an estimated \$33 billion in foreign direct investments in 69 developing and transition member countries.

### International Centre for Settlement of Investment Disputes (ICSID)

ICSID provides facilities for the settlement — by conciliation or arbitration — of investment disputes between governments and private foreign investors. It was established under the 1966 *Convention on the Settlement of Investment Disputes between States and Nationals of Other States*, which has been ratified by 131 countries. Recourse to the Centre is voluntary, but once the parties have consented to arbitration neither can unilaterally withdraw its consent.

The Centre is an autonomous organization with close links to the Bank, and all of its members are also members of the Bank. Its Administrative Council, chaired by the World Bank's President, consists of one representative of each country that has ratified the Convention.

## International Monetary Fund (IMF)

Established at the Bretton Woods Conference in 1944, the International Monetary Fund:

- facilitates international monetary cooperation;
- promotes exchange rate stability and orderly exchange arrangements;
- assists in the establishment of a multilateral system of payments and the elimination of foreign exchange restrictions;
- assists members by temporarily providing financial resources to correct maladjustments in their balance of payments.

The financial resources of IMF consist primarily of the subscription ("quotas") of its 182 member countries, which currently total SDR 210 billion, or about $300 billion. Quotas are determined by a formula based upon the relative economic size of the members. IMF has authority to create and allocate to its members international financial reserves in the form of "Special Drawing Rights (SDRs)".

IMF's main financial role is to provide temporary credits to members experiencing balance of payments difficulties. In return, members borrowing from IMF agree to undertake policy reforms to correct the problems that underlie these difficulties. The amounts that IMF members may borrow are limited in proportion to their quotas.

IMF also offers concessional assistance to low-income member countries *(see Chapter 3, page 137)*.

IMF's governing body, the Board of Governors, in which all member countries are represented, meets annually. Day-to-day work is conducted by the 24-member Executive Board, advised by the Interim Committee.

IMF has a staff of about 2,700 from 123 countries, headed by a Managing Director who is selected by the Executive Board. Its administrative annual budget is about $650 million.

IMF publishes the *World Economic Outlook* twice a year, as well as the annual *International Capital Markets* report.

Managing Director: Mr. Horst Koehler (Germany)
Headquarters: 700 19th Street NW, Washington, D.C. 20431, USA
Tel.: (1 202) 623 7000; Fax: (1 202) 623 4661
E-mail: publicaffairs@imf.org
Internet: www.imf.org

## International Civil Aviation Organization (ICAO)

The International Civil Aviation Organization makes it safer and easier to fly from one country to another. Created in 1944, it sets international standards and regulations necessary for the safety, security, efficiency and regularity of air transport, and serves as the medium for cooperation in all fields of civil aviation among its 185 Contracting States.

ICAO has an Assembly, its sovereign body, comprising delegates from all Contracting States, and a Council of representatives of 33 nations elected by the Assembly. The Assembly meets at least once every three years: it decides ICAO policy and examines any matters not specifically referred to the Council. The Council is the executive body, and carries out Assembly directives.

The budget for 2000 was $52.6 million. ICAO has a staff of 793.

President of the Council: Dr. Assad Kotaite (Lebanon)
Secretary General: Mr. R.C. Costa Pereira (Brazil)
Headquarters: 999 University Street, Montreal, Quebéc H3C 5H7, Canada
Tel.: (1) (514) 954 8219; Fax: (1) (514) 954 6077
E-mail: icaohq@icao.org
Internet: www.icao.org

## International Maritime Organization (IMO)

The International Maritime Organization, which began functioning in 1959, is responsible for improving the safety of shipping engaged in international trade and for preventing marine pollution from ships.

IMO provides the machinery for governments to cooperate in formulating regulations and practices relating to technical matters affecting international shipping; to facilitate the adoption of the highest practicable standards of maritime safety and efficiency in navigation; and to protect the marine environment through prevention and control of pollution from ships.

Currently, some 40 conventions and protocols and some 800 codes and recommendations have been produced and globally implemented (*see Chapter 3, page 149*).

In 1983, IMO established the World Maritime University in Malmö, Sweden, which provides advanced training for administrators, educators and others involved in shipping at the senior level. The IMO International Maritime Law Institute, Valletta, Malta, was established in 1989 to train lawyers in international maritime law. The IMO International Maritime Academy, Trieste, Italy, established in 1989, offers specialized short courses in a variety of maritime disciplines.

IMO's governing body, the Assembly, consists of all member states and meets every two years. It elects the 32-member Council, which is IMO's executive organ and meets twice a year.

IMO's budget for 2000-2001 was $56.3 million. It has a staff of about 300.

Secretary-General: Mr. William A. O'Neil (Canada)
Headquarters: 4 Albert Embankment, London SE1 7SR, England
Tel.: (44 207) 735 76 11; Fax: (44 207) 587 32 10
E-mail: info@imo.org
Internet: www.imo.org

## International Telecommunication Union (ITU)

The International Telecommunication Union is an international organization within which governments and the private sector coordinate global telecommunication networks and services. Founded in Paris in 1865 as the International Telegraph Union, ITU took its present name in 1934 and became a United Nations specialized agency in 1947.

ITU's mandate covers the following areas:
- a technical area: to promote the development and efficient operation of telecommunication facilities, in order to improve the efficiency of telecommunication services and their availability to the public;
- a policy area: to promote the adoption of a broader approach to the issues of telecommunications in the global information economy and society;
- a development area: to promote and offer technical assistance to developing countries in the field of telecommunications, to promote the mobilization of the human and financial resources needed to develop telecommunications, and to promote the extension of the benefits of new technologies to people everywhere.

ITU is composed of 189 member states and nearly 600 sector members (scientific and industrial companies, public and private operators, broadcasters, regional and international organizations). Its governing body is the Plenipotentiary Conference, which meets every four years and which elects the 46-member ITU Council that meets annually.

ITU has a staff of 740. Its budget for the 2000-2001 biennium was $23 million.

Secretary-General: Mr. Yoshio Utsumi (Japan)
Headquarters: Place des Nations, CH-1211 Geneva 20, Switzerland
Tel.: (41 22) 730 5111; Fax: (41 22) 733 7256
E-mail: itumail@itu.int
Internet: www.itu.int

## Universal Postal Union (UPU)

The Universal Postal Union is the specialized institution that regulates international postal services. Established by the Berne Treaty of 1874, it became a United Nations specialized agency in 1948.

The UPU plays a leadership role in promoting the continued revitalization of postal services. With 189 member countries, it is the primary vehicle for cooperation between postal services. It advises, mediates and renders technical assistance. Among its principal objectives are the promotion of universal postal service, growth in mail volumes through the provision of up-to-date postal products and services, and improvement in the quality of postal service for customers. In so doing, the UPU fulfils its basic mission of promoting and developing communication between all the people of the world.

The Universal Postal Congress is the supreme authority of the UPU. Meeting every five years, it examines strategic issues of concern to the postal sector and lays down the general programme of activities. The twenty-third Congress is to take place in Abidjan, Côte d'Ivoire, in 2004.

UPU's budget for 2000 was $22.5 million. Its has a staff of 151.

Director-General: Mr. Thomas E. Leavey (USA)
Headquarters: Weltpoststrasse 4, Case Postale 3000, Berne 15, Switzerland
Tel.: (41 31) 350 31 11; Fax: (41 31) 350 31 10
E-mail: info@upu.int
Internet: www.upu.int

## World Meteorological Organization (WMO)

The World Meteorological Organization, a United Nations specialized agency since 1951, provides authoritative scientific information on atmospheric environment, the Earth's freshwater resources and climate issues. It develops weather-forecasting services, including seasonal forecasting, and through international collaboration contributes to tracking of global weather conditions, makes possible the rapid exchange of weather information and promotes activities in operational hydrology.

WMO operates various major programmes on issues including climate, the atmosphere, applied meteorology, the environment and water resources. These programmes provide the basis for better preparation and forewarning of severe weather events such as tropical cyclones, El Niño, floods, droughts and other natural disasters, saving both lives and property, and improve our understanding of the environment and the climate. WHO has drawn attention to issues of major concern, such as ozone layer depletion, global warming and diminishing water resources.

WMO has 185 members, comprising 179 states and 6 territories, all of which maintain their own meteorological and hydrological services. Its governing body, the World Meteorological Congress, meets every four years. The 36-member Executive Council meets annually.

WMO has a staff of 246. The budget for 2000-2003 was $152 million.

Secretary-General: Dr. G.O.P. Obasi (Nigeria)
Headquarters: 7 bis, Avenue de la Paix, CH-1211 Geneva 2, Switzerland
Tel.: (41 22) 730 8111; Fax: (41 22) 730 8181
E-mail: ipa@gateway.wmo.ch
Internet: www.wmo.ch

## World Intellectual Property Organization (WIPO)

The World Intellectual Property Organization was established in 1970 and became a United Nations specialized agency in 1974. Its objectives are to promote the protection of intellectual property throughout the world through cooperation among its 175 member states, and to ensure administrative cooperation among the Unions established to afford protection in the field of intellectual property.

The principal Unions so established are:
• the Paris Union, officially the International Union for the Protection of Industrial Property;
• the Berne Union, officially the International Union for the Protection of Literary and Artistic Works.

Intellectual property comprises two main branches: industrial property, chiefly inventions, trademarks, industrial designs and appellations of origin; and copyright, mainly of literary, musical, artistic, photographic and audiovisual works. WIPO administers 21 international treaties, 15 on industrial property and 6 on copyright.

WIPO's three governing bodies are: the General Assembly, comprised of WIPO member states which are members of the Paris and/or Berne Union, and which meets every two years; the Conference, comprised of all member states, which also meets every two years; and the 72-member Coordination Committee, which meets every year.

WIPO's programme and budget are established biennially by its governing bodies. Its 2000-2001 budget was about $248 million. WIPO has a staff of 765.

Director-General: Dr. Kamil Idris (Sudan)
Headquarters: 34 Chemin des Colombettes, 1211 Geneva 20, Switzerland
Tel.: (41 22) 338 91 11; Fax: (41 22) 733 54 28
E-mail: PUBLICINF.mail@wipo.int
Internet: www.wipo.int

## International Fund for Agricultural Development (IFAD)

The International Fund for Agricultural Development, a multilateral financial institution established in 1977 following a decision by the 1974 World Food Conference, is mandated to combat hunger and rural poverty in the developing countries.

The Fund mobilizes resources for improved food production and better nutrition among the poor in developing countries, focusing on the needs of the poorest rural communities. Chronic hunger and malnutrition almost always accompany extreme poverty — 75 per cent of which is in rural areas.

IFAD provides direct financing through loans and grants, and mobilizes additional resources for its projects and programmes. Lending terms and conditions vary according to the country's gross national product per capita. IFAD works with many other institutions, including the World Bank, regional development banks, other regional financial agencies and United Nations agencies. Many of these institutions co-finance IFAD projects.

IFAD is financed by voluntary contributions from governments, special contributions, loan repayments and investments income. The annual commitment for new projects and grants is around $450 million. The Fund has a staff of 266.

The governing body, the Governing Council, is made up of all member States and meets annually. The Executive Board, consisting of 18 members and 18 alternate members, oversees the Fund's operations and approves loans and grants.

President: Mr. Lennart Bage (Sweden)
Headquarters: Via del Serafico 107, 00142 Rome, Italy
Tel.: (39 06) 54 591; Fax: (39 06) 504 3463
E-mail: ifad@ifad.org
Internet: www.ifad.org

## United Nations Industrial Development Organization (UNIDO)

The mandate of the United Nations Industrial Development Organization is to promote industrial development and cooperation. Established by the General Assembly in 1966, it became a United Nations specialized agency in 1985.

UNIDO helps to improve the living conditions of people and promote global prosperity by offering tailor-made solutions for the sustainable industrial development of developing countries and countries in transition. It cooperates with governments, business associations and the private industrial sector to build industrial capabilities for meeting the challenges and spreading the benefits of globalization of industry.

To support its services, UNIDO has engineers, economists and technology and environment specialists in Vienna, as well as professional staff in its network of Investment Promotion Service offices and field offices. Field offices are headed by UNIDO Regional and Country Representatives.

UNIDO's 168 member states meet every two years at the General Conference, which approves the budget and work programme. The Industrial Development Board, comprising 53 member States, makes recommendations relating to the planning and implementation of the programme and budget.

UNIDO has a staff of some 650 at headquarters, and appointed about 1,830 experts in 1999 serving worldwide. Its budget for 2000-2001 was $133 million. Additional funds are increasingly mobilized from multilateral and bilateral sources.

Director-General: Mr. Carlos Magariños (Argentina)
Headquarters: Vienna International Centre, A-1400 Vienna, Austria
Tel.: (43 1) 26026/0; Fax: (43 1) 269 2669
E-mail: unido-pinfo@unido.org
Internet: www.unido.org

## International Atomic Energy Agency (IAEA)

The International Atomic Energy Agency serves as the world's central intergovernmental forum for scientific and technical cooperation in the peaceful uses of nuclear energy, and as the international inspectorate for the application of nuclear safeguards and verification measures covering civilian nuclear programmes. It was set up in 1957 as an autonomous agency under the aegis of the United Nations.

The Agency provides technical assistance to its 131 member states in the development of self-sufficient nuclear science programmes. Almost half of the Agency's work focuses on programmes that can be applied in areas such as food and agriculture, health, industry and hydrology and environmental pollution, especially marine.

IAEA helps states to verify their compliance with international treaties, meant to ensure that nuclear materials are not diverted for military purposes. Some 200 inspectors are deployed worldwide to more than 1,000 installations and other locations covered under the IAEA Safeguards Programme.

IAEA's governing bodies are the General Conference, in which all member states are represented and which meets annually; and the Board of Governors, made up of 35 member states.

IAEA has a staff of 2,133. Its regular budget for 2000 was $224 million, with extrabudgetary contributions amounting to $80 million.

Director-General: Mr. Mohamed ElBaradei (Egypt)
Headquarters: Vienna International Centre, Wagramerstrasse 5,
P.O. Box 100, A-1400 Vienna, Austria
Tel.: (43 1) 2600-0; Fax: (43 1) 2600-7
E-mail: official.mail@iaea.org
Internet: www.iaea.org

## Preparatory Commission for the Comprehensive Nuclear-Test-Ban Treaty Organization (CTBTO)

The Preparatory Commission for the Comprehensive Nuclear-Test-Ban Treaty Organization (*see Chapter 2, page 113*) was established on 19 November 1996 at a Meeting of States Signatories to the Treaty held in New York. As an international organization financed by the States Signatories, it consists of two organs: a plenary body composed of all the States Signatories — also known as the Preparatory Commission — and the Provisional Technical Secretariat. The main task of the Preparatory Commission is to establish the global verification regime foreseen in the Treaty, so that it will be operational by the time the Treaty enters into force. The Commission has three subsidiary bodies; Working Group A on administrative and budgetary matters; Working Group B on verification issues; as well as the Advisory Group on financial, budgetary and associated administrative issues.

Executive Secretary: Mr. Wolfgang Hoffmann (Germany)
Headquarters: Vienna International Centre, P.O.Box 1200, A-1400 Vienna, Austria
Tel: (431) 26030 6159; Fax: (431) 26030 55877
E-mail: info@ctbto.org
Internet: www.ctbto.org

## Organisation for the Prohibition of Chemical Weapons (OPCW)

The Organisation for the Prohibition of Chemical Weapons' main task is the implementation of the Convention on the Prohibition of the Development, Production, Stockpiling and Use of Chemical Weapons and on their Destruction (*see Chapter 2, page 116*). The Convention, which entered into force on 29 April 1997, is the first international disarmament agreement that provides for the elimination of an entire category of weapons of mass destruction.

The Conference of the States Parties is the principal organ of OPCW: composed of all members, it meets annually. The Executive Council supervises the OPCW's day-to-day activities: it consists of 41 representatives elected for two-year terms from among the member states. The Technical Secretariat has the primary responsibility for the activities mandated by the Convention, including carrying out verification, providing assistance if chemical weapons are used and promoting international cooperation in the peaceful use of chemistry. The Scientific Advisory Board provides specialized advice in areas of science and technology related to the Convention.

OPCW has a staff of some 500, and an annual budget of $56 million.

Director-General: Mr. Rogelio Pfirter (Argentina)
Headquarters: Johan de Wittlaan 32, 2517 The Hague, The Netherlands
Tel.: (31 70) 416 3300; Fax: (31 70) 306 3535
E-mail: webmaster@opcw.org
Internet: www.opcw.org

## World Tourism Organization (WTO)

Dating back to 1925, the World Tourism Organization is the leading international organization in the field of travel and tourism. It serves as a global forum for tourism policy issues and a practical source of tourism know-how. Its membership includes 138 countries and territories, as well as more than 350 affiliate members representing local government, tourism associations and private-sector companies, including airlines, hotel groups and tour operators.

An intergovernmental body entrusted by the United Nations with the promotion and development of tourism, WTO signed a cooperation agreement with the United Nations in 1977. Through tourism, WTO aims to stimulate economic growth and job creation, provide incentives for protecting the environment and heritage of tourist destinations, and promote understanding among nations.

WTO's supreme organ, the General Assembly, is made up of the full and associate members. It meets every two years to approve the budget and work programme, and to debate major topics of the tourism sector. The Executive Council is WTO's governing board: composed of 26 members elected by the Assembly, it meets twice a year. The six regional commissions — Africa, the Americas, East Asia and the Pacific, Europe, the Middle East and South Asia — composed of the members from the region, meet at least once a year.

WTO has a staff of 80 and a biennial budget of some $18 million.

Secretary-General: Francesco Frangialli (France)
Headquarters: Capitán Haya 42, 28020 Madrid, Spain
Tel.: (34) 91 567 81 00; Fax: (34) 91 571 37 33
E-mail: omt@world-tourism.org
Internet: www.world-tourism.org

## World Trade Organization (WTO)

The World Trade Organization was established in 1995, replacing the General Agreement on Tariffs and Trade (GATT) as the only international body dealing with the global rules of trade between nations. It is not a specialized agency, but has cooperative arrangements and practices with the United Nations.

The purpose of WTO is to help trade flow smoothly, in a system based on rules; to impartially settle trade disputes between governments; and to organize trade negotiations. At its heart are the some 60 WTO agreements, the legal ground rules for international commerce and trade policy.

The principles on which these agreements are based include: non-discrimination (the "most-favoured nation" clause), freer trade, encouraging competition, and extra provisions for less developed countries. One of WTO's objectives is to reduce protectionism.

Since its establishment, WTO has been the forum for successful negotiations to open markets in telecommunications, in information technology equipment and financial services. It has been involved in settling more than 190 trade disputes, and it continues to oversee implementation of the agreements reached in the 1986-1994 Uruguay Round of world trade talks.

WTO has 135 member countries. Its governing body, the Ministerial Conference, meets every two years; the General Council carries out the day-to-day work.

WTO's budget for 2000 was $77.1 million. It has a staff of 500.

Director-General: Dr. Supachai Panitchpakdi (Thailand)
Headquarters: Centre William Rappard, 154 Rue de Lausanne,
CH-1211 Geneva 21, Switzerland
Tel.: (41 22) 739 51 11; Fax: (41 22) 731 42 06
E-mail: enquiries@wto.org
Internet: www.wto.org

# PART TWO

## Chapter 2

**International Peace and Security**

# INTERNATIONAL PEACE AND SECURITY

One of the primary purposes of the United Nations — and a central part of its mandate — is the maintenance of international peace and security. Since its creation, the United Nations has often been called upon to prevent disputes from escalating into war, to persuade opposing parties to use the conference table rather than force of arms, or to help restore peace when conflict does break out. Over the decades, the United Nations has helped to end numerous conflicts, often through actions of the Security Council — the primary organ for dealing with issues of international peace and security.

During the 1990s, there have been major changes in the patterns of conflict and in the international community's response to them. One reason is that more than 90 per cent of recent conflicts have taken place within, rather than between, states.

The United Nations has therefore reshaped and enhanced the range of instruments at its command, emphasizing conflict prevention, continually adapting peacekeeping operations to meet new challenges, increasingly involving regional organizations, and strengthening post-conflict peace-building. Civil conflicts have raised complex issues regarding the response of the international community, including the dilemma of whether to intervene to protect endangered civilians (*see box on page 71*).

To deal with civil conflicts, the Security Council has authorized complex and innovative peacekeeping operations. In El Salvador and Guatemala, in Cambodia and in Mozambique, the United Nations played a major role in ending conflict and fostering reconciliation.

Other conflicts, however — in Somalia, Rwanda and the former Yugoslavia — often characterized by ethnic violence, brought new challenges to the United Nations peacemaking role. Confronted with the problems encountered in these conflicts, the Security Council did not establish any operation from 1995 to 1997.

But the essential role of United Nations peacekeeping has once more been dramatically reaffirmed. Continuing crises in the Democratic Republic of the Congo, the Central African Republic, East Timor, Kosovo and Sierra Leone led the Council to establish five new missions in 1998-1999. A sixth one was created in 2000 to support the peace process between Ethiopia and Eritrea.

The experience of recent years has also led the United Nations to focus as never before on peace-building — action to support structures that will strengthen and consolidate peace. Experience has shown that keeping peace, in the sense of avoiding military conflict, is not sufficient for establishing a secure and lasting peace. Such security can only be achieved by helping countries to foster economic development, social justice, human rights protection, good governance and the democratic process. No other institution has the multilateral experience, competence, coordinating ability and impartiality that the United Nations brings in support of these tasks. This has been demonstrated by the complex and challenging peace-building tasks entrusted to the United Nations in East Timor and Kosovo.

The **Security Council**, the **General Assembly** and the **Secretary-General** all play major, complementary roles in fostering peace and security. United Nations activities cover the principal areas of *prevention (see page 70), peacemaking (see page 72), peacekeeping (see page 73), enforcement (see page 77)* and *peace-building (see page 78)*. These types of engagement must overlap or take place simultaneously if they are to be effective.

## The Security Council

The United Nations Charter — an international treaty — obligates Member States to settle their disputes by peaceful means, in such a manner that international peace and security, and justice, are not endangered. They are to refrain from the threat or use of force against any state, and may bring any dispute before the Security Council.

The Security Council *(see also Chapter 1, page 8)* is the United Nations organ with primary responsibility for maintaining peace and security. Under the Charter, Member States are obliged to accept and carry out its decisions. Recommendations of other United Nations bodies do not have the mandatory force the decisions of the Security Council have, but can influence situations as they express the opinion of the international community.

When a dispute is brought to its attention, the Council usually urges the parties to settle their dispute by peaceful means. It may make recommendations to the parties for a peaceful settlement. It may appoint special representatives or ask the Secretary-General to use his good offices. In some cases the Council itself undertakes investigation and mediation.

When a dispute leads to fighting, the Council seeks to bring it to an end as quickly as possible. Often the Council has issued ceasefire directives that have been instrumental in preventing wider hostilities. In support of a peace process, the Council may deploy military observers or a peacekeeping force to an area of conflict.

Under *Chapter VII* of the Charter, the Council is empowered to take measures to enforce its decisions. It can impose embargoes and sanctions, or authorize the use of force to ensure that mandates are fulfilled.

In some cases, the Council has authorized, under Chapter VII, the use of military force by a coalition of Member States or by a regional organization or arrangement. But the Council takes such action only as a last resort, when peaceful means of settling a dispute have been exhausted, and after determining that a threat to the peace, a breach of the peace or act of aggression exists.

Also under Chapter VII, the Council has established international tribunals to prosecute persons accused of serious violations of international humanitarian and human rights law, including genocide.

## The General Assembly

The United Nations Charter (article 11) empowers the General Assembly to "consider the general principles of cooperation in the maintenance of international peace and security" and "make recommendations ... to the Members or to the Security Council or to both". The Assembly offers a means for finding consensus on difficult issues, providing a forum for the airing of grievances and diplomatic exchanges. To foster the maintenance of peace, it has held special or emergency special sessions on issues such as disarmament, the question of Palestine or the situation in Afghanistan.

The General Assembly considers peace and security issues in its First (Disarmament and International Security) Committee and in its Fourth (Special Political and Decolonization) Committee. Over the years, the Assembly has helped promote peaceful relations among nations by adopting declarations on peace, the peaceful settlement of disputes and international cooperation.

The Assembly in 1980 approved the establishment in San José, Costa Rica, of the **University for Peace**, an international institute for studies, research and dissemination of knowledge on peace-related issues.

The Assembly has designated the opening day of its regular annual session in September as **International Day of Peace**.

# Conflict prevention

The main strategies for preventing disputes from escalating into conflict, and for preventing the recurrence of conflict, are preventive diplomacy, preventive deployment and preventive disarmament.

*Preventive diplomacy* refers to action to prevent disputes from arising, to resolve them before they escalate into conflicts or to limit the spread of conflicts when they occur. It may take the form of mediation, conciliation or negotiation. Early warning is an essential component of prevention, and the United Nations carefully monitors political and other developments around the world to detect threats to international peace and security, thereby enabling the Security Council and the Secretary-General to carry out preventive action.

Envoys and Special Representatives of the Secretary-General are engaged in mediation and preventive diplomacy throughout the world. In some trouble spots, the mere presence of a skilled Special Representative can prevent the escalation of tension. This work is often undertaken in close cooperation with regional organizations (*see page 77, below*).

Complementing preventive diplomacy are preventive deployment and preventive disarmament. *Preventive deployment* — the fielding of peacekeepers to forestall probable conflict — is intended to provide a "thin blue line" to help contain conflicts by building confidence in areas of tension. To date, the only specific instances are the United Nations missions in the former Yugoslav Republic of Macedonia[1] and in the Central African Republic (*see page 88, below*). Preventive deployment has been considered in other conflicts and remains a valuable option.

*Preventive disarmament* seeks to reduce the number of small arms in conflict-prone regions. In El Salvador, Mozambique and elsewhere, this has entailed demobilizing combat forces as well as collecting and destroying their weapons as part of an overall peace

---

[1]United Nations action in the former Yugoslav Republic of Macedonia is an example of successful "preventive deployment". Concerned about being drawn into the Yugoslav conflict (*see page 104*), the country in 1992 requested the deployment of United Nations observers. The Security Council agreed and dispatched a peacekeeping contingent to the country's borders with Yugoslavia and Albania. The 1,100-strong United Nations Preventive Deployment Force monitored developments in the border areas that could threaten the country's territory or undermine its stability. The country repeatedly requested the extension of the mission, which stayed until 1999 and stands as a model for future preventive operations.

# The question of intervention

Should the international community intervene in a country to stop gross, systematic and widespread violations of human rights? The question was raised in 1998 by Secretary-General Kofi Annan, generating wide debate.

In the wake of genocide, crimes against humanity and war crimes in Central Africa, the Balkans and elsewhere, the Secretary-General has argued that the international community should agree on legitimate and universal principles, within the framework of international law, for protecting civilians against massive and systematic human rights violations.

The legal framework, Mr. Annan has said, is provided by universal norms embodied in the Charter, international humanitarian law, human rights law and refugee law. The concept of intervention covers a wide range of actions, including, in some circumstances, the Security Council intervening in internal conflicts by authorizing the creation of "safe corridors" and "safe areas" in conflict zones, imposing sanctions against recalcitrant states or taking other measures. At the same time, Mr. Annan has warned that such coercive action will have the support of the world's people only if it is fairly and consistently applied.

In the ensuing debate, one group of nations has maintained that, in the face of massive human rights violations and crimes against humanity, the responsibility of the international community to prevent violations is paramount. Thus, in the last resort, human rights can be legitimately protected through the use of force authorized by the Security Council.

A second group of nations has raised three major questions: Where does humanitarian assistance stop and interference in the internal affairs of states begin? How does one distinguish between humanitarian imperatives and political or economic motivations? Is humanitarian intervention valid only for weak states, or for all states without distinctions? These nations have called for a broad dialogue, and urged that any decision be based on the consensus of Member States.

A third group of states has argued that the notion of humanitarian intervention has the potential to undermine the Charter, eroding the sovereignty of states and threatening legitimate governments and the stability of the international system. They have emphasized that all measures to protect human rights should be taken only with respect for the independence, sovereignty and territorial integrity of all countries, and the will of the government and people of the country concerned.

The moral rights and wrongs of this complex issue have continued to be debated, and the principles involved are likely to be tested again when a major humanitarian crisis challenges the international community.

agreement. Destroying yesterday's weapons prevents their being used in tomorrow's wars.

# Peacemaking

Peacemaking refers to the use of diplomatic means to persuade parties in conflict to cease hostilities and to negotiate a peaceful settlement of their dispute. The United Nations provides various means through which conflicts may be contained and resolved, and their root causes addressed. The Security Council may recommend ways to resolve a dispute or request the Secretary-General's mediation. The **Secretary-General** may take diplomatic initiatives to encourage and maintain the momentum of negotiations.

The Secretary-General plays a central role in peacemaking, both personally and by dispatching special envoys or missions for specific tasks, such as negotiation or fact-finding. Under the Charter, the Secretary-General may bring to the attention of the Security Council any matter which may threaten the maintenance of international peace and security.

To help resolve disputes, the Secretary-General may use "good offices" for mediation or exercise preventive diplomacy. The impartiality of the Secretary-General is one of the United Nations great assets. In many instances, the Secretary-General has been instrumental in averting a threat to peace or in securing a peace agreement.

For instance, action by the Secretary-General led in 1988 to the end of the war between Iran and Iraq that had raged since 1980. In Afghanistan, mediation by the Secretary-General and his envoy led to the 1988 agreements that resulted in the withdrawal of Soviet troops from the country. Cases such as Cambodia, Central America, Cyprus, the Middle East, Mozambique and Namibia reflect the many different ways the Secretary-General becomes involved as a peacemaker (*see pages 81-109, below*).

---

## Who commands peacekeeping operations?

Peacekeeping operations are established by the Security Council and directed by the Secretary-General, often through a Special Representative; depending on the mission, the Force Commander or the Chief Military Observer is responsible for the military aspects.

The United Nations has no military force of its own, and Member States provide, on a voluntary basis, the personnel, equipment and logistics required for an operation. Member States carefully negotiate the terms of their participation, including command and control arrangements, and retain ultimate authority over their own military forces. Peacekeepers wear their country's uniform: they are identified as peacekeepers only by a United Nations blue helmet or beret and a badge.

---

# Peacekeeping

United Nations peacekeeping operations are a crucial instrument at the disposal of the international community to advance international peace and security. The role of peacekeeping was internationally recognized in 1988, when the United Nations peacekeeping forces received the Nobel Peace Prize.

While not specifically envisaged in the Charter, the United Nations pioneered peacekeeping in 1948 with the establishment of the United Nations Truce Supervision Organization in the Middle East (*see page 95*).[2]

Peacekeeping operations and their deployment are authorized by the Security Council, with the consent of the host government and usually of the other parties involved. They may include military and police personnel, together with civilian staff. Operations may involve military observer missions, peacekeeping forces or a combination of both. Military observer missions are made up of unarmed officers, typically to monitor an agreement or a ceasefire. The soldiers of the peacekeeping forces have weapons, but in most situations can use them only in self-defence.

The military personnel of peacekeeping operations are voluntarily provided by Member States and are financed by the international community. Participating states are compensated at a standard rate from a special peacekeeping budget (*see Chapter 1, page 20*).

Peacekeeping operations were expected to cost around $2 billion in 2000 — about 0.15 per cent of world military spending. Operations are financed through the peacekeeping budget and include

---

[2]The intervention in Korea in 1950 was not a United Nations peacekeeping operation. In June 1950, the United States and the United Nations Commission on Korea informed the United Nations that the Republic of Korea had been attacked by forces from North Korea. The Security Council recommended that Member States furnish the necessary assistance to the Republic of Korea to repel the attack and restore peace and security. In July, the Council recommended that Member States providing military forces make them available to a unified command under the United States; 16 nations made troops available. This force, known as the United Nations Command and authorized by the Council to fly the United Nations flag, was not a United Nations peacekeeping operation but an international force acting under the unified command. The Soviet Union, which had been absent from the Security Council in protest against the Chinese Nationalist government representing China at the United Nations, deemed the Council's decisions illegal on the grounds that two permanent members (the Soviet Union and China) were absent. Fighting continued until July 1953, when an armistice agreement was signed.

troops from many countries: this "burden-sharing" can offer extraordinary efficiency in human, financial and political terms.

Since 1948, over 750,000 military, police and civilian personnel from some 110 countries have served in these operations; more than 1,650 of them have lost their lives.

Conflicts today are a complex mix: their roots may be essentially internal, but they are complicated by cross-border involvement, either by states or by economic interests and other non-state actors. Re-

---

## Current peacekeeping operations*

- United Nations Truce Supervision Organization (UNTSO, established 1948), in the Middle East (strength: military 150; civilian 218);
- United Nations Military Observer Group in India and Pakistan (UNMOGIP, 1949) (military 46; civilian 62);
- United Nations Peacekeeping Force in Cyprus (UNFICYP, 1964) (military 1,213; civilian police 33; civilian 187);
- United Nations Disengagement Observer Force (UNDOF, 1974), in the Syrian Golan Heights (military 1,034; civilian 124);
- United Nations Interim Force in Lebanon (UNIFIL, 1978) (military 5,802; civilian 483);
- United Nations Iraq-Kuwait Observation Mission (UNIKOM, 1991) (military 1,096; civilian 208);
- United Nations Mission for the Referendum in Western Sahara (MINURSO, 1991) (military 230; civilian police 31; civilian 398);
- United Nations Observer Mission in Georgia (UNOMIG, 1993) (military 103; civilian 240);
- United Nations Mission in Bosnia and Herzegovina (UNMIBH, 1995) (military 5; civilian police 1,808; civilian 1,772);
- United Nations Mission of Observers in Prevlaka (UNMOP, 1996), in Croatia (military 27; civilian 9);
- United Nations Interim Administration Mission in Kosovo (UNMIK, 1999) (military 39; civilian police 4,411; civilian 3,920);
- United Nations Mission in Sierra Leone (UNAMSIL, 1999) (military 10,386; civilian police 34; civilian 399);
- United Nations Transitional Administration in East Timor (UNTAET, 1999) (military 7,889; civilian police 1,398; civilian 2,655).
- United Nations Observer Mission in the Democratic Republic of the Congo (MONUC, 1999) (military 207; civilian 358; authorized strength of 5,537 military when conditions allow).
- United Nations Mission in Ethiopia and Eritrea (UNMEE, 2000) (military 1,777; civilian 183; authorized strength of 4,400 military).

*As of December 2000. For a list of all operations, see Part Three, page 298.

---

# United Nations peacekeeping operations, 2000

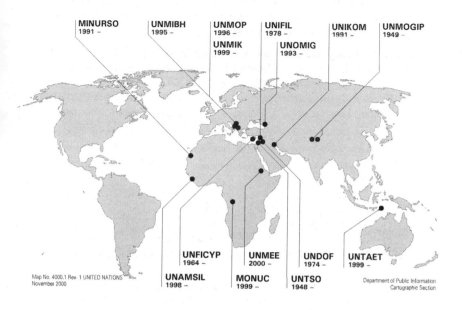

MINURSO 1991 –
UNMIBH 1995 –
UNMOP 1996 –
UNMIK 1999 –
UNIFIL 1978 –
UNOMIG 1993 –
UNIKOM 1991 –
UNMOGIP 1949 –

Map No. 4000.1 Rev. 1 UNITED NATIONS
November 2000

UNFICYP 1964 –
UNAMSIL 1998 –
UNMEE 2000 –
MONUC 1999 –
UNDOF 1974 –
UNTSO 1948 –
UNTAET 1999 –

Department of Public Information
Cartographic Section

cent conflicts in Africa have shown the deadly mix of civil strife and illegal export of natural resources — primarily diamonds — to fuel arms purchases. In addition, the consequences of conflicts can quickly become international because of illegal arms flows, terrorism, drug trafficking, refugee flows and environmental degradation.

United Nations operations, because of their universality, offer unique advantages as a means to address conflicts. Their universality adds to their legitimacy and limits the implications for the host country's sovereignty. Peacekeepers from outside a conflict can foster discussion among warring parties while focusing global attention upon local concerns, opening doors that would otherwise remain closed for collective peace efforts.

Certain prerequisites for the success of an operation have become increasingly clear. These include a genuine desire on the part of combatants to resolve their differences peacefully; a clear mandate; strong political support by the international community; and the provision of the resources necessary to achieve the operation's objectives.

This support may require positive engagement by non-state actors. Recent conflicts in Africa have shown how civil strife may be exploited by private interests for financial gain; yet at the same time, an influx of private capital, if coordinated with international efforts to promote peace, may make an essential contribution to the recovery of a post-conflict economy.

The international community has drawn lessons from past operations, and is working to strengthen the United Nations peacekeeping capacity in a number of areas. A blueprint for reform was provided by the Secretary-General's Panel on Peace Operations, chaired by Ambassador Lakhdar Brahimi, which issued its report in 2000.[3]

The Security Council and other bodies are now tackling the major issues at stake, which include:

- enhancing preparedness;
- speeding up deployment;
- strengthening the deterrent capacities of peacekeepers; and
- ensuring full political and financial support by Member States.

Operations can take many forms, and are constantly evolving in the light of changing circumstances. Among the tasks discharged by peacekeeping operations over the years are:

- *Maintenance of ceasefires and separation of forces.* By providing "breathing space," an operation based on a limited agreement between parties can foster an atmosphere conducive to negotiations.
- *Preventive deployment.* Deployed before conflict breaks out, an operation can provide a reassuring presence and a degree of transparency which favour political progress.
- *Protection of humanitarian operations.* In many conflicts, civilian populations have been deliberately targeted as a means to gain political ends. In such situations, peacekeepers have been asked to provide protection and support for humanitarian operations. However, such tasks can place peacekeepers in difficult political positions, and can lead to threats to their own security.
- *Implementation of a comprehensive peace settlement.* Complex, multi-dimensional operations, deployed on the basis of comprehensive peace agreements, can assist in such diverse tasks as providing humanitarian assistance, monitoring human rights, observing elections and coordinating support for economic reconstruction.

---

[3] *Report of the Panel on United Nations Peace Operations*, A/55/305-S/2000/809, 21 August 2000. Also available at www.un.org/peace/reports/peace_operations.

No catalogue of such roles can be exhaustive. Future conflicts are likely to continue to present complex challenges to the international community. An effective response will require courageous and imaginative use of the tools for peace.

## Cooperating with regional organizations

In the search for peace, the United Nations has been increasingly cooperating with regional organizations and other actors and mechanisms provided for in Chapter VIII of the Charter. It has worked closely with the Organization of American States in Haiti, the European Union in the former Yugoslavia, the Economic Community of West African States in Liberia and Sierra Leone, and the Organization of African Unity (OAU) in Western Sahara, the Great Lakes region, Sierra Leone and Ethiopia and Eritrea (*see below*).

United Nations military observers have cooperated with peace-keeping forces of regional organizations in Liberia, Sierra Leone, Georgia and Tajikistan (*see below*).

In the former Yugoslavia, the United Nations has cooperated with the Council of Europe and the Organization for Security and Cooperation in Europe (OSCE) in the areas of human rights, electoral assistance, peacemaking and economic development. The complex mission in Kosovo has brought together the United Nations, the European Union and OSCE (*see below*).

# Enforcement

Under Chapter VII of the Charter, the Security Council can take enforcement measures to maintain or restore international peace and security. Such measures range from economic sanctions to international military action.

## Sanctions

The Council has resorted to mandatory sanctions as an enforcement tool when peace was threatened and diplomatic efforts had failed. In the last decade, sanctions have been imposed against Iraq, the former Yugoslavia, Libya, Haiti, Liberia, Rwanda, Somalia, UNITA forces in Angola, Sudan, Sierra Leone, the Federal Republic of Yugoslavia (including Kosovo), Afghanistan, and Ethiopia and Eritrea (*see below*). The range of sanctions has included comprehensive economic and trade sanctions, or more specific measures such as arms embargoes, travel bans and financial or diplomatic restrictions.

The use of sanctions seeks to apply pressure on a state or entity to comply with the objectives set by the Security Council without resorting to the use of force. Sanctions thus offer the Council an important tool to enforce its decisions. The universal character of the United Nations makes it an especially appropriate body to establish and monitor sanctions.

At the same time, many states and humanitarian organizations have expressed concerns at the possible adverse impact of sanctions on the most vulnerable segments of the population, such as women and children. Concerns have also been expressed at the negative impact sanctions can have on the economy of third countries, which have to interrupt trade and economic relations with the sanctioned state.

It is increasingly accepted that the design and application of sanctions need to be improved. The negative effects of sanctions can be reduced either by incorporating humanitarian exceptions directly in Security Council resolutions, or by better targeting them. So-called "smart sanctions"—which seek to pressure those in power rather than the population at large, thus reducing humanitarian costs—have been gaining support. Smart sanctions may for instance involve freezing the financial assets and blocking the financial transactions of élites or entities whose behaviour triggered sanctions in the first place.

### Authorizing military action

When peacemaking efforts fail, stronger action by Member States may be authorized under Chapter VII of the Charter. The Security Council has authorized coalitions of Member States to use "all necessary means", including military action, to deal with a conflict — as it did to restore the sovereignty of Kuwait after its invasion by Iraq (1991); to establish a secure environment for humanitarian relief operations in Somalia (1992); to contribute to the protection of civilians at risk in Rwanda (1994); to restore the democratically elected government in Haiti (1994); to protect humanitarian operations in Albania (1997); and to restore peace and security in East Timor (1999) (*see below*).

These actions, though sanctioned by the Security Council, were entirely under the control of the participating states. They were not United Nations peacekeeping operations — which are established by the Security Council and directed by the Secretary-General.

## Peace-building

Peace-building involves actions to prevent the resurgence of conflict and support structures and practices that strengthen and solidify peace.

## An interim administrator

The United Nations has increasingly played a role in helping to administer countries in transition. Requested to step in after a conflict, the Organization has carried out wide-ranging tasks in this new form of peace-building — on occasions taking up the full range of government powers while working with local political and civil leaders to build a self-sustaining government.

An example of such an administrative role took place in Cambodia in 1992-1993, following years of civil war. As specified in the 1991 peace agreement, the Security Council established the United Nations Transition Authority in Cambodia, which ran key sectors of the country's administration. After the 1993 elections, the mission relinquished its powers to the new government.

Another peacekeeping operation with administrative responsibilities was the United Nations Transitional Authority in Eastern Slavonia, Baranja and Western Sirmium, which was deployed from 1996 to 1998 to assist in the peaceful integration of that area into Croatia.

In 1999, the Security Council established the United Nations Interim Administration Mission in Kosovo, with legislative, executive and judiciary powers (*see page 107*). The mission has been running the administration of the province, pending its final status.

Also in 1999, the Security Council established the United Nations Transitional Administration in East Timor, with legislative and executive authority (*see page 285*). The mission is helping to develop social services, assist in reconstruction and build East Timor's capacity towards nationhood.

---

*Preventive peace-building* involves the broad range of long-term political, institutional and developmental activities seeking to address the root causes of conflict. *Post-conflict peace-building* encompasses all efforts to prevent the recurrence of conflict and to foster the consolidation of a peace process, thereby laying the foundation for sustainable peace.

United Nations peace-building consists of five main activities. The first, in the *military and security* area, includes disarmament, demobilization, reintegration of combatants and destruction of arms. The second involves *humanitarian activities*, such as repatriation of refugees and care for children affected by the conflict. Political action is another area, which involves institution-building and fostering good governance, constitutional reforms and elections. Another area is human rights, encompassing human rights monitoring, reform of the judiciary and the police, and investigation of abuses. Finally, *economic and social measures* include the reconstruction of infrastructure destroyed in a conflict, the alleviation of economic and social injustice and the creation of conditions for good governance and economic development.

By addressing the root causes of conflict, peace-building becomes an important component of efforts to promote a peaceful evolution of crises. In some cases, including Haiti, Guinea-Bissau and the Central African Republic, a full-fledged civil war may not have taken place, but peace-building can foster stabilization and conflict prevention.

Peace-building involves action by a wide array of organizations of the United Nations system, including the World Bank, by regional economic and other organizations, by non-governmental organizations (NGOs) and local citizens' groups. Peace-building has played a prominent role in United Nations operations in Cambodia, El Salvador, Guatemala, Mozambique, Liberia, Bosnia and Herzegovina and Sierra Leone, as well as most recently in Kosovo and East Timor.

United Nations assistance has often been instrumental in building and consolidating democracy. This has at times entailed assisting armed opposition movements to transform themselves into political parties, fully integrated into political life, as happened in Mozambique, El Salvador and Guatemala.

Representatives of the Secretary-General have often been appointed to coordinate peace-building activities and to head peace-building support offices. Such offices exist for instance in Liberia, Guinea-Bissau and the Central African Republic. Their aim is to help prevent the resumption of conflict and promote lasting peace.

## Election monitoring

The United Nations broke new ground in 1989, when it supervised the entire election process that led to the independence of Namibia (*see Chapter 7, pages 280-281*). Since then, the United Nations has monitored, at government request, elections in Nicaragua and Haiti (1990), Angola (1992), Cambodia (1993), El Salvador, South Africa and Mozambique (1994), Eastern Slavonia (Croatia) and Liberia (1997), and the Central African Republic (1998 and 1999) (*see below*). It also observed the 1993 referendum in Eritrea (*see pages 91-92, below*) and the 1999 popular consultation in East Timor (*see Chapter 7, page 284*).

The degree of United Nations involvement depends upon factors such as the requests received from governments, provisions of peace agreements, or mandates from the Security Council. The United Nations has played a variety of roles ranging from technical assistance to the actual conduct of the electoral process.

United Nations observers typically follow the electoral campaign, the registration of voters and the organization of the polls. On election day, they are deployed to polling stations throughout the country, observe voting and vote counting, and issue a final statement on the validity of the elections.

Various entities assist in organizing and conducting elections. The **Electoral Assistance Division** in the Department of Political Affairs helps states to conduct free and fair elections. It has provided various forms of electoral assistance to more than 80 countries, including coordination and support, advisory services, logistics, training, computer applications and short-term observation. The United Nations Development Programme (UNDP) provides technical support to the election process, helps countries to establish electoral structures and coordinates United Nations electoral assistance in the field. The Office of the High Commissioner for Human Rights helps to train election officials, to establish guidelines for drafting electoral laws and procedures, and to set up information activities on human rights and elections.

## Building peace through development

A central tool of United Nations action to consolidate peace is development assistance. Many organizations — including UNDP, the United Nations Children's Fund (UNICEF), the World Food Programme and the Office of the United Nations High Commissioner for Refugees (UNHCR) — play roles in the recovery stage, which is crucial for providing opportunities for displaced persons and restoring confidence in national and local institutions (*see also Chapter 5, pages 249-252*).

The United Nations can help repatriate refugees, clear landmines, repair infrastructure, mobilize resources and stimulate economic recovery. While war is the worst enemy of development, a healthy and balanced development is the best form of conflict prevention.

## United Nations action for peace

### Africa

### Southern Africa

At the end of the 1980s, with the cold war waning, the United Nations was able to reap the fruits of many years of efforts aimed at ending wars that had plagued southern Africa. The decline of the apartheid regime in South Africa, whose influence extended to the bordering

# Africa: a United Nations priority

Africa has been a major focus of United Nations action in the last decade. The Organization has addressed the challenge posed by protracted conflicts and long-standing disputes in the continent in innovative ways — and at the highest level. In their Millennium Declaration in September 2000, world leaders resolved to give full support, including taking special measures to help Africa tackle its peace and development issues.

The Security Council has held several special meetings on Africa at the ministerial level. In 1997, the Council expressed "grave concern" over the number and intensity of conflicts in the continent and called for an international effort to promote peace and security. In 1998, meeting at the level of Foreign Ministers, the Council stated its determination to make its response to conflict more effective, and adopted three resolutions on the destabilizing effects of illicit arms flows, on arms embargoes and on conflict prevention in Africa.

In January 2000, the Security Council held a month-long series of meetings on the challenges facing Africa. At the initiative of the United States, which presided over the Council that month, the body dealt with major peace and security issues, such as conflict resolution, refugees and internally displaced people, and HIV/AIDS. The focus on Africa helped to draw world attention to the continent's plight.

The Council also called for a strengthening of United Nations cooperation with other organizations in conflict prevention and resolution. United Nations peace efforts have involved close collaboration with the Organization of African Unity (OAU) and subregional organizations, such as the Economic Community of West African States (ECOWAS) and the Southern Africa Development Community (SADC).

The Secretary-General has made of Africa one of his priorities, taking action to prevent or contain disputes both personally and through his 15 special envoys to the continent. In his 1998 report to the Council on the causes of conflict in Africa and on promoting durable peace, he urged that African nations demonstrate the will to rely on political rather than military responses; that Africa embrace good governance and ensure respect for human rights, democratization and accountable public administration; and that it enact reforms promoting economic growth. For its part, the international community should provide stronger political support, as well as debt relief and market access for African exports, the Secretary-General said.

United Nations efforts have taken many forms over the years, including the campaign against apartheid in South Africa, active support for independence in Namibia and some 20 peacekeeping operations. In addition to the operations described in the following pages, three peacekeeping operations in Somalia, deployed from 1992 to 1995, attempted to restore peace and provide relief aid. Another operation, deployed from 1993 to 1997, helped to bring to an end the eight-year civil war in Liberia.

But peace and security in Africa are challenged by structural constraints in the wider economic, social and human rights sphere. Many conflicts have made apparent the link between war and dire poverty. The connection is nowhere more apparent than in issues relating to refugees and internally displaced persons, HIV/AIDS, foreign debt, environmental degradation and the persistent economic crisis. In the economic and social sphere as well, Africa is a priority concern of the United Nations (*see Chapter 3, page 134*).

"frontline" states, and which had supported opposition forces in Angola and Mozambique (*see below*), was a major factor in these efforts.

In 1988, South Africa agreed to cooperate with the Secretary-General to ensure the independence of **Namibia** (*see page 280*). In 1992, the government of **Mozambique** and the Mozambican National Resistance (RENAMO) signed a peace agreement to end a long and debilitating civil war. As part of the agreement, the United Nations Operation in Mozambique, deployed in 1993, successfully monitored the ceasefire, the demobilization of forces, and the country's first multi-party elections, held in 1994.

**Angola**. The civil war in Angola, fueled by external political and economic interests, has proved more intractable. There, the government and the opposition force, the National Union for the Total Independence of Angola (UNITA) have been engaged in an intermittent yet devastating civil war since the country's independence in 1975.

The United Nations has long been involved in efforts to bring peace and reconciliation. Efforts have included mediation by the Secretary-General and his envoys, the organization of peace talks, the imposition of a Security Council arms and oil embargo against UNITA forces, and the monitoring of national elections.

The Security Council has established four successive peacekeeping missions (*see Part Three, pages 299-301*). The first, in 1989, monitored the withdrawal of pro-government Cuban troops from Angola. The second, from 1991, sought to monitor a ceasefire, verify demobilization of combatants and observe the 1992 elections — whose results were rejected by UNITA, making the country plunge again into war.

Mediation by the Secretary-General's Special Representative, Mr. Alioune Blondin Beye — who was killed in a plane crash in June 1998 while on a peace mission — brokered the 1994 Lusaka peace accord, which led to a fragile peace. The accord provided for a ceasefire and for UNITA's integration into the government and the armed forces. To back the accord and to help the parties to achieve peace and national reconciliation, a third mission was set up in 1995. In a peace-building effort, the Secretary-General visited Angola in 1997 to promote reconciliation and the installation of a government of national unity and reconciliation, which was inaugurated in April 1997. The United Nations Observer Mission in Angola (MONUA) was established in 1997 to help restore peace and assist in the transition.

But after four years of relative peace, the conflict flared up again in December 1998, exacting a heavy toll on the civilian population —

with some 750,000 people becoming internally displaced. The Security Council strengthened sanctions against UNITA for failing to meet its obligations under the Lusaka peace accord.

In December 1998, a United Nations charter flight crashed in an area of military operations, killing all 14 people aboard. In January 1999, another United Nations charter plane came under fire in the same area and crashed, killing all nine people aboard.

The Council in December 1998 reiterated that the main responsibility for the deterioration of the peace process lay with UNITA, and in February 1999 allowed MONUA's mandate to expire. However, the Council stressed the need for a continued United Nations presence, and in October 1999 established the United Nations Office in Angola (UNOA), to explore measures to restore peace and assist in capacity-building, humanitarian assistance and human rights promotion. United Nations agencies have continued to address the grave humanitarian and development crisis in the country.

## Central Africa

The Great Lakes region of Central Africa has been the focus of particular concern for the United Nations. Decades of ethnic tension, which culminated in the Rwandan genocide of 1994 (*see below*), created a climate of instability affecting all neighbouring states. The Secretary-General in 2000 appointed as his new Special Representative for the region Mr. Berhanu Dinka, who has been deeply involved in international efforts to help resolve the continuing crises, particularly in Burundi and the Democratic Republic of the Congo. In the latter country, the Security Council has established a peacekeeping mission to assist in implementing a ceasefire agreement. On the humanitarian front, United Nations agencies have continued to address the emergencies resulting from the mass movements of refugees and displaced people.

**Rwanda.** United Nations involvement in Rwanda started in 1993, when Rwanda and Uganda requested the deployment of military observers along their common border to prevent the military use of the area by the Rwandese Patriotic Front (RPF). In response, the Security Council established the United Nations Observer Mission Uganda-Rwanda.

Fighting had broken out in Rwanda in 1990 between the mainly Hutu government and the Tutsi-led RPF, operating from Uganda. A peace agreement was reached in 1993, providing for a transitional government and for elections. At the request of Rwanda and the RPF, the Security Council in 1993 set up the United Nations Assistance Mission for Rwanda (UNAMIR), to help the parties implement the agreement. But the transitional government was never established.

In April 1994, the Presidents of Rwanda and of Burundi were killed while returning from peace talks in Tanzania, when their plane was shot down as it was landing in Kigali, Rwanda's capital. This set off a wave of massacres, in which the Prime Minister, other Ministers and UNAMIR peacekeepers were among the first victims. The killings, targeting Tutsis and moderate Hutus, were mainly carried out by the Hutu-dominated army and militias.

UNAMIR sought to arrange a ceasefire, without success, and its personnel came under attack. After some countries unilaterally withdrew their contingents, the Security Council in April reduced UNAMIR's strength from 2,548 to 270. However, UNAMIR managed to shelter thousands of Rwandese.

The Security Council in May imposed an arms embargo against Rwanda and increased UNAMIR's strength to up to 5,500 troops. But it took nearly six months for Member States to provide them.

In July, RPF forces took control of Rwanda, ending the civil war and establishing a broad-based government. Out of a population of 7.9 million, some 800,000 people had been killed, some 2 million had fled to other countries and as many as 2 million were internally displaced. A United Nations humanitarian appeal raised $762 million, making it possible to respond to the enormous humanitarian challenge.

A Commission of Experts established by the Security Council reported in September that "overwhelming evidence" proved that Hutu elements had perpetrated acts of genocide against the Tutsi group. In November, the Security Council established the International Tribunal for Rwanda to prosecute those responsible for genocide and war crimes (*see Chapter 6, page 268*).

Meanwhile, while Rwandan refugees returned to the country en masse, large numbers of Rwandan Hutus took refuge in Eastern Zaire, including elements involved in the genocide. From there, those elements launched attacks into western Rwanda.

At the request of Rwanda, the Security Council terminated UNAMIR's mandate in 1996. United Nations agencies have continued to provide humanitarian aid and to assist in the return of refugees.

In 1999, the Secretary-General accepted the findings of the independent inquiry, headed by former Swedish Prime Minister Ingvar Carlsson, which he had commissioned to look into the United Nations actions during the genocide. The panel concluded that the failure to stop the genocide was shared by the United Nations Secretariat, the Security Council and the Member States. The Secretary-General expressed "deep remorse" over the United Nations failure to stop the genocide, and reiterated his commitment to make sure the Organization never again falters in stopping mass slaughter.

**Burundi**. The United Nations Office in Burundi has participated in international efforts to help resolve the crisis in that country, where a long-standing internal conflict led in 1993 to a coup attempt in which the first democratically elected President, a Hutu, and six Ministers were killed. This ignited factional fighting in which at least 150,000 people died in the following three years.

In 1996, the government and President, who had been put in place in 1994 through an agreement between the Hutu majority and the Tutsi minority, were deposed by a Tutsi-led military coup. The Security Council condemned the coup and urged the military leaders to restore constitutional order. To encourage negotiations between the new government and the rebels, as well as the return of constitutional rule, neighbouring countries imposed an economic embargo on Burundi. But fighting between the largely Tutsi army and Hutu rebels followed, resulting in massive internal displacements of people. During 1996 and 1997, some 500,000 people were forcibly transferred to "regroupment camps" as a security measure, and an additional 300,000 people fled to Tanzania to escape the continuing violence.

In 1996, former Tanzanian President Julius Nyerere began mediation efforts with the strong backing of the international community. A new transitional Constitution, providing for a political partnership between Hutus and Tutsis, came into being in 1998, and a Transitional National Assembly was inaugurated. Parties to the conflict also agreed on a ceasefire. In 1999, the neighbouring countries suspended the economic sanctions.

In 2000, following the death of Mr. Nyerere, former South African President Nelson Mandela succeeded him as Facilitator of the peace process in Burundi. His diplomatic efforts, strongly supported by the Security Council, led to the Peace and Reconciliation Agreement signed in Arusha, Tanzania, in August 2000. Welcoming the agreement, the Security Council urged the parties that remained outside the peace process to participate fully in the process.

**Democratic Republic of the Congo**. Following the 1994 massacres in Rwanda and the establishment of a new government there, some 1.2 million Rwandese Hutus — including elements who had taken part in the genocide — fled to the Kivu province of eastern Zaire, an area inhabited, among others, by ethnic Tutsis. There, a rebellion started in 1996, pitting Zairean Tutsis, led by Laurent Désiré Kabila, against the pro-Hutu army of President Mobutu Sese Seko. Kabila's Alliance of Democratic Forces for the Liberation of Zaire/Congo (ADFL), aided by Rwanda and Uganda, took Kinshasa, the capital, in 1997, establishing the Democratic Republic of the Congo. The civil war resulted in more than 450,000 refugees and internally displaced people.

In 1998, a rebellion against the Kabila government started in Kivu, and within weeks the rebels had seized large areas of the country. Angola, Chad, Kenya, Namibia and Zimbabwe promised President Kabila military support. The Angolan army recaptured several towns in the south-west, and a rebel push towards Kinshasa was turned back with help from Angolan, Namibian and Zimbabwean troops. However, the rebels maintained their grip on the eastern regions. The rebel movement, the Congolese Rally for Democracy (RCD), was supported by Rwanda and Uganda. The Security Council called for a ceasefire and the withdrawal of foreign forces, and urged states not to interfere in the country's internal affairs. Uganda signed a peace agreement with the Kabila government in April 1999. In May, the RCD split into two factions.

Efforts by the Secretary-General, the OAU and the South African Development Community (SADC) led in July 1999 to the Lusaka Ceasefire Agreement. Signed by the Democratic Republic of the Congo, along with Angola, Namibia, Rwanda, Uganda and Zimbabwe, it provided for an end of hostilities and for the holding of an inter-Congolese dialogue. The two rebel factions signed the agreement in August. To help implement the agreement, the Council in August authorized the deployment of 90 United Nations military liaison officers to strategic areas in the country and to the capitals of the signatory states.

To maintain liaison with the parties, assist in implementing the agreement and monitor security conditions, the Security Council in November established the **United Nations Mission in the Democratic Republic of the Congo (MONUC)**, incorporating the personnel it had authorized earlier on. In February 2000, the Council expanded the size and mandate of the mission, which was to monitor implementation of the ceasefire, support disarmament and demobilization, and provide support to the Facilitator of the National Dialogue, designated with the assistance of the OAU. The Council authorized the use of force by MONUC to protect United Nations personnel and civilians under imminent threat of violence, and made the deployment of the mission to its authorized strength of 5,500 contingent on adequate conditions of access, security and cooperation. Continued fighting has to date prevented full deployment and limited the functioning of the military observers in the field.

**Republic of the Congo.** In 1997, factional tension, heightened by an attempt by government forces to disarm the militia of former President Denis Sassou-Nguesso ahead of the presidential elections, called for July, escalated into full-scale fighting between Sassou-Nguesso's supporters and government forces and militia loyal to the incumbent President, Pascal Lissouba. The Security Council called for an end to the violence and a negotiated solution to the crisis.

During mediation efforts by President Omar Bongo of Gabon, assisted by the joint OAU/United Nations special representative, a request was made for establishing a peacekeeping operation in the country. The Secretary-General sent a mission to assess the modalities of such an operation. After four months of fighting, Mr. Sassou-Nguesso seized power.

Meanwhile, with 650,000 people displaced by the civil war, the United Nations launched a $17.7 million appeal to meet their needs. The signing of a peace agreement in 1999 and better security conditions led to the return of hundreds of thousands of displaced people.

**Central African Republic.** Following mutinies in the country's armed forces, several African states formed an International Mediation Committee that brokered the 1997 Bangui Agreements between the mutineers and the government. The peace agreements outlined a framework for national reconciliation, and provided for an amnesty law and for disarmament. African states then sent an inter-African force to facilitate implementation of the agreements and assure security.

The Security Council in 1998 established the United Nations Mission in the Central African Republic (MINURCA), which replaced the inter-African force and helped to maintain security and stability, promote dialogue and create an environment conducive to free and fair elections.

MINURCA's electoral unit established a presence throughout the country, and monitored legislative (1998) and presidential elections (1999) that took place without major incidents. MINURCA played a crucial role in maintaining law and order and in delivering electoral materials. The elections, which saw the re-election of President Ange-Felix Patassé, were a crucial step towards national reconciliation within the framework of the Bangui Agreements. MINURCA assisted in the transition until its mandate ended in 2000. To support efforts to consolidate peace and reconciliation, strengthen democratic institutions and help to mobilize international resources for reconstruction, the United Nations established a Peace-Building Support Office (BONUCA).

## West Africa

**Sierra Leone**. The United Nations became involved in Sierra Leone in 1995, when the Secretary-General appointed a Special Envoy, Mr. Berhanu Dinka, to mediate in the civil war. In 1991, fighters of the Revolutionary United Front (RUF) had launched a war from the east of the country to overthrow the government. With the support of Nigerian and Guinean troops, Sierra Leone's army had tried at first to defend the government, but in 1992 the army itself had overthrown the government. Despite the change of power, the RUF continued its attacks.

The Special Envoy, working in collaboration with the OAU and the Economic Community of West African States (ECOWAS), negotiated a settlement and the return to civilian rule. Elections were held in 1996, and the army relinquished power to the winner, Ahmed Tejan Kabbah. But the RUF did not participate in the election and continued hostilities.

The Special Envoy assisted in negotiating the 1996 Abidjan Peace Accord between the government and the RUF. But it was derailed by another military coup in 1997, with the army joining forces with the RUF and forming a ruling junta. President Kabbah and his government went into exile in Guinea. The Security Council imposed an oil and arms embargo and authorized ECOWAS to ensure its implementation, using troops of the monitoring group of ECOWAS, ECOMOG.

In 1998, responding to an attack by supporters of the junta, ECOMOG launched a military attack that led to the collapse of the junta. President Kabbah was returned to office, and the Security Council terminated the embargo. In June, the Council established the United Nations Observer Mission in Sierra Leone (UNOMSIL), headed by the Secretary-General's Special Representative, Francis G. Okelo, which monitored the security situation and efforts to disarm combatants and restructure the security forces. Unarmed UNOMSIL teams, under ECOMOG protection, documented atrocities and human rights abuses against civilians.

Fighting continued, with the rebel alliance gaining control of more than half of the country. During an offensive to retake Freetown, the capital, the alliance in January 1999 overran most of the city. All UNOMSIL personnel were evacuated, but the Special Representative and the Chief Military Observer continued to perform their duties, maintaining contacts with all parties and monitoring the situation. Later that month, ECOMOG troops retook Freetown and reinstalled the civilian government. The war resulted in some 700,000 internally displaced persons and some 450,000 refugees in neighbouring countries.

The Special Representative, in consultation with West African States, started diplomatic efforts to open up a dialogue with the rebels. Negotiations between the government and the rebels led to the Lomé Peace Agreement, signed in July, to end the war and form a government of national unity.

The Security Council in October decided to replace UNOMSIL with a larger mission, the **United Nations Mission in Sierra Leone (UNAMSIL)**, to assist the parties in putting into effect the agreement and to assist in disarming, demobilizing and reintegrating the estimated 45,000 combatants. In February 2000, following the announcement that the ECOMOG troops would be withdrawn, the Council increased the strength of UNAMSIL to 11,000 troops.

But in April, members of the RUF attacked United Nations forces after ex-combatants came forward to disarm. Four peacekeepers were killed, and close to 500 United Nations personnel were taken hostage by RUF forces amid renewed fighting. In May, the RUF leader, Foday Sankoh, was arrested by the police, and by the end of the month around half of the hostages had been released. The Security Council increased UNAMSIL's strength to 13,000 troops to help restore peace in the country. In July, UNAMSIL staged a rescue operation, bringing to safety the remaining hostages.

The Security Council in August started the process of setting up a special court to try those responsible for war crimes. After a Security Council delegation visited Sierra Leone in October, the Council recommended establishing a mechanism to coordinate an overall strategy for the country, comprised of the United Nations, the Freetown government, Member States and ECOWAS.

**Guinea Bissau**. In June 1998, fighting erupted between government forces and army rebels in Guinea Bissau, over the dismissal of the army chief of staff for allegedly allowing the smuggling of arms to a Senegalese separatist movement. At the request of the government,

Guinea and Senegal sent troops to assist government forces loyal to President Joao Bernardo Vieira. The Secretary-General condemned the military confrontation and the Security Council called on the mutineers to lay down their arms and restore constitutional order. ECOWAS and the Community of Portuguese Speaking Countries (CPLP) took action to address the crisis.

In July, talks under CPLP auspices led to a ceasefire and the signing of a memorandum of understanding. The Secretary-General renewed his call for the return to constitutional order, and the United Nations issued a $28 million appeal to assist the some 350,000 internally displaced people.

In November, the government and the military junta reached an agreement in Abuja, Nigeria, providing for a government of national unity and for elections, as well as for the withdrawal of foreign troops and the deployment of an ECOMOG interposition force. The Security Council welcomed the agreement as a step towards national reconciliation.

A government of national unity was inaugurated in February 1999 and Guinean and Senegalese troops withdrew in March in accordance with the peace agreement. In April, the United Nations set up a Peace-building Support Office to promote reconciliation and strengthen democratic institutions. The Office helped build the judiciary, speed up trials and advance women's rights. But no elections took place and the peace accord broke down in May. Fighting resumed, and rebel troops ousted President Vieira.

Following elections in November 1999 and January 2000, a new government was formed in February, and a new National Assembly was inaugurated. The new President, Mr. Kumba Yala, offered five ministerial posts to members of the former military junta. The United Nations Support Office has continued to help the new government in the transitional period.

## Ethiopia-Eritrea

With the collapse of the military government in Ethiopia in 1991, the Eritrean People's Liberation Front (EPLF) announced the formation of a provisional government and the holding of a referendum to determine the wishes of the Eritrean people regarding their status in relation to Ethiopia. The head of the Referendum Commission in 1992 invited the United Nations to observe the referendum process.

The General Assembly established the United Nations Observer Mission to Verify the Referendum in Eritrea (UNOVER), which observed the organization and holding of the 1993 referendum.

Ninety-nine per cent of the voters favoured independence; shortly thereafter, Eritrea declared independence and joined the United Nations.

In 1998, fighting broke out between Ethiopia and Eritrea over disputed border areas. The Security Council demanded an end to the hostilities and offered technical support for the delimitation and demarcation of the border. The Secretary-General called for an end of hostilities so as to give a chance to mediation efforts by the United States and Rwanda. The OAU subsequently took the lead in the mediation effort.

In May 2000, the Security Council imposed an arms embargo against the two countries. In June, a cessation of hostilities agreement proposed by the OAU was reached in Algiers. To assist in implementing the agreement, the Security Council in July established the **United Nations Mission in Ethiopia and Eritrea (UNMEE)**, involving the deployment of military observers and infantry battalions along the border. In September, the Council authorized the deployment of up to 4,420 military personnel to monitor the end of hostilities and assist in ensuring the observance of the security commitments agreed by the two countries.

*(On Western Sahara, see Chapter 7, page 281.)*

## The Americas

In 1998, the Secretary-General was able to report that, for the first time in decades, not one of Central America's countries was plagued by internal conflict. The United Nations was instrumental in bringing peace to the region, in one of its most complex and successful peacemaking and peacekeeping efforts.

The United Nations became involved in Central America in 1989, when Costa Rica, El Salvador, Guatemala, Honduras and Nicaragua requested its assistance in their collective agreement to end the conflicts that were disrupting the region, promote democratic elections and pursue democratization and dialogue.

The Security Council established the United Nations Observer Group in Central America (ONUCA), which was deployed in all five countries to verify that they cease assistance to irregular and insurrectionist forces, and not allow their territory to be used for attacks into other countries.

**Nicaragua.** The five countries also agreed to draw up a plan for demobilizing the Nicaraguan resistance, also known as "contras". Nicaragua announced it would hold elections under international and United

Nations monitoring. At Nicaragua's request, the United Nations Observation Mission for the Verification of Elections in Nicaragua (ONUVEN) observed the preparation and holding of the 1990 elections — the first United Nations-observed elections in an independent country.

The success of ONUVEN helped create conditions for the voluntary demobilization of the "contras". ONUCA oversaw that demobilization in 1990, as decided by the Security Council, at sites in Honduras and Nicaragua, where some 22,000 "contras" turned in their weapons to United Nations observers. ONUCA remained in Central America until 1992.

**El Salvador.** Meanwhile, as requested by the government and the Farabundo Martí National Liberation Front (FMLN), the Secretary-General began assisting in talks aimed at ending the civil war in El Salvador. To verify the first major accord, achieved in 1990, the Security Council established the United Nations Observer Mission in El Salvador (ONUSAL).

Negotiations brokered by the Secretary-General and his personal envoy culminated in the 1992 peace accords, which put an end to a 12-year conflict that had claimed some 75,000 lives. In one of the most comprehensive operations in United Nations history, ONUSAL monitored the accords, and verified the demobilization of combatants and the respect by both parties of their human rights commitments.

ONUSAL also assisted in bringing about reforms needed to tackle the root causes of the civil war — such as judicial reforms, the establishment of a new civilian police, and the transfer of land to former combatants and landholders. At the request of the government, ONUSAL observed the 1994 elections. Its mandate ended in 1995.

**Guatemala.** At the request of the government and the Guatemalan National Revolutionary Unity (URNG), the United Nations from 1991 observed talks aimed at ending the civil war, which had lasted over three decades and resulted in some 200,000 people killed or missing.

In 1994, the parties concluded accords providing for the United Nations to verify all agreements reached, as well as to establish a human rights mission. The General Assembly established the **United Nations Human Rights Verification Mission in Guatemala (MINUGUA)**.

The United Nations-moderated talks led to various other agreements on political, social and human rights issues. A ceasefire was reached in 1996, and finally the parties signed the peace agreement which ended the last and longest of Central America's conflicts. The region was at peace for the first time in 36 years.

In 1997, a military observer group attached to MINUGUA oversaw the demobilization of URNG forces. MINUGUA has remained in the country to verify compliance with the accords, while United Nations agencies have continued to address the social and economic roots of conflict throughout the region.

**Haiti.** In 1990, after the departure of "Life President" Jean-Claude Duvalier and a series of short-lived governments, Haiti's provisional government requested the United Nations to observe that year's elections. The United Nations Observer Group for the Verification of the Elections in Haiti observed the preparation and holding of the elections, at which Mr. Jean-Bertrand Aristide was elected President.

But in 1991 a military coup ended democratic rule, and the President went into exile. The Organization of American States (OAS) and the United Nations condemned the coup and began diplomatic efforts for the return to democratic rule. The Secretary-General, at the request of the General Assembly, appointed a special envoy for Haiti, who was also appointed special envoy by the OAS.

In response to the worsening situation, a joint United Nations/OAS mission, the International Civilian Mission in Haiti (MICIVIH), was deployed in the country in 1993 to monitor the human rights situation and investigate violations.

In an effort to restore constitutional rule, the Security Council imposed an oil and arms embargo in 1993 and a trade embargo in 1994, while the special envoy held a series of talks with the military rulers. Finally, the Council in 1994 authorized Member States to form a multinational force and use "all necessary means" to facilitate the return to democratic rule. As the force was about to intervene, the United States and the military rulers reached an agreement aimed at avoiding further violence. The United States-led multinational force deployed peacefully in the country, President Aristide returned, and the embargo was lifted.

As decided by the Security Council, a United Nations peacekeeping mission took over from the multinational force in 1995, assisting the government in maintaining security and stability and helping to create the country's first national civil police. Meanwhile, MICIVIH continued to promote human rights and build the capacity of national human rights institutions.

Against the background of a continuing political crisis, the General Assembly in 2000 created a new peace-building mission, the **Inter-**

**national Civilian Support Mission in Haiti,** which took over from previous peacekeeping missions and MICIVIH. Its task was to assist the government in developing democratic institutions, in particular in the areas of human rights, justice and public security.

## Asia

### The Middle East

The United Nations has been concerned with the question of the Middle East from its earliest days. It has formulated principles for a peaceful settlement and dispatched various peacekeeping operations, and continues to support efforts towards a just, lasting and comprehensive solution to the underlying political problems.

The question has its origin in the issue of the status of Palestine. In 1947, Palestine was a Territory administered by the United Kingdom under a Mandate from the League of Nations: it had a population of some 2 million, two thirds Arabs and one third Jews. The General Assembly in 1947 endorsed a plan, prepared by the United Nations Special Committee on Palestine, for the partition of the Territory: it provided for creating an Arab and a Jewish state, with Jerusalem under international status. The plan was rejected by the Palestinian Arabs, the Arab states and other states.

On 14 May 1948, the United Kingdom relinquished its Mandate and the Jewish Agency proclaimed the state of Israel. The following day, the Palestinian Arabs, assisted by Arab states, opened hostilities against the new state. The hostilities were halted through a truce called for by the Security Council and supervised by a Mediator appointed by the General Assembly, assisted by a group of military observers which came to be known as the **United Nations Truce Supervision Organization (UNTSO)** — the first United Nations observer mission.

As a result of the conflict, some 750,000 Palestine Arabs lost their homes and livelihoods and became refugees. To assist them, the General Assembly in 1949 established the **United Nations Relief and Works Agency for Palestine Refugees in the Near East (UNRWA)** *(see Chapter 5, page 255)*, which has since been a major provider of assistance and a force for stability in the region.

Unresolved, Arab-Israeli hostilities led again to warfare in 1956, 1967 and 1973, each conflict leading Member States to call for United Nations mediation and peacekeeping missions. The 1956 conflict saw the deployment of the first full-fledged peacekeeping force, the United Nations Emergency Force, which oversaw troop with-drawals and contributed to peace and stability.

The 1967 war involved fighting between Israel and Egypt, Jordan and Syria, during which Israel occupied the Sinai peninsula, the Gaza Strip, the West Bank of the Jordan River, including East Jerusalem, and part of Syria's Golan Heights. The Security Council called for a ceasefire, and subsequently dispatched observers to supervise the ceasefire in the Egypt-Israel sector.

The Council, by *resolution 242 (1967)*, defined principles for a just and lasting peace. These are:

- "withdrawal of Israel armed forces from territories occupied in the recent conflict"; and
- "termination of all claims or states of belligerency and respect for and acknowledgement of the sovereignty, territorial integrity and political independence of every state in the area and their right to live in peace within secure and recognized boundaries, free from threats or acts of force". The resolution also affirmed the need for "a just settlement of the refugee problem".

After the 1973 war between Israel, and Egypt and Syria, the Security Council adopted *resolution 338 (1973)*, which reaffirms the principles of resolution 242 and calls for negotiations aimed at "a just and durable peace". These resolutions remain the basis for an overall settlement in the Middle East.

To monitor the 1973 ceasefire, the Security Council established two peacekeeping forces. One of them, the **United Nations Disengagement Observer Force (UNDOF)**, established to supervise the disengagement agreement between Israel and Syria, is still in place on the Golan Heights. The other operation was UNEF II in the Sinai.

In the following years, the General Assembly called for an international peace conference on the Middle East, under United Nations auspices. In 1974, the Assembly invited the Palestine Liberation Organization to participate in its work as an observer. In 1975, it established the **Committee on the Exercise of the Inalienable Rights of the Palestinian People.**

Bilateral negotiations between Egypt and Israel, mediated by the United States, led to the Camp David accords (1978) and the Egypt-Israel peace treaty (1979): Israel withdrew from the Sinai, which was returned to Egypt. Israel and Jordan concluded a peace treaty in 1994.

**Lebanon**. Meanwhile, southern Lebanon had become the theatre of hostilities between Palestinian groups on the one hand, and Israeli forces and its local Lebanese auxiliary on the other. After Israeli forces invaded southern Lebanon in 1978, following a Palestinian commando raid in Israel, the Security Council called upon Israel to withdraw, and established the **United Nations Interim Force in Lebanon (UNIFIL)** to confirm the Israeli withdrawal, restore international peace and security, and assist Lebanon in re-establishing its authority in the area.

In 1982, after intense exchanges of fire in southern Lebanon and across the Israel-Lebanon border, Israeli forces moved into Lebanon, reaching and surrounding Beirut. Israel withdrew from most of the country in 1985, but kept control of a strip of land in southern Lebanon, where Israeli forces and its local Lebanese auxiliary remained, and which partly overlapped UNIFIL's area of deployment. Hostilities between Lebanese groups and Israeli and auxiliary forces continued.[4]

Over the years, the Security Council maintained its commitment to Lebanon's integrity, sovereignty and independence, while the Secretary-General sought to persuade Israel to leave the security zone. Israel maintained that the zone was a temporary arrangement governed by its security concerns. UNIFIL sought to contain the conflict and protect the population.

Israel withdrew its forces in May 2000, in accordance with the 1978 Security Council resolutions and in cooperation with the United Nations, with the Secretary-General verifying completion of the withdrawal in June. As Israel pulled out, the Security Council endorsed the Secretary-General's operational plan to assist Lebanon in re-establishing its authority. The Council called on all parties to cooperate with the United Nations in its efforts to stabilize the situation.

**The Middle East peace process**. In 1987, the Palestinian uprising (*intifada*) began in the occupied territories of the West Bank and Gaza Strip in a call for Palestinian independence and statehood. The Palestine National Council proclaimed in 1988 the state of Palestine. The General Assembly acknowledged that proclamation and decided to designate the Palestine Liberation Organization as "Palestine", without prejudice to its observer status.

Following talks in Madrid, and subsequently Norwegian-mediated negotiations, Israel and the Palestine Liberation Organization established mutual recognition on 10 September 1993. Three days later,

---

[4] At the height of the conflict, a number of foreigners were taken hostage. In 1991, "quiet diplomacy" by the Secretary-General and his envoy led to the release of nine Western hostages held in Lebanon and 91 Lebanese prisoners held by Israel.

Israel and the Palestine Liberation Organization signed in Washington, D.C., the Declaration of Principles on Interim Self-Government Arrangements. The agreement opened the way to an interim Palestinian self-government and to successive Israeli withdrawals from the occupied Palestinian territory.

Welcoming the agreement, the Secretary-General pledged the assistance of United Nations agencies and programmes. The United Nations created a task force on the social and economic development of Gaza and Jericho, and appointed a special coordinator for United Nations assistance, who has been overseeing the work of the programmes and agencies involved.

The transfer of powers from Israel to the Palestinian Authority in the Gaza Strip and Jericho began in 1994. In 1995, Israel and the Palestine Liberation Organization signed an agreement on Palestinian self-rule in the West Bank, providing for the withdrawal of Israeli troops and the handover of civil authority to an elected Palestinian Council.

Elections for the Council and the presidency of the Palestinian Authority were held in 1996. Yasser Arafat, Chairman of the Palestine Liberation Organization, was elected President of the Authority.

The peace process was reactivated with the signing of a 1999 interim agreement leading to further redeployment of Israeli troops from the West Bank, agreements on prisoners, the opening of safe passage between the West Bank and Gaza, and resumption of negotiations on permanent status issues.

Major problems between Israel and the Palestinian remained unresolved. At the end of September 2000, a new wave of protests and violence began in the occupied Palestinian territory. International efforts were directed at calming the situation on the ground and bringing the two parties back to the negotiating table to resume the peace process. A few months before the outbreak of this second Palestinian *intifada*, high-level peace talks, under United States mediation, had taken place at Camp David. These talks ended inconclusively. Among the unresolved issued remained the staus of Jerusalem; a resolution to the Palestinian refugee question; security; borders; and Israeli settlements. As in previous years, the General Assembly in 2000 reaffirmed the right of the Palestinian people to self-determination, including the option of a state.

## India-Pakistan

The United Nations has continued to be concerned with the decades-old dispute between India and Pakistan over Kashmir. The issue dates back to the 1940s, when the state of Jammu and Kashmir was one of the princely states that became free, under the partition plan and the India Independence Act of 1947, to accede to India or Pakistan. The Hindu Maharaja of mostly Muslim Kashmir signed his state's instrument of accession to India in 1947.

The Security Council first discussed the issue in 1948, following India's complaint that tribesmen and others, with Pakistan's support and participation, were invading Kashmir and that fighting was taking place. Pakistan denied the charges and declared Kashmir's accession to India illegal.

The Council recommended measures to stop the fighting, including the use of observers, and to create conditions for a plebiscite. It established a United Nations Commission for India and Pakistan, which made proposals on a ceasefire and troop withdrawals, and proposed that the issue be decided by plebiscite. Both sides accepted, but could not agree on the modalities for the plebiscite. Since 1949, the **United Nations Military Observer Group in India and Pakistan (UNMOGIP)** has been observing the ceasefire in Kashmir.

Following the 1972 India-Pakistan agreement defining a Line of Control in Kashmir, the parties undertook to settle their difference peacefully and achieve a final settlement. After the agreement, India maintained that the mandate of UNMOGIP had lapsed, a position not accepted by Pakistan. The Secretary-General has maintained that only the Security Council can terminate the mission, and has consistently expressed his readiness to facilitate the search for an overall solution.

## Iraq

The United Nations response to Iraq's invasion of Kuwait in 1990 illustrates the range of options it has at its disposal in the pursuit of restoring international peace and security. The Security Council immediately condemned the invasion, demanded Iraq's withdrawal, and imposed comprehensive sanctions against Iraq. At the 1990 session of the General Assembly, all Member States condemned Iraq's action.

At the same time, the United Nations undertook many initiatives to avert war. The Secretary-General met with the Iraqi President and the Foreign Minister, and was in constant contact with the political leaders involved in the crisis.

The Security Council set 15 January 1991 as the deadline for Iraq's compliance with the Council's resolutions, and authorized Member States cooperating with Kuwait to use "all necessary means" to implement these resolutions and restore international peace and security in the area. Faced with Iraq's non-compliance, on 16 January coalition forces allied to restore Kuwait's sovereignty began attacks against Iraq. These forces acted in accordance with the Council's authorization, but not under the direction or control of the United Nations. Hostilities were suspended in February, after the Iraqi forces had left Kuwait.

By *resolution 687* (1991), the Security Council set terms for a ceasefire, demanded that Iraq and Kuwait respect the border's inviolability, called for deploying United Nations observers, took action on compensation for war damages, and decided that Iraq's weapons of mass destruction should be eliminated.

The Council established a demilitarized zone along the border. To monitor the zone, it set up an observer mission, the **United Nations Iraq-Kuwait Observation Mission (UNIKOM)**.

Under resolution 687, an Iraq-Kuwait Boundary Demarcation Commission was established, made up of one representative from Iraq, one from Kuwait and three independent experts appointed by the Secretary-General. Iraq stopped participating in its work in 1992. The Commission demarcated the boundary as agreed by Iraq and Kuwait in 1932 and again in 1963. Iraq informed the Secretary-General in 1994 that it recognized Kuwait's sovereignty, territorial integrity and international boundaries.

Resolution 687 also dealt with the elimination of Iraq's weapons of mass destruction. To verify implementation of this provision, the Security Council established the United Nations Special Commission (UNSCOM), with powers of no-notice inspection. The International Atomic Energy Agency (IAEA) was asked to undertake similar tasks in the nuclear area, with UNSCOM assistance.

UNSCOM and IAEA uncovered and eliminated much of Iraq's banned weapons programmes and capabilities, including nuclear, chemical and biological warfare programmes. But despite their achievements, UNSCOM and IAEA were unable to determine that Iraq had fulfilled all the obligations it had accepted.

Iraq frequently hindered UNSCOM's task, and a conflict was averted in February 1998, when the Secretary-General mediated in Baghdad an agreement with Iraq allowing unlimited access for United Nations weapons inspectors.

But in October Iraq suspended cooperation with UNSCOM, pending Security Council agreement to lift the oil embargo. Iraq stated that there were no more proscribed weapons in the country, while UNSCOM said it did not have the evidence that Iraq had fully complied with resolution 687. In response, the United Kingdom and the United States launched in December air strikes on Iraq.

The Security Council in 1999 created a new weapons monitoring system replacing UNSCOM, the **United Nations Monitoring, Verification and Inspection Commission (UNMOVIC)**. Iraq was to provide full cooperation, unrestricted access and provision of information to United Nations arms inspection teams. The Council expressed its intention to lift economic sanctions, dependent on Iraq's cooperation with UNMOVIC and IAEA, which would be reviewed every 120 days.

The Secretary-General in 2000 appointed a coordinator for the return of missing property and missing persons from Iraq to Kuwait. Some 600 Kuwaitis and others were still unaccounted for since the Gulf War.

**Oil-for-food programme**. In 1991, a Security Council resolution offered Iraq the opportunity to export limited amounts of oil, under specified conditions, to provide funds for purchasing humanitarian goods. That resolution was never implemented.

In 1995, the Council authorized states to import up to $1 billion worth of oil and oil products from Iraq every 90 days, for a total of 180 days, to generate resources for importing humanitarian goods for the needs of the Iraqi people. While sanctions have remained in place, the "oil-for-food" programme between the United Nations and Iraq was launched in 1996. A Sanctions Committee of the Security Council has since been monitoring the implementation of the programme, authorizing the supply of food, medicine and other humanitarian items.

In 1998, the Security Council expanded the "oil-for-food" programme by authorizing Iraq to sell $5.2 billion worth of oil over a six-month period. The authorization was repeatedly renewed. In 1999, the Council lifted the cap on the amount of oil Iraq is allowed to sell under the 1986 scheme.

The Council in 2000 extended the programme by a further 180 days, beginning 9 June 2000, and invited the Secretary-General to appoint independent experts to prepare a comprehensive analysis of the humanitarian situation in Iraq.

**Humanitarian programme**. The Secretary-General launched in 1991 the **United Nations Humanitarian Programme for Iraq**, which has promoted the return of those displaced and provided humanitarian assistance to the population. He also appointed a coordinator of the humanitarian work of the United Nations system and other relief agencies.

The humanitarian situation has remained critical. Economic sanctions have taken a severe toll on the most vulnerable people, especially children. In 1999, a UNICEF survey revealed that mortality rate for children under 5 had more than doubled over the previous 10 years.

Addressing the Security Council in 2000, the Secretary-General said that the humanitarian situation in Iraq posed a moral dilemma for the United Nations. The Organization had always been on the side of the vulnerable and the weak, and had always sought to relieve suffering, yet in the case of Iraq, it was accused of causing suffering to an entire population. The only satisfactory outcome of any such situation was for the state that was the object of sanctions to return to full compliance with the Council's decisions, so that sanctions could be ended as quickly as possible.

## Tajikistan

Following the breakup of the Soviet Union, Tajikistan became independent in 1991. The country soon faced a social and economic crisis, regional and political tensions, and differences between secularists and pro-Islamic traditionalists. A civil war erupted in 1992, and the Tajik opposition — a coalition of Islamic and other groups — seized power. After suffering defeat in 1992, most of the opposition forces went into Afghanistan; from there, they carried out attacks into Tajikistan. The war resulted in an estimated 50,000 deaths, some 400,000 refugees and 600,000 internally displaced persons.

From 1993, a Special Representative of the Secretary-General mediated between the government and the opposition. Talks under his auspices led to a ceasefire agreement signed in Tehran in 1994. The Security Council in 1994 established the United Nations Mission of Observers in Tajikistan (UNMOT) to assist the Joint Commission — composed of government and opposition representatives — to monitor the agreement.

United Nations-sponsored negotiations led to the signing of a peace agreement in Moscow in 1997: it provided for a transitional period during which the agreement was to be implemented, thus creating the political, legislative and security environment under which new parliamentary elections could be held. The Security Council gave UNMOT the mandate to assist in implementing the peace agreement and help promote reconciliation. UNMOT cooperated closely with a peacekeeping force of the Commonwealth of Independent States (CIS) and a mission of the Organization for Security and Cooperation in Europe (OSCE).

Acknowledging progress in implementing the peace agreement, the Security Council in 1999 welcomed the declaration by the opposition on disbanding its armed units and the Supreme Court's decision to lift restrictions on activities by opposition parties. The country's first-multi-party parliamentary elections were held in February 2000, marking the completion of the transitional phase set forth in the 1997 peace agreement. UNMOT withdrew in May, and the United Nations established a Peace-Building Office to consolidate peace and promote democracy.

*(On East Timor, see Chapter 7, page 283).*

## Europe

### Cyprus

The **United Nations Peacekeeping Force in Cyprus (UNFCYP)** has been supervising a ceasefire and maintaining a buffer zone between the Greek Cypriot National Guard and Turkish Forces since 1974, when a *coup d'état* by Greek Cypriot and Greek elements favouring union of the country with Greece was followed by military intervention by Turkey and the de facto division of the island. Since 1974, the Secretary-General and his envoy have been seeking to resolve the decades-old dispute between the Greek-Cypriot and Turkish-Cypriot communities. The Secretary-General has used his good offices to bring the two sides together in search of a comprehensive settlement. In 1999, the Secretary-General and his new Special Adviser on Cyprus initiated a process of fresh rounds of proximity talks between the two sides, with the strong support of the Security Council.

### Georgia

The relations between the Abkhaz and the Georgians have been tense for decades. Renewed attempts in 1990 by the local authorities in Abkhazia (north-western region of Georgia) to separate from the Republic of Georgia, which had become independent in 1991, escalated in 1992 into a series of armed confrontations. Hundreds of people died and some 30,000 fled to the Russian Federation. An envoy of the Secretary-General, appointed in 1993, began mediation among the parties. A ceasefire agreement was reached later that year, and to verify compliance with it, the Security Council established the **United Nations Observer Mission in Georgia (UNOMIG)**.

But fighting resumed, turning into civil war in September 1993 and leading to the displacement of some 250,000 people. Another ceasefire was reached in Moscow in 1994. The parties agreed to the deployment of a peacekeeping force of the Commonwealth of Independent States (CIS) to monitor compliance with the agreement, with UNOMIG monitoring implementation of the agreement and observing the operation of the CIS force.

Over the years, successive Special Representatives of the Secretary-General have conducted negotiations towards a lasting settlement. The Security Council has stressed the need for a comprehensive settlement, which should include the political status of Abkhazia on the basis of the full respect for the sovereignty and territorial integrity of Georgia and the return of refugees and internally displaced persons to Abkhazia. At a meeting held under United Nations auspices in 1997, both sides agreed to establish a Coordinating Council and, within its framework, three working groups to address the military, political and economic aspects of the peace process. A United Nations office for the protection and promotion of human rights in Abkhazia was established in 1996.

## The Balkans

**Former Yugoslavia**. The Federal Socialist Republic of Yugoslavia was a founding Member of the United Nations. In 1991, two republics of the Federation, Slovenia and Croatia, declared independence. Croatian Serbs, supported by the national army, opposed the move, and war between Serbia and Croatia broke out.

The European Community sought to resolve the crisis, without success. The Security Council in 1991 imposed an arms embargo on Yugoslavia, and the Secretary-General appointed a personal envoy to support the European Community's peace effort.

To create the conditions for a settlement, the Security Council in 1992 established the United Nations Protection Force (UNPROFOR), which was initially deployed in Croatia. Meanwhile, the war had extended to Bosnia and Herzegovina, which had declared independence — an act supported by Bosnian Croats and Muslims but opposed by Bosnian Serbs — and had seen the intervention of the Serb and Croatian armies. To end the bloodshed in Bosnia, the Security Council in May imposed economic sanctions on the Federal Republic of Yugoslavia, consisting by then of Serbia and Montenegro.

The war intensified, with widespread reports of ethnic cleansing and the largest refugee crisis in Europe since the Second World War.

The Security Council in 1993 created, for the first time, an international court to prosecute war crimes (*see Chapter 6, page 268*).

In Bosnia, UNPROFOR sought to protect the delivery of humanitarian aid, and subsequently to protect Sarajevo, the capital, and other towns that had been declared "safe areas" in 1993 by the Security Council. But while peacekeeping commanders requested 35,000 troops, the Security Council authorized 7,600.

To deter continuing attacks against Sarajevo, the North Atlantic Treaty Organization (NATO) authorized in 1994 air strikes at the Secretary-General's request. In response to the air strikes, Bosnian Serb forces in 1995 detained about 400 UNPROFOR observers, using some as "human shields".

Fighting intensified in 1995. Croatia launched major offensives against its Serb-populated areas. NATO responded to the Bosnian Serbs' constant shelling of Sarajevo with massive air strikes. Bosnian Serb forces took over the "safe areas" of Srebrenica and Zepa, killing some 7,000 unarmed men and boys in Srebrenica — the worst massacre in Europe since the Second World War. In a 1999 report, the Secretary-General acknowledged the errors of the United Nations and Member States in their response to the ethnic cleansing campaign that culminated in Srebrenica, and stated that the tragedy "will haunt our history forever".

Talks sponsored by the Contact Group (France, Germany, Italy, Russia, the United Kingdom and the United States) led to an agreement between Bosnia, Croatia and Yugoslavia to end the war in Bosnia. The agreement provided for Bosnia to consist of two entities, a Bosnian-Croat federation and a Serb republic. A peace initiative led by the United States resulted in other agreements. Finally, peace talks in Dayton, United States, culminated in the 1995 peace agreement between Bosnia-Herzegovina, Croatia and Yugoslavia that ended the 42-month war. Over 230 United Nations personnel died in the conflict. To help ensure compliance with the agreement, the Security Council authorized the deployment of a multinational, NATO-led, 60,000-strong Implementation Force.

In Bosnia and Herzegovina, the Security Council established a United Nations International Police Task Force, which in 1996 became part of a larger **United Nations Mission in Bosnia and Herzegovina (UNMIBH)**. The mission has facilitated the return of refugees and displaced persons, fostered peace and security, and helped to build up common state institutions.

The Council in 1996 established the **United Nations Mission of Observers in Prevlaka (UNMOP)**, to monitor the demilitarization of the Prevlaka peninsula, a strategic area in Croatia contested by Yugoslavia.

(*On the* United Nations Transitional Authority in Eastern Slavonia, Baranja and Western Sirmium, *see page 79, above*).

**Kosovo.** In 1989, the Federal Republic of Yugoslavia revoked local autonomy in Kosovo, a province in southern Yugoslavia historically important to Serbs that was more than 90 per cent ethnically Albanian. Kosovo Albanians dissented, boycotting Serbian state institutions and authority in a quest for self-rule.

Tensions increased as the Kosovo Liberation Army (KLA), which surfaced in 1996 with a call for armed rebellion for independence, launched attacks against Serb officials and Albanians who collaborated with the Serb administration. The Serb authorities responded with mass arrests, increasing the explosiveness of the situation. In 1997, the Contact Group urged authorities in Belgrade and Kosovo to join a peaceful dialogue and create conditions for refugees to return. It also called on Belgrade to enhance Kosovo's status within Yugoslavia and to protect the rights of the ethnic Albanian population.

Fighting erupted in March 1998 as the Serbian police swept the Drenica region, ostensibly looking for KLA members. The Contact Group, the European Union, the OSCE and the Security Council condemned the use of force by the Serbian police and denounced terrorist actions by the KLA. The international community indicated that neither independence nor the current situation were acceptable, and called for an enhanced status for Kosovo within Yugoslavia.

To foster peace and stability in Kosovo, the Security Council imposed an arms embargo against Yugoslavia, including Kosovo. Despite international efforts, the situation deteriorated into an open war between the KLA and Serbian security forces.

The Security Council called for a ceasefire and for the withdrawal of Serbian forces. A United Nations mission visited Kosovo in October to assess the situation. Negotiations between U.S. Ambassador Richard Holbrooke and Yugoslav President Slobodan Milosevic led to a ceasefire agreement in October: it established limits for Yugoslav military and police presence in Kosovo, which was verified by the OSCE's Kosovo Verification Mission. But the accord failed to bring peace and security to the province. As the violence and breaches to the ceasefire increased, the Secretary-General warned the Security Council about the danger of a renewal of hostilities.

At the invitation of France and the United States, both sides in 1999 attended talks in Rambouillet, France. The Kosovo Albanian delegation signed an agreement that offered Kosovo autonomy and provided for the deployment of a NATO peacekeeping force, which would be authorized to have access throughout Yugoslavia. Stating that this arrangement would violate its sovereignty, Yugoslavia refused to sign, and peace talks were abandoned.

Following warnings to Yugoslavia, and against the backdrop of a Serbian offensive in Kosovo, NATO commenced in March 1999 air strikes against Yugoslavia. The Security Council found itself deeply divided, as some states condemned the strikes as a unilateral use of force violating the United Nations Charter, while others said the action would prevent a humanitarian catastrophe resulting from Serbian attacks on Kosovo Albanians. The Secretary-General said it was tragic that diplomacy had failed, but there were times when "the use of force may be legitimate in the pursuit of peace". At the same time, he stressed that the Security Council, which has the primary responsibility for maintaining peace and security, should be involved in any decision to resort to the use of force.

Yugoslav forces launched a major offensive against the KLA, while Yugoslavia began mass deportations of ethnic Albanians from Kosovo, causing an unprecedented outflow of some 850,000 refugees. UNHCR and other humanitarian agencies rushed to assist the refugees in Albania and the former Yugoslav Republic of Macedonia.

In June, Yugoslavia accepted a peace plan proposed by the Group of Eight (G-8 — comprising the seven Western industrialized nations and Russia). The Security Council endorsed the plan and decided to deploy both a civil and security presence in Kosovo. It authorized Member States to establish an international security presence to deter hostilities, demilitarize the KLA and facilitate the return of refugees, and requested the Secretary-General to establish an interim international civilian administration, under which the people of the province could enjoy substantial autonomy and self-government.

Following the withdrawal of Yugoslav forces from Kosovo, NATO suspended its air bombing campaign, and a 50,000-strong multinational force (KFOR) entered the province to provide a security presence. The **United Nations Interim Administration Mission in Kosovo (UNMIK)** immediately established a presence on the ground.

The Mission was unprecedented in its complexity and scope. The Security Council vested in UNMIK authority over the territory and people of Kosovo, including all legislative and executive powers, as well as the administration of the judiciary. The Mission, headed by the Secretary-General's Special Representative, Bernard Kouchner, had four pillars: civil administration, under the United Nations itself; humanitarian assistance, led by UNHCR; democratization and institution-building, led by the OSCE; and economic reconstruction, managed by the European Union. It was a unique team effort, bringing together four international organizations under the umbrella of the United Nations.[5]

At least 841,000 refugees of the some 850,000 who fled during the war returned, and the first priority was to equip them for the rigours of the coming winter.

That accomplished, UNMIK made significant progress towards re-establishing normal life and ensuring long-term economic reconstruction. The UNMIK administration was set up in all five regions and 29 municipalities. Over 30 regulations were issued, covering such issues as the appointment and removal of judges, banking, licensing, the establishment of a central fiscal authority and a Kosovo budget. UNMIK also established a dialogue with leaders of ethnic communities, restored utilities, opened schools and began paying stipends to about 70,000 public service workers.

A Joint Interim Administrative Structure (JIAS) was established, involving representatives of all ethnic groups and headed by the Interim Administrative Council, to ensure the political participation of the population. The body allowed the involvement of the people of Kosovo in decision-making and the elimination of parallel institutions. Work began on establishing 20 Departments under the JIAS. The Kosovo Transitional Council, comprising all political parties as well as representatives of civil society, religious and other groups, acted as an advisory body.

Some 3,000 UNMIK police officers were deployed throughout the territory, and a Kosovo Police Service that included representatives from minorities was built up. Demilitarization of the KLA was completed in September 1999, and the reintegration of its members in civil society continued.

In the months following the ceasefire, some 210,000 non-Albanian Kosovars left Kosovo for Serbia and Montenegro. To facilitate their safe return, a joint Committee on Returns was established in May 2000.

The overwhelming security challenge remained the protection of non-Albanian minorities, such as Serbs and Romas. Despite significant progress, the overall situation remained tense. Intimidation,

---

[5]UNHCR phased out as an UNMIK pillar by the end of June 2000, but maintained its presence in the region.

murders and violence against the non-Albanian population continued. Remaining ethnic minorities lived in several isolated enclaves
guarded by KFOR. To break the circle of impunity, aggravated by a
dysfunctional judiciary system, UNMIK started appointing international judges and prosecutors.

Under the plan outlined by the Security Council in 1999, UNMIK
was to organize and conduct elections. UNMIK became fully involved in the preparation of municipal elections, which took place in
October 2000. Most Serbs, however, did not participate in the elections, citing lack of security and the inability of internally displaced
Serbs to return to Kosovo.

# Disarmament

Since the birth of the United Nations, the goals of multilateral disarmament and arms limitation have been central to its efforts to maintain international peace and security. The Organization has given highest
priority to reducing and eventually eliminating nuclear weapons, destroying chemical weapons and strengthening the prohibition against
biological weapons — all of which pose the greatest threat to humankind. While this objective has remained constant over the years, the
scope of deliberations and negotiations is changing as political reali-
ties and the international situation evolve.

The international community is now considering more closely the
excessive and destabilizing proliferation of small arms and light
weapons and the massive deployment of landmines — phenomena
that threaten the economic and social fabric of societies and kill and
maim civilians, mainly women and children. It is also beginning to
consider the need for multilaterally negotiated norms against the
spread of ballistic missile technology for military purposes and to explore the impact that developments in information and telecommunications technologies can have for international security.

The essential role of the United Nations in these areas is to assist
Member States in establishing new norms and in strengthening and
consolidating existing agreements. The growing complexity of connections among individuals, organizations and nations necessitates a
multilateral, inclusive approach that will benefit all.

## Disarmament machinery

The United Nations machinery for disarmament was established by
the Charter and subsequent decisions of the General Assembly.

## Multilateral disarmament and arms regulation agreements

- A chronology of important international disarmament and arms regulation measures concluded through negotiations in multilateral and regional fora includes:

- *1959 Antarctic Treaty*: demilitarizes the continent and bans the testing of any kind of weapon in the continent.

- *1963 Treaty Banning Nuclear Weapon Tests in the Atmosphere, in Outer Space and under Water (Partial Test-Ban Treaty)*: restricts nuclear testing to underground sites only.

- *1967 Treaty for the Prohibition of Nuclear Weapons in Latin America and the Caribbean (Treaty of Tlatelolco)*: prohibits testing, use, manufacture, storage, or acquisition of nuclear weapons by the countries of the region.

- *1967 Treaty on Principles Governing the Activities of States in the Exploration and Use of Outer Space, including the Moon and Other Celestial Bodies (Outer Space Treaty)*: mandates that outer space be used for peaceful purposes only and that nuclear weapons not be placed or tested in outer space.

- *1968 Treaty on the Non-Proliferation of Nuclear Weapons (NPT)*: the non-nuclear-weapon states agree never to acquire nuclear weapons and, in exchange, are promised access to and assistance in the peaceful uses of nuclear energy; nuclear-weapon states pledge to carry out negotiations relating to cessation of the nuclear arms race and to nuclear disarmament, and not to assist in any way in the transfer of nuclear weapons to non-nuclear-weapon states.

- *1971 Treaty on the Prohibition of the Emplacement of Nuclear Weapons on the Sea-Bed and the Ocean Floor and in the Subsoil Thereof (Sea-bed Treaty)*: bans the emplacement of nuclear weapons, or any weapon of mass destruction, on the seabed or ocean floor.

- *1972 Convention on Bacteriological (Biological) Weapons (BWC)*: bans the development, production and stockpiling of biological and toxin agents, and provides for the destruction of such weapons and their means of delivery.

- *1980 Convention on Certain Conventional Weapons (CCW)*: prohibits certain conventional weapons deemed excessively injurious or having indiscriminate effects. It is considered an umbrella agreement, to which additional agreements can be added. As of 2000, it contains four Protocols. Protocol I bans weapons which explode fragments that are undetectable by X-ray within the human body; Amended Protocol II (1995) limits the use of certain types of mines, booby-traps, and other devices; Protocol III bans incendiary weapons designed to set fire to targets; and Protocol IV bans the use of blinding laser weapons.

- *1985 South Pacific Nuclear Free Zone Treaty (Treaty of Rarotonga)*: bans the stationing, acquisition or testing of nuclear explosive devices and the dumping of nuclear waste within the zone.

- *1990 Treaty on Conventional Armed Forces in Europe (CFE Treaty)*: limits the numbers of various conventional armaments in a zone stretching from the Atlantic Ocean to the Urals.

- *1993 Chemical Weapons Convention (CWC)*: prohibits the development, production, stockpiling and use of chemical weapons and requires their destruction.

- *1995 Southeast Asia Nuclear-Weapon-Free Zone Treaty (Treaty of Bangkok)*: bans the development or stationing of nuclear weapons on the territories of the states party to the treaty.

- *1996 African Nuclear-Weapon-Free Zone Treaty (Treaty of Pelindaba)*: bans the development or stationing of nuclear weapons on the African continent.

- *1996 Comprehensive Nuclear-Test-Ban Treaty (CTBT)*: places a worldwide ban on nuclear test explosions of any kind and in any environment.

- *1997 Mine Ban Convention: prohibits the use, stockpiling, production and transfer of anti-personnel mines and provides for their destruction.*

(For status of ratification of these agreements, see www.un.org/Depts/dda/index.html)

The Charter gives the **General Assembly** the chief responsibility of considering "the general principles of cooperation in the maintenance of international peace and security, including the principles governing disarmament and the regulation of armaments" (article 11). The Assembly has two subsidiary bodies dealing with disarmament issues: the Disarmament and International Security Committee (the First Committee), which meets during the regular session and deals with all disarmament issues on the agenda of the Assembly; and the United Nations Disarmament Commission, a specialized deliberative body that focuses on specific issues.

---

## Bilateral agreements

The 1972 *Treaty on the Limitation of Anti-Ballistic Missile Systems (ABM Treaty)* limited the number of anti-ballistic missile systems of the United States and the Soviet Union to one each. A 1997 "demarcation" agreement between the United States and the Russian Federation distinguished between "strategic", or long-range ABMs, which are still prohibited, and "non-strategic" or shorter-range ABMs, which are not.

The 1987 United States-Soviet Union *Intermediate- and Shorter-Range Nuclear Forces Treaty (INF Treaty)* eliminated an entire class of nuclear weapons, which includes all land-based ballistic and cruise missiles with a range of 500 to 5,500 km. By the end of 1996, all the weapons slated for destruction under the provisions of the Treaty had been eliminated.

The 1991 United States–Soviet Union *Strategic Arms Limitation and Reduction Treaty (START I)* placed a ceiling of 6,000 warheads on 1,600 deployed long-range nuclear missiles for each side by 2001, thereby reducing the 1991 stockpile levels by about 30 per cent.

The 1992 *Lisbon Protocol to START I* committed the Russian Federation, Belarus, Kazakhstan and Ukraine, as successor states to the Soviet Union, to abide by the START I Treaty; Belarus, Kazakhstan and Ukraine were to adhere to the NPT as non-nuclear-weapon states. By 1996, these three states had removed all nuclear weapons from their territories.

The 1993 *Strategic Arms Limitation and Reduction Treaty II (START II)* committed both parties to reduce the number of warheads on long-range nuclear missiles to 3,500 on each side by 2003, and eliminated ICBMs (intercontinental ballistic missiles) equipped with MIRVs (multiple independently targetable re-entry vehicles). A 1997 agreement extended the deadline for destruction of the launching systems — missile silos, bombers and submarines — to the end of 2007.

Agreement was reached in 1997 to begin START III negotiations on further reductions in nuclear weapons stocks, once START II has entered into force. Talks are taking place, but formal negotiations have not yet begun.

---

The **Conference on Disarmament** is the single multilateral negotiating forum for disarmament agreements. This body, which works strictly on the basis of consensus in matters that touch the national security interests of states, has a limited membership of 66 and a unique relationship with the General Assembly. It defines its own rules and develops its own agenda, but takes into account the recommendations of the Assembly and reports to it annually. The Conference successfully negotiated both the Chemical Weapons Convention and the Comprehensive Nuclear-Test-Ban Treaty (*see below*). Since 1997, the Conference has not engaged in any negotiations due to lack of consensus among its members on disarmament priorities.

In the United Nations Secretariat, the **Department for Disarmament Affairs** (*see Chapter 1, page 27*) implements the decisions of the Assembly in matters of disarmament.

The **United Nations Institute for Disarmament Research (UNIDIR)** (*see Chapter 1, page 48*) undertakes research on disarmament and international security issues, in particular on emerging problems and the foreseeable consequences of disarmament.

The **Advisory Board on Disarmament Matters** advises the Secretary-General on matters of arms limitation and disarmament, as well as on the implementation of the United Nation Disarmament Information Programme, and serves as the Board of Trustees of UNIDIR.

## Weapons of mass destruction

### Nuclear weapons

Through sustained efforts, the world community has achieved numerous agreements aimed at reducing nuclear arsenals, excluding their deployment from certain regions and environments (e.g., outer space, ocean floor), limiting their proliferation and ending testing. Despite these achievements, nuclear weapons and their proliferation remain a major threat to peace and a major challenge to the international community.

In 1996, the International Court of Justice examined the legal aspects of the threat or use of nuclear weapons, and in an advisory opinion affirmed that states are under an obligation "to pursue in good faith *and bring to a conclusion* negotiations leading to nuclear disarmament in all its aspects" (emphasis added). Issues of vital concern in this area include the development of ballistic missiles and missile defence systems, the possibility of clandestine nuclear weapon programmes, the danger of nuclear-weapon proliferation, nuclear tests in South Asia and the need for key states to ratify the Comprehensive Nuclear-Test-Ban Treaty.

### Bilateral agreements on nuclear weapons

While international efforts to contain nuclear weapons continue in different fora, it has been generally understood that the nuclear-weapon powers hold special responsibility for maintaining a stable international security environment. During and after the cold war, the two major powers arrived at agreements that have significantly reduced the threat of nuclear war (*see box*).

### Multilateral agreements on nuclear weapons and non-proliferation

The 1968 Treaty on the Non-Proliferation of Nuclear Weapons (NPT), which was extended indefinitely in 1995, is considered the cornerstone of the global nuclear non-proliferation regime. The 2000 Review Conference of the Parties to the NPT adopted a final document in which the nuclear-weapon states made "an unequivocal undertaking … to accomplish the total elimination of their nuclear arsenals". The Conference agreed that there should be increased transparency about nuclear-weapon capabilities, as well as a diminishing role for nuclear weapons in security policies.

To verify obligations assumed under the NPT, states parties are required to accept the nuclear safeguards of the International Atomic Energy Agency (IAEA) (*see below*). By the end of 1999, there were 224 safeguards agreements with 140 states (and with Taiwan, China), including 127 comprehensive safeguards agreements pursuant to the NPT. However, 55 states parties to the NPT have yet to meet their treaty obligation to conclude a safeguards agreement with IAEA.

In addition to the NPT, the treaties of Tlatelolco, Rarotonga, Bangkok and Pelindaba (*see below*) require non-nuclear-weapon states to apply IAEA safeguards.

In 1996, an overwhelming majority of Members of the General Assembly adopted the *Comprehensive Nuclear-Test-Ban Treaty* (*CTBT*), which banned any nuclear-test explosions anywhere — an objective originally proposed in 1954 and sought for four decades. The Treaty thus extended the 1963 partial prohibition on nuclear test explosions to all environments. With nearly 150 signatory states participating in the Preparatory Commission for the **Comprehensive Nuclear-Test-Ban-Treaty Organization (CTBTO)**, based in Vienna, preparations are under way in the Provisional Technical Secretariat, established in 1997, to ensure that an international monitoring system is operational by the time the Treaty enters into force. The

Agreement to Regulate the Relationship between the United Nations and the Preparatory Commission for the CTBTO was signed in 2000 (*see also Chapter 1, page 61*).

## Nuclear-weapon-free zones

In a development that was to herald a new movement in regional arms control, the signing of the 1967 *Treaty for the Prohibition of Nuclear Weapons in Latin America and the Caribbean* (*Treaty of Tlatelolco*) established for the first time a nuclear-weapon-free zone in a populated area of the world.

Since then, three other zones have been established: in the South Pacific (*Treaty of Rarotonga, 1985)*, South-East Asia (*Treaty of Bangkok, 1995*) and Africa (*Treaty of Pelindaba*, 1996). By virtue of such treaties, the whole of the populated southern hemisphere has nuclear-weapon-free status, greatly reducing the chance of nuclear proliferation (*see map on page 115*). Proposals have been made for establishing nuclear-weapon-free zones in Central Asia, Central Europe and South Asia, as well as for a zone free of weapons of mass destruction in the Middle East. The concept of a single nuclear-weapon-free state was acknowledged by the international community in 1998, when the General Assembly supported Mongolia's self-declaration of its territory free from nuclear weapons.

## Preventing nuclear proliferation

The **International Atomic Energy Agency (IAEA)** plays a prominent role in international efforts aimed at preventing the proliferation of nuclear weapons. IAEA serves as the world's inspectorate for the application of nuclear safeguards and verification measures covering civilian nuclear programmes.

Under agreements concluded with states, IAEA inspectors regularly visit nuclear facilities to verify records on the whereabouts of nuclear material, check IAEA-installed instruments and surveillance equipment, confirm inventories of nuclear material, and prepare detailed reports. Taken together, these and other safeguards measures provide independent, international verification that governments are living up to their commitment to peaceful uses of nuclear energy.

To verify the implementation of the 224 safeguards agreements currently in force in 140 states (and in Taiwan, China), 200 IAEA experts conduct daily on-site inspections in every part of the world, for a total of some 2,500 safeguards inspections a year. Their aim is to ensure that the nuclear material held in 900 nuclear installations in some 70 countries is not diverted away from legitimate peaceful uses to military purposes. IAEA thus contributes to international security,

# Nuclear-weapon-free zones

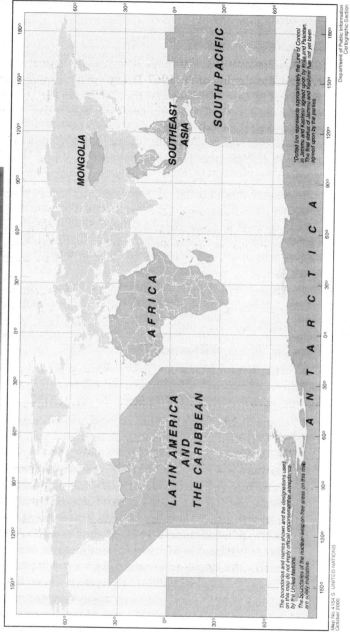

OUTER SPACE

MONGOLIA

AFRICA

SOUTHEAST ASIA

SOUTH PACIFIC

LATIN AMERICA AND THE CARIBBEAN

ANTARCTICA

The boundaries and names shown and the designations used on this map do not imply official endorsement or acceptance by the United Nations.

The boundaries of the nuclear-weapon-free areas on this map are solely indicative.

*Dotted line represents approximately the Line of Control in Jammu and Kashmir agreed upon by India and Pakistan. The final status of Jammu and Kashmir has not yet been agreed upon by the parties.

Map No. 4154 S  UNITED NATIONS
October 2000

Department of Public Information
Cartographic Section

and reinforces efforts to halt the spread of arms and move towards a world free of nuclear weapons.

Various types of safeguards agreements can be concluded with IAEA. Those in connection with the NPT, the *Model Protocol Additional to Existing Safeguards Agreements,* the *Treaty of Tlatelolco*, the *Treaty of Pelindaba* and the *Treaty of Rarotonga* (*see above*) require non-nuclear-weapon states to submit their entire nuclear-fuel-cycle activities to IAEA safeguards. Other types of agreement cover safeguards at single facilities. IAEA safeguards under the NPT are an integral part of the international regime for non-proliferation and play an indispensable role in ensuring implementation of the Treaty.

## Removing the threat of chemical and biological weapons

The entry into force in 1997 of the *Chemical Weapons Convention (CWC)* completed a process that started in 1925, when the Geneva Protocol prohibited the use of poison gas weapons. The Convention created, for the first time in the history of international arms control, a stringent international verification regime (involving collection of information on chemical facilities and routine global inspection) to oversee states parties' compliance with treaty obligations. Established for that purpose in The Hague, the Netherlands, the **Organisation for the Prohibition of Chemical Weapons (OPCW)** had conducted, by October 2000, a total of 850 inspections in 44 states parties. Through its inspections, it confirmed inactivation of all of the 60 chemical weapon production facilities that had been declared under the terms of the convention. The Agreement concerning the relationship between the United Nations and the OCPW was signed in 2000 (*see also Chapter 1, page 62*).

Unlike the CWC, the 1972 *Biological Weapons Convention (BWC)*, which entered into force in 1975, does not provide for a verification mechanism. Negotiations have been held since 1995 to elaborate a protocol to strengthen the BWC by establishing a system of measures to promote compliance with the Convention and the implementation of its provisions on technical cooperation and assistance. Many states have urged its conclusion prior to the fifth BWC Review Conference, scheduled for 2001. In the meantime, states parties exchange, as a confidence-building measure, detailed information each year on such items as their high-risk biological research facilities. Universalizing and implementing the BWC, as well as the CWC, and preventing the proliferation of these weapons to non-party states represent a major task ahead for the international community.

# The fight against landmines

Since the 1980s, the United Nations has been addressing the problems posed by the millions of deadly landmines scattered in over 60 countries. Each year thousands of people — most of them children, women and the elderly — are maimed or killed by these "silent killers". Meanwhile, new landmines continue to be deployed in various countries around the world.

Since 1994, the General Assembly has included "Assistance in Mine Action" in its agenda. International conventions have been created to address the problem, including the United Nations–sponsored Inhumane Weapons Convention (1980), which was strengthened in 1996 to apply to mine use in internal conflicts and to stipulate that all mines must be detectable. In 1997, the combined efforts of a group of Member States, including Canada and Norway, in partnership with NGOs, led to a landmark convention banning the production, use and export of anti-personnel landmines (*see page 118*).

The **United Nations Mine Action Service** acts as the focal point for mine action and coordinates all mine-related activities of United Nations agencies, funds and programmes. Governments have increasingly asked the United Nations to start and oversee mine clearance programmes as part of peacekeeping missions, during humanitarian emergencies, and in response to the long-term problems caused by landmines and unexploded ordnance. Today, thousands of personnel, both international and local, work in United Nations-supported programmes in nearly 30 countries — conducting mine-awareness training, assisting victims, marking, mapping and clearing minefields and surveying their impact.

These activities are under way in several of the most affected countries — in South-East Asia, throughout Africa, in Central and South America and in the Balkans. They have shown that effective and vital action against landmines is possible: with the right mixture of skills, commitment and resources, the problem can be resolved effectively, and lives in the affected areas can return to normal.

## Conventional weapons, confidence-building and transparency

**Small arms, light weapons and practical disarmament.** An estimated 40 to 60 per cent of the world's trade in small arms is illicit. Controlling the proliferation of illicit weapons is a necessary first step towards the non-proliferation of small arms. A United Nations Conference on the Illicit Trade in Small Arms and Light Weapons in All Its Aspects is scheduled for 2001. Within the United Nations system, a mechanism called "Coordinating Action on Small Arms" was put in place in 1998 to coordinate small arms control activities throughout the system.

The General Assembly in 1996 invited interested states to establish a group in order to assist states that faced problems arising out of post-conflict situations. Subsequently, a group of "interested states in practical disarmament measures" was set up to examine and support concrete projects of practical disarmament, particularly as designed and initiated by affected countries. At the group's recommendation, the Secretary-General created in 1998 a Trust Fund which has supported a number of projects — including that in Albania, where the civilian population was encouraged to voluntarily surrender weapons in exchange for community development incentives.

**Anti-personnel mines.** The growing proliferation and indiscriminate use of anti-personnel landmines around the world has been a particular focus of attention. In 1995, a review of the *Convention on Certain Conventional Weapons* (so-called *Inhumane Weapons Convention or CCW*) produced *Amended Protocol II,* strengthening restrictions on certain uses, types (self-destroying and detectable) and transfers of landmines.

Not satisfied with what they considered an inadequate response to a serious humanitarian crisis, a group of like-minded states negotiated an agreement on a total ban on all anti-personnel landmines — the *Convention on the Prohibition of the Use, Stockpiling, Production and Transfer of Anti-personnel Mines on Their Destruction* (*Mine-Ban Convention*), which was opened for signature in 1997 in Ottawa, Canada. By the end of 2000, it had been ratified by 109 states.

The Convention has spurred the campaign to reduce needless human suffering by increasing resources for mine clearance, mine awareness and mine assistance. It has been proposed that the Conference on Disarmament negotiate a ban on mines transfers, a measure which a number of states that have not adhered to the Convention would find acceptable.

**Register of Conventional Arms.** To enhance the level of transparency in arms transfers, thus contributing to confidence-building and security among states, the General Assembly established in 1992 the *United Nations Register of Conventional Arms.* The arrangement allows for governments to provide information on a voluntary basis on their transfers to other states of major weapons systems, such as aircraft, tanks, battleships, artillery and missiles. Such data are compiled and published annually by the United Nations as official documents, available to the general public including through the United Nations web site (*see address on page120*). Another global mechanism designed to promote transparency in military matters is the United Nations system for the standardized reporting of military expenditures, introduced in 1980.

**Prevention of an arms race in outer space.** Matters related to outer space have been pursued in international fora along two separate lines: those related to peaceful applications of space technology and those related to the prevention of an arms race in that environment. These issues have been discussed in the General Assembly, in the Committee on the Peaceful Uses of Outer Space and its subsidiary bodies (*see page 120, below*) and in the Conference on Disarmament. The discussions have contributed to the conclusion of a number of international agreements concerning both peaceful and military aspects of the use of outer space (*see list on page 110, above*).

Reflecting the importance of preventing the militarization of outer space, the General Assembly first special session on disarmament (1978) called for international negotiations on the issue. Since 1982, the Conference on Disarmament has had on its agenda an item entitled "Prevention of an arms race in outer space"; but little progress has been made to date in efforts to negotiate a multilateral agreement, owing to continuing differences in perception among its members.

**Relationship between disarmament and development.** The question of using for development purposes resources released through general disarmament under effective international control has been long debated among Member States. An international conference on the relationship between disarmament and development was held in 1987, and adopted a Programme of Action. But despite the end of the cold war, little interest was evinced among Member States, as the "peace dividend" did not materialize. A high-level Steering Group on Disarmament and Development, established in 1999 in the United Nations Secretariat, has stressed the need to revisit disarmament and development in the light of the changes that have taken place in the international situation since the 1987 conference.

**Regional approaches to disarmament.** The United Nations supports initiatives towards disarmament undertaken at the regional and subregional levels, and promotes security and confidence-building measures among states within a region. The activities of the United Nations regional centres for peace and disarmament in Africa (Lomé, Togo), Asia and the Pacific (Katmandu, Nepal) and Latin America and the Caribbean (Lima, Peru), include assisting Member States in implementing the guidelines and recommendations for regional approaches to disarmament within the context of global security, adopted by the Disarmament Commission in 1993. In fostering regional disarmament, the United Nations works together with regional governmental and non-governmental organizations, such as the Organization of African Unity (OAU), the Arab League and the Organization of American States (OAS).

**Disarmament information and outreach activities**. The United Nations undertakes information and outreach activities in the framework of its *Disarmament Information Programme*. Its purpose is to inform and educate the international community and generate public understanding and support for the objectives of the United Nations in the field of arms control and disarmament. The Programme offers a variety of activities: publications, special events, meetings, seminars, panel discussions, exhibits and a web site (*www.un.org/Depts/dda/index.html*).

The *United Nations Disarmament Fellowship Programme*, launched by the General Assembly in 1978, has trained over 500 public officials from about 150 countries, many of whom are now in positions of responsibility in the field of disarmament within their own governments.

## Peaceful uses of outer space

The United Nations works to ensure that outer space be used for peaceful purposes and that the benefits from space activities be shared by all nations. This concern in the peaceful uses of outer space began soon after the launch of the Sputnik — the first man-made satellite — by the Soviet Union in 1957, and has kept in step with the advances in space technology. The United Nations has played an important role, by developing international space law and by promoting international cooperation in space science and technology.

The main intergovernmental body in this field is the **United Nations Committee on the Peaceful Uses of Outer Space**. It reviews the scope of international cooperation in peaceful uses of outer space, devises programmes and directs United Nations technical cooperation, encourages research and dissemination of information, and contributes to the development of international space law. Set up by the General Assembly in 1959, it is made up of 61 Member States.

The Committee has two Subcommittees:
• The **Scientific and Technical Subcommittee** is the focal point of international cooperation in space technology and research;
• The **Legal Subcommittee** works to ensure the development of a legal framework concomitant to the rapid technological development of space activities.

The Committee and its Subcommittees meet annually to consider questions put before them by the General Assembly, reports submitted to them and issues raised by Member States. Working on the basis of consensus, the Committee makes recommendations to the General Assembly.

## Legal instruments

The work of the Committee and its Legal Subcommittee has resulted in the adoption by the General Assembly of five legal instruments, all of which are in force:

- The 1966 *Treaty on Principles Governing the Activities of States in the Exploration and Use of Outer Space, including the Moon and Other Celestial Bodies (Outer Space Treaty)* provides that space exploration shall be carried out for the benefit of all countries, irrespective of their degree of development. It seeks to maintain outer space as the province of all humankind, free for exploration and use by all states, solely for peaceful purposes, and not subject to national appropriation;

- The 1967 *Agreement on the Rescue of Astronauts, the Return of Astronauts and the Return of Objects Launched into Outer Space (Rescue Agreement)* provides for aiding the crews of spacecraft in case of accident or emergency landing, and establishes procedures for returning to the launching authority a space object found beyond the territory of that authority;

- The 1971 *Convention on International Liability for Damage Caused by Space Objects (Liability Convention)* provides that the launching state is liable for damage caused by its space objects on the Earth's surface, to aircraft in flight and to space objects of another state or persons or property on board such objects;

- The 1974 *Convention on Registration of Objects Launched into Outer Space (Registration Convention)* provides that launching states maintain registries of space objects and provide information on objects launched to the United Nations. Under this Convention, the Office for Outer Space Affairs maintains a United Nations Registry on objects launched into outer space. Information has been provided by all launching states and by the European Space Agency (ESA);

- The 1979 *Agreement Governing Activities of States on the Moon and Other Celestial Bodies (Moon Agreement)* elaborates the principles relating to the Moon and other celestial bodies set out in the 1966 Treaty, and sets up the basis to regulate the future exploration and exploitation of natural resources on those bodies.

On the basis of the work of the Committee and its Legal Subcommittee, the General Assembly has adopted sets of principles, including the following, on the conduct of space activities:

- The *Principles governing the use by States of artificial Earth satellites for international direct television broadcasting* (1982) recognize that such use has international political, economic, social and cultural implications. Such activities should promote the dissemination and exchange of information and knowledge, foster development, and respect the sovereign rights of states, including the principle of non-intervention.

- The *Principles relating to remote sensing of the Earth from outer space* (1986) state that such activities are to be conducted for the benefit of all countries, respecting the sovereignty of all states and peoples over their natural resources, and for the rights and interests of other states. Remote sensing is to be used to preserve the environment and to reduce the impact of natural disasters.

- The *Principles on the use of nuclear power sources in outer space* (1992) recognize that such sources are essential for some space missions, but that their use should be based on a thorough safety assessment. The Principles provide guidelines for the safe use of nuclear power sources and for notification of a malfunction of a space object where there is a risk of re-entry of radioactive material to the Earth.

- The *Declaration on international cooperation in the exploration and use of outer space for the benefit and in the interest of all States, particularly developing countries* (1996) provides that states are free to determine all aspects of their participation in international space cooperation on an equitable and mutually acceptable basis, and that such cooperation should be conducted in ways that are considered most effective and appropriate by the countries concerned.

## Office for Outer Space Affairs

The Vienna-based **United Nations Office for Outer Space Affairs** serves as the secretariat for the Committee on the Peaceful Uses of Outer Space, and assists developing countries in using space technology for development.

The Office disseminates space-related information to Member States through its International Space Information System. Through its *United Nations Programme on Space Applications,* it provides technical advisory services to Member States in conducting pilot projects, and undertakes training and fellowship programmes in such ar-

## UNISPACE conferences

The United Nations has organized three major United Nations Conferences on the Exploration and Peaceful Uses of Outer Space, all held in Vienna. The first conference (1968) examined the practical benefits deriving from space research and exploration, and the extent to which non-space countries, especially developing countries, might enjoy them. The second conference (UNISPACE '82) reflected the growing involvement of all nations in outer space activities: it assessed the state of space science and technology, considered the applications of space technology for development, and discussed international space cooperation.

The third conference (UNISPACE III, 1999), in its Vienna Declaration on Space and Human Development, outlined a wide variety of actions to protect the global environment and manage natural resources; increase use of space applications for human security, development and welfare; protect the space environment; increase developing countries' access to space science and its benefits; and enhance training and education opportunities, especially for young people.

The conference also called for the implementation of a global system to manage natural disaster mitigation, relief and prevention; the improvement of educational programmes and satellite-related infrastructure to promote literacy; and the international coordination of activities related to near-Earth objects. A Space Generation Forum, organized for and by young professionals and university students, contributed to the outcome of the conference. The event brought together governments, intergovernmental bodies, civil society and, for the first time, the private sector.

Endorsing the Vienna Declaration, the General Assembly in 1999 declared 4 to 10 October World Space Week to celebrate each year the contributions of space science and technology to the betterment of the human condition.

---

eas as remote sensing, satellite communication, satellite meteorology and basic space science.

The Office provides technical assistance to the Regional Centres for Space Science and Technology Education and to the Network of Space Science and Technology Education and Research Institutions for Central-Eastern and South-Eastern Europe, affiliated with the United Nations. These bodies help to develop skills and knowledge of scientists and researchers in those aspects of space science and technology that can contribute to sustainable development. The Centre in Asia and the Pacific became operational in India in 1996; the Centres in Morocco and in Nigeria in 1999. Centres in West Asia and in Latin America and the Caribbean are being planned.

The Office works in close cooperation with organizations such as ESA, the International Astronautical Federation (IAF) and the Committee on Space Research (COSPAR).

In addition, other United Nations organizations are active in areas such as space communication, satellite meteorology, space science and remote sensing. To coordinate the space activities of the United Nations system, an *Inter-Agency Meeting on Outer Space Activities* convenes once a year.

(*For further information, see* www.oosa.unvienna.org).

# PART TWO

## Chapter 3

## Economic and Social Development

# ECONOMIC AND SOCIAL DEVELOPMENT

Although most people associate the United Nations with the issues of peace and security, the vast majority of the Organization's resources are in fact devoted to advancing the Charter's pledge to "promote higher standards of living, full employment and conditions of economic and social progress and development". United Nations development efforts have profoundly affected the lives and well-being of millions of people throughout the world. Guiding the United Nations endeavours is the conviction that lasting international peace and security are possible only if the economic and social well-being of people everywhere is assured.

Many of the economic and social transformations that have taken place globally in the last five decades have been significantly affected in their direction and shape by the work of the United Nations. As the global centre for consensus-building, the United Nations has set priorities and goals for international cooperation to assist countries in their development efforts and to foster a supportive global economic environment.

This consensus has been expressed through a series of *International Development Decades*, the first beginning in 1961. These broad statements of policy and goals, while emphasizing certain issues of particular concern in each decade, have consistently stressed the need for progress on all aspects of development, social as well as economic, and the importance of narrowing the disparities between industrialized and developing countries.

As a forum for innovative thinking, the United Nations has been responsible for formulating and promoting key new developmental objectives on the international agenda, such as sustainable development. It has articulated the need for incorporating issues such as the advancement of women, human rights, environmental protection and good governance into the development paradigm.

International debate on economic and social issues has increasingly reflected the commonality of interests between rich and poor countries in solving the many problems that transcend national boundaries. Issues such as refugee populations, organized crime, drug trafficking and AIDS are seen as global problems requiring coordinated action. The impact of persistent poverty and unemployment in one region can be quickly felt in others, not least through migration, social disruption and conflict. Similarly, in the age of a

## Making globalization work for all

In their Millennium Declaration, in September 2000, world leaders stressed that ensuring globalization becomes a positive force for all represents the central challenge before the international community. People must feel included if globalization is to succeed, Secretary-General Kofi Annan said in his report to the Millennium Summit, entitled *We the Peoples: the role of the United Nations in the 21st century.**

The benefits of globalization are obvious, the Secretary-General said: faster growth, higher living standards, new opportunities for countries and individuals. Yet a backlash has begun, because these benefits are so unequally distributed, and because the global market is not yet underpinned by rules based on shared social objectives.

Global companies should be guided by the concept of global "corporate citizenship", and apply good practices wherever they operate — promoting equitable labour standards, respect for human rights and protection of the environment.

For its part, the United Nations must "ensure that globalization provides benefits not just for some, but for all; that opportunity exists not merely for the privileged, but for every human being everywhere". The Organization must "broker differences among states" and forge "coalitions for change" by opening up further to the participation of the many actors involved in globalization — civil society, the private sector, parliamentarians, local authorities, scientific associations, educational institutions.

Above all, "we must put people at the centre of everything we do", Mr. Annan said. "Only when that begins to happen will we know that globalization is indeed becoming inclusive, allowing everyone to share its opportunities".

---

*United Nations, 2000, ISBN 92-1-100844-1, E.00.1.16. Also available at www.un.org/millennium/sg/report.

---

global economy, financial instability in one country is immediately felt in the markets of others.

There is also growing consensus on the role played by democracy, human rights, popular participation, good governance and the empowerment of women in fostering economic and social development.

## Coordinating development activities

Despite advances on many fronts, gross disparities in wealth and well-being continue to characterize the world. Reducing poverty and redressing inequalities, both within and between countries, remain fundamental goals of the United Nations.

The United Nations system works in a variety of ways to promote its economic and social goals — by formulating policies, advising

## The United Nations competitive advantage

The United Nations system has unique strengths in promoting development worldwide:

- Its *universality*: all countries have a voice when policy decisions are made;
- Its *impartiality*: it does not represent any particular national or commercial interest, and can thus develop special relations of trust with countries and their people to provide aid with no strings attached;
- Its *global presence*: it has the world's largest network of country offices for delivering assistance for development;
- Its *comprehensive mandate*, encompassing development, security, humanitarian assistance, human rights and the environment;
- Its *commitment* to "the peoples of the United Nations".

governments on their development plans, setting international norms and standards, and mobilizing funds for development programmes totalling over $30 billion annually. It is through the work of its various Funds and Programmes and its family of specialized agencies, in areas as diverse as education, air safety, environmental protection and labour conditions, that the work of the Organization touches the lives of people everywhere.

The **Economic and Social Council (ECOSOC)** (*see Chapter 1, page 10*) is the principal body coordinating the economic and social work of the United Nations and its operational arms. It is also the central forum for discussing international economic and social issues and for formulating policy recommendations.

Under ECOSOC, the **Committee for Development Policy**, made up of 24 experts working in their personal capacity, acts as an advisory body on emerging economic, social and environmental issues. It also sets the criteria for the designation of "least developed countries" (LDCs).

The **United Nations Development Group**, comprised of Secretariat bodies as well as the development Funds and Programmes, assists in the management and coordination of development work within the Organization. This executive body works to enhance cooperation between policy-making entities and the distinct operational programmes.

Within the United Nations Secretariat, the **Department of Economic and Social Affairs (DESA)** (*see Chapter 1, page 29*) gathers and analyses economic and social data; carries out policy analysis and coordination; and provides substantive and technical support to Member States in the social and economic sphere. Its substantive support to intergovernmental processes facilitates the task of

Member States to set norms and standards and agree on common courses of action in relation to global challenges. DESA thus constitutes a crucial interface between global policies and national action, and among research, policy and operational activities at the national and international levels.

The five **Regional Commissions** (*see Chapter 1, page 32*) facilitate similar exchanges of economic and social information and policy analysis in the regions of Africa, Asia and the Pacific, Europe, Latin America and the Caribbean, and Western Asia.

The various **United Nations Funds and Programmes** deal with operational activities for development in programme countries. The **United Nations Specialized Agencies** are engaged as well in providing support and assistance to the development efforts of countries. At a time of increasingly limited resources, both human and financial, enhanced coordination and cooperation among the various arms of the system are vital if development goals are to be realized.

## Economic development

The world has witnessed enormous economic development in recent decades, but the generation of wealth and prosperity has been very uneven — so uneven that economic imbalances are seen to exacerbate social problems and political instability in virtually every region of the world. The end of the cold war and the accelerating integration of the global economy have not solved persistent problems of extreme poverty, indebtedness, underdevelopment and trade imbalance.

One of the founding principles of the United Nations is the conviction that economic development for all peoples is the surest way to achieve political, economic and social security. It is a central preoccupation of the Organization that nearly half of the world's population, most of them in Africa, Asia and Latin America and the Caribbean, still has to make do on less than $2 per day. Nearly 1 billion people are illiterate, and over 1 billion lack access to safe water. Worldwide, some 140 million workers are out of work altogether, and at least 750 million are underemployed.

The United Nations continues to be the single institution dedicated to finding ways to ensure that economic expansion and globalization are guided by policies aimed at ensuring human welfare, sustainable development, the eradication of poverty, fair trade policies and the reduction of crippling foreign debt.

The United Nations urges the adoption of macroeconomic policies that address current imbalances, particularly the growing gap between the North and South, the persistent problems of the least developed countries, and the unprecedented needs of the countries in transition from centralized to market economies. All over the world, United Nations programmes of assistance promote poverty reduction, child survival, environmental protection, women's progress and human rights. For millions in poor countries, these programmes *are* the United Nations.

## Official development assistance

Through their policies and loans, the lending institutions of the United Nations system have, collectively, an enormous influence on the economies of developing countries. This is especially true for the least developed countries (LDCs), which include 48 nations whose extreme poverty and indebtedness have marginalized them from global growth and development. These nations, most of which are in Africa, are the focus of several United Nations assistance programmes, as well as a priority of international development cooperation. Donor countries have agreed to commit 0.15 per cent of their gross national product (GNP) to this group of nations.

Small island developing states (*see also page 202*), landlocked developing countries and countries with economies in transition also suffer from critical problems requiring special attention from the international community, and are similarly priorities in the assistance programmes of the United Nations system.

Official development assistance (ODA) to all developing countries has averaged around $55 billion a year in the 1990s (*see box on page 132*).

United Nations ODA is derived from two sources: grant assistance from United Nations specialized agencies, funds and programmes, which has averaged around $4.5 billion a year; and loans from lending institutions of the United Nations system, such as the World Bank and the International Fund for Agricultural Development (IFAD).

ODA from the United Nations agencies, funds and programmes is widely distributed among 130 countries. In 1998, the latest year for which a detailed breakdown is available, humanitarian assistance received the largest single share of United Nations grant-financed development activities, accounting for one fifth of total outlays of $5.2 billion, followed by the health sector.

The World Bank provides loans totalling over $25 billion a year, and IFAD provides over $400 million a year in loans and grants. In addition, the International Monetary Fund offers various forms of support to countries in financial difficulties.

## Financing development

In 1980, industrialized countries pledged at the General Assembly to devote 0.7 per cent of their gross national product (GNP) for official development assistance (ODA) to developing countries. But that target has been reached by only a few countries — currently Denmark, Finland, Norway, and Sweden. On average, ODA has remained at less than half of the targeted level, or about 0.3 per cent of industrialized countries' GNP, falling in real terms with the end of the cold war. In 1999, ODA, at $56 billion, represented a mere 0.24 per cent of the GNP of the 21 main donor countries. The largest donor continued to be Japan, followed by the United States, France and Germany.

In the past, official development finance from northern governments represented the bulk of the financial resources going into developing countries. But in the last few years, private investment in developing countries has increased dramatically, and private investments and loans now far outweigh official flows. Of total net resource flows of $240 billion to developing countries in 1998, $147 billion was private flows, and only $88 billion was official flows, including non-ODA funds.

Both the World Bank and the United Nations Conference on Trade and Development carefully monitor these flows and point to serious problems that still must be addressed. In 1999, for example, developing countries received only 24 per cent of foreign direct investment. Africa's share was a mere 1.2 per cent.

Reflecting concern over these issues, the General Assembly has decided to convene in 2002 an international consultation on financing for development. The high-level meeting is to address, among other things, the continuing high level of indebtedness and the mobilization of innovative domestic and private resources for development, as well as international resources, and governance of the international monetary, financial and trade systems.

---

But the activities of the United Nations system have been affected by the marked decline of the share of ODA in total resource flows (*see box above*). The share of United Nations system development grants in total ODA has averaged around 8 per cent.

As general (core) resources provided to United Nations agencies and bodies have declined, there has been a relatively rapid increase in non-core resources provided for specific programmes, projects or funds. In addition, while all countries contribute to development cooperation, over 90 per cent of core resources is provided by only 15 industrial countries. The traditional donor base has been static, despite significant changes in the global economy.

## Promoting development worldwide

The **United Nations Development Programme (UNDP)** (*see also Chapter 1, page 38*) is the developing countries' development agency, committed to making a pivotal contribution to halving world poverty by 2015. UNDP provides sound policy advice and helps build institutional capacity that generates equitable economic growth.

UNDP's global network of 134 country offices, with programmes in 174 countries and territories, helps people to help themselves. Current priorities include the use of information technology for development, combating the spread of HIV/AIDS, promoting sustainable trade and helping to address the effects of conflict and natural disasters. UNDP is often asked to support rebuilding societies in the aftermath of war and humanitarian emergencies (*see Chapter 2, page 81 and Chapter 5, page 249*). UNDP is a hands-on organization, with 85 per cent of its staff working in the countries where people need help.

Ninety per cent of UNDP's core programme funds go to the 66 countries that are home to 90 per cent of the world's extremely poor (*see page 160, below*). UNDP and its funds provide annually around $2 billion in development assistance. Contributions to UNDP are voluntary, and come from nearly every government in the world. Countries that receive UNDP-administered assistance contribute to project costs through personnel, facilities, equipment and supplies.

To ensure maximum impact from global development resources, UNDP coordinates its activities with other United Nations funds and programmes and the international financial institutions, including the World Bank and the International Monetary Fund. In addition, UNDP's country and regional programmes draw on the expertise of developing country nationals and NGOs. Seventy-five per cent of all UNDP-supported projects are implemented by local organizations.

At the country level, UNDP promotes an integrated approach to the provision of United Nations development assistance. In several developing countries, it has established a **United Nations Development Assistance Framework (UNDAF)** made up of United Nations teams under the leadership of the local United Nations Resident Coordinator, who is usually the Resident Representative of UNDP. The Frameworks articulate a coordinated response to the main development challenges identified for the United Nations by governments.

Resident Coordinators serve as coordinators of humanitarian assistance in cases of human disasters, natural disasters and complex emergency situations (*see Chapter 5, pages 249-250*).

UNDP — together with the World Bank and the United Nations Environment Programme — is one of the managing partners of the

## Africa — a United Nations priority

The United Nations, reflecting the concern of the international community, has made the critical socio-economic conditions in Africa a priority concern. In affirming its commitment to support the region's development, it has devised special programmes to find durable solutions to external debt and debt-service problems, to increase foreign direct investment, to enhance national capacity-building, to deal with the shortage of domestic resources for development, to facilitate the integration of the African countries into international trade and to tackle AIDS.

The General Assembly in 1991 adopted the New Agenda for Development of Africa in the 1990s. To put the Agenda into practice and help accelerate development in the decade to 2005, the Assembly launched in 1996 the United Nations System-wide Special Initiative on Africa. The Initiative is designed to rationalize and maximize the impact of the United Nations extensive programmes in the region, including those of UNDP, UNICEF and the financial institutions, through more effective coordination at headquarters and at the country level. Its focus is on forging partnerships to address priorities already identified by African countries.

The Jobs for Africa Programme, an integral part of the Initiative, aims to develop and strengthen the capacity of national and regional institutions and networks in 10 participating countries to combat poverty by generating employment. The Africa 2000 initiative of UNDP, which provides support to rural women for sustainable development activities, has sponsored over 700 projects. Led by UNESCO, UNICEF and the World Bank, education activities under the Special Initiative focus on improving primary education in 16 countries where primary school environment is low.

The Joint United Nations Programme on AIDS (UNAIDS) has intensified its campaign against HIV/AIDS in Africa. Seeking as broad a base as possible for its campaign, UNAIDS has brought together governments, regional bodies, development agencies, non-governmental organizations (NGOs) and the corporate sector, including pharmaceutical corporations, under an umbrella group known as the International Partnership Against AIDS in Africa.

The Secretary-General and United Nations agencies have called on industrialized countries to ease Africa's economic hurdles — by arranging deeper debt relief, by lowering tariffs that penalize African exports and by increasing official development assistance.

The United Nations is tying its work into other development undertakings, such as the Tokyo International Conference on African Development, the Heavily Indebted Poor Countries Debt Initiative and the Alliance for African Industrialization.

Global Environment Facility (*see page 197, below*) and is one of the sponsors of the **Joint United Nations Programme on HIV/AIDS (UNAIDS)** (*see page 167, below*).

## Lending for development

The **World Bank** (*see also Chapter 1, page 52*) works to strengthen economies and expand markets, with the aim of improving the quality of life for people everywhere, especially the poorest. Unlike aid programmes, the Bank does not make grants: it lends money to developing countries — and the loans are repaid.

Developing countries borrow from the Bank because they need capital, technical assistance and policy advice. There are two types of Bank lending. The first type is for developing countries that are able to pay near-market interest rates. The money for these loans comes largely from investors around the world, who buy bonds issued by the Bank.

The second type of loan goes to the poorest countries, which are usually not creditworthy in the international financial markets and are unable to pay near-market interest rates on the money they borrow. Lending to the poorest countries is done by a World Bank affiliate, the **International Development Association (IDA)**. IDA credits are free of interest, carry a low 0.75 per cent annual administrative charge, and are very long-term — 35 or 40 years, including 10 years grace. Countries with per capita incomes of less than $895 are eligible for IDA credits, but most credits go to countries that are much poorer. But again, the credits are repaid. Funded largely by contributions from the richer member countries, IDA lends an average of about $6 billion a year (*see also page 162, below*).

Under its regulations, the Bank can lend only to governments, but it works closely with local communities, NGOs and private enterprise. Its projects are designed to assist the poorest sectors of the population. Successful development requires that governments and communities "own" their development projects. The Bank encourages governments to work closely with NGOs and civil society to strengthen participation by people affected by Bank-financed projects. NGOs based in borrowing countries collaborate in about half of Bank-supported projects.

The Bank encourages the private sector by advocating stable economic policies, sound government finances, and open, honest and accountable governance. It supports many sectors in which private-sector development is making rapid inroads — finance, power, telecommunications, information technology, oil and gas and industry. The Bank's regulations prohibit the Bank from lending directly to the private sector. But a Bank affiliate — the **International Finance Corporation (IFC)** — exists expressly to invest in private-sector enterprises (*see page 138, below*). Another affiliate, the

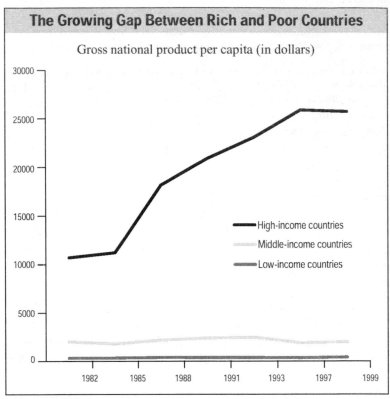

## The Growing Gap Between Rich and Poor Countries

Gross national product per capita (in dollars)

- High-income countries
- Middle-income countries
- Low-income countries

1982 1985 1988 1991 1993 1997 1999

*Source*: World Bank

**Multilateral Investment Guarantee Agency (MIGA),** facilitates private-sector investment to developing countries (*see page 139, below*).

The Bank does much more than lend money: it also routinely includes technical assistance in the projects it finances. This may cover advice on issues such as the overall size of a country's budget and where the money should be allocated, or how to set up village health clinics, or what sort of equipment is needed to build a road. The Bank funds a few projects each year devoted exclusively to providing expert advice and training. It also trains people from borrowing countries on how to create and carry out development programmes.

In the area of sustainable development, the Bank supports projects for reforestation, pollution control and land management; invests in water, sanitation and agriculture to combat the environmental problems that afflict the poor; promotes economic policies and national environmental action plans which help to conserve natural resources; and is the main funder of the Global Environment Facility (*see page 197, below*).

## Lending for stability

Many countries turn to the **International Monetary Fund (IMF)** (*see also Chapter 1, page 54*), a United Nations specialized agency, when internal or external factors seriously undermine their balance-of-payments position, fiscal stability or capacity to meet debt service commitments. The IMF offers advice and policy recommendations to overcome these problems, and often makes financial resources available to member countries in support of economic reform programmes under a range of policies and facilities.

Members with balance-of-payments problems generally avail themselves of the IMF's financial resources by "purchasing" reserve assets — in the form of other members' currencies and Special Drawing Rights — with an equivalent amount of their own currencies. The IMF levies charges on these loans, and requires that members repay the loans by repurchasing their own currencies from the IMF over a specified time.

The main IMF facilities are:

• *Stand-by arrangements,* designed to provide short-term balance-of-payments assistance for deficits of a temporary or cyclical nature; must be repaid within 5 years.

• *Extended Fund Facility,* designed to support medium-term programmes aimed at overcoming balance-of-payment difficulties stemming from macroeconomic and structural problems; must be repaid within 10 years.

• *Poverty Reduction and Growth Facility,* a concessional facility designed for the low-income member countries with the explicit goal of reducing poverty. Members qualifying for funding may borrow up to 140 per cent of their quota under a three-year arrangement (and up to 185 per cent under exceptional circumstances). Loans carry an annual interest rate of 0.5 per cent; repayments are made beginning 5 1/2 years and ending 10 years after disbursement.

• *Compensatory Financing Facility,* which provides timely financing for members experiencing temporary export shortfalls or excesses in cereal import costs.

• *Contingent Credit Lines,* which aim to prevent the spread of a crisis by enabling countries that are pursuing sound policies to have quick access to financing should a crisis threaten.

- *Supplemental Reserve Facility,* which provides financial assistance in financial crises for exceptional balance-of-payments difficulties due to a large short-term financing need resulting from a sudden and disruptive loss of market confidence. Repayments are expected within 1 1/2 year, but can be extended to 2 1/2 years.

To provide debt relief to heavily indebted poor countries following sound policies, the IMF and the World Bank jointly provide, under the Heavily Indebted Poor Countries Initiative, exceptional assistance to eligible countries to reduce their external debt burdens to sustainable levels, enabling them to service their debts without the need for further debt relief. It is a comprehensive approach to debt relief, involving multilateral, official, bilateral and commercial creditors.

Surveillance is the process by which the IMF appraises its members' exchange rate policies through a comprehensive analysis of the general economic situation and policies of each member. The IMF carries out surveillance through annual consultations with individual countries; multilateral surveillance twice a year; regional surveillance through discussion with regional groupings; as well as precautionary arrangements, enhanced surveillance and programme monitoring, which provide a member with close IMF monitoring in the absence of the use of IMF resources.

The IMF provides technical assistance to its members in several broad areas: the design and implementation of fiscal and monetary policy; institution-building, such as the development of central banks or treasuries; and the collection and refinement of statistical data. It also provides training to member countries' officials at the IMF institutes in Washington, D.C., Abidjan, Côte d'Ivoire, Singapore and Vienna.

### Investment and development

As foreign direct investment has continued to expand dramatically, developing countries have increasingly opened up their economies to such investment. Various parts of the United Nations system monitor and assess developments, and, such as FAO (*see page 143, below*), UNDP (*see page 133, above*) and UNIDO (*see page 145, below*), assist developing-country governments in attracting investment.

Two affiliates of the World Bank — the International Finance Corporation and the Multilateral Investment Guarantee Agency — help promote investment in developing countries. Through its advisory work, the **International Finance Corporation (IFC)** helps governments create conditions that stimulate the flow of both domestic and foreign private savings and investment. IFC stimulates and mobilizes private investment in the developing world by demonstrating that investments there can be profitable. Since its founding in 1956, IFC has committed more than $26.7 billion of its own funds, and has arranged $17.9 billion in syndications and underwriting for 2,264 companies in 132 developing countries.

The **Multilateral Investment Guarantee Agency (MIGA)** is an investment insurance affiliate to the Bank. Its goal is to facilitate the flow of private investment for productive purposes to developing member countries by offering to investors long-term political risk insurance — that is, coverage against the risks of expropriation, currency transfer, war and civil disturbance — and by providing advisory services. MIGA carries out promotional programmes, disseminates information on investment opportunities and provides technical assistance that enhances the investment promotion capabilities of countries. MIGA guarantees have facilitated an estimated $33 billion in foreign direct investment in 69 developing countries.

The **United Nations Conference on Trade and Development (UNCTAD)** assists developing countries to promote inward investment and improve their investment climate. It also assists government agencies to improve the general understanding of global trends in foreign direct investment flows and related policies, as well as the interrelationship between foreign direct investment, trade, technology and development. The results of its work are presented in the annual *World Investment Report* and other studies, which are the basis for policy discussions in UNCTAD's **Commission on Investment, Technology and Related Financial Issues.**

UNCTAD, through its **Division on Investment Technology and Enterprise Development,** promotes understanding on investment, enterprise development and technological capacity building, and assists governments to formulate and carry out policies and activities in this area.

## Trade and development

International trade has been growing strongly at an annual rate of 10 per cent since the mid-1980s, enabling various developing countries to enjoy remarkable gains in prosperity and growth. But major disparities persist, with many of the poorest countries still participating only marginally in international trade.

Ensuring the integration of all countries in global trade is the task of the **United Nations Conference on Trade and Development (UNCTAD)** — the focal point within the United Nations for dealing with development-related issues in the areas of trade, finance, tech-

## Foreign direct investment and development

Foreign direct investment continues to be a driving force in the global economy. The continuing expansion of investment flows underscores the central role played by transnational corporations in both industrialized and developing countries. According to UNCTAD's *World Investment Report 2000*:

- Foreign direct investment inflows by transnational corporations rose to $865 billion in 1999, and have suspassed $1 trillion in 2000;
- The number of transnational corporations worldwide has continued to expand — up to 63,000 in 2000;
- The around 690,000 foreign affiliates of the world's transnationals sold about $14 trillion of goods and services in 1999 — almost double the volume of global exports: international production has become more important than international trade in delivering goods and services to foreign markets;
- The largest 100 non-financial transnationals hold a dominant position in the global production system: in 1998 they held over $2 trillion in foreign assets, had foreign sales amounting to $2 trillion and employed more than 6 million people in their foreign affiliates;
- Since 1995, for the first time, two corporations from developing countries have been in the list of the world's 100 biggest corporations: Daewoo Corporation (Republic of Korea) and Petroleos de Venezuela.

---

nology, investment and sustainable development. UNCTAD works to maximize the trade, investment and development opportunities of developing countries, and to help them face the challenges arising from globalization and to integrate into the world economy on an equitable basis.

UNCTAD pursues these goals through research and policy analysis, intergovernmental deliberations, technical cooperation, and interaction with civil society and the business sector.

In particular, UNCTAD:

- Examines trends in the global economy and evaluates their impact upon development;
- Helps developing countries, particularly the least developed, to maximize the positive impact of globalization and liberalization by helping them integrate into the international trading system and become actively involved in international trade negotiations;
- Examines global trends in foreign direct investment flows and their impact on trade, technology and development;
- Helps developing countries to attract investment;
- Helps developing countries to develop enterprises and entrepreneurship;

## Promoting equitable trade

Intergovernmental negotiations under UNCTAD's auspices have resulted in:

- Agreement on a Generalized Systems of Preferences (1971), which facilitates the preferential treatment of over $70 billion of developing-country export to industrialized countries annually;
- Agreement on a Global System of Trade Preferences (1989) among developing countries;
- International commodity agreements, including those for cocoa, sugar, natural rubber, jute and jute products, tropical timber, tin, olive oil and wheat;
- The Common Fund for Commodities, which provides financial backing for the operation of international stocks and for research and development projects in the area of commodities;
- Debt relief: more than 50 developing countries have benefited from debt relief of over $6.5 billion since a resolution on the retroactive adjustment of terms of the ODA debt of low-income developing countries was approved in 1978;
- Guidelines for international action on debt rescheduling (1980);
- Agreement on a Global Framework for Transit Transport Cooperation between Landlocked and Transit Developing Countries and the Donor Community (1995); and
- United Nations Conventions in the area of maritime transport: on a Code of Conduct for Liner Conferences (1974), on International Carriage of Goods by Sea (1978), on International Multimodal Transport of Goods (1980), on Conditions for Registration of Ships (1986) and on Maritime Liens and Mortgages (1993).

UNCTAD also brought about the only universal, voluntary code on competition — the 1980 agreement on a set of multilateral principles and rules to control restrictive business practices — which is reviewed every five years. The agreement was reviewed most recently in 2000, in close cooperation with the World Bank and the World Trade Organization, to increase both efficiency and equity in competition matters.

---

- Helps developing countries and countries with economies in transition to improve the efficiency of their trade-supporting services;
- Promotes global electronic commerce by facilitating access to information technologies, particularly through its Trade Point Programme (*see page 142, below*).

UNCTAD promotes enterprise development, particularly for small and medium-sized enterprises, through regular intergovernmental discussions and through technical cooperation. The Commission on Enterprise, Business Facilitation and Development and its expert meetings examine ways to formulate and carry out effective enterprise development strategies.

UNCTAD's technical cooperation activities involve over 300 projects in more than 100 countries, for which it provides about $24 million annually. Some interregional projects include:

- The *Automated System for Customs Data*, using state-of-the-art technology, helps governments modernize customs procedures and management. Used by more than 60 countries, the system is fast becoming the internationally accepted standard for customs automation.

- The *Advance Cargo Information System* helps African countries to develop their transport sector, using computer technology to track cargo along land and sea routes.

- The *EMPRETEC Programme* promotes small and medium-sized enterprise development. An information network provides entrepreneurs with access to business databases.

- The *Trade Point Programme* involves the creation of trade facilitation centres to reduce transaction costs and provide small and medium-sized enterprises with better access to trade-related information, services and global networks, using modern information technology such as the Internet. Thanks to the Trade Points, all connected countries and enterprises exchange "Electronic Trade Opportunities" and other types of information regarding trade regulations, banking practices and market intelligence.

(*For UNCTAD's work in science and technology, see page 156, below.*)

The **International Trade Centre UNCTAD/WTO (ITC)** (*see also Chapter 1, page 36*) is the focal point in the United Nations system for technical cooperation with developing countries in trade promotion. It works with developing countries and countries with economies in transition to set up trade promotion programmes to expand their exports and improve their import operations.

ITC's field of specialization covers six areas:

- Product and market development;
- Development of trade support services;
- Trade information;
- Human resource development;
- International purchasing and supply management;
- Needs assessment and programme design for trade promotion.

Technical cooperation projects in trade promotion are carried out by ITC specialists working in close liaison with local trade officials. National projects often take the form of a broad-based package of services to expand country exports and improve import operations.

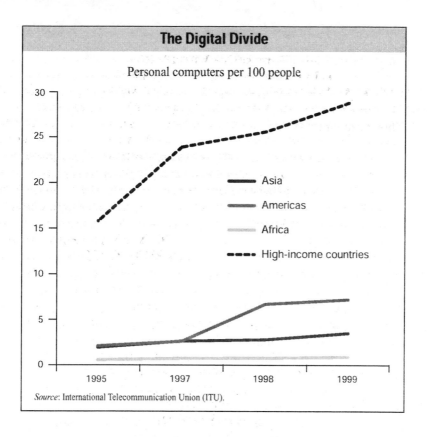

**The Digital Divide**

Personal computers per 100 people

- Asia
- Americas
- Africa
- High-income countries

*Source*: International Telecommunication Union (ITU).

## Agricultural development

The majority of people on the planet continue to live in rural areas and derive their livelihood, directly or indirectly, mostly from agriculture. In recent decades, rural poverty has spread and deepened and, in the rush to industrialization, insufficient investment has been made in the agricultural sector. The United Nations has addressed this imbalance in a variety of ways.

The **Food and Agriculture Organization of the United Nations (FAO)** *(see also Chapter 1, page 50, and page 163, below)* is the lead agency for agriculture, forestry, fisheries and rural development. It gives practical help to developing countries through a wide range of technical assistance projects. A specific priority is to encourage rural development and sustainable agriculture — a long-term strategy for increasing food production and food security while conserving and managing natural resources.

In promoting sustainable agricultural development, FAO encourages an integrated approach, with environmental, social and economic considerations included in the formulation of development projects. In some areas, for example, particular combinations of crops can improve agricultural productivity, provide a source of fuel wood for local villagers, improve soil fertility and reduce the impact of erosion.

On average, FAO has some 1,800 field projects operating at any one time. They range from integrated land management projects to policy and planning advice to governments in areas as diverse as forestry and marketing strategies. FAO usually takes one of three roles: implementing its own programme; executing a programme on behalf of other agencies and donors; or providing advice and management assistance to national projects.

FAO's Investment Centre assists developing countries in formulating investment projects in agricultural and rural development. Each year, this assistance helps mobilize some $3 billion for investment projects, including external funds of over $2 billion.

FAO is active in land and water development, plant and animal production, forestry, fisheries, economic, social and food security policy, investment, nutrition, food standards and food safety, and commodities and trade. For instance:

- A programme in nine southern African countries helps rural populations to improve their living standards and nutrition by fish farming. Small water bodies are brought into production, integrating aquaculture with farming. Small farmers have thus expanded food production for consumption and trade.
- Poor farmers in Sri Lanka have been encouraged to form informal groups for income-generating activities, such as land reclamation or small-scale processing. Groups are taught how to gain economic advantages by, for example, buying fertilizer in bulk and marketing crops together. Some 4,000 poor farmers have benefited from the project.
- A project in Mali has established revolving funds to allow women's groups to buy seeds, fertilizers, water pumps and grinding mills. The women have created home and market gardens, selling surplus vegetables in newly established weekly markets. Village women have thus developed activities to expand food production, increase income, improve health and gain access to water.
- Using integrated pest management techniques promoted by FAO, 200,000 Indonesian rice farmers have increased yields and reduced the use of pesticides, helping protect the environment and

food quality while saving the government $120 million a year in pesticide subsidies.

The **International Fund for Agricultural Development (IFAD)** (*see also Chapter 1, page 59, and page 164, below*) finances agricultural development projects that alleviate rural poverty and improve nutrition in the developing world. The Fund's participatory, grass-roots approach gives it a comparative advantage over other institutions. Its small but efficient institutional structure enables the Fund to detect and react to new demands in the rural sector in a flexible and timely manner. In fulfilling its mandate, IFAD provides direct funding and mobilizes resources for programmes specifically designed to promote the economic advancement of the rural poor, mainly by improving the productivity of farm activities.

IFAD's beneficiaries are the poorest of the world's people: small farmers, the rural landless, nomadic pastoralists, artisanal fisherfolk, indigenous people and — across all groups — poor rural women.

The bulk of IFAD's resources are made available to poor countries on highly concessional terms, repayable over 40 years, including a grace period of 10 years, and a 0.75 per cent service charge per annum.

Since its establishment in 1977, IFAD has financed 548 loans for projects in 114 countries, to which it has committed over $6.8 billion in loans and grants. Recipient countries have contributed $6.9 billion, and donors have provided $5.8 billion in cofinancing. These projects have helped more than 250 million people.

## Industrial development

Globalization of industry has created unprecedented industrial challenges and opportunities for developing countries and countries with economies in transition. The **United Nations Industrial Development Organization (UNIDO)** (*see also Chapter 1, page 60*) is the specialized agency helping these countries to pursue sustainable industrial development in the new global environment. UNIDO provides tailor-made solutions to today's industrial problems by assisting governments, business associations and the private industrial sector with packages of integrated services addressing three priority areas:

- *Competitive economy,* including industrial policy formulation and implementation, continuous improvements and quality management, and investment and technology promotion;
- *Sound environment,* including environmental policies, energy efficiency and cleaner production; and

- *Productive employment,* including policies supporting small- and medium-size enterprises, entrepreneurship development and women entrepreneurs.

Acting as a global forum for industrial development, UNIDO brings together representatives of government, industry, and the public and private sectors from developed and developing countries, as well as from countries with economies in transition. Through its technical cooperation programmes, UNIDO puts into effect the task of sustaining an economically efficient, socially desirable and ecologically sound pace of industrial development.

Together with member states, UNIDO has developed integrated packages of service modules designed to meet the specific requirements of countries in strengthening industrial capacities and achieving a cleaner and sustainable industrial development.

UNIDO's Investment and Technology Promotion Offices promote business contacts between industrialized countries and developing countries and countries with economies in transition. They are financed by the countries in which they are located: Bahrain, China, France, Greece, Italy, Japan, Poland, Republic of Korea and Slovakia. The Russian Federation is host to the UNIDO Centre for International Industrial Cooperation. In addition, UNIDO has 29 field offices all over the world.

### Labour

Concerned with both the economic and social aspects of development, the **International Labour Organization (ILO)** *(see also Chapter 1, page 49)* is one of the specialized agencies that predates the United Nations, as it was established in 1919. Its long and diverse work in the setting and monitoring of labour standards in the workplace has provided the framework of international labour standards and guidelines that have been adopted in national legislation in virtually all countries.

ILO is guided by the principle that social stability and integration can be sustained only if they are based on social justice, particularly the right to employment with fair compensation in a healthy workplace. Over the decades, ILO has helped to create such hallmarks as the eight-hour day, maternity protection, child-labour laws, and a whole range of policies that promote safety in the workplace and peaceful industrial relations *(see also Chapter 4, page 230)*.

Specifically, ILO engages in:
- The formulation of international policies and programmes to promote basic human rights, improve working and living conditions and enhance employment opportunities;

- The creation of international labour standards — backed by a unique system to supervise their application — to serve as guidelines for national authorities in putting sound labour policies into practice;
- An extensive programme of technical cooperation, formulated and carried out in partnership with beneficiaries, to help countries make these policies effective;
- Training, education, research and information activities to help advance all these efforts.

**Decent work.** The central purpose of ILO is to promote opportunities of decent work for all people. The International Labour Conference has approved four objectives that must converge on this primary goal. They are:
- Promote and realize fundamental principles and rights at work;
- Create greater opportunities for women and men to secure decent employment and income;
- Enhance the coverage and effectiveness of social protection for all;
- Strengthen dialogue among governments, labour and business.

To implement these objectives, ILO is focusing on such areas as health and safety at work, the promotion of small and medium-sized enterprises, the elimination of discrimination and gender inequality, the progressive abolition of child labour and the promotion of the *ILO Declaration on Fundamental Principles and Rights at Work*, adopted by the International Labour Conference in 1998.

**Technical cooperation.** ILO's technical cooperation focuses on support for democratization, poverty alleviation through employment creation, and the protection of workers. In particular, ILO helps countries to develop their legislation and take practical steps towards putting ILO standards into effect — for instance by developing occupational health and safety departments, social security systems and worker education programmes. Projects are carried out through close cooperation between recipient countries, donors and ILO, which maintains a network of area and regional offices worldwide. ILO has technical cooperation programmes in some 140 countries and territories; in the last decade, it spent an average of some $130 million annually on technical cooperation projects.

ILO's **International Training Centre,** located in Turin, Italy, carries out training for senior and mid-level managers in private and public enterprises, leaders of workers' and employers' organizations, government officials and policy makers. Some 70,000 people from 172 countries have been trained since the Centre opened in 1965.

ILO's **International Institute for Labour Studies**, located in Geneva, promotes policy research and public discussion of emerging issues of concern to ILO. The organizing theme is the relationship between labour institutions, economic growth and social equity. The Institute acts as a global forum on social policy, maintains international research networks and carries out educational programmes.

## International aviation

In 1999 alone, some 1.5 billion passengers flew on over 20 million flights, while nearly 30 million tonnes of manufactured goods were shipped by air. The safe and orderly growth of international flight is overseen by a United Nations specialized agency, the **International Civil Aviation Organization (ICAO)** (*see also Chapter 1, page 55*).

ICAO works to encourage the design and operation of civil aircraft; to support the development of airways, airports and air navigation facilities; and to meet the need of the public for safe, regular, efficient and economic international air transport.

To meet those objectives, ICAO:

- Has adopted international standards and recommendations which are applied to the design and performance of aircraft and much of their equipment; the performance of airline pilots, flight crews, air traffic controllers, and ground and maintenance crews; and security requirements and procedures at international airports;
- Formulates visual and instrument flight rules, as well as the aeronautical charts used for international navigation. Aircraft telecommunications systems, radio frequencies and security procedures are also its responsibility;
- Works towards minimizing the impact of aviation on the environment through reductions in aircraft emissions and through noise limits;
- Facilitates the movement of aircraft, passengers, crews, baggage, cargo and mail across borders, by standardizing customs, immigration, public health and other formalities.

ICAO meets requests from developing countries for help in improving air transport systems and training for aviation personnel. It has helped to establish regional training centres in several developing countries, and has enabled thousands of students to attend training schools registered with ICAO. The agency has dispatched technical cooperation experts to more than 100 countries, and is involved in some 120 projects each year, with average annual expenditures of $54 million.

ICAO is now developing a satellite-based system to meet the future communications, navigation, surveillance and air traffic management needs of civil aviation. The system applies the latest technology in satellites and computers, data links and deck avionics to cope with expanding operational needs. This integrated global system will increase safety, and improve the way air traffic services are organized and operated. The system, which has been endorsed by ICAO member states, is now in its implementation phase.

ICAO cooperates with the International Air Transport Association, the Airports Council International, the International Federation of Airline Pilot Associations and the International Council of Aircraft Owner and Pilot Associations.

## International shipping

In 1958, collisions between ships caused the loss of 56,000 tons of merchant shipping, while grounding or striking wrecks resulted in the loss of 115,000 tons. Nearly half of these casualties were caused by navigational error or deficiency. The same year, the **International Maritime Organization (IMO)** was established (*see also Chapter 1, page 56*), issuing the first safety measures in 1959. Four decades later, losses have dropped dramatically, with over 96 per cent of the world's merchant fleets adhering to three key safety conventions developed by IMO.

Thanks to this United Nations specialized agency, measures to improve the safety of international shipping and to prevent marine pollution from ships are in force worldwide (*for IMO action against pollution, see page 204, below*). IMO is also involved in legal matters, including liability and compensation issues and the facilitation of international maritime traffic.

The adoption of maritime legislation is IMO's best known responsibility. IMO has adopted around 40 conventions and protocols, most of them updated in line with changes taking place in world shipping.

When IMO began operations, its chief concern was to develop international treaties and other legislation concerning safety and marine pollution prevention. This was largely completed by the late 1970s, and the agency has subsequently concentrated on keeping legislation up to date and ensuring that it is ratified by as many countries as possible. This has been so successful that some conventions now apply to more than 98 per cent of world merchant shipping tonnage.

The main IMO treaties on maritime safety include:
* *International Regulations for Preventing Collisions at Sea (COLREG), 1972;*

- *International Convention for Safe Containers (CSC),* 1972;

- *International Convention for the Safety of Life at Sea (SOLAS),* 1974;

- *International Convention on Standards of Training, Certification and Watchkeeping for Seafarers (STCW),* 1978;

- *International Convention on Maritime Search and Rescue (SAR),* 1979.

Other measures introduced by IMO concern the safety of containers, bulk cargoes, liquefied gas tankers, fishing vessels and other ship types. Special attention has been paid to crew standards. Safety standards around the world have improved considerably since the late 1970s, when these treaties began to enter into force and the number of ratifications rose to record levels.

IMO works to establish communications systems guaranteeing greater safety at sea. The enormous strides made in communications technology have made it possible for IMO to introduce major improvements in the marine distress system. A global search and rescue system was initiated in the 1970s. The *International Maritime Satellite Organization (Inmarsat),* established in 1979, has greatly improved the provision of radio and other messages to ships. A further advance was made in 1999, when the *Global Maritime Distress and Safety System* became fully operational: a ship in distress anywhere in the world is virtually guaranteed assistance, even if its crew does not have time to radio for help, as the message is transmitted automatically.

Various IMO conventions address liability and compensation issues — among them the 1971 *Convention relating to Civil Liability in the Field of Marine Carriage of Nuclear Materials,* the 1976 *Convention on Limitation of Liability for Maritime Claims* and the 1996 *Convention on Liability and Compensation for Damage in Connection with the Carriage of Hazardous and Noxious Substances by Sea.*

IMO's technical cooperation programmes aim to support the implementation of its international standards and regulations, particularly in developing countries, and to assist governments in operating a shipping industry successfully. The emphasis is on training, and perhaps the best example is IMO's **World Maritime University** in Malmö, Sweden, which provides advanced training for the men and women involved in maritime administration, education and management.

# Telecommunications

Telecommunications have become a key to the global delivery of services: banking, tourism, transportation and the information industry all depend on quick and reliable global telecommunications. The sector is being revolutionized by powerful trends, such as globalization, deregulation, restructuring, value-added network services, intelligent networks and regional arrangements. Such developments have transformed telecommunications from its earlier status of public utility to one having strong links with commerce and trade. The global telecommunications market is expected to grow over the next decade to some $1,000 billion.

Against this background works the **International Telecommunication Union (ITU)** (*see also Chapter 1, page 56*), the world's oldest intergovernmental organization, dating back to 1865. Within ITU, the public and private sectors coordinate global telecommunication networks and services.

Specifically, ITU:

- Develops standards which foster the interconnection of national communications infrastructures into global networks, allowing the seamless exchange of information — be it data, faxes or phone calls — across the world;
- Works to integrate new technologies into the global telecommunications network, allowing for the development of new applications, such as the Internet, electronic mail, multimedia and electronic commerce;
- Adopts international regulations and treaties governing the sharing of the radio frequency spectrum and satellite orbital positions — finite natural resources which are used by a wide range of equipment including television and radio broadcasting, mobile telephones, satellite-based communications systems, aircraft and maritime navigation and safety systems, and wireless computer systems;
- Strives to expand and improve telecommunications in the developing world by providing policy advice, technical assistance, project management and training, and by fostering partnerships between telecommunications administrations, funding agencies and private organizations.

For instance, ITU approved in 2000 a set of characteristics for broadband radio local area networks (LAN) that promote the global portability of computer equipment. The agency has played a major role in the introduction of the third-generation mobile phone system (IMT-2000) by allocating its radio frequency spectrum and by providing the forum to reach global agreements on the elements of the system. ITU recommendations have resulted in many of the standards for electronic signatures in electronic commerce. The agency is now assisting developing countries to participate in e-commerce by helping them to acquire the necessary technology and build the soft and hard infrastructure.

In addition to its 189 member states, ITU is made up of some 600 sector members, representing scientific and industrial companies, public and private operators and broadcasters, and regional and international organizations.

## International postal service

Despite enormous technological progress in telecommunications, mail volume continues to increase in real terms, and the postal network remains the world's largest and densest network. Some 6.2 million postal employees working in over 700,000 post offices all over the world handle an annual total of 430 billion letters, printed matter items and parcels in the domestic service, and almost 10 billion in the international service. The United Nations specialized agency regulating this service is the **Universal Postal Union (UPU)** (*see also Chapter 1, page 57*).

The UPU forms a single postal territory of countries for the reciprocal exchange of letter-post items. Every member state agrees to transmit the mail of all other members by the best means used for its own mail. The primary vehicle of cooperation between national postal services, the UPU works to secure the improvement of international postal services, to provide postal customers in every country with harmonized and simplified procedures for their international mail, and to make available a universal network of up-to-date products and services.

The UPU sets indicative rates, maximum and minimum weight and size limits, and the conditions of acceptance of letter-post items — priority and non-priority items, letters, aerogrammes, postcards, printed matter and small packets. It prescribes the methods for calculating and collecting transit charges (for letter-post items passing through one or more countries) and terminal dues (for imbalance of mails). It also establishes regulations for registered and air mail, and for items requiring special precautions, such as infectious and radioactive substances.

Thanks to the UPU, new products and services are integrated into the international postal network. In this way, such services as registered letters, postal money orders, international reply coupons, small packets, postal parcels and expedited mail services have been made available to most of the world's citizens.

The agency has taken a strong leadership role in certain activities, such as the application of Electronic Data Interchange (EDI) technology by the postal administrations of member countries and the monitoring of quality of postal services on a global scale.

The UPU provides technical assistance through multi-year projects aimed at optimizing national postal services. It also conducts short projects which may include study cycles, training fellowships, and the expertise of development consultants who carry out on-the-spot studies on training, management or postal operations. The UPU has also made international financial institutions increasingly aware of the need for investment in the postal sector.

Around the world, postal services are making a determined effort to revitalize the postal business. As part of a communications market that is experiencing explosive growth, they have to adapt to a rapidly changing environment, becoming more independent, self-financing enterprises and providing a wider range of services. The UPU is playing a leadership role in promoting this revitalization.

## Intellectual property

Intellectual property has become a central issue in international trade relations. Over 3.7 million patents, 11 million registrations of trademarks and 1.3 million registrations of industrial design are in force around the world. Each year, around 1 million books and 5,000 feature films are produced, and 3 billion copies of disks and tapes are sold. In today's knowledge-based economy, intellectual property is a tool for promoting wealth creation as well as economic, social and cultural development.

A United Nations specialized agency, the **World Intellectual Property Organization (WIPO)** (*see also Chapter 1, page 59*) is responsible for promoting the protection of intellectual property all over the world through cooperation among states, and for administering various international treaties dealing with the legal and administrative aspects of intellectual property.

Intellectual property comprises two main branches: industrial property, which primarily means inventions, trademarks, industrial designs, and appellations of origin; and copyright, covering chiefly literary, musical, artistic, photographic and audiovisual works.

WIPO carries out many tasks related to the protection of intellectual property, such as administering international treaties, assisting governments, organizations and the private sector, monitoring developments in the field, and harmonizing and simplifying rules and practices.

WIPO's **Arbitration and Mediation Centre** helps individuals and companies from around the world to resolve their disputes. Since 1999, the Centre has also been providing services for resolving domain name disputes in the generic top level domains of the Internet (.com, .net, .org). It is also providing domain name dispute resolution services for some country administrators.

WIPO administers 21 treaties covering crucial aspects of intellectual property, some dating back to the 1880s. Two key treaties are the *Paris Convention for the Protection of Industrial Property* (1883) and the *Berne Convention for the Protection of Literary and Artistic Works* (1886).

A fundamental part of WIPO's activities is the progressive development and application of international norms and standards. WIPO is constantly alert to the need to develop new norms and standards in keeping with advances in technology and business practices, as well as in response to specific concerns such as traditional knowledge, folklore, biodiversity and biotechnology.

Through its development cooperation activities, WIPO offers to developing countries expert advice with respect to international patent applications, trademark registration and deposits of industrial designs. It encourages developing countries to make full use of the intellectual property system to foster domestic creative activity, attract investment and facilitate the transfer of technology.

Legal and technical assistance includes advice and expertise in drafting and revising national legislation. Training programmes are organized for a range of beneficiaries, including policy makers, officials and students. Assistance is offered to countries for the automation of their national intellectual property offices.

WIPO also provides services for international applications of industrial property rights. Four WIPO treaties, covering inventions (patents), trademarks and industrial design, ensure that one international registration of filing will have effect in any of the signatory states. The services provided by WIPO under these treaties simplify and reduce the cost of making individual applications or filings in all the countries in which protection for a given intellectual property right is sought.

## Global statistics

Governments, public institutions and the private sector rely heavily on accurate and comparable statistics at national and global levels, and the United Nations has served as a global focal point for statistics since its founding. Guided by the Statistical Commission — the United Nations intergovernmental body for statistics — the **Statistics Division** of the Secretariat provides a broad range of statistics and services for producers and users of statistics worldwide.

Its data publications and Internet services include the *Statistical Yearbook, Monthly Bulletin of Statistics, World Statistics Pocketbook* and specialized publications covering demographic statistics, national accounts, international merchandise trade, industrial commodities production, and energy. Studies on the world's women, disabled persons and human settlements are published regularly.

The Division seeks to improve national capabilities in developing countries, and assists them through advisory services, training support and workshops organized annually worldwide.

The **Statistical Commission,** supported by the Division, develops statistical methodology on national accounts, merchandise trade, environment statistics, social and gender indicators, and demographic statistics — including population and housing censuses, sample surveys, and vital statistics and civil registration. This functional Commission of ECOSOC, made up of 24 Member States, also ensures coordination of methodological standards among all international statistical services. (*See also* www.un.org/esa/unsd/global.htm *and* www.un.org/Depts/unsd).

## Public administration

A country's public sector is arguably the most important component in the successful implementation of its national development programmes. The new opportunities created by globalization, the information revolution and democratization have dramatically affected the state and how it functions. Managing the public sector in an environment of unremitting change has become a demanding challenge for national decision-makers, policy developers and public administrators.

The United Nations, through its *Programme in Public Administration and Finance*, assists countries in their efforts to strengthen, improve and reform their governance systems and administrative institutions. Managed by DESA's **Division for Public Economics and Public Administration,** the Programme assists governments to ensure that their public economic, administrative and financial institutions function in an effective, responsive and democratic manner. It promotes sound public policies, effective and responsive public administration, efficient service delivery and openness to change.

Activities range from assisting African governments in developing national programmes for improving the ethics in public-sector policies, to innovation in the delivery of public services in Latin America, to civil service reform in Asia. Many activities foster South-South cooperation, by emphasizing its successes through the dissemination of best practices and the promotion of further cooperation, including through the United Nations Online Network of Regional Institutions for Capacity Building in Public Administration and Finance.

### Science and technology for development

Since the 1960s, the United Nations has been promoting the application of science and technology for the development of its Member States. The **Commission on Science and Technology for Development,** a functional commission of ECOSOC, examines science and technology questions and their implications for development; promotes the understanding of science and technology policies in respect of developing countries; and formulates recommendations on science and technology matters within the United Nations system. Made up of 33 Member States and meeting every two years, the Commission selects different themes for its intersessional work and its deliberations. The theme for 1999-2000 was national capacity-building in biotechnology, with particular attention to agriculture, agro-industry, health and the environment.

**UNCTAD** provides substantive and secretariat support to the Commission. In addition, UNCTAD promotes policies favouring technological capacity-building, innovation and technology flows to developing countries. It provides technical assistance in the area of information technologies, and promotes technological capacity-building to individual enterprises through cooperative arrangements among firms, such as partnerships and networking.

FAO, IAEA, ILO, UNDP, UNIDO and WMO all address scientific and technological issues within their specific mandates. Science for development is also an important element in the work of UNESCO (*see page 191, below*).

### Social development

Inextricably linked to economic development, social development has been a cornerstone of the work of the United Nations from its inception. Over the decades, the United Nations has emphasized the social aspects of development to ensure that the aim of better lives for all people remains the central target of overall development efforts.

## Recent major world conferences

- World Conference on Education for All, 1990, Jomtien, Thailand
- World Summit for Children, 1990, New York
- United Nations Conference on Environment and Development (UNCED), 1992, Rio de Janeiro
- World Conference on Human Rights, 1993, Vienna
- International Conference on Population and Development, 1994, Cairo
- World Summit for Social Development, 1995, Copenhagen
- Fourth World Conference on Women: Action for Equality, Development and Peace, 1995, Beijing
- Second United Nations Conference on Human Settlements (Habitat II), 1996, Istanbul
- World Food Summit, 1996, Rome

Special sessions of the General Assembly review progress for each of the major conferences at five-year intervals, following up to the Conferences on Population and Development (1999), Women (2000), Social Development (2000), Human Settlements (2001), Children (2001) and Sustainable Development (2002). The third United Nations Conference on the Least Developed Countries is scheduled for 2001.

In its early years, the United Nations organized ground-breaking research and data-gathering in the areas of demographics, health and education, which witnessed the compilation — often for the first time — of reliable data on social indicators on a global scale. It also undertook efforts to protect the cultural heritage, from architectural monuments to languages, reflecting concern for those societies particularly vulnerable to the rapid processes of change.

The Organization has been in the forefront of supporting government efforts to extend social services relating to health, education, family planning, housing and sanitation to all people. In addition to developing models for social programmes, the United Nations has helped to integrate economic and social aspects of development. Its evolving policies and programmes have always stressed that the components of development — social, economic, environmental and cultural — are interconnected and cannot be pursued in isolation.

Globalization and liberalization are posing new challenges to social development. There is growing concern with achieving a more equitable sharing of the benefits of globalization. Many governments, which have made great sacrifices in economic reforms and liberalization, feel they have yet to reap the anticipated benefits of globalization. These benefits, moreover, have not been equally distributed, not even in the developed countries. For more than half of

## World Summit for Social Development

The World Summit for Social Development (Copenhagen, 1995) was part of a series of global conferences convened by the United Nations, with the objective of enriching the international agenda and to raise awareness of major issues, through cooperation of Member States and participation of other development actors. Some 117 heads of state and government, supported by ministers representing another 69 countries, adopted the *Copenhagen Declaration on Social Development* and the *Programme of Action.*

Governments pledged to confront the profound social problems of the world by addressing three core issues common to all countries: eradication of poverty, promotion of full employment, and promotion of social integration, particularly of the disadvantaged groups. The Summit signaled the emergence of a collective determination to treat social development as one of the highest priorities of national and international policies, and to place the human person at the centre of development.

Five years later, a special session of the General Assembly (Geneva, 2000) reaffirmed the centrality of more equitable, socially just and people-centred societies. It agreed on new initiatives, including creating a coordinated international strategy on employment, developing innovative sources of public and private funding for social development and poverty eradication programmes, and setting for the first time a global target for poverty reduction — halving the proportion of people living in extreme poverty by 2015.

Many new national policies and programmes have been initiated following the Summit. Social development has been given increased priority in national and international policy objectives. States have recognized the importance of making social improvement an integral part of development strategy at the national and international levels, as well as to place people at the centre of development. The Summit has also led the United Nations system to refocus its activities.

However, national and international policy responses have been uneven. Despite these advances, there has been little progress in some key areas, and evident regress in others. Inequality within and among states has continued to grow.

---

the world's population who have not benefited from it, the new global economy has often deepened feelings of despair that the weak will never be able to compete with the already strong and powerful. There is a need to better direct the benefits of liberalized trade and investment towards reducing poverty, increasing employment and promoting social integration.

The United Nations work in the social area has become ever more closely associated with a "people-centred" approach that places individuals, families and communities at the centre of development strategies. The Organization has placed new emphasis on social development, in part out of concern that economic and political problems have dominated the international agenda, sometimes at the expense of social issues, such as health, education and population, or of social groups, such as women, children and the elderly.

Reflecting this concern, most of the recent global conferences convened by the United Nations (*see box on page 157*) have focused on the problems of social development in order to compensate for this shortcoming. In a related effort to encourage allocation of increasingly scarce national resources to the social sector, the 1995 World Summit for Social Development urged countries to adopt the 20/20 *formula* — an initiative which calls on developing country governments to set aside at least 20 per cent of their budgets for basic social services, and, correspondingly, on donor governments to earmark 20 per cent of their official development assistance for such services.

The diverse issues of social development, the United Nations argues, are challenges for developing and developed countries alike. To differing degrees, all societies are confronted by the problems of unemployment, social fragmentation and persistent poverty. And a growing number of social problems — from forced migration to drug abuse, organized crime and the spread of diseases — can be successfully tackled only through concerted international action.

The United Nations addresses the issues of social development through the **General Assembly** and the **Economic and Social Council (ECOSOC)**, where system-wide policies and priorities are set and programmes endorsed. One of the Assembly's six main committees, the **Social, Humanitarian and Cultural Committee**, takes up agenda items relating to the social sector.

Under ECOSOC, the main intergovernmental body dealing with social concerns is the **Commission for Social Development.** Made up of 46 Member States, the Commission advises ECOSOC and governments on social policies and on the social aspects of development.

Within the Secretariat, the **Division for Social Policy and Development** of the Department of Economic and Social Affairs services these bodies, providing research, analysis and expert guidance. System-wide, there are many specialized agencies, funds, programmes and offices that address different aspects of social development.

## Reducing poverty

Governments, often in collaboration with the United Nations system, have made significant progress in reducing poverty worldwide. Since the 1960s, life expectancy in developing countries has increased from

46 to 64 years, infant mortality rates have been halved, the proportion of children enrolled in primary school has increased by more than 80 per cent, and the access to safe drinking water and basic sanitation has doubled.

Despite these gains, no less than 1.2 billion people are currently living on less than $1 a day (*see map on page 162*). With growing inequality within and among countries, more than 100 million people live in poverty in the richer countries of North America, Asia and Europe, where over 35 million are jobless. Globally, 113 million children are still not in school, and nearly 1.3 billion people do not have access to clean water. In at least 55 countries, mostly in Africa, Eastern Europe and the former Soviet Union, per capita incomes have declined over the last decade. In Asia, the sudden economic downturn has left large numbers of people without jobs or income. The challenge towards the eradication of poverty remains enormous.

The United Nations system has made poverty reduction a priority. The General Assembly has proclaimed 1997-2006 the **International Decade for the Eradication of Poverty**: the objective is to eradicate absolute poverty, and substantially reduce overall global poverty through decisive national action and international cooperation. In their Millennium Declaration, world leaders resolved to halve, by 2015, the number of people living on less than $1 a day, as well as setting a number of other targets in the fight against poverty and disease.

A key player is the **United Nations Development Programme (UNDP)**, which has made poverty alleviation its main focus area. UNDP sees poverty as a complex phenomenon, involving people's lack of empowerment, as well as lack of income and basic services.

UNDP works to strengthen the capacity of governments and civil society organizations to address the whole range of factors that contribute to poverty: for instance, to increase food security; improve the availability of shelter and basic services; generate employment opportunities; increase people's access to land, credit, technology, training and markets; and enable people to participate in the political processes that shape their lives. The heart of UNDP's anti-poverty work lies in empowering the poor.

The international financial institutions of the United Nations system play a central role in funding numerous programmes that focus on the social aspects of poverty eradication. In 1999, 25 per cent of **World Bank** lending went to health, nutrition and education programmes. The Bank seeks to increase poor people's employment and earning opportunities by investing in human resource development — health, education and family planning. The world's largest

# Millennium Declaration targets for poverty, disease and the environment

At the Millennium Summit in September 2000, world leaders committed themselves to the following targets:

- By 2015, cut in half the proportion of the world's people whose income is less than one dollar a day and the proportion of people unable to reach or afford safe drinking water.

- Also by 2015, ensure that both male and female children everywhere will be able to complete a full course of primary schooling and have equal access to all levels of education.

- Reduce maternal mortality by three-quarters and under-five child mortality by two thirds.

- Halt and reverse the spread of HIV/AIDS, malaria and other major diseases.

- Provide special assistance to children orphaned by HIV/AIDS.

- By 2020, achieve significant improvement in the lives of at least 100 million slum dwellers.

- Promote gender equality and the empowerment of women as ways to combat poverty, hunger and disease and to stimulate sustainable development.

- Develop and implement strategies that give young people everywhere a chance to find decent and productive work.

- Encourage the pharmaceutical industry to make essential drugs more widely available and affordable for all who need them in developing countries.

- Develop partnerships with the private sector and civil society organizations in pursuit of development and poverty eradication.

- Ensure that the benefits of new technologies—especially information and communication technologies—are available to all.

In the Millennium Declaration world leaders also resolved to take action on a number of environmental issues, namely:

- Ensure the entry into force of the Kyoto Protocol, preferably by 2002, and begin the required reduction in emissions of greenhouse gases.

- Press for full implementation of the Convention on Biological Diversity and the Convention to Combat Desertification, especially in Africa.

- Stop unsustainable exploitation of water resources by developing water management strategies at the regional, national and local levels.

- Intensify cooperation to reduce the number and effects of natural and man-made disasters.

- Ensure free access to information on the human genome sequence.

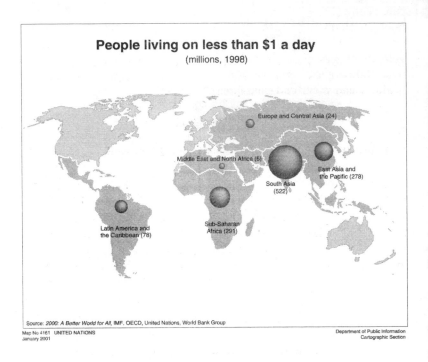

**People living on less than $1 a day**
(millions, 1998)

Europe and Central Asia (24)

Middle East and North Africa (6)

East Asia and the Pacific (278)

South Asia (522)

Latin America and the Caribbean (78)

Sub-Saharan Africa (291)

Source: *2000: A Better World for All*, IMF, OECD, United Nations, World Bank Group

Map No 4161  UNITED NATIONS
January 2001

Department of Public Information
Cartographic Section

lender for human resources development, it loaned $8.6 billion in 1999 for agriculture, water and sanitation, education, population, health and nutrition, and social programmes. It also helps borrowing countries to design social safety nets for the poorest, most vulnerable groups.

As a development institution focused on poverty reduction, the Bank favours investing in people by providing basic social services to the poor, from building roads to educating girls. Its Social Protection sector has been developing ways to better assist vulnerable individuals, households and communities for whom a disruptive shock — such as economic downturns or natural disasters — would aggravate poverty. To address such vulnerability, the Bank supports publicly mandated unemployment and old-age insurance, for example, or income support to the groups most in need of social protection.

The Bank's **International Development Association (IDA)** is the largest source of donor funds for basic social services in the poorest countries. Funds from IDA, for example, have ensured that African pupils have received over 5 million textbooks, that over 6,700 health care centres have been built and staffed in Asia, and that 9.5 million poor people in Latin America have benefited from social investment projects. IDA lends on average about $5 to $6 billion a year for development projects. Since 1960, IDA has lent some $115 billion to over 100 countries, making basic investments in primary education, health, clean water and sanitation.

## Fighting hunger

Food production has increased at an unprecedented rate over the past 50 years, outpacing the doubling of world population over the same period. Despite rapid population growth, food production per capita increased by nearly 25 per cent from 1990 to 1997. But 830 million people — more than the whole population of Europe — do not have enough to eat. The United Nations has made it clear that hunger, and famine in particular, result not so much from the scarcity of food as from the poverty of the affected populations, who are unable to purchase food.

Most of the United Nations bodies fighting hunger have important social programmes to advance food security for the poorer sectors of the population, particularly in rural areas. Since its establishment, the **Food and Agriculture Organization of the United Nations (FAO)** has been working to alleviate poverty and hunger by promoting agricultural development, improved nutrition and the pursuit of food security — the access of all people at all times to the food they need for an active and healthy life.

FAO's **Committee on World Food Security** is responsible for monitoring, evaluating and consulting on the international food security situation. It analyses food needs, assesses availability and stock levels, and monitors policies aimed at food security. FAO, through its *Global Information and Early Warning System*, also oversees an extensive monitoring system with the assistance of satellite surveillance, which monitors conditions affecting food production and alerts governments and donors to any potential threat to food supplies.

FAO's *Special Programme for Food Security* targets the 83 countries that are home to the vast majority of the world's chronically hungry people. The Programme seeks to increase food production and to make conditions better for farming families. During a pilot phase, farmers choose and demonstrate selected technologies to increase food production. Successful strategies are then made widely available during an expansion phase.

At the World Food Summit (Rome, 1996), hosted by FAO, 186 countries approved a *Declaration* and *Plan of Action on World Food Security* aiming to halve hunger by 2015 and outlining ways to achieve universal food security.

The **International Fund for Agricultural Development (IFAD)** provides development funding to combat rural poverty and hunger in the poorest regions of the world. To ensure that development aid actually reaches those who need it most, IFAD involves the rural poor, both men and women, in their own development. This means identifying their needs, building on their own knowledge and skills, and promoting successful traditional livelihoods and resource management.

The social dimensions of IFAD's work include the organization and mobilization of farming and fishing associations in poor communities. Using loans to finance basic inputs such as seeds, fertilizers, tools and nets to buy food-processing equipment or to start up micro-enterprises, millions of rural women and men have been able to organize beyond the levels of subsistence and lift their families and communities out of poverty. Over the past two decades, IFAD has financed 548 loans for projects in 114 countries. For every dollar of its own resources channelled to the poor, IFAD has mobilized two dollars from other donors and host governments, for a total of $19.3 billion in project costs.

IFAD has helped more than 250 million rural poor, once marginalized, to participate in their national economies. Once organized, the rural poor are excellent repayers, with a loan-repayment rate of 97 per cent, a fact that has stimulated the establishment of small-loan programmes around the world.

Hunger afflicts one out of seven people on Earth. The **World Food Programme (WFP)** (*see also Chapter 1, page 42*) is the largest food-aid organization in the world, providing food aid to more than 89 million people worldwide in 1999. WFP buys more goods and services from developing countries, in an effort to reinforce their economies, than any other United Nations agency.

WFP regularly delivers two thirds of the world's emergency food assistance, saving millions of lives (*see Chapter 5, page 251*). Over the past three decades, WFP has invested about $24 billion to combat hunger, promote development and provide relief assistance throughout the world.

Where people are chronically hungry, WFP provides "food-for-work" assistance, helping them to become self-reliant. In "food-for-work" programmes, WFP pays workers with food to build roads and ports in

Ghana, repair dykes in Bangladesh, terrace hillsides in Guatemala and re-plant forests in Ethiopia. These programmes prepare people to help them-selves and to reduce reliance on international food assistance.

"Food-for-growth" projects target needy people at the most critical time of their lives — babies, schoolchildren, pregnant women and the elderly. WFP feeds hundreds of thousands of schoolchildren around the world every day. In countries like Haiti, Pakistan and Morocco, food aid is also used to draw vulnerable mothers and children to health clinics, encourage poor women to attend literacy and repro-ductive health classes, and induce parents to send their daughters to school.

United Nations programmes have proved over and over again that hunger and poverty can be overcome with socially relevant and care-fully planned programmes that address the longer-term needs of the affected populations. Many countries that once received food aid are now among the largest markets for food exports — countries like South Korea, Mexico and China. And some countries that received food aid have recently become donors to WFP, like Croatia and Mo-rocco.

## Health

In most parts of the world, people live longer, infant mortality is de-creasing and illnesses are kept in check as more people have access to basic health services, immunization, clean water and sanitation. The United Nations has been deeply involved in many of these advances, particularly in developing countries, by supporting health services, fighting infectious diseases, delivering essential drugs, making cities healthier and providing health assistance in emergencies.

Infectious diseases, however, remain a major global threat. Up to 45 per cent of deaths in Africa and South-East Asia in 1998 are thought to have been due to an infectious disease, while 48 per cent of premature deaths (under age 45) worldwide are thought to have an infectious cause. Factors have included increased drug resistance, constantly expanding global travel and the emergence of new dis-eases. However, the causes and the solutions for most infectious dis-eases are known, and illness and death can in most cases be avoided at an affordable cost.

For decades, the United Nations system has been in the forefront of the fight against disease through the creation of policies and systems that address the social dimensions of health problems. **UNICEF** fo-cuses on child and maternal health and the **United Nations Popula-tion Fund** focuses on reproductive health and family planning. The

## On the verge of a polio-free world

When the Global Polio Eradication Initiative was launched in 1988, there were an estimated 350,000 cases of the paralyzing disease worldwide. After a concerted campaign to immunize millions of children under five during National Immunization Days, that figure dropped to around 7,000 reported cases of polio in 1999 (and no more than 20,000 estimated cases).

There have been tremendous gains. Three million people in the developing world, who would have been paralyzed, are walking because they have been immunized against polio. Tens of thousands of public health workers and millions of volunteers have been trained. "Cold chains" and transport and communications systems for immunization have been strengthened. Nearly 2 billion children worldwide have been immunized during National Immunization Days in the last five years, including 130 million children in a single day in India. In 1998, 470 million children — more than two thirds of the world's children — were reached as part of this effort. A network of over 140 polio laboratories has been established.

The successes have been possible through an unprecedented partnership for health spearheaded by WHO, UNICEF, the United States Centers for Disease Control and Prevention, and Rotary International, which alone will have contributed $500 million to the campaign by 2005. Health ministries, donor governments, foundations, corporations, celebrities, the United Nations Secretary-General, former South African President Nelson Mandela, philanthropists and millions of health workers and volunteers have each played their part.

Now the challenge for interrupting polio transmission is to reach every child. Thirty countries are endemic, mainly in sub-Saharan Africa and South-East Asia. Critical for eradicating polio is improving disease surveillance, establishing access to children in conflict countries, maintaining political commitment and meeting funding requirements. The public health savings of polio eradication, once immunization stops, are estimated to be $1.5 billion a year.

---

specialized agency coordinating global action against disease is the **World Health Organization (WHO)** *(see also Chapter 1, page 51)*. WHO has set ambitious goals for achieving health for all, making reproductive health available, building partnerships and promoting healthy lifestyles and environments.

WHO and its member states aim at the attainment of the highest possible level of health — a goal WHO views as "one of the fundamental rights of every human being". The World Health Assembly, WHO's governing body comprised of all member states, has promoted this goal through the campaign "Health for All": its aim is the attainment of levels of well-being ensuring that all people may lead socially and economically productive lives.

## The UN combats HIV/AIDS

HIV/AIDS has become a development disaster of global proportions. More than 34 million people are living with HIV/AIDS, and 18.8 million people have already died from the disease. The epidemic is still expanding at the rate of more than 5 million new infections a year. In some African countries, AIDS has resulted in a much shorter life expectancy.

To tackle this global threat, seven United Nations agencies have pooled their resources in the Joint United Nations Programme on HIV/AIDS (UNAIDS) — the leading advocate for a worldwide response aimed at preventing transmission, providing care and support, reducing the vulnerability of individuals and communities, and alleviating the impact of the epidemic. With a budget of $140 million for the 2000-2001 biennium and a staff of 111 professionals worldwide, UNAIDS operates as a catalyst and coordinator of action on AIDS rather than as a direct funding or implementing agency. Priority areas include:

- young people;
- highly vulnerable populations;
- prevention of mother-to-child HIV transmission;
- community standards of AIDS care;
- vaccine development;
- special initiatives for hard-hit regions, including Africa (*see box on page 134*).

UNAIDS works together with governments, corporations, media, religious organizations community groups, and networks of people living with HIV/AIDS. In developing countries, UNAIDS staff and representatives of co-sponsoring organizations share information, plan coordinated action and decide on joint financing of major AIDS activities. The main objective is to support the host country's effort to mount an effective response.

UNAIDS also seeks to increase commitment against AIDS among political leaders, to promote world research on AIDS and to foster an environment supportive of people affected by HIV/AIDS. The participating agencies are UNICEF, UNDP, UNFPA, UNESCO, WHO, the World Bank and the United Nations Drug Control Programme. (*See also* www.unaids.org).

In their Millennium Declaration, world leaders resolved by 2015 to have halted and begun to reverse the spread of HIV/AIDS and to provide special assistance to children orphaned by the disease. The General Assembly will hold a special session in June 2001 to help mobilize the political will and resources needed to combat HIV/AIDS.

---

WHO was the driving force behind various historic achievements. One was the global eradication of smallpox in 1980, achieved after a 10-year campaign. Another, along with its partners (*see box on page 166*) was the elimination of poliomyelitis from the Americas in

1994 — the first step towards the goal of certifying the world polio-free by 2005.

Between 1980 and 1995 a joint UNICEF-WHO effort raised global immunization coverage against six killer diseases — polio, tetanus, measles, whooping cough, diphtheria and tuberculosis — from 5 to 80 per cent, saving the lives of some 2.5 million children a year.

A similar initiative is the Global Alliance for Vaccines and Immunization, which is extending immunization services to include protection against hepatitis B, which kills some 1 million people a year, and haemophilus influenza type B, which kills 900,000 children under age five annually. The Global Alliance, launched in 1999 with initial funds from the Bill and Melinda Gates Foundation, incorporates WHO, UNICEF, the World Bank, the United Nations Foundation and private sector partners.

Guinea-worm disease is on the threshold of eradication and, thanks to new and better methods of treatment, leprosy is also being overcome. River blindness has been virtually eliminated from the 11 West African countries once affected — an achievement benefiting millions. WHO is now targeting elephantiasis for elimination as a public health problem.

WHO's priorities in the area of communicable diseases are: to reduce the impact of malaria and tuberculosis through global partnership; to strengthen surveillance, monitoring and response to global communicable disease problems; to reduce the impact of diseases through intensified and routine prevention and control; and to generate new knowledge, intervention methods, implementation strategies and research capabilities for use in developing countries.

But as well as fighting infectious disease, WHO is a key player in promoting primary health care, delivering essential drugs, making cities healthier and promoting healthy lifestyles and environments.

**A motor for health research.** Working with its partners in health research, WHO gathers data on current conditions and needs, particularly in developing countries. These range from epidemiological research in remote tropical forests to monitoring the progress of genetic research. WHO's tropical disease research programme is tackling the resistance of the malaria parasite to the most commonly used drugs, and is fostering the development of new drugs and diagnostics against tropical infectious diseases. Research also helps to improve national and international surveillance of epidemics, and to develop preventive strategies for new and emerging diseases that integrate laboratory discoveries with the latest information from the field.

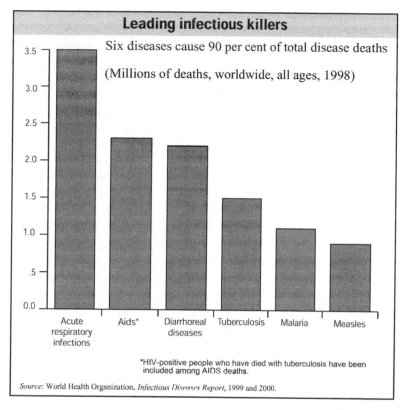

**Leading infectious killers**

Six diseases cause 90 per cent of total disease deaths

(Millions of deaths, worldwide, all ages, 1998)

Acute respiratory infections | Aids* | Diarrhoreal diseases | Tuberculosis | Malaria | Measles

*HIV-positive people who have died with tuberculosis have been included among AIDS deaths.

*Source*: World Health Organization, *Infectious Diseases Report*, 1999 and 2000.

**Standard setting.** WHO establishes international standards on biological and pharmaceutical substances. It has developed the concept of "essential drugs" as a basic element of primary health care.

WHO works with countries to ensure the equitable supply of safe and effective drugs at the lowest possible cost and with the most effective use. To this end, it has developed a "Model List" of some 306 drugs and vaccines considered essential to help prevent or treat over 80 per cent of all health problems. Nearly 160 countries have adapted the list to their own requirements. WHO also cooperates with member states, civil society and the pharmaceutical industry to develop new essential drugs for priority health problems in poor and middle-income countries, and to continue production of established essential drugs.

Through the international access afforded to the United Nations, WHO oversees the global collection of information on communicable diseases, compiles comparable health and disease statistics, and sets international standards for safe food, as well as for biological and pharmaceutical products. It also provides unmatched evaluation of the cancer-producing risks of pollutants, and has put into place the universally accepted guidance for global control of HIV/AIDS (*see box*).

## Human settlements

In 1900, only one in 10 people lived in towns. Today, almost 3 billion people — nearly half of humanity — live in towns and cities. Already 23 cities — 18 of them in the developing world — have populations exceeding 10 million.

One result of this rapid increase in the urban population is that millions of the world's poor are now concentrated in slums and squatter settlements —living in housing conditions that are below the minimum standards necessary for healthy families and communities.

Addressing this problem is the **United Nations Human Settlements Programme (UN-Habitat)** (*see also Chapter 1, page 45*), the lead agency within the United Nations system for coordinating activities in the field of human settlements. Habitat's operational activities focus on promoting housing for all, improving urban governance, reducing urban poverty, improving the living environment, and managing disaster mitigation and post-conflict rehabilitation. The Centre has some 240 technical programmes and projects in 86 countries, with an annual budget of $70 million.

At Habitat II, the Second United Nations Conference on Human Settlements (Istanbul, Turkey, 1996), the *Habitat Agenda* was agreed — a global plan of action in which governments committed themselves to the goals of adequate shelter for all and sustainable urban development. Habitat is the focal point for implementing the Agenda, assessing progress in its implementation at the international, regional, national and local levels, and monitoring global trends and conditions.

Habitat is now preparing Istanbul + 5, the special session of the General Assembly in June 2001 to review the worldwide implementation of the Agenda.

In 2000-2001, Habitat launched two global campaigns:

*Campaign for secure tenure.* Security of tenure is a fundamental requirement for the progressive integration of the urban poor in the city, and is one of the most important components of housing rights. This rights-based campaign is backed by a work programme offering assistance in key policy areas, including land markets and tenure reform. Access to urban services and infrastructure, particularly water and sanitation, are vital elements of the strategy. Habitat is also providing policy advice and technical support in urban transport policy and in housing finance, with an emphasis on micro-credit and micro-enterprise.

*Campaign on urban governance.* In many cities, poor governance and inappropriate policies have led to environmental degradation, increased poverty, low economic growth and social exclusion. Urban governance can be defined as an efficient and effective response to urban problems by democratically elected and accountable local governments, working in partnership with civil society. This campaign focuses on promoting inclusiveness: if urban poverty is to be reduced, marginalized groups must be given a voice in decision-making. The campaign fosters consensus-building between local governments and civil society in establishing development priorities.

The aim of both campaigns is to reduce urban poverty through policies that emphasize equity, sustainability and social justice. Partnerships with governments, local authorities, NGOs and the private sector are crucial to their success.

Other programmes include:

- *Best Practices and Local Leadership Programme*, a global network of government agencies, local authorities and civil society organizations dedicated to identifying and disseminating best practices in improving the living environment and to applying lessons learned to policy development and capacity-building.

- *Cities Alliance,* a Habitat-World Bank initiative to improve the living conditions of the urban poor and the socio-economic and environmental viability of cities. Its two components are city development strategies and upgrading of low-income settlements.

- *Sustainable Cities Programme*, a Habitat-United Nations Environment Programme (UNEP) initiative that builds capacities in urban environmental planning and management, using participatory methods. The programme works with over 40 cities and 30 partner organizations around the world.

- *Urban Management Programme*, a major technical cooperation programme monitored by UNDP that seeks to strengthen the efforts of some 80 cities in developing countries towards poverty reduction, participatory governance and urban environment.

- *Safer Cities Programme*, which helps to establish a community-wide consultation process to reduce crime and address its causes through the development of crime-prevention measures, methods and strategies.

- *Water in African Cities*, a Habitat-UNEP initiative that supports effective water management and protection of water resources from urban pollution.
- *Disaster Management Programme*, which assists national and local governments, as well as communities, to carry out post-disaster reconstruction and rehabilitation programmes.
- *Localizing Agenda 21*, which translates the human settlements components of *Agenda 21* (*see below, page 195*) into action at the local level, by stimulating joint venture initiatives in selected medium-size cities.
- *Global Urban Observatory*, which monitors the implementation of the Habitat Agenda by developing and applying policy-oriented urban indicators, and by sharing lessons learned through best practices.

## Education

Great strides have been made in education in the past decades: the number of children in schools has risen from 599 million in 1990 to 681 million in 1998. But more than 113 million children — nearly two thirds of them girls in developing countries — have no access to primary education, and many who start attending are forced to leave because of poverty or family and social pressures. Despite enormous literacy efforts, at least 875 million adults remain illiterate — exactly the same figure as 10 years ago.

Research has shown the close relationship between access to education and improved social indicators. Schooling has a special multiplier effect for women. A woman who is educated, for example, will typically be healthier, have fewer children and have more opportunities to increase household income. Her children, in turn, will experience lower mortality rates, better nutrition and better overall health. For this reason, girls and women are the focus of education programmes of many United Nations agencies.

Many parts of the United Nations system are involved in the funding and development of a variety of education and training programmes. These range from traditional basic schooling to technical training for human resource development in areas such as public administration, agriculture and health services, to public awareness campaigns to educate people about HIV/AIDS, drug abuse, human rights, family planning, and many other issues. **UNICEF**, for example, devotes 14 per cent of its annual programme expenditure to education, with special attention to basic education and girls' schooling (*see below, page 181*).

The lead organization in the area of education is the **United Nations Educational, Scientific and Cultural Organization (UNESCO)** (*see also Chapter 1, page 50, and page 191, below*): together with other partners, it works to ensure that all children are enrolled in schools that are child-friendly, and that have trained teachers providing quality education.

UNESCO is providing the secretariat for the most ambitious United Nations interagency campaign ever launched to achieve universal, quality-based primary education by 2015, on the basis of a *Framework for Action* adopted by 181 nations in 2000 at the World Education Forum in Dakar, Senegal. This goal was reconfirmed by world leaders in their Millennium Declaration in September 2000.

At the Forum, governments committed themselves to achieve quality education for all, with a particular emphasis on girls and other groups such as working children and children affected by war. Donor countries and institutions pledged that no nation committed to basic education would be thwarted by lack of resources. The Forum drew from the results of the largest, most comprehensive and statistically rigorous stocktaking of education in history, encompassing a two-year Education for All Assessment and six high-level regional conferences held in 1999 and 2000.

UNESCO's innovative interdisciplinary project, "Educating for a sustainable future", helps member states to improve and reorient their national education and training activities dealing with the environment, population and development, including health education and the prevention of drug abuse and AIDS.

Under its programme of promoting lifelong education for all, UNESCO supports and fosters national projects to renovate education systems and develop alternative strategies to make lifelong education accessible to all. The programme also seeks to widen access to basic education and improve its quality, reform higher education systems throughout the world and promote adult and continuing education.

Some 5,700 schools in 162 countries are involved in UNESCO's Associated Schools Project, an international network elaborating ways and means for enhancing the role of education in learning to live together in a world community. Some 5,000 UNESCO Clubs in more than 120 countries, mainly comprising teachers and students, carry out a wide range of educational and cultural activities.

## Research and training

Academic work in the form of research and training is carried out by a number of specialized United Nations organizations. This work is aimed at enhancing understanding of the global problems we face, as well as fostering the human resources required for the more technical aspects of economic and social development.

The mission of the **United Nations University (UNU)** (*see also Chapter 1, page 46*) is to contribute, through research and capacity building, to efforts to resolve the pressing global problems of concern to the United Nations, its peoples and Member States. An international community of scholars, UNU is a bridge between the United Nations and the international academic community, a think-tank for the United Nations system, and a builder of capacities, particularly in developing countries. The UNU cooperates with over 30 United Nations entities and more than 100 research institutions around the world.

UNU's academic work addresses specific issues of concern to the United Nations. Its current thematic focus covers five areas: peace, governance, development, the environment, and science, technology and society. Academic activities are carried out at the **UNU Centre** in Tokyo, and through research and training centres and programmes located in various parts of the world. These include:

- **UNU World Institute for Development Economics Research (UNU/WIDER)**, Helsinki, Finland (established 1985), which focuses on development economics;
- **UNU Institute for New Technologies (UNU/INTECH)**, Maastricht, the Netherlands (1990), which examines the social and economic impact of new technologies;
- **UNU Institute for Natural Resources in Africa (UNU/INRA)**, Accra, Ghana (1990), which focuses on natural resources management;
- **UNU International Institute for Software Technology (UNU/IIST)**, Macau, China (1992), which concentrates on software technologies for development;
- **UNU Institute of Advanced Studies (UNU/IAS)**, Tokyo, Japan (1995), which works on eco-restructuring for sustainable development;
- **UNU Programme for Biotechnology in Latin America and the Caribbean (UNU/BIOLAC)**, Caracas, Venezuela (1988), which focuses on biotechnology and society;
- **UNU International Leadership Academy (UNU/ILA)**, Amman, Jordan (1995), which focuses on leadership development;

- **UNU International Network on Water, Environment and Health (UNU/INWEH)**, Hamilton, Ontario, Canada (1996), which focuses on water, environment and health;
- **UNU Food and Nutrition Programme for Human and Social Development**, Ithaca, New York, United States (1975), which focuses on food and nutrition capacity-building;
- **UNU Geothermal Training Programme (UNU/GTP)**, Reykjavik, Iceland (1979), which works on geothermal research, exploration and development;
- **UNU Fisheries Training Programme (UNU/FTP)**, Reykjavik, Iceland (1998), which carries out fisheries research and development;
- **Initiative on Conflict Resolution and Ethnicity (INCORE)**, Ulster, Northern Ireland, United Kingdom (1993), which focuses on ethnic, political and religious conflict; and
- **UNU Governance Programme (UNU/GP)**, Barcelona, Spain (1992), which works with a consortium of research entities in the area of governance.

The **United Nations Institute for Training and Research (UNITAR)** (*see also Chapter 1, page 47*) works to enhance the effectiveness of the United Nations in its work in peace and security and development through training and research. Each year, UNITAR designs and organizes some 120 training programmes for about 4,000 participants, benefiting individuals and institutions in Member States as well as diplomats posted at the United Nations. Current programmes cover international affairs management; environmental management training; and debt, economic and financial management and public administration.

Training and learning for managers and high officials of the United Nations system is provided at the **United Nations Staff College (UNSC)**. The pre-eminent in-house training and learning arm of the system, the Staff College provides a wide range of training courses, fosters the sharing of knowledge and best practices throughout the system, and enhances collaboration among United Nations officials working in key areas of the Secretary-General's reforms—such as peacekeeping, United Nations partnerships, communication and organizational development. The overall goal is to foster a cohesive and effective management culture throughout the United Nations. The College is located in Turin, on the campus of the International Training Centre of the ILO: this partnership facilitates the exchange of training resources and expertise (see www.itcilo.it/unscp).

The **United Nations Research Institute for Social Development (UNRISD)** (*see also Chapter 1, page 48*) engages in research on the social dimensions of contemporary problems affecting development. Working through an extensive network of national research centres, the Institute collaborates with governments, development agencies, grass-roots organizations and scholars on the formulation of development policies. Current research themes include social policy and development; democracy, governance and human rights; civil society and social movements; and technology and society.

*(On the **International Research and Training Institute for the Advancement of Women (INSTRAW)** see page 180, below).*

## Population and development

The rapid growth of world population became an urgent concern of the United Nations in the 1960s. World population doubled between 1960 and 1999, passing the 6 billion mark in October 1999. While the growth rate has slowed — from 2 per cent to 1.3 per cent between 1969 and 1999 — global population is still rising by about 77 million people a year, with 95 per cent of this growth in developing regions. The United Nations estimates there would be between 7.9 billion and 10.9 billion people in 2050, with 9.3 billion the most likely projection, depending in part on the effectiveness of family planning programmes.

Over the decades, the United Nations has been carrying out operational activities in many developing countries. Various parts of the Organization have worked together to build national statistical offices, take censuses, make projections and disseminate reliable data. The United Nations quantitative and methodological work, particularly its authoritative estimates and projections of population size and change, has been pioneering. This has led to significant increase in national capacities to plan ahead, to incorporate population policies into development planning and to take sound economic and social decisions.

Rapid population growth has weighed heavily on the Earth's resources and environment, often outstripping efforts towards development. The United Nations has addressed the relationship between population and development in many ways, placing special emphasis on the advancement of the rights and status of women, which is seen as key to social and economic progress.

The **Commission on Population and Development,** made up of 47 Member States, is charged with studying and advising ECOSOC on population changes and their effects on economic and social conditions. It has primary responsibility for reviewing the implementation of the *Programme of Action* of the 1994 International Conference on Population and Development (*see below*).

The **Population Division** of the United Nations Department of Economic and Social Affairs serves as the secretariat of the Commission. It also provides the international community with up-to-date and scientifically objective information on population and development, and undertakes studies on population levels, trends, estimates and projections, as well as on population policies and the link between population and development. The Division maintains major databases, including the *World Population Projections to 2150* and the *Global Review and Inventory of Population Policies* (*GRIPP*). It also coordinates the *Population Information Network* (*POPIN*), which promotes the use of the Internet to facilitate global sharing of population information.

The **United Nations Population Fund (UNFPA)** (*see also Chapter 1, page 40*), which leads the operational population activities of the United Nations system, helps developing countries and countries with economies in transition find solutions to their population problems. It assists states to improve reproductive health and family planning services on the basis of individual choice, and to formulate population policies in support of efforts towards sustainable development. It also promotes awareness of population problems and ways to deal with them, and assists governments in dealing with population issues in ways best suited to each country's needs.

The largest internationally funded source of population assistance, UNFPA manages one fourth of global population assistance. It is primarily a funding organization: many of the projects and programmes it supports are carried out by governments, United Nations agencies and NGOs.

Its core programme areas are:

* *reproductive health of women* — including family planning, sexual health and safe motherhood — which helps people achieve their desired family size and enjoy greater freedom in planning their lives, saves lives, supports the fight against HIV/AIDS and contributes to slower and more balanced population growth;

* *population and development strategies,* which assist countries in drawing up policies with population issues built in, help them design strategies to improve the quality of life of their people and assist them to develop their own capacity for population programmes;

177

- *advocacy*, to promote women's equality, maintain political commitment and increase awareness and resources for population and development.

Other special programmes cover youth, ageing, HIV/AIDS control and prevention, and population and the environment. UNFPA does not provide any support for abortion services. Rather, it seeks to prevent abortion by helping to increase access to family planning.

UNFPA is the lead United Nations organization for advancing the *Programme of Action* endorsed at the International Conference on Population and Development (Cairo, 1994) and reviewed by a special session of the General Assembly in 1999. The Programme focuses on meeting the needs of individual women and men rather than achieving demographic targets. Key to this approach is empowering women and providing them with more choices through expanded access to education, health services and employment opportunities.

UNFPA also addresses the reproductive health needs of adolescents. Programmes seek to prevent teenage pregnancy, reduce recourse to abortion, prevent HIV/AIDS and sexually transmitted diseases, and improve access to reproductive health services and information.

The ability of parents to choose the number and spacing of their children is an essential component of reproductive health. While the number of couples using family planning has risen dramatically in recent years, at least 350 million couples worldwide lack access to a full range of family planning methods.

Surveys show that an additional 120 million women would currently be using a modern family planning method if more accurate information, affordable services and appropriate counselling were available, and if husbands, extended families and communities were more supportive. UNFPA works with governments, the private sector and NGOs to meet people's family planning needs.

### The advancement of women

Ongoing efforts to overcome poverty have underscored the crucial role that women play in social and economic development. In the developing world, for example, women manage 50 to 80 per cent of food production, processing and marketing, and run 70 per cent of small enterprises. The United Nations, in its action to eradicate poverty, supports women's empowerment and enjoyment of their human rights through its development assistance activities. Gender equality and the advancement of women are cross-cutting issues relevant to all aspects of the work of the United Nations.

The **Commission on the Status of Women** (*see also Chapter 4, page 234*), under ECOSOC, examines progress towards women's equality throughout the world and makes recommendations for promoting women's rights in the political, economic and social fields. The 45-Member Commission has prepared four global conferences on women's issues, including the Fourth World Conference on Women (Beijing, 1995), and monitors implementation of the resulting *Platform for Action.*

The **Committee on the Elimination of Discrimination against Women** (*see also Chapter 4, page 220*), *supported by the* **Division for the Advancement of Women (DAW)** in the Department of Economic and Social Affairs, monitors adherence to the *United Nations Convention on the Elimination of All Forms of Discrimination against Women.* The recommendations of the 23-expert Committee have contributed to a better understanding of women's economic and social rights, their political and civil rights and the means to ensure the enjoyment of these rights.

In addition to the work done by DAW to advance the global agenda on women's issues and to stimulate the adoption of a gender perspective throughout the United Nations system, all the organizations of the United Nations family address women and gender issues in their policies and many of their programmes. Women are central to UNICEF's work for children. Much of UNFPA's mandate revolves around women's health and reproductive rights. UNDP, UNESCO, WFP, ILO and others have active gender programmes and targets.

Within DAW, the **Special Adviser of the Secretary-General on Gender Issues and Advancement of Women** plays a key role in promoting widespread attention to women's issues and applying a gender perspective in the work of the United Nations. The Special Adviser is also the Chairperson of the Inter-agency Committee on Women and Gender Equality of the Administrative Committee on Coordination, which meets twice a year.

In addition, two other entities have an exclusive focus on women's issues.

The **United Nations Development Fund for Women (UNIFEM)** (*see also Chapter 1, page 39*) is a voluntary fund that provides financial support and technical assistance to innovative programmes promoting women's human rights, their economic and political empowerment, and gender equality. UNIFEM works primarily in three areas:

• strengthening women's economic capacity as entrepreneurs and producers;

- increasing women's participation in governance, leadership and decision-making; and
- promoting women's human rights to make development more equitable.

UNIFEM helps women in more than 100 countries to improve the quality of life for themselves and their families. It supports innovative programmes benefiting women; provides direct technical and financial support to women's initiatives; and disseminates information to women's groups regarding best practices and lessons learned from the successes and failures of its diverse programmes.

For example, a UNIFEM global micro-credit campaign that provides seed money for starting small businesses, promoted in cooperation with the private sector, NGOs and governments, has reached 10.3 million of the world's poorest women.

The **International Research and Training Institute for the Advancement of Women (INSTRAW)** (*see also Chapter 1, page 46*) undertakes research and training by utilizing new information and communication technologies to contribute to the advancement of women and support their access into the information society of the 21$^{st}$ century.

This mandate was enhanced in 1999, when the General Assembly endorsed the establishment of the Gender Awareness Information and Networking System (GAINS) as the new working method of INSTRAW. Through GAINS (www.un-instraw-gains.org), INSTRAW will use new information technologies to:
- conduct collaborative research electronically to address critical areas of concern for the achievement of gender equality;
- produce, manage and disseminate gender-related knowledge and information for policy-making to improve women's lives at all levels;
- pull together, systematize and make easily accessible through an electronic database gender-related knowledge, information and training tools and methods;
- provide a practical mechanism for women's empowerment through e-training and capacity building methods using distance education and on-line training.

Operating as a "virtual workshop on gender", GAINS features a mechanism for international consultation, dialogue and networking; a think-tank and a platform for research and network of trainers to work collaboratively in the achievement of gender equality; an international network of regional nodes and national focal points serving as outreach and feedback arms for effective decentralization from global to local; and an international network of information technology specialists to assist women in entering the information society.

(*On women's issues, see also* www.un.org/womenwatch).

## Assistance to children

As the United Nations sees the family as the primary unit of society, it has always placed special emphasis on children and women. Despite great progress in improving conditions for families, 11 million children in the developing world continue to die each year from preventable or easy-to-treat illnesses. The healthy development of many millions more is stifled by poverty, lack of education, discrimination and the trauma of war, exploitation and abuse.

Since 1946, the **United Nations Children's Fund (UNICEF)** (*see also Chapter 1, page 41*) has been working with governments, local communities and other partners in more that 160 countries, territories and areas to protect children's rights by providing them with health care, nutrition, education, and safe water and sanitation. Emphasis is placed on low-cost, community-based programmes in which people are encouraged to take an active part.

As the only United Nations organization exclusively dedicated to children, UNICEF speaks on their behalf and promotes the full implementation of the *Convention on the Rights of the Child* (*see Chapter 4, page 221*). UNICEF is also guided by the *Convention on the Elimination of All Forms of Discrimination against Women* (*see Chapter 4, page 220*).

UNICEF cooperates with governments, other United Nations agencies and international organizations to ensure that children get the best possible start in life to assure them full realization of their rights. Its programmes cover health, education, nutrition and breast-feeding, water and sanitation. It also cooperates with partners in programmes to help adolescents acquire life skills to survive and influence events which relate to their lives.

Millions of children and women are victims of war, violence and exploitation, and 250 million children work in hazardous conditions in order to survive. UNICEF supports special projects to reduce the suffering of these children and women, helping to provide education, counselling and care.

In many countries, girls still face discrimination that often threatens their lives and well-being. They often receive less food and medical care than boys, and far less education: 73 million girls aged 6 to 11, compared with 57 million boys, do not go to primary school. Paying special attention to schooling, UNICEF works to improve the

## Promoting child health

Considerable progress has been made to improve the welfare of children. Under-five mortality rates and child nutrition have continued to improve globally. Improvements in numbers of children being exclusively breastfed and access to safe water, as well as reductions in gender gaps, have been achieved in numerous countries. UNICEF has been behind many of these advancements.

- Immunization programmes supported by WHO and UNICEF (*see page 168*) prevent more than 2.5 million child deaths every year. Polio is on the verge of being eradicated (*see box, page 166*). UNICEF's ultimate objective is to ensure that every child on the planet is immunized against vaccine-preventable disease, and that new and underused vaccines against diseases like hepatitis B, meningitis and yellow fever are made affordable to poor countries.

- By iodizing salt, the world has achieved great success in preventing mental retardation in children as a result of iodine deficiency. By the end of 1999, close to 70 per cent of the world's population was using iodized salt. UNICEF continues working with traditional partners like Kiwanis International, donors and local salt manufacturers in the affected countries to ensure that all salt is iodized.

- Children affected by vitamin A deficiency face a high risk of death from diseases such as measles and pneumonia. Three million children exhibit the eye damage that is a sign of vitamin A deficiency. Overall, an estimated 100 million children under age 5 are at increased risk of illness and death. UNICEF helps countries remedy this easily preventable health problem by distributing vitamin A capsules to children at risk, by assisting in the fortification of food with vitamin A, and by informing people about the need to eat fruits and vegetables rich in the vitamin.

- More than 1 billion people lacked access to clean drinking water and sanitation in 1999, and almost 2.4 billion had inadequate or no sanitation. About 3 million children still die from diarrhoeal and other water-related diseases. These are the challenges that UNICEF, working with governments and other partners, aims to surmount by providing wells, pumps and improvements of other sources of water supplies.

- Every year about 600,000 women — many only in their teens — die and millions of others suffer disabling and lifelong injuries from causes related to pregnancy and childbirth. UNICEF helps train community health workers and midwives to provide prenatal care and hygienic delivery practices.

- UNICEF recommends breastmilk as the most wholesome nourishment for an infant up to six months. Thereafter, it should continue for 2 years or beyond, together with supplemental feeding. The Baby-Friendly Hospital initiative, which promotes breastfeeding in the health care system, is expanding globally, with the support of UNICEF, WHO and other partners.

---

lives of girls and change the beliefs and practices that undermine their potential.

UNICEF is fully committed to helping end the discrimination and customary practices which deny girls their rights. Of specific concern are issues like denial of schooling opportunities, gender biases that diminish girls' worth, and female genital mutilation — to which an estimated 2 million girls in at least 28 countries are subjected every year. Its Global Girls Education Programme, operating in more than 60 countries, links national and global resources, guiding countries in transforming educational systems to become gender sensitive and to achieve equitable and quality education for both girls and boys.

Every day, more than 1,600 children under 15 years of age become infected with the virus that causes AIDS; 13.2 million of children worldwide had lost their parents to the disease by 2000. Communities must be supported as they care for orphaned children. Access to education, life skills training, health services and confidential testing and counselling must be improved if the disease is to be contained. UNICEF supports programmes for AIDS orphans and works with governments and NGOs in addressing issues of HIV/AIDS prevention, care and rights of those infected.

## Social integration

There are several social groups that the United Nations has come to recognize as requiring special attention, including youth, the elderly, people with disabilities, minorities, and indigenous populations. Their concerns are addressed by the General Assembly, ECOSOC and the Commission for Social Development. Specific programmes for these groups are carried out within the United Nations Department of Social and Economic Affairs (DESA).

The United Nations has been instrumental in defining and defending the human rights of vulnerable groups (*see Chapter 4*). It has helped to formulate international norms, standards and recommendations for action regarding these social groups, and strives to highlight their concerns through research and data gathering, as well as through special years and decades intended to encourage international action (*see Part Three, page 310*).

### Families in the development process

There are critical family issues confronting policy and decision makers globally, such as strengthening the family's ability to meet its own needs, balancing work and familial responsibilities, curbing domestic violence and alleviating poverty.

By proclaiming 1994 as the International Year of the Family, with the theme "Family: Resources and Responsibilities in a Changing World", the General Assembly helped to bring the subject of the family into the international dialogue on the issue of development. The Assembly also convened in 1994 in New York an International Conference on Families. As a result of the Year, governments formulated national action plans on the family, established ministries devoted to the family and passed family-oriented legislation.

Follow-up action by governments has involved the development, implementation and evaluation of family-related policies and programmes within the context of the Year's framework. Activities in this area are the responsibility of DESA's Division for Social Policy and Development. The Division also promotes international cooperation in the field of family research, strengthens links between the United Nations and civil society, works with NGOs and research and academic institutions, and provides technical assistance through the United Nations Trust Fund on Family Activities.

The United Nations promotes the annual worldwide observance of the International Day of Families, 15 May, which provides an opportunity to increase awareness of issues relating to the family as the basic unit of society, as well as to promote appropriate action.

### Youth

The General Assembly has adopted several resolutions and campaigns specific to youth, and the Secretariat has overseen the related programmes and information campaigns.

- In 1965, the General Assembly adopted the *Declaration on the Promotion among Youth of the Ideals of Peace, Mutual Respect and Understanding between Peoples,* stressing the importance of the role of youth in today's world.
- Two decades later, the General Assembly proclaimed 1985 International Youth Year: Participation, Development, Peace, and adopted guidelines for further planning and suitable follow-up in the field of youth — a global long-term strategy for youth work. The United Nations has promoted implementation of the guidelines, assisting governments in developing youth policies and programmes.
- In 1995 — the tenth anniversary of the Year — the United Nations adopted the *World Programme of Action for Youth to the Year 2000 and Beyond,* an international strategy to address the problems of young people and to increase opportunities for their participation in society. It also called for a World Conference of Ministers Responsible for Youth to meet regularly under the aegis of the United Nations. The first session of that Conference (Lisbon, 1998) was convened by Portugal, in cooperation with the United Nations, to focus on the implementation of the World Programme of Action; it did so by adopting a *Lisbon Declaration on Youth* and recommendations for initiatives at the national, regional and world levels.
- The General Assembly also indicated that a **World Youth Forum** of the United Nations system could contribute to realizing the

World Programme of Action by promoting joint initiatives. In that regard, DESA's Division for Social Policy and Development has convened three sessions of the World Youth Forum to: increase the channels of communication between youth NGOs and the youth-related bodies of the United Nations system; attune such channels to the youth-related projects and activities of the United Nations system; and promote implementation of the World Programme of Action through joint youth NGO-United Nations system initiatives. The fourth session of the Forum, convened in partnership with the Senegal National Youth Council, will be held in 2001 on the theme "Empowering Youth for Action".

- The United Nations Youth Fund supports projects involving young people through operational activities. It provides seed-money grants to governments and NGOs in support of catalytic and innovative action in the field of youth.

### Older persons

During the past 50 years, the average life expectancy has climbed globally by about 20 years, to its current level of 66 years. At the same time, fertility has been declining. The combined result is a global expansion in both the numbers and proportion of older persons.

The populations of different countries are ageing at varying rates. Developing country populations are ageing later than developed countries, but at a much greater pace. By 2030, an estimated 70 per cent of the world's older population will reside in developing countries.

The ageing of populations is posing new and unprecedented challenges and opportunities for the organization of individual lives and the socio-economic and cultural environment.

For the later years to flourish, the earlier years need to be adjusted for continuing education, skills upgrading, healthy lifestyles and saving.

For ageing societies to flourish, systems and facilities need to be adjusted for age-appropriate use and access, as well as enhanced availability of adult education, gradual retirement, part-time work arrangements, and intergenerational contracts for sustainable income security and health care in old age.

In response to global ageing, the United Nations has taken several initiatives:

- The World Assembly on Ageing (Vienna, 1982) adopted the *International Plan of Action on Ageing*. The Plan recommends action in such sectors as employment and income security, health and nutrition, housing, education and social welfare. It sees older persons as a diverse and active population group with wide-ranging capabilities and, at times, particular health-care needs.

- The *United Nations Principles for Older Persons*, adopted by the General Assembly in 1991, established universal standards pertaining to the status of older persons in five areas: independence, participation, care, self-fulfilment and dignity.
- In 1992 — the tenth anniversary of the adoption of the Plan of Action — the Assembly held an International Conference on Ageing: it adopted the *Proclamation on Ageing*, laying out the main direction for further implementing the Plan of Action, and proclaimed 1999 the International Year of Older Persons.
- The conceptual framework for the Year's observance called for exploring four dimensions: the situation of older persons; lifelong individual development; relationships between generations; and the relationship between development and the ageing of populations. The Year's unifying theme, "Towards a society for all ages", will continue to be promoted throughout the next decades.
- The General Assembly in 1999 met to follow up on the International Year; 64 countries addressed the meeting and offered wide support to the Year's objectives. The ongoing process of facilitating movement towards a society for all ages is elaborated in the *Policy Framework for a Society for All Ages* and the *Research Agenda on Ageing for the 21$^{st}$ Century*.
- Creating a new "architecture" for ageing and transmitting it onto the world stage and into policy has been the focus of the United Nations Programme on Ageing. The process of updating the 1982 International Plan of Action, as well as developing a Long Term Strategy on Ageing, is under way, and will be presented to the second world assembly on ageing, to be held in Spain in 2002.

(*On minorities, indigenous peoples and disabled persons, see Chapter 4, pages 237-240.*)

## Uncivil society: crime, illicit drugs and terrorism

Transnational organized crime, illicit drug trafficking and terrorism have become social, political and economic forces capable of altering the destinies of countries and regions. Recent trends include large-scale bribery of public officials, the growth of "crime multinationals", and trafficking in human beings. The use of terrorism to intimidate communities large and small and to sabotage economic development is a further threat that requires effective international cooperation. The United Nations is addressing these threats to good governance, social equity and justice for all citizens, and is orchestrating a global response.

The Vienna-based **Office for Drug Control and Crime Prevention** (*see also Chapter 1, page 37*) leads the international effort to combat drug trafficking, organized crime and international terrorism — what the Secretary-General has called the "uncivil" elements of society. The Office is comprised of the **United Nations International Drug Control Programme (UNDCP)** and the **Centre for International Crime Prevention.**

## Drug control

More than 200 million people abuse drugs worldwide. Drug abuse is responsible for lost wages, soaring health-care costs, broken families and deteriorating communities. In particular, injecting drug use is fueling the rapid spread of HIV/AIDS and hepatitis in many parts of the world.

There is a direct link between drugs and an increase in crime and violence. Drug cartels undermine governments and corrupt legitimate businesses. Revenues from illicit drugs fund some of the most deadly armed conflicts.

The financial toll is staggering. Enormous sums are spent to strengthen police forces, judicial systems and treatment and rehabilitation programmes. The social costs are equally jarring: street violence, gang warfare, fear, urban decay and shattered lives.

The United Nations is addressing the global drug problem on many levels. The **Commission on Narcotic Drugs**, a functional commission of ECOSOC, is the main intergovernmental policy-making and coordination body on international drug control. Made up of 53 Member States, it analyses the world drug abuse and trafficking problem and develops proposals to strengthen international drug control. It monitors implementation of the international drug control treaties and the guiding principles and measures adopted by the General Assembly. It also directs the activities of UNDCP.

The Commission has five subsidiary bodies to promote cooperation and coordination at the regional level in Africa, Asia and the Pacific, Europe, Latin America and the Caribbean, and the Near and Middle East.

The **International Narcotics Control Board** is a 13-member, independent, quasi-judicial body that monitors governments' compliance with the international drug control treaties and assists them in this effort. It strives to ensure that drugs are available for medical and scientific purposes and to prevent their diversion into illegal channels. It sets limits on the amounts of narcotic drugs needed by countries for medical and scientific purposes. It also sends investigative missions and technical visits to drug-affected countries.

A series of treaties, adopted under United Nations auspices, require that governments exercise control over production and distribution of narcotic and psychotropic substances, combat drug abuse and illicit trafficking, and report to international organs on their actions. These treaties are:

- The *Single Convention on Narcotic Drugs* (1961), which seeks to limit the production, distribution, possession, use and trade in drugs exclusively to medical and scientific purposes, and obliges states parties to take special measures for particular drugs such as heroin. The 1972 *Protocol* to the Convention stresses the need for treatment and rehabilitation of drug addicts.
- The *Convention on Psychotropic Substances* (1971), which establishes an international control system for psychotropic substances. It responds to the diversification and expansion of the spectrum of drugs, and introduces controls over a number of synthetic drugs.
- The *United Nations Convention against Illicit Traffic in Narcotic Drugs and Psychotropic Substances* (1988), which provides comprehensive measures against drug trafficking, including provisions against money laundering and the diversion of precursor chemicals. The main framework for international cooperation against drug trafficking, it provides for the tracing, freezing and confiscation of proceeds and property derived from drug trafficking, extradition of drug traffickers, and transfer of proceedings for criminal prosecution. States parties commit themselves to eliminate or reduce drug demand.

The **United Nations International Drug Control Programme (UNDCP)** provides leadership for all United Nations drug control activities. It helps to prevent developments that could aggravate drug production, trafficking and abuse; assists governments in establishing drug control structures and strategies; provides technical assistance in drug control; promotes the implementation of drug control treaties; and acts as a worldwide centre of expertise and repository of information.

UNDCP's approach to the global drug problem is multifaceted: community-based programmes for drug abuse prevention, treatment and rehabilitation involve NGOs and civil society; alternative development assistance provides new economic opportunities to populations economically dependent on the cultivation of illicit crops which are to be eradicated; better training and technology to curb drug trafficking makes law enforcement agencies more effective; and assistance to the business community and NGOs helps them create programmes to reduce drug demand. For instance:

- The *Global Illicit Crops Monitoring Programme,* carried out in Afghanistan, Laos, Myanmar, Bolivia, Colombia and Peru, integrates satellite sensing, aerial surveillance and on-the-ground assessment, in order to enable countries to gain a wide-ranging picture of illicit growing areas and trends.

- The *Global Assessment Programme* supplies accurate and current statistics on illicit drug consumption worldwide. Having an accurate picture of drug abuse trends is crucial for finding the best strategies for prevention, treatment and rehabilitation.

- The *Legal Assistance Programme* works with states to implement drug control treaties by helping to draft legislation and train judicial officials. More than 1,700 key personnel have received legal training, and over 140 countries have received legal assistance.

At the 1998 special session of the General Assembly devoted to countering the world drug problem, the world's governments developed a truly global drug control strategy. They pledged to work together to streamline strategies and to strengthen practical activities aimed at curtailing both illicit drug production and consumption. These included: campaigns to reduce drug demand; programmes to restrict availability of materials that can be used in drug production; efforts to improve judicial cooperation among countries to better control drug trafficking; and stepped-up efforts to eradicate illicit drug crops.

## Crime prevention

Crime is increasing in scope, intensity and sophistication. It threatens the safety of citizens around the world and hampers the social and economic development of countries. Globalization has opened up new forms of transnational crime. Multinational criminal syndicates have expanded the range of their operations from drug and arms trafficking to money laundering. Traffickers move as many as 4 million illegal migrants each year, generating gross earning of up to $7 billion. A country plagued by corruption is likely to attract investment levels 5 per cent lower than those of a relatively uncorrupt country, and to lose up to 1 per cent of economic growth per year.

The **Commission on Crime Prevention and Criminal Justice**, made up of 40 Member States, is a functional body of ECOSOC. It formulates international policies and coordinates activities in crime prevention and criminal justice.

The **Centre for International Crime Prevention** carries out the mandates established by the Commission, and is the United Nations office responsible for crime prevention, criminal justice and criminal law reform. It pays special attention to combating transnational organized crime, corruption, terrorism and trafficking in human beings.

The Centre's strategy is based on the twin pillars of international cooperation and the provision of assistance for international efforts. It also fosters a culture based on integrity and respect for the law, and promotes the participation of civil society in preventing and combating crime and corruption.

The Centre supports the development of new international legal instruments to deal with the challenges of global crime. It supported the completion by Member States of the *United Nations Convention against Transnational Organized Crime* and its three protocols, adopted by the General Assembly in 2000. The Centre is now promoting its ratification by states and assisting them through technical cooperation in putting it into effect.

The Centre provides technical cooperation to strengthen the capacity of governments to reform legislation and modernize their criminal justice systems. In cooperation with UNICRI (*see below*), the Centre launched in 1999 three programmes addressing major priority concerns of the international community: the *Global Programme against Corruption,* the *Global Programme in Trafficking in Human Beings* and the *Global Studies on Organized Crime.*

The Centre promotes and facilitates the application of United Nations standards and norms in crime prevention and criminal justice as cornerstones of humane and effective criminal justice systems — which are basic requisites for fighting national and international crime. More than 100 countries have relied on these standards for elaborating national legislation and policies, leading to a common foundation for the fight against international crime that is respectful of human rights and the needs of individuals.

Emerging trends in crime and justice are analyzed, databases developed, global surveys issued and information gathered and disseminated. Country-specific needs assessments and early warning measures are undertaken — for example on the escalation of terrorism.

The *Global Programme against Money Laundering*, a joint undertaking of the Centre and UNDCP, assists governments in confronting criminals who launder the proceeds of crime through the international financial system. Estimates of laundered money are as high as $500 billion a year. In close cooperation with international anti-money laundering organizations, the Programme provides governments, law enforcement and financial intelligence units with anti-money laundering schemes, advises on improved banking and financial policies, and assists national financial investigation services.

The **United Nations Interregional Crime and Justice Research Institute (UNICRI)** (*see Chapter 1, page 47*) operates as the interregional research arm of the Centre. It undertakes and promotes action-oriented research aimed at the prevention of crime and the treatment of offenders, and contributes, through research and information dissemination, to formulating improved policies in crime prevention and control.

As decided by the General Assembly, a **United Nations Congress on the Prevention of Crime and the Treatment of Offenders** is held every five years, to provide a forum to exchange policies and to stimulate progress in the fight against crime. Participants include criminologists, penologists and senior police officers, as well as experts in criminal law, human rights and rehabilitation. (*For United Nations action against terrorism, see Chapter 6, page 270*).

## Science, culture and communication

The United Nations sees cultural and scientific exchanges, as well as communication, as instrumental to the advancement of international peace and development. In addition to its central work around education (*see page 172, above*), the **United Nations Educational, Scientific and Cultural Organization (UNESCO)** focuses its activities on three other areas: science in the service of development; cultural development — heritage and creativity; and communication, information and informatics.

### Science

The major programme, *Sciences in the service of development,* fosters the advancement, transfer and sharing of knowledge in the natural, physical, social and human sciences. UNESCO's intergovernmental programmes include *Man and the Biosphere;* the programme of the *Intergovernmental Oceanographic Commission;* the *Project on Environment and Development in Coastal Regions;* the *Management of Social Transformations Programme;* the *International Hydrological Programme*; and the *International Geological Correlation Programme.* In addition, through education and training initiatives, UNESCO helps to correct the imbalance in scientific and technological manpower, 90 per cent of which is concentrated in the industrialized countries.

In the wake of advances in cloning living beings, the UNESCO member states adopted in 1997 the *Universal Declaration on the Human Genome and Human Rights* — the first international text on the ethics of genetic research. The Declaration sets universal ethical standards on human genetic research and practice that balance the freedom of scientists to pursue their work with the need to safeguard human rights and protect humanity from potential abuses.

In the social and human sciences, UNESCO focuses on teaching human rights and democracy, combating all forms of discrimination, improving the status of women, and encouraging action to solve the problems faced by youth, such as education for the prevention of AIDS.

## Cultural development

UNESCO's cultural activities are concentrated on safeguarding cultural heritage. Under the 1972 *Convention on the Protection of the World Cultural and Natural Heritage,* 161 states have pledged international cooperation to protect 630 outstanding sites in 118 countries — protected towns, monuments and natural environments that have been placed on the *World Heritage List.* Sites threatened by neglect are included in the *List of World Heritage in Danger.*

A 1970 UNESCO convention prohibits the illicit import, export and transfer of cultural property, and a 1995 convention favours the return of stolen or illegally exported cultural objects to their country of origin.

Cultural activities also concentrate on promoting the cultural dimension of development; encouraging creation and creativity; preserving cultural identities and oral traditions; and promoting books and reading.

## Communication, information and informatics

UNESCO has asserted itself as a world leader in promoting press freedom and pluralistic, independent media. Its major programme in this area seeks to promote the free flow of information and to strengthen the communication capacities of developing countries.

UNESCO promotes press freedom and independence and seeks to reinforce media pluralism. It assists member states in adapting their media laws to democratic standards, and in pursuing editorial independence in public and private media.

When violations of press freedom occur, the UNESCO Director-General intervenes through diplomatic channels or public statements. At the initiative of UNESCO, 3 May is observed as **World Press Freedom Day**.

To reinforce communication infrastructures and human resources in developing countries, UNESCO provides training and technical expertise, and helps to develop national and regional media projects, especially through its *International Programme for the Development of Communication.*

UNESCO helps developing countries set up their own informatics systems and to secure access to global information flows through information highways. The emphasis in the programme is on training, on establishing computer networks linking scientific and cultural institutions, as well as on hooking them up to the Internet.

The new communication technologies, by multiplying the possibilities for producing, disseminating and receiving information on an unprecedented scale, are leading to an extension of the principle of "free flow of ideas". UNESCO seeks to ensure that as many people as possible benefit from the opportunities that these technologies provide. The social and cultural impact of such technologies, and the policy approaches to legal and ethical issues related to cyberspace, are also questions of concern to UNESCO.

## Sustainable development

In the first decades of the United Nations, environmental concerns rarely appeared on the international agenda. The related work of the Organization emphasized natural resources exploration and utilization while seeking to ensure that developing countries, in particular, would be able to maintain control over their own natural resources. During the 1960s, there were some agreements made regarding marine pollution, especially oil spills (*see page 204, below*). But with increasing evidence of the deterioration of the environment on a global scale, the international community has since the 1970s shown escalating alarm over the impact of development on the ecology of the planet and human well-being. The United Nations has been a leading advocate for environmental concerns, and a leading proponent of "sustainable development".

The relationship between economic development and environmental degradation was first placed on the international agenda in 1972, at the United Nations Conference on the Human Environment, held in Stockholm. After the Conference, governments set up the **United Nations Environment Programme (UNEP)**, which today continues

## The Earth Summit

At the United Nations Conference on Environment and Development (UNCED) (Rio de Janeiro, 1992), also known as the Earth Summit, the world's nations agreed on an approach to development that would protect the environment while ensuring economic and social development, and laid the foundation for a global partnership between developing and industrialized countries, based on common but differentiated needs and responsibilities, to ensure a healthy future for the planet.

The Summit adopted Agenda 21, a plan of action for addressing both environment and development goals in the 21st century; the Rio Declaration on Environment and Development, which defines the rights and responsibilities of states; and the Statement of Forest Principles, guidelines for the sustainable management of forests worldwide. The assembled world leaders signed the conventions on climate change and on biological diversity (*see pages 200 and 203, below*).

The Rio Declaration, among other things, states that scientific uncertainty should not delay measures to prevent environmental degradation where there are threats of serious or irreversible damage; that eradicating poverty and reducing disparities in global living standards are "indispensable" for sustainable development; and that the developed countries acknowledge the responsibility that they bear in the international pursuit of sustainable development in the view of the pressures their societies place on the global environment and of the technologies and financial resources they command.

The Summit called for several major initiatives in other key areas of sustainable development. These included a global conference on small island developing states, a convention on desertification, and an agreement on highly migratory and straddling fish stocks (*see below*).

The General Assembly in 1997 held a special session (Earth Summit + 5) on the implementation of Agenda 21. Member States grappled with differences among them on how to finance sustainable development globally, but emphasized that putting Agenda 21 into practice was more urgent than ever. The session's final document recommended measures to this end, including: adopting legally binding targets to reduce emission of greenhouse gases leading to climate change; moving more forcefully towards sustainable patterns of energy production, distribution and use; and focusing on poverty eradication as a prerequisite for sustainable development.

The 10-year follow-up to the Earth Summit will be held in 2002.

---

to act as the leading global environmental agency (*see page 198, below*).

In 1973, the United Nations set up the **Sudano-Sahelian Office (UNSO)** to spearhead efforts to reverse the spread of desertification in West Africa. Action was slow, however, to integrate environmental concerns into national economic planning and decision-making.

Overall, the environment has continued to deteriorate, and such problems as global warming, ozone depletion and water pollution have grown more serious, while the destruction of natural resources has accelerated at an alarming rate.

The 1980s witnessed landmark negotiations among Member States on environmental issues, including treaties protecting the ozone layer and controlling the movement of toxic wastes (*see below*). The World Commission on Environment and Development, established in 1983 by the General Assembly, brought about a new understanding and sense of urgency to the need for a new kind of development — a development that would ensure economic well-being for present and future generations while protecting the environmental resources on which all development depends. The Commission's 1987 report to the General Assembly put forward the concept of *sustainable development* as an alternative approach to one simply based on unconstrained economic growth.[1]

After considering the report, the General Assembly called for the United Nations Conference on Environment and Development *(see box)*.

Today, awareness of the need to support and sustain the environment is reflected in virtually all areas of United Nations work. Thanks to the groundbreaking work since 1972, new mechanisms have been created; dynamic partnerships between the Organization and governments, NGOs, the scientific community and the private sector are bringing new knowledge and concrete action to the environmental problems that are shared by all nations. The United Nations maintains that the need to protect the environment must be integral to all economic and social development activities. Economic and social development goals cannot be achieved unless the environment is protected and its services preserved.

## Agenda 21

Governments took an historic step towards ensuring the future of the planet when they adopted at the Earth Summit *Agenda 21*, a comprehensive plan for global action in all areas of sustainable development.

In *Agenda 21*, governments outlined a detailed blueprint for action which could move the world away from its present unsustainable model of economic growth towards activities that will protect and re-

---

[1] In the words of the Commission, a development "which meets the needs of the present without compromising the ability of future generations to meet their own needs".

new the environmental resources on which growth and development depend. Areas for action include protecting the atmosphere; combating deforestation, soil loss and desertification; preventing air and water pollution; halting the depletion of fish stocks; and promoting the safe management of toxic wastes. *Agenda 21* also addresses patterns of development which cause stress to the environment: poverty and external debt in developing countries, unsustainable patterns of production and consumption, demographic stress and the structure of the international economy.

The action programme recommends ways to strengthen the part played by major groups — women, trade unions, farmers, children and young people, indigenous peoples, the scientific community, local authorities, business, industry and NGOs — in achieving sustainable development.

The United Nations was requested to support national efforts to put *Agenda 21* into effect, and has taken steps to integrate the concept of sustainable development into all relevant policies and programmes. Income-generating projects increasingly take into account environmental consequences. Development assistance programmes are increasingly directed towards women, given their central roles as producers of goods, services and food and as caretakers of the environment. The moral and social imperatives for alleviating poverty are given additional urgency by the recognition that poverty eradication and environmental quality go hand in hand.

To ensure full support for giving effect to *Agenda 21* worldwide, the General Assembly established in 1992 the **Commission on Sustainable Development**. A functional commission of ECOSOC, the 53-member body monitors and reports on implementation of *Agenda 21* and the other Earth Summit agreements; supports and encourages action by governments, business, industry and other non-governmental groups to bring about the social and economic changes needed for sustainable development; and helps to coordinate environment and development activities within the United Nations.

The United Nations Department of Economic and Social Affairs, through its **Division for Sustainable Development**, provides the Secretariat for the Commission and responds to requests for policy recommendations to facilitate the implementation of sustainable development. It also provides analytical, technical and information services, of which a key element is the forging of partnerships among the governmental, non-governmental and international actors.

# Changing human behaviour

Achieving sustainable development worldwide depends largely on changing patterns of production and consumption — what we produce, how it is produced and how much we consume. Finding ways to change these patterns, particularly in the industrialized countries, was first put on the international agenda at the Earth Summit. Since then, the Commission on Sustainable Development has spearheaded a programme of work, in cooperation with organizations both within and outside the United Nations, aimed at challenging the behaviour of individual consumers, households, industrial concerns, businesses and governments.

Central to the issue is the fact that using fewer resources and wasting less is simply better business. It saves money and generates higher profits. It also protects the environment by conserving natural resources and creating less pollution. In doing so, we sustain the planet for the enjoyment and well-being of future generations.

The Commission's work programme in this area focuses on projected trends in consumption and production; the impact on developing countries, including trade opportunities; assessment of the effectiveness of policy instruments; progress by countries through their time-bound voluntary commitments; and extension and revision of United Nations guidelines for consumer protection. Discussions on these issues have involved business and industry, governments, international organizations, the academic community and NGOs.

## Financing sustainable development

At the Earth Summit, it was agreed that most financing for *Agenda 21* would come from within each country's public and private sectors. However, new and additional external funds were considered necessary to support developing countries' efforts to implement sustainable development practices and protect the global environment.

Launched in 1991 and restructured in 1994, the **Global Environment Facility (GEF)** has twice been entrusted with channelling these funds. In 1994, 34 nations pledged $2 billion to the GEF, and in 1998, 36 nations pledged $2.75 billion more. GEF funds are the primary means by which the goals of the Conventions on Biological Diversity and on Climate Change are achieved on the ground.

GEF projects — principally carried out by UNDP, UNEP and the World Bank — conserve and sustainably use biological diversity, address global climate change, reverse the degradation of international waters, and phase out substances that deplete the ozone layer. Work to stem the pervasive problem of land degradation is also eligible for funding.

GEF currently funds close to 700 projects in 140 developing nations and countries with economies in transition. It has allocated $3 billion and raised another $8 billion in co-financing from recipient governments, international development agencies, private industry and NGOs.

## Action for the environment

While the whole United Nations system is engaged in environmental protection in diverse ways, its lead agency in this area is the **United Nations Environment Programme (UNEP)** (*see also Chapter 1, page 37*). Created to be the environmental conscience of the United Nations system, UNEP assesses the state of the world's environment and identifies issues requiring international cooperation; helps formulate international environmental law; and helps to integrate environmental considerations in the social and economic policies and programmes of the United Nations system.

UNEP helps solve problems that cannot be handled by countries acting alone. It provides a forum to build consensus and to forge international agreements. In doing so, it strives to enhance the participation of business and industry, the scientific and academic community, NGOs, community groups and others in achieving sustainable development.

One of the functions of UNEP is the promotion of scientific knowledge and information on the environment. Research and synthesis of environmental information, promoted and coordinated at regional and global levels by UNEP, has generated a variety of *State-of-the-Environment* reports, and created worldwide awareness of emerging environmental problems — some of which triggered international negotiations of several environmental conventions.

Through the worldwide network of centres making up the **Global Resource Information Database (GRID)**, UNEP facilitates and coordinates the collection and dissemination of the best possible data and information at the regional level. **UNEP-INFOTERRA** is a global network for environmental information exchange and scientific and technical query response services; it is comprised of national consortia providing an integrated environmental information service in over 175 countries.

UNEP acts to protect oceans and seas and promote the environmentally sound use of marine resources under its *Regional Seas Programme,* which now covers over 140 countries. This programme works towards the protection of shared marine and water resources through 13 Conventions or Action Plans, and is one of UNEP's major successes. Regional conventions and action plans for which UNEP provides the secretariat cover Eastern Africa, West and Central Africa, the Mediterranean, the Caribbean, the East Asian seas and the north-west Pacific.

Coastal and marine areas cover some 70 per cent of the Earth's surface and are vital to the planet's life-support system. Most pollution comes from industrial wastes, mining, agricultural activities and emissions from motor vehicles, some of which occurs thousands of miles inland. UNEP sponsored talks which led in 1995 to the adoption by 110 governments of the *Global Programme of Action for the Protection of the Marine Environment from Land-based Activities* — a milestone in international efforts to protect oceans, estuaries and coastal waters from pollution caused by human activities on land. The Programme, with a Coordination Office in The Hague, provides for plans to deal with perhaps the most serious threat to the marine environment: the flow of chemicals, pollutants and sewage into the sea.

UNEP's Paris-based **Division of Technology, Industry and Economics** is of central importance to United Nations efforts to encourage decision makers in government, industry and business to adopt policies, strategies and practices that are cleaner and safer, use natural resources more efficiently, and reduce pollution risks to people and the environment. The Division facilitates the transfer of green technologies; helps countries to build capacities for the sound management of chemicals and the improvement of chemical safety worldwide; supports the phase-out of ozone-depleting substances in developing countries and countries with economies in transition; and works with the private sector to integrate environmental considerations in company activities, practices and products.

**UNEP Chemicals** makes information from its **International Register of Potentially Toxic Chemicals (IRPTC)** available to those people who need to use them. Some 70,000 chemicals are in use today, and IRPTC provides vital information for decisions on chemical safety. Information on more than 8,000 chemicals is distributed cost-free to over 100 countries, while a query response service handles thousands of requests annually.

In collaboration with FAO, UNEP facilitated the negotiation of the *Rotterdam Convention on Prior Informed Consent Procedures for Certain Hazardous Chemicals and Pesticides in International Trade* (1998). The Convention gives importing countries the power to decide which chemicals they want to receive and exclude those they cannot manage safely.

Over the years, UNEP has been the catalyst for the negotiation of other international agreements that form the cornerstone of the United Nations efforts to halt and reverse damage to the planet. The historic *Montreal Protocol* (1987) and its subsequent Amendments seek to preserve the ozone layer in the upper atmosphere. The *Basel Convention on the Control of Hazardous Wastes and Their Disposal* (1989) has reduced the danger of pollution from toxic waste. The *Convention on International Trade in Endangered Species* (1973) is universally recognized for its achievements in controlling the trade in wildlife products. UNEP assisted African governments in developing the *Lusaka Agreement on Cooperative Enforcement Operations Directed at Illegal Trade in Wild Fauna and Flora* (1994), and provides its secretariat on an interim basis. UNEP has also helped to negotiate and implement the Conventions on biological diversity, desertification and climate change; it now administers and provides the secretariat functions for these treaties.

UNEP is now facilitating the negotiation of a legally binding treaty to reduce and eliminate releases of certain persistent organic pollutants — highly toxic pesticides and industrial chemical that are highly mobile and accumulate in the food chain. The resulting convention is expected to be adopted in 2001.

## Climate change and global warming

There is substantial evidence that human activities contribute to the build-up of "greenhouse gases" in the atmosphere, leading to a gradual rise in global temperatures. In particular, carbon dioxide is produced when fossil fuels are burned to generate energy, or when forests are cut down and burned. According to the Intergovernmental Panel on Climate Change, climate models predict that global temperatures will rise by about 1 to 3.5 degrees centigrades by 2100. This projected change is larger than any climate change experienced over the last 10,000 years — with potentially significant impact on the global environment.

To counter global warming, the 1992 *United Nations Framework Convention on Climate Change* was developed and signed in Rio. Under the Convention, developed countries agreed to reduce emissions of carbon dioxide and other "greenhouse" gases they release into the atmosphere to 1990 levels by 2000. These countries, which together account for 60 per cent of annual carbon dioxide emissions, also agreed to transfer to developing countries technology and information that would help them respond to the challenges of climate change. By December 2000, 186 countries had ratified the Convention.

United Nations negotiations on climate change are supported by the work the **Intergovernmental Panel on Climate Change (IPCC)**, which was organized jointly in 1988 by UNEP and WMO. The Panel, a worldwide network of 2,500 leading scientists and experts, reviews scientific research on the issue. In 1989, its finding that human activities could possibly cause changes in the global climate system led to negotiations on the Climate Change Convention. By 1995, with access to new and more powerful computer models, the Panel found that there was "discernible human influence on the global climate".

The evidence presented by IPCC scientists was clear: the 1992 target, even if reached on time, would not prevent global warming and its associated problems. Additional reductions would be necessary. In 1997, countries which had ratified the Convention met in Kyoto, Japan and agreed on a legally binding *Protocol* under which developed countries are to reduce their collective emissions of six greenhouse gases by 5.2 per cent between 2008 and 2012, taking 1990 levels as the baseline.

### Ozone depletion

The ozone layer is a thin layer of gas in the upper atmosphere (about 12 to 45 kilometres above the ground) which shields the Earth's surface from the sun's damaging ultraviolet rays. Exposure to increased ultraviolet radiation is known to result in skin cancer, and to cause unpredictable damage to plants, algae, the food chain and the global ecosystem.

UNEP helped to negotiate and now administers the historic *Vienna Convention for the Protection of the Ozone Layer* (1985), and the *Montreal Protocol* (1987) and its *Amendments*. Under these agreements, developed countries have banned the production and sale of chlorofluorocarbons, a chemical that depletes the ozone layer. Developing countries must stop production by 2010. Schedules are in place to phase out other ozone-depleting substances.

In 1998, a UNEP–WMO assessment of ozone depletion, prepared by more than 200 scientists from around the world, confirmed the effectiveness of the Montreal Protocol. According to the assessment, the combined total abundance of ozone-depleting compounds in the lowest part of the atmosphere peaked in 1994 and is now slowly declining. If measures had not been taken in accordance with the Protocol, the ozone depletion would have been much more serious and would have continued for many more decades. But even though the Protocol is working well to reduce the use and release of ozone-depleting substances, the life of chemicals already released in the atmosphere means that the depletion will continue for years to come.

Scientists predict that the Earth's protective ozone shield will start to recover in the near future and will fully recover by 2050 — provided the Protocol continues to be vigorously enforced.

## Small islands

Some 40 small island developing states and territories share a number of disadvantages, including a narrow range of resources, economic isolation, degradation of land and marine environments, and possible sea-level rise caused by climate change.

As requested by the Earth Summit, the United Nations held the Global Conference on the Sustainable Development of Small Island Developing States (Barbados, 1994). The Conference highlighted the economic and ecological vulnerability of these states, and adopted a programme of action setting forth policies, actions and measures to be taken at the national and international levels in support of the sustainable development of these states.

The General Assembly followed up on the Conference at a special session in 1999. It reviewed progress in implementing the programme of action, and set forth recommendations for priority areas requiring urgent action, as well as the means of implementation.

## Forests

By 1995, the international community, which had adopted a non-binding statement on forest principles at the Earth Summit, was ready to discuss additional measures necessary to ensure the sustainable development of the world's forests. The Intergovernmental Panel on Forests, set up by the Commission on Sustainable Development, concluded its work in 1997 by adopting some 100 action-specific proposals for the conservation, management and sustainable development of forests.

Responding to the continuing need for a central forum on forests, governments attending the Earth Summit + 5 established the **Intergovernmental Forum on Forests**, to promote and monitor implementation of these proposals and to consider what additional measures, including an international legally binding agreement, might be needed to ensure the sustainable development of forests.

The Forum recommended in 2000 the establishment of a United Nations Forum on Forests, to promote the implementation of the proposals for action resulting from five years of intergovernmental deliberations.

# Desertification

One quarter of the Earth's land is threatened by desertification, according to UNEP estimates. Over 250 million people are directly affected, and the livelihoods of over 1 billion people in more than 100 countries are jeopardized, as farming and grazing land becomes less productive. Drought can trigger desertification, but human activities — overcultivation, overgrazing, deforestation, poor irrigation — are usually the main causes.

A United Nations treaty seeks to address this problem: the *Convention to Combat Desertification in those Countries Experiencing Serious Drought and/or Desertification, Particularly in Africa*. The treaty, to which 172 countries are parties, provides the framework for all activity to combat desertification. It focuses on improving land productivity, rehabilitation of land, conservation and management of land and water resources. It emphasizes popular participation and an "enabling environment" for local people to help themselves reverse land degradation. It contains criteria for the preparation by affected countries of national action programmes, and gives an unprecedented role to NGOs in preparing and carrying out action programmes.

Various United Nations agencies provide assistance to combat desertification. UNDP funds activities to combat desertification through the **Sudano-Sahelian Office (UNSO)**, which helps develop policies, provides technical advice, and supports desertification control and dryland management programmes. A special IFAD programme has mobilized $400 million, plus another $350 million in co-financing, for projects in 25 African countries threatened by desertification. Similarly, the World Bank organizes and funds programmes aimed at protecting fragile drylands and increasing their agricultural productivity on a sustainable basis, while FAO promotes sustainable agricultural development through a wide range of practical help to governments.

## Biodiversity, pollution and overfishing

**Biodiversity** — the variety of plant and animal species — is essential for human survival. The protection and conservation of the diverse range of species of animal and plant life and their habitats is the aim of the *United Nations Convention on Biological Diversity* (1992), to which 180 states are parties. The Convention obligates states to conserve biodiversity, ensure its sustainable development, and provide for the fair and equitable sharing of benefits from the use of genetic resources. A protocol to ensure the safe use of genetically modified organisms was adopted in 2000 (*see Chapter 6, page 264*).

Protection of endangered species is also enforced under the 1973 *Convention on International Trade in Endangered Species*, administered by UNEP. The 151 states parties meet periodically to update the list of which plant and animal species or products, such as ivory, should be protected by quotas or outright bans.

**Acid rain.** Caused by emissions of sulphur dioxide from industrial manufacturing processes, "acid rain" has been significantly reduced in much of Europe and North America thanks to the 1979 *Convention on Long-Range Transboundary Air Pollution*. The Convention, to which 47 states are parties, is administered by the United Nations Economic Commission for Europe.

**Hazardous wastes and chemicals.** To regulate the 3 million tons of toxic waste that crosses national borders each year, Member States negotiated in 1989 the *Basel Convention on the Control of Transboundary Movements of Hazardous Wastes and their Disposal*, administered by UNEP. The treaty, to which 142 states are parties, was strengthened in 1995 to ban the export of toxic waste to developing countries, which often do not have the technology for safe disposal.

**High seas fishing.** The overfishing and near exhaustion of many species of commercially valuable fish and the increasing incidence of violence over fishing on the high seas led governments at the Earth Summit to call for measures to conserve and sustainably manage fish which migrate across broad areas of the ocean or move between more than one country's exclusive economic zone. The 1995 *United Nations Agreement on Straddling Fish Stocks and Highly Migratory Fish Stocks*, signed by some 60 countries, provides for these species to be subject to quotas designed to ensure the continued survival of fish in the future, as well as steps for peacefully resolving disputes on the high seas.

## Protecting the marine environment

The oceans cover two thirds of the Earth's surface, and protecting them has become one of the United Nations' primary concerns. UNEP's work, particularly its diverse efforts to protect the marine environment, has focused world attention on the oceans and seas (*see page 198, above*). The **International Maritime Organization (IMO)** (*see also Chapter 1, page 56*) is the United Nations specialized agency responsible for measures to prevent marine pollution from ships and improve the safety of international shipping. In spite of the dramatic expansion of world shipping, oil pollution from ships was cut by around 60 per cent during the 1980s and the number of oil spills during the last two decades has been greatly reduced. This is partly due to the introduction of better methods of controlling the disposal of wastes, and partly to the tightening of controls through conventions.

The pioneer *International Convention for the Prevention of Pollution of the Sea by Oil* was adopted in 1954, and IMO took over responsibility for it in 1959. In the late 1960s, a number of major tanker accidents led to further action. Since then, IMO has developed many measures to prevent accidents at sea and oil spills, to minimize their consequences, and to combat marine pollution — including that caused by the dumping into the seas of wastes generated by land-based activities.

The main treaties are:
* *International Convention Relating to Intervention on the High Seas in Cases of Oil Pollution Casualties (Intervention)*, 1969;
* *Convention on the Prevention of Marine Pollution by Dumping of Wastes and Other Matters (LC)*, 1972;
* *International Convention on Oil Pollution Preparedness, Response and Cooperation (OPRC)*, 1990.

IMO has also tackled the environmental threats caused by routine operations such as the cleaning of oil cargo tanks and the disposal of engine-room wastes — in tonnage terms a bigger menace than accidents. The most important of these measures is the 1973 *International Convention for the Prevention of Pollution from Ships*, as modified by its 1978 *Protocol (MARPOL 73/78)*. It covers not only accidental and operational oil pollution, but also pollution by chemicals, packaged goods, sewage and garbage. Amendments to the Convention adopted in 1992 oblige all new tankers to be fitted with double hulls or a design that provides equivalent cargo protection in the event of a collision or grounding.

Two IMO treaties — the *International Convention on Civil Liability for Oil Pollution Damage (CLC)* and the *International Convention on the Establishment of an International Fund for Oil Pollution Damage (FUND)* — establish a system for providing compensation to those who have suffered financially as a result of pollution. The treaties, adopted in 1969 and 1971 and revised in 1992, enable victims of oil pollution to obtain compensation much more simply and quickly than had been possible before. (*For IMO action in international shipping, see page 149, above*).

## Meteorology, climate and water

From weather prediction to climate-change research and tropical-storm forecasting, the **World Meteorological Organization**

**(WMO)** *(see also Chapter 1, page 58)* coordinates global scientific efforts to improve accurate weather information and other services for public, private and commercial use, including the airline and shipping industries. WMO's activities contribute to the safety of life and property, economic and social development, and the protection of the environment.

Within the United Nations, WMO provides the authoritative scientific voice on the state and behaviour of the Earth's atmosphere and climate. The agency:

- Facilitates international cooperation in establishing networks of stations for making meteorological, hydrological and other observations;
- Promotes the rapid exchange of meteorological information, the standardization of meteorological observations, and the uniform publication of observations and statistics;
- Furthers the application of meteorology to aviation, shipping, water problems, agriculture and other activities;
- Promotes operational hydrology; and
- Encourages research and training.

The backbone of WMO's activities, the *World Weather Watch* programme, offers up-to-the-minute worldwide weather information through observation systems and telecommunication links operated by member states, with 9 satellites, 3,000 aircraft, 10,000 land observation stations, 7,300 ship stations, and 900 moored and drifting buoys carrying automatic weather stations. Each day, high-speed links transmit data and weather charts through 3 World, 34 Regional and 185 National Meteorological Centres, which cooperate in preparing weather analyses and forecasts. Thus ships and airplanes, research scientists, the media and the public are given a constant supply of timely weather data.

It is through WMO that the complex agreements on weather standards, codes, measurements and communications are established internationally. A *Tropical Cyclone Programme* assists more than 50 countries vulnerable to cyclones to minimize destruction and loss of life by improving forecasting and warning systems and disaster preparedness.

With climate change an issue of growing concern, the *World Climate Programme*, by collecting and preserving climate data, helps governments to plan in response to the changing situation. It aims at using climate information to improve economic and social planning; to improve understanding of climate processes through research; and to detect and warn governments of impending climate variations or changes, either natural or man-made, which could affect critical human activities. To assess all available information on climate change, WMO and UNEP established in 1988 the Intergovernmental Panel on Climate Change (*see page 201, above*).

The *Atmospheric Research and Environment Programme* coordinates research on the structure and composition of the atmosphere, the physics and chemistry of clouds, weather modification, tropical meteorology, and weather forecasting. It helps member states to conduct research projects, to disseminate scientific information, and to incorporate the results of research into forecasting and other techniques. In particular, under the *Global Atmosphere Watch*, some 340 stations in 80 countries constitute a global network to monitor the levels of greenhouse gases in the atmosphere.

Weather-related agricultural losses may approach 20 per cent of annual production in some countries. The *Applications of Meteorology Programme* helps countries to apply meteorology to the protection of life and property and to social and economic development. It seeks to improve public weather services; increase safety of sea and air travel; reduce the impact of desertification; and improve agriculture and the management of water, energy and other resources. In agriculture, for instance, prompt meteorological advice can mean a substantial reduction in losses caused by droughts, pests and disease.

The *Hydrology and Water Resources Programme* helps to assess, manage and conserve global water resources. It promotes global cooperation in evaluating water resources and developing hydrological networks and services, including data collection and processing, hydrological forecasting and warning, and the supply of meteorological and hydrological data for design purposes. The programme, for instance, facilitates cooperation within water basins shared between countries, and provides specialized forecasting in flood-prone areas, thus helping to preserve life and property.

The *Education and Training Programme* encourages the exchange of scientific knowledge through courses, seminars and conferences. Training programmes place several hundred specialists from all over the world in advanced courses each year.

The *Technical Cooperation Programme* helps developing countries to obtain technical expertise and equipment for improving their national meteorological and hydrological services. It fosters the transfer of technology, as well as of meteorological and hydrological knowledge and information.

The *Regional Programme* supports the implementation of programmes and activities that have a regional focus. Support is pro-

vided through five WMO regional and sub-regional offices throughout the world.

## Natural resources and energy

The United Nations has long been assisting countries in managing
their natural resources. As early as 1952, the General Assembly declared that developing countries have "the right to determine freely the
use of their natural resources" and that they must use such resources
towards realizing their economic development plans in accordance
with their national interests.

An ECOSOC body composed of government-nominated experts,
the 24-member **Committee on Energy and Natural Resources for
Development**, develops guidelines on policies and strategies for
ECOSOC and governments, in cooperation with the Commission on
Sustainable Development. It is divided in two sub-groups of 12 members each. The **Sub-group on Energy** reviews trends and issues of
energy development, as well as coordination of United Nations system activities in the field of energy. The **Sub-group on Water Resources** considers issues related to the integrated management of
land and water resources, as well as coordination of United Nations
system activities in this field.

**Water resources**. The United Nations has long been addressing the
global crisis caused by growing demands on the world's water resources to meet human, commercial and agricultural needs. The 1977
United Nations Water Conference, the 1992 International Conference
on Water and the Environment, the 1992 Earth Summit and the International Drinking Water Supply and Sanitation Decade (1981-1990)
all focused on this vital resource. The Decade helped some 1.3 billion
people in the developing countries gain access to safe drinking water.

Today 20 per cent of the world's population face water shortages;
that figure will rise to 30 per cent by 2025, affecting 50 countries.
Water shortage has many causes, including inefficient use, degradation of water by pollution, and overexploitation of groundwater re-
serves. Action is needed to achieve a better management of scarce
freshwater resources, especially management of water supply and demand, as well as of quantity and quality.

The activities of the United Nations system are geared towards the
sustainable development of fragile and finite freshwater resources,
which are coming under increasing stress from population growth,
pollution and increasing demand for agricultural and industrial purposes. For instance, the Department of Economic and Social Affairs

has a sizeable programme of technical cooperation in water resources development; FAO promotes efficient use and conservation of water resources to achieve food security, and UNDP and the World Bank cooperate in the *Joint Water and Sanitation Programme*. The Commission on Sustainable Development has considered ways to increase access to water through market mechanisms, including pricing, while ensuring that poor people can afford water.

**Energy.** Much of the world's energy is produced and used in ways that may not be sustained if overall consumption continues to increase substantially. *Agenda 21* emphasizes that all energy sources need to be used in ways that protect the atmosphere, human health and the environment.

While fossil-fuel use in developed countries is slowly stabilizing, many polluting emissions are on the increase. In many developing countries, rapid growth in fossil-fuel use is leading to severe pollution. Global energy consumption is projected to more than double by 2050. At the same time, over 1.8 billion people, mostly in rural areas of developing countries, do not have access to commercial energy services.

Many entities of the United Nations system are active in a variety of projects and programmes in the field of energy, often in the form of education and training, generation of awareness and capacity-building. Most of the projects seek to assist specific countries to meet their energy objectives. Other activities reflect the changing energy situation and the environmental impact of the development and use of energy resources.

**Technical cooperation.** The United Nations maintains an active programme of technical cooperation in the field of natural resources and energy. In water and mineral resources, the United Nations system provides technical cooperation assistance and advisory services, emphasizing environmental protection, investment promotion, legislation and sustainable development. In energy, technical cooperation is organized under three programmes involving global energy efficiency, renewable energy, and cleaner fossil fuel technologies and production processes.

During the last two decades, hundreds of technical cooperation and pre-investment projects in natural resources and energy involving hundreds of millions of dollars have been implemented by the United Nations and its family of organizations. A roughly equivalent amount was provided by the recipient governments in the form of national staff, facilities and local operating costs. As a result, each year some 300 field projects assist developing countries in the sustainable development of their natural resources. Such projects strengthen national capacities, stimulate further investment and promote sustainable development.

## Nuclear safety

Today, 433 nuclear reactors produce almost 17 per cent of the world's electricity. In eight countries, over 40 per cent of energy production comes from nuclear power. In this area, the **International Atomic Energy Agency (IAEA)** (*see also Chapter 1, page 61*), an international organization in the United Nations family, fosters the development of peaceful uses of atomic energy, and establishes standards for nuclear safety and environmental protection.

IAEA serves as the world's central intergovernmental forum for scientific and technical cooperation in the nuclear field. It provides a focal point for exchanging information and drawing up of guidelines and norms in the area of nuclear safety, as well as for the submission to governments, at their request, of ways to improve the safety of reactors and avoid the risk of accidents. It also plays a prominent role in international efforts aimed at ensuring the use of nuclear technology for sustainable development.

The Agency's responsibility in the area of nuclear safety has increased as nuclear-power programmes have grown and public attention has focused on safety aspects. IAEA formulates basic standards for radiation protection and issues regulations and codes of practice on specific types of operations, including the safe transport of radioactive materials. It facilitates emergency assistance to member states in the event of a radiation accident, under the *Convention on Assistance in the Case of a Nuclear Accident or Radiological Emergency* and the *Convention on Early Notification of a Nuclear Accident.*

Other international treaties for which IAEA is the depositary include the *Convention on Physical Protection of Nuclear Material,* the *Vienna Convention on Civil Liability for Nuclear Damage,* the *Convention on Nuclear Safety,* and the *Joint Convention on the Safety of Spent Fuel Management and on the Safety of Radioactive Waste Management* — the first legal instrument to address those issues on a global scale.

IAEA aids and advises member countries on atomic energy programmes, and fosters the exchange of scientific and technical information. Its technical cooperation activities to promote the peaceful uses of atomic energy help countries in the critical areas of water, health, nutrition, medicine and food production. A prime example is the work related to mutation breeding, through which nearly 2,000 new beneficial varieties of crops have been developed using radiation-based technology.

In the current debate on energy options to curb carbon dioxide emissions contributing to global warming, IAEA has stressed the benefits of nuclear power as an energy source free of greenhouse and other toxic gas emissions.

IAEA collects and disseminates information on virtually every aspect of nuclear science and technology through its *International Nuclear Information System* (*INIS*) in Vienna. With UNESCO, it operates the **International Centre for Theoretical Physics** in Trieste, Italy, and maintains three laboratories for studies in basic uses. IAEA works with FAO in research on atomic energy in food and agriculture, and with WHO on radiation in medicine and biology. IAEA's **Marine Environment Laboratory** in Monaco carries out worldwide marine pollution studies with UNEP and UNESCO. (*On IAEA's work to prevent nuclear proliferation, see Chapter 2, page 114*).

# PART TWO

## Chapter 4

### Human Rights

# HUMAN RIGHTS

One of the great achievements of the United Nations is the creation of a comprehensive body of human rights law, which, for the first time in history, provides us with a universal and internationally protected code of human rights, one to which all nations can subscribe and to which all people can aspire. Not only has the Organization painstakingly defined a broad range of internationally accepted rights — including economic, social and cultural, as well as political and civil rights; it has also established mechanisms with which to promote and protect these rights and to assist governments in carrying out their responsibilities.

The foundations of this body of law are the United Nations Charter and the Universal Declaration of Human Rights, adopted by the General Assembly in 1948. Since then, the United Nations has gradually expanded human rights law to encompass specific standards for women, children, disabled persons, minorities, migrant workers and other vulnerable groups, who now possess rights that protect them from discriminatory practices that had long been common in many societies.

Rights have been extended through groundbreaking General Assembly decisions that have gradually established their universality, indivisibility and interrelatedness with development and democracy. Education campaigns have tirelessly informed the world's public of their inalienable rights, while numerous national judicial and penal systems have been enhanced with United Nations training programmes and technical advice. The United Nations machinery to monitor compliance with human rights covenants has acquired a remarkable cohesiveness and weight among Member States.

The United Nations High Commissioner for Human Rights has been working to strengthen and coordinate United Nations work for the protection and promotion of all human rights of all persons around the world. The Secretary-General has made human rights the central theme that unifies the Organization's work in the key areas of peace and security, development, humanitarian assistance and economic and social affairs. Virtually every United Nations body and specialized agency is involved to some degree in the protection of human rights.

# Human rights instruments

At the San Francisco Conference in 1945 at which the United Nations was established, some 40 non-governmental organizations (NGOs) representing women, trade unions, ethnic organizations and religious groups joined forces with delegations, mostly from smaller countries, and pressed for more specific language on human rights than proposed by other states. This determined lobbying resulted in bold provisions on human rights being incorporated into the *Charter of the United Nations*, laying the foundation for the post-1945 era of international law-making.

The Charter Preamble explicitly reaffirms "faith in fundamental human rights, in the dignity and worth of the human person, in the equal rights of men and women and of nations large and small". Article 1 establishes that one of the principal tasks of the United Nations is to promote and encourage "respect for human rights and for fundamental freedoms for all without distinction as to race, sex, language, or religion". Other provisions commit states to take action in cooperation with the United Nations to achieve universal respect for human rights.

## International Bill of Human Rights

Three years after the United Nations began work, the General Assembly laid the cornerstone of contemporary human rights law: the *Universal Declaration of Human Rights*, which was intended as a "common standard of achievement for all peoples". It was adopted on 10 December 1948, the day now observed worldwide as **International Human Rights Day**. Its 30 articles spell out basic civil, cultural, economic, political and social rights that all human beings in every country should enjoy (*see box on facing page*).

The provisions of the Universal Declaration are considered to have the weight of customary international law because they are so widely accepted and used as a yardstick for measuring the conduct of states. Many newly independent countries have cited the Universal Declaration or included its provisions in their basic laws or constitutions.

The broadest legally binding human rights agreements negotiated under United Nations auspices are the two International Covenants — one on Economic, Social and Cultural Rights and the other on Civil and Political Rights. These agreements, adopted by the General Assembly in 1966, take the provisions of the Universal Declaration a step further by translating these rights into legally binding commitments and setting up bodies to monitor the compliance of states parties. Most of the world's countries are parties to the Covenants.

# Defining universal rights

The Universal Declaration of Human Rights is the cornerstone of the wide-ranging body of human rights law created over the decades.

Its Articles 1 and 2 state that "all human beings are born equal in dignity and rights" and are entitled to all the rights and freedoms set forth in the Declaration "without distinction of any kind such as race, colour, sex, language, religion, political or other opinion, national or social origin, property, birth or other status".

Articles 3 to 21 set forth the civil and political rights to which all human beings are entitled, including:

- The right to life, liberty and security;
- Freedom from slavery and servitude;
- Freedom from torture or cruel, inhuman or degrading treatment or punishment;
- The right to recognition as a person before the law; the right to judicial remedy; freedom from arbitrary arrest, detention or exile; the right to a fair trial and public hearing by an independent and impartial tribunal; the right to be presumed innocent until proved guilty;
- Freedom from arbitrary interference with privacy, family, home or correspondence; freedom from attacks upon honour and reputation; the right to protection of the law against such attacks;
- Freedom of movement; the right to seek asylum; the right to a nationality;
- The right to marry and to found a family; the right to own property;
- Freedom of thought, conscience and religion; freedom of opinion and expression;
- The right to peaceful assembly and association;
- The right to take part in government and to equal access to public service. Articles 22 to 27 set forth the economic, social and cultural rights to which all human beings are entitled, including:
- The right to social security;
- The right to work; the right to equal pay for equal work; the right to form and join trade unions;
- The right to rest and leisure;
- The right to a standard of living adequate for health and well-being;
- The right to education;
- The right to participate in the cultural life of the community.

The concluding Articles, 28 to 30, recognize that everyone is entitled to a social and international order in which the human rights set forth in the Declaration may be fully realized; that these rights may only be limited for the sole purpose of securing recognition and respect of the rights and freedoms of others and of meeting the requirements of morality, public order and the general welfare in a democratic society; and that each person has duties to the community in which she or he lives.

The Universal Declaration, together with the two International Covenants on Human Rights and their Optional Protocols, comprise the International Bill of Human Rights.

## Economic, social and cultural rights

The *International Covenant on Economic, Social and Cultural Rights* entered into force in 1976, and has 143 states parties (all figures as of December 2000). The human rights that the Covenant seeks to promote and protect are of three kinds:

- The right to work in just and favourable conditions;
- The right to social protection, to an adequate standard of living and to the highest attainable standards of physical and mental well-being;
- The right to education and the enjoyment of benefits of cultural freedom and scientific progress.

The Covenant provides for the realization of these rights without discrimination of any kind. It also requires states parties to submit periodic reports to the **Committee on Economic, Social and Cultural Rights**, a body established by the Economic and Social Council (ECOSOC), on how they have been implementing its provisions. This 18-member body of experts studies these reports and discusses them with representatives of the governments concerned. Its comments on the Covenant aim to help states parties in their task of implementation, as well as to bring to their attention deficiencies in reports and procedures. The Committee also makes recommendations to states parties based on its review of their reports.

## Civil and political rights

The *International Covenant on Civil and Political Rights* and the *First Optional Protocol* to that Covenant both entered into force in 1976. The Covenant has 147 states parties; the Protocol 98.

- The Covenant deals with such rights as freedom of movement; equality before the law; the right to a fair trial and presumption of innocence; freedom of thought, conscience and religion; freedom of opinion and expression; peaceful assembly; freedom of association, participation in public affairs and elections; and protection of minority rights.
- It prohibits arbitrary deprivation of life; torture, cruel or degrading treatment or punishment; slavery and forced labour; arbitrary arrest or detention and arbitrary interference with privacy; war propaganda, and advocacy of racial or religious hatred.

The Covenant has two Protocols. The *First Optional Protocol* (1966) provides for recourse procedures that extend to individuals the right of petition. The *Second Optional Protocol* (1989) aims at the abolition of the death penalty and has 43 states parties.

The Covenant established an 18-member **Human Rights Committee**, which considers reports submitted periodically by states parties on measures taken to implement the Covenant's provisions. For states parties to the *First Optional Protocol*, the Committee also considers communications from individuals who claim to be victims of violations of any of the rights set forth in the Covenant. The Committee considers communications from individuals in closed meetings; their letters and other documentation remain confidential. The findings of the Committee, however, are made public and are reproduced in the Committee's annual report to the General Assembly.

## Other conventions

The Universal Declaration has served as the inspiration for some 80 conventions and declarations that have been concluded within the United Nations on a wide range of issues. Six of the conventions have established expert bodies that monitor compliance by states parties of the rights set out in that convention. When states ratify these treaties, they agree to have their human rights legislation and practices reviewed by independent expert bodies.

- The *Convention on the Prevention and Punishment of the Crime of Genocide* (1948), a direct response to the atrocities of the Second World War, defines the crime of genocide as the commission of certain acts with intent to destroy a national, ethnic, racial or religious group, and commits States to bringing to justice alleged perpetrators. It has 132 states parties.
- The *Convention Relating to the Status of Refugees* (1951) defines the rights of refugees, especially their right not to be forcibly returned to countries where they are at risk, and makes provisions for various aspects of their everyday lives, including their right to work, education, public assistance and social security, and their right to travel documents (*see page 254*). It has 137 states parties. The *Protocol relating to the Status of Refugees* (1967) ensures the universal application of the Convention, which was originally designed for refugees from the Second World War. The Protocol has 136 states parties.
- The *International Convention on the Elimination of All Forms of Racial Discrimination* (1966) is one of the most widely ratified treaties, with 157 states parties. Beginning with the premise that

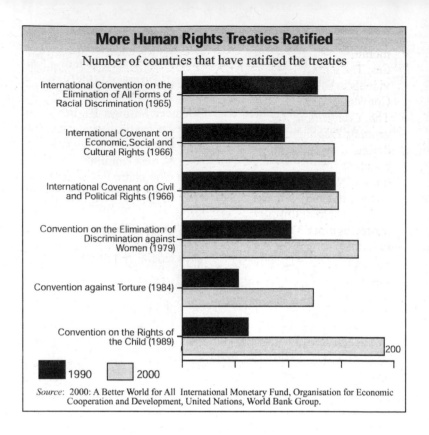

**More Human Rights Treaties Ratified**

Number of countries that have ratified the treaties

- International Convention on the Elimination of All Forms of Racial Discrimination (1965)
- International Covenant on Economic, Social and Cultural Rights (1966)
- International Covenant on Civil and Political Rights (1966)
- Convention on the Elimination of Discrimination against Women (1979)
- Convention against Torture (1984)
- Convention on the Rights of the Child (1989)

200

■ 1990   □ 2000

*Source*: 2000: A Better World for All  International Monetary Fund, Organisation for Economic Cooperation and Development, United Nations, World Bank Group.

any policy of racial superiority based on racial differences is unjustifiable, scientifically false and morally and legally condemnable, it defines "racial discrimination" and commits states parties to take measures to abolish it in both law and practice. The Convention established a monitoring body, the **Committee on the Elimination of Racial Discrimination**, to consider reports from states parties — as well as petitions from individuals alleging a violation of the Convention, if the state concerned has accepted this optional procedure of the Convention.

- The *Convention on the Elimination of All Forms of Discrimination against Women* (1979), with 166 states parties, guarantees women's equality before the law and specifies measures to eliminate discrimination against women with respect to political and public life, nationality, education, employment, health, marriage and the family. The Convention established the **Committee on the Elimination of Discrimination against Women** as the body to monitor its implementation and consider reports from states parties. The *Optional Protocol* to the Convention (1999) allows individuals to submit to the Committee complaints on violations of the Convention.

- The *Convention Against Torture and Other Inhuman or Degrading Treatment or Punishment* (1984), with 123 states parties, defines torture as an international crime, holds states parties accountable for preventing it and requires them to punish the perpetrators. No exceptional circumstances may be invoked to justify torture, nor may a torturer offer a defence of having acted under orders. The monitoring body set up by the Convention, the **Committee against Torture**, reviews reports of states parties and can initiate investigations on countries where it believes the practice of torture is systematic.
- The *Convention on the Rights of the Child* (1989) recognizes the particular vulnerability of children and brings together in one comprehensive code protections for children concerning all categories of human rights. The Convention firmly guarantees non-discrimination and recognizes that the best interests of the child must guide all actions. Special attention is paid to children who are refugees, disabled, or members of minorities. States parties are to provide guarantees for children's survival, development, protection and participation. The Convention is the most broadly ratified treaty, with 191 states parties. The **Committee on the Rights of the Child**, established by the Convention, oversees its implementation and considers reports submitted by states parties.
- The *International Convention on the Protection of the Rights of All Migrant Workers and Members of Their Families* (1990) defines basic rights and principles as well as measures to protect migrant workers, whether legal or illegal, throughout the process of migration. Unfortunately the Convention is not yet in force, because only 15 countries have ratified it to date. When it does enter into force, a monitoring committee will be set up.

The Universal Declaration and other United Nations instruments have also inspired several regional agreements, such as the *European Convention on Human Rights*, the *American Convention on Human Rights* and the *African Charter of Human and Peoples Rights*.

### Other standards

In addition, the United Nations has adopted many other standards and rules on the protection of human rights. These "declarations", "codes of conduct", "principles", etc. are not treaties which states become party to, but have nevertheless a profound influence, not least because they are carefully drafted by states and adopted by consensus. Among the most important of these:

- The *Declaration on the Elimination of All Forms of Intolerance and of Discrimination Based on Religion and Belief* (1981) affirms the right of everyone to freedom of thought, conscience and religion and the right not to be subject to discrimination on the grounds of religion or other beliefs.

- The *Declaration on the Right to Development* (1986) established that right as "an inalienable human right by virtue of which each person and all peoples are entitled to participate in, contribute to and enjoy economic, social, cultural and political development in which all human rights and fundamental freedoms can be fully realized". It adds that "equality of opportunity for development is a prerogative both of nations and of individuals".

- The *Declaration on the Rights of Persons Belonging to National or Ethnic, Religious and Linguistic Minorities* (1992) proclaims the right of minorities to enjoy their own culture; to profess and practise their own religion; to use their own language; and to leave any country, including their own, and to return to their country. The Declaration calls for action by states to promote and protect these rights.

- The *Declaration on Human Rights Defenders* (1998) seeks to recognize, promote and protect the work of human rights activists all over the world. It enshrines the right of everyone, individually and in association with others, to promote and strive to protect human rights at the national and international levels, and to participate in peaceful activities against human right violations. States are to take all necessary measures to protect human rights defenders against any violence, threats, retaliation, pressure or any other arbitrary action.

Other important non-treaty standards include the *Standard Minimum Rules for the Treatment of Prisoners* (1957), the *Basic Principles on the Independence of the Judiciary* (1985), the *Body of Principles for the Protection of All Persons under Any Form of Detention or Imprisonment* (1988) and the *Declaration on the Protection of All Persons from Enforced Disappearance* (1992).

# Human Rights Conference

The second World Conference on Human Rights (Vienna, 1993) reaffirmed the universality and central role of human rights.

The Conference revealed tensions around many issues — such as national sovereignty, universality, the role of NGOs and the question of impartiality and non-selectivity of international human rights action. But in the *Vienna Declaration and Programme of Action*, the 171 participating states proclaimed that human rights had become the "legitimate concern of the international community", and that "all human rights are universal, indivisible, interdependent and interrelated".

The Declaration states that "while the significance of national and regional particularities and various historical, cultural and religious backgrounds must be borne in mind, it is the duty of states, regardless of their political, economic and cultural systems, to promote and protect all human rights and fundamental freedoms."

It reaffirms the right to development as a universal right and the inextricable relationship between human rights and development, adding that "democracy, development and respect for human rights and fundamental freedoms are interdependent and mutually reinforcing".

# Human rights machinery

## Commission on Human Rights

The major United Nations body working to promote and protect human rights is the **United Nations Commission on Human Rights**, which was established in 1946 by ECOSOC. The Commission provides overall policy guidance, studies human rights problems, develops and codifies new international norms and monitors the observance of human rights around the world. As the principal intergovernmental policy-making body for human rights at the United Nations, the Commission is authorized to discuss human rights situations anywhere in the world and to examine information from states, NGOs and other sources.

The Commission provides a forum for states, intergovernmental organizations and NGOs to voice their concerns about human rights issues. Made up of 53 Member States elected for three-year terms, the Commission meets for six weeks each year in Geneva. States as well as NGOs present information on situations of concern to them; the governments involved often submit replies. In light of the examination of such situations, fact-finding groups or experts may be designated, on-the-spot visits may be organized, discussions with governments pursued, assistance provided and violations condemned.

If a particular situation is deemed sufficiently serious, the Commission may order an investigation by either a group of independent experts (Working Group) or an individual (Special Rapporteur/Representative). Based on information received from these experts, the Commission then calls upon the government concerned to bring about needed changes.

In 1947, the Commission on Human Rights established the **Subcommission on the Promotion and Protection of Human Rights** (formerly the Subcommission on Prevention of Discrimination and Protection of Minorities). Meeting annually, it consists of 26 experts who serve in their personal capacity, not as state representatives. Originally dedicated to the issues of discrimination and minority protection, the Subcommission has over the years greatly expanded its scope of concern to cover a broad range of human rights issues. It has initiated many studies, particularly on the development of legal rules, and makes recommendations to the Commission on Human Rights. NGOs take part in the work of the Subcommission.

Three major Working Groups function under the Subcommission: on Indigenous Populations, on Contemporary Forms of Slavery and on Minorities.

## High Commissioner for Human Rights

The **United Nations High Commissioner for Human Rights** is the United Nations official with principal responsibility for United Nations human rights activities. Appointed for a four-year term, the High Commissioner is charged with many tasks, including: promoting and protecting the effective enjoyment by all of all human rights; promoting international cooperation for human rights; stimulating and coordinating action on human rights in the United Nations system; assisting in developing new human rights standards; and promoting ratification of human rights treaties. The High Commissioner is also mandated to respond to serious violations of human rights and to undertake action to prevent violations.

The current High Commissioner is Mary Robinson, former President of Ireland. Under the direction and authority of the Secretary-General, the High Commissioner reports on her activities to the Commission on Human Rights and through ECOSOC to the General Assembly. In her work to secure respect for human rights and prevent violations, the High Commissioner engages in a dialogue with governments. Within the United Nations system, she works to strengthen and streamline the United Nations human rights machinery to make it more efficient and effective.

The **Office of the High Commissioner for Human Rights (OHCHR)** (*see also Chapter 1, page 44*) is the focal point for United Nations human rights activities and serves as the secretariat for the Commission on Human Rights, the treaty bodies (expert committees monitoring treaty compliance) and other United Nations human rights organs. It also undertakes human rights field activities, and provides advisory services and technical assistance (*see box*). In addition to the regular budget, some of its activities are financed through voluntary or trust funds.

The High Commissioner has taken concrete steps to institutionalize cooperation and coordination with other United Nations bodies involved in human rights, such as the United Nations Children's Fund (UNICEF), the United Nations Educational, Scientific and Cultural Organization (UNESCO), the United Nations Development Programme (UNDP), the Office of the United Nations High Commissioner for Refugees (UNHCR) and the United Nations Volunteers. Similarly, the Office works in the area of peace and security in close cooperation with the Departments of the United Nations Secretariat. The Office is part of the Inter-agency Standing Committee, which oversees the international response to humanitarian emergencies (*see Chapter 5, page 248*).

### Field presence

A priority of the United Nations human rights programme is the realization of human rights in practical terms. Accordingly, OHCHR is carrying out field activities in close to 30 countries, involving more than 200 officials. In addition to technical assistance, field offices often carry out monitoring and protection functions, such as information gathering, investigation of human rights situations and report of violations. This field presence also contributes to strengthening national capacities in human rights legislation, administration and education, helping governments take corrective measures when needed.

### Education and information

For the United Nations, education is a fundamental human right and one of the most effective instruments for human rights promotion. Human rights education, whether in formal or non-formal settings, seeks to advance a universal culture of human rights through innovative teaching methods, the spreading of knowledge and the modification of attitudes.

The **United Nations Decade for Human Rights Education (1995-2004)** seeks to increase global awareness and foster a universal culture of human rights. It has already led some 40 countries to promote human

# Technical cooperation programme

Since human rights are best protected when they are rooted in the local culture, the United Nations has increased its efforts to promote and protect human rights at the national and local level. International human rights norms cannot be applied unless they are incorporated in national legislation and supported by national institutions.

Many obstacles at the national level still hinder the universal enjoyment of human rights. Various Member States do not have the infrastructure that would allow them to effectively promote and protect the rights of their citizens. This is particularly true of countries that are just recovering from deadly civil wars.

The United Nations has therefore strengthened its advisory services to governments and expanded its technical cooperation programmes in the wider framework of promoting democracy, development and human rights, and strengthening the capacity of states to advance such rights in their laws and practice.

The Programme of Technical Cooperation for Human Rights, supervised by the Office of the High Commissioner, manages some 200 projects annually in some 50 countries. They are carried out mainly in developing countries and countries in transition towards democracy, which request the Office's expertise to establish national human rights structures. The Programme, with an annual budget of some $1.7 million, is financed by the United Nations regular budget as well as by voluntary contributions, which have totalled more than $20 million since 1987.

The Office helps governments to identify the different aspects of their human rights problems, and to define policies, especially by formulating and enacting broad national plans of action. Such plans define national priorities in human rights protection and promotion, set objectives and frames of reference, and involve human rights actors from both national institutions and NGOs.

The Office provides advice for enacting legislative reforms that affect the enjoyment of human rights, such as penal codes, prison regulations, judicial and legal practices, and freedom of expression and association. Detailed technical assistance is provided in incorporating international human rights standards in national laws and policies, and to establish national institutions promoting human rights, democracy and the rule of law. Among them are the Ombudsmen, who deal with complaints from individuals, and the National Commissions for Human Rights, which monitor the actions of the government and can help it to observe its human rights obligations under national accords for human rights protection.

In addition to national programmes, the Office carries out global or thematic programmes — such as human rights education, and training for peacekeeping forces.

---

rights education, among other things by including it in their school curricula. Various countries have adopted national action plans and involved national institutions in this effort.

A key source of human rights information is the OHCHR Web site (www.unhchr.ch).

## Promoting and protecting human rights

The role and scope of United Nations action in promoting and protecting human rights continue to expand, but the central mandate remains: to ensure that the human dignity of the ultimate constituents, the "peoples of the United Nations", in whose name the Charter was written, is fully respected. Through the international machinery, the United Nations is at work on many fronts:

- **As global conscience** — The United Nations has set a pace in establishing international standards of acceptable behaviour by nations, and kept the attention of the international community focused on human rights practices that threaten to undermine those standards. Human rights declarations and conventions are adopted by the General Assembly, underscoring their universality.
- **As lawmaker** — An unprecedented codification of international law has taken place. Those human rights pertaining to women, children, prisoners and detainees, and mentally disabled persons, as well as violations such as genocide, racial discrimination and torture, to name just a few, are now a major part of international law which at one time focused almost exclusively on relations between states.
- **As monitor** — The United Nations plays a central role in ensuring that human rights are not just defined in the abstract, but also put into practice. The International Covenants on Civil and Political Rights and on Economic, Social and Cultural Rights (1966) are among the earliest examples of treaties that empower international bodies to monitor how states live up to their commitments. Treaty bodies, Special Rapporteurs and Working Groups of the Commission on Human Rights (*see box, page 229*) each have procedures and mechanisms to monitor compliance with international standards and investigate allegations of violations. Their decisions on specific cases carry a moral weight that few governments are willing to defy.
- **As nerve-centre** — OHCHR receives communications from groups and individuals claiming violations of their human rights. More than 100,000 complaints are received per year. OHCHR refers these communications to the appropriate United Nations bodies and mechanisms, taking into account the implementation procedures established by conventions and resolutions. Requests

for urgent intervention can be addressed to OHCHR by fax (41 22 - 917 9003) and e-mail (webadmin.chr@unog.ch).

- **As defender** — When a Rapporteur or a chairman of a working group receives information that a serious human rights violation is about to be committed — such as torture or imminent extrajudicial execution — he or she addresses an urgent message to the state concerned, requesting clarification and appealing for guaranteeing the rights of the alleged victim. Such appeals are made in particular by the Special Rapporteurs on torture and on arbitrary executions, as well as the Working Groups on disappearances and on arbitrary detention.
- **As researcher** — The data compiled by the United Nations on human rights issues is indispensable to the development and application of human rights law. For example, several country studies provided the basis of an instrument being drafted to protect the rights of indigenous peoples. OHCHR prepares studies and reports requested by United Nations bodies on human rights issues, pointing the way towards policies, practices and new institutions which can enhance respect for human rights.
- **As forum of appeal** — Under the First Optional Protocol to the International Covenant on Civil and Political Rights, the International Convention on the Elimination of All Forms of Racial Discrimination, the Convention Against Torture and the Optional Protocol to the Convention on the Elimination of All Forms of Discrimination against Women, individuals can bring complaints against states that have accepted the appeal procedure, once all domestic remedies have been exhausted. Also, under procedures established by the Commission on Human Rights, the Commission itself, its Subcommission on the Promotion and Protection of Human Rights and their Working Groups hear numerous complaints annually submitted by NGOs or individuals.
- **As fact-finder** — The Commission on Human Rights has established mechanisms to monitor and report on the incidence of certain kinds of abuses, and on violations in a specific country. The mechanisms entrusted with this politically sensitive, humanitarian and sometimes dangerous task are **Special Rapporteurs/Representatives** or **Working Groups** (*see box*). They gather facts, keep contact with local groups and government authorities, conduct on-site visits when governments permit, and make recommendations on how respect for human rights might be strengthened.
- **As discreet diplomat** — The Secretary-General and the High Commissioner for Human Rights confidentially raise human rights concerns with Member States on items such as the release of pris-

# Special Rapporteurs and Working Groups

The Special Rapporteurs and Working Groups on human rights are on the front lines of human rights protection, investigating violations and intervening in individual cases and emergency situations.

These independent human rights experts and groups of experts are established by the Commission on Human Rights and the Economic and Social Council, and report to the Commission, the Council and the General Assembly. In preparing their reports, they use all resources, including individual communications and information from NGOs. Much of their research is done in the field, conducting interviews with both authorities and victims and gathering on-site evidence. They also utilize an urgent-action procedure to intercede with governments at the highest level (*see page 228*). Their reports are made public, thus contributing to publicize violations and the responsibility of governments.

These experts examine, monitor and publicly report on human rights situations in specific countries, or on major phenomena of human rights violations around the world.

- Country-specific Special Rapporteurs and Representatives currently report on Afghanistan, Burundi, Cambodia, Democratic Republic of the Congo, Equatorial Guinea, Haiti, Iran, Iraq, Myanmar, Palestinian occupied territories, Rwanda, Somalia, Sudan and former Yugoslavia. In addition, mandates have been entrusted to the Secretary-General to prepare reports on Cyprus, East Timor, Kosovo, and occupied Arab Territories.

- Thematic Special Rapporteurs, Representatives and Working Groups currently report on enforced or involuntary disappearances, summary executions, torture, arbitrary detention, racial discrimination, violence against women, the sale of children, religious intolerance, internally displaced persons, migrants, human rights defenders, freedom of expression, independence of the judiciary, restitution and compensation of victims, mercenaries, structural adjustment and foreign debt, extreme poverty, right to development, right to education, right to food, right to housing, and adverse effects of shipping and dumping toxic and dangerous products and wastes.

oners, commutation of death sentences and other issues. The Commission on Human Rights may ask the Secretary-General to intervene or send an expert to examine a human rights situation with a view to preventing flagrant violations. The Secretary-General also undertakes such efforts of quiet diplomacy in the exercise of his "good offices", thus helping establish the United Nations legitimate concern and curb abuses.

## Right to development

The recognition that grinding poverty and underdevelopment affect the enjoyment of human rights has long been part of the approach of the United Nations to human rights, reflected first in the Universal Declaration itself. The *Declaration on the Right to Development*, adopted by the General Assembly in 1986, marked a turning point in efforts to make this recognition a reality, and has had practical implications for the way in which national and international development policies are pursued.

In the Vienna Declaration, states attached a high priority to the right to development, and this is explicitly reflected in the mandate of the High Commissioner. The Commission on Human Rights in 1998 appointed an **Independent Expert on the Right to Development**. The Commission also established in 1998 a **Working Group** to monitor progress and develop strategies for implementing the right to development.

## The rights of labour

Defining and protecting the rights of labour is another major area of concern for the United Nations. One of the principal bodies of the **International Labour Organization (ILO)**, the tripartite **International Labour Conference** — which is made up of government, employer and worker representatives — has set international standards through a series of conventions and recommendations. Ratification by states creates binding obligations to put the provisions of these conventions into effect. Recommendations provide guidance on policy, legislation and practice.

Over the years, the governments of member states and their employers' and workers' organizations have built up a system of international standards in all work-related matters. Altogether, some 183 Conventions and 191 Recommendations have been adopted. While many are concerned with matters such as labour administration, industrial relations, employment policy, working conditions, social security, occupational safety and health, others relate to ensuring basic human rights in the workplace, and to issues such as the employment of women, children and special categories, such as migrant workers and the disabled.

ILO's supervisory procedure to ensure the application of its conventions in law and practice is the most advanced of all such international procedures. It is based on the objective evaluation by independent experts of the manner in which obligations are complied with, and on the examination of cases by the ILO's tripartite bodies.

There is a special procedure to investigate complaints of infringements of freedom of association.

The ILO has brought about many landmark conventions:

- *On Forced Labour* (1930): requires the suppression of forced or compulsory labour in all its forms;
- *On Freedom of Association and Protection of the Right to Organize* (1948): establishes the right of workers and employers to form and join organizations without prior authorization; lays down guarantees for the free functioning of such organizations;
- *On Right to Organize and Collective Bargaining* (1949): provides for protection against anti-union discrimination, for protection of workers' and employers' organizations, and for measures to promote collective bargaining;
- *On Equal Remuneration* (1951): calls for equal pay and benefits for work of equal value;
- *On Discrimination* (1958): calls for national policies to promote equality of opportunity and treatment, and to eliminate discrimination in the workplace on grounds of race, colour, sex, religion, political opinion, extraction or social origin;
- *On Minimum Age* (1973): aiming at the abolition of child labour, it stipulates that the minimum age for employment shall not be less than the age of completion of compulsory schooling;
- *On Worst Forms of Child Labour* (1999): prohibits child slavery, debt bondage, prostitution and pornography, dangerous work, and forcible recruitment for armed conflict.

In addition, the General Assembly has taken a number of measures to protect the rights of migrant workers (*see page 240, below*).

## The struggle against discrimination

### Apartheid

One of the great successes that demonstrated the ways in which the United Nations can bring an end to major injustices in the world is its role in the abolition of South Africa's apartheid rule. Practically from its inception, the United Nations was involved in the struggle against apartheid, a system of institutionalized racial segregation and discrimination imposed by the South African government.

When, in 1994, the newly elected President of South Africa, Nelson Mandela, addressed the General Assembly, he observed that it was the first time in its 49 years that the Assembly had been addressed by a South African head of state drawn from among the African majority. Welcoming the vanquishing of apartheid, he said: "That historic change has come about not least because of the great efforts in which the United Nations engaged to ensure the suppression of the apartheid crime against humanity."

Condemned by the United Nations in 1966 as a "crime against humanity" incompatible with the Charter and the Universal Declaration of Human Rights, the issue of apartheid was on the agenda of the General Assembly from 1948 until the end of apartheid in 1994. During the 1950s, the General Assembly repeatedly appealed to the South African government to abandon apartheid in the light of the principles of the Charter.

- The United Nations Special Committee against Apartheid, established in 1962 by the General Assembly to keep the racial policies of South Africa under review, became the focal point in the efforts of the international community to promote a comprehensive programme of action against apartheid
- The General Assembly in 1973 adopted the *International Convention on the Suppression and Punishment of the Crime of Apartheid.*
- The Security Council instituted a voluntary arms embargo against South Africa in 1963, and made it mandatory in 1977 after determining that the country's aggressions against its neighbours and its potential nuclear capability constituted a threat to international peace and security — the first time the Council took such action against a Member State.
- The General Assembly called for a sports boycott of South Africa in 1971, a move which had a continuing impact on public opinion in South Africa and abroad, and adopted in 1985 the *International Convention Against Apartheid in Sports.*
- Among its many censures of South Africa, the General Assembly did not accept its credentials to the Assembly's regular sessions from 1970 through 1974, thereby refusing to allow the South African delegation to participate in its work. South Africa did not participate in further proceedings of the Assembly until the end of apartheid in 1994.
- In 1985, when the South African government proclaimed a state of emergency and escalated repression, the Security Council, for the first time, called on governments to take significant economic measures against South Africa under Chapter VII of the Charter.
- The transition from the apartheid government to a non-racial democracy, facilitated by a National Peace Accord between the government and major political parties in 1990, was fully supported

by the United Nations. Two Security Council resolutions in 1992 emphasized the involvement by the international community in facilitating the transition. To strengthen the structures of the peace accord, the Security Council in 1992 deployed the United Nations Observer Mission in South Africa (UNOMSA). The mission observed the 1994 elections that led to the establishment of a non-racial and democratic government. With the installation of the new government and the adoption of the first non-racial, democratic constitution, the apartheid system came to an end.

## Racism

In 1963, the General Assembly adopted the *United Nations Declaration on the Elimination of All Forms of Racial Discrimination*. The Declaration affirms the fundamental equality of all persons and confirms that discrimination between human beings on the grounds of race, colour or ethnic origin is a violation of the human rights proclaimed in the Universal Declaration and an obstacle to friendly and peaceful relations among nations and peoples.

Two years later, the General Assembly adopted the *International Convention on the Elimination of All Forms of Racial Discrimination*, which obliges states parties to adopt legislative, judicial, administrative and other measures to prevent and punish racial discrimination.

The General Assembly in 1993 proclaimed the **Third Decade to Combat Racism and Racial Discrimination (1993-2003)** and called on all states to take measures to combat new forms of racism, especially through laws, administrative measures, education and information.

Also in 1993, the Commission on Human Rights appointed a **Special Rapporteur on Contemporary Forms of Racism, Racial Discrimination, Xenophobia and Related Intolerance**. His mandate is to examine incidents worldwide of contemporary forms of racism; racial discrimination; any form of discrimination against blacks, Arabs and Muslims; xenophobia; anti-Semitism; and related intolerance, as well as governmental measures to overcome them.

As decided by the General Assembly, the third **World Conference against Racism, Racial Discrimination, Xenophobia and Related Intolerance** will be held in South Africa in 2001. It will focus on practical measures to eradicate racism, including measures of prevention, education and protection. Previous conferences were held in Geneva in 1978 and 1983.

# The rights of women

Equality for women has been a focus of the work of the United Nations since its founding in 1945 and the establishment of the Commission on the Status of Women in 1946 as a special body to deal with women's issues. The United Nations has been a staunch ally in the struggle to attain women's rights universally and the efforts to ensure that women have equal access to public life and to opportunities in all aspects of economic and social development (*see also Chapter 3, pages 178-181*).

In recent years, the organizations of the United Nations family have all undertaken reviews of their work to ensure that women are better represented in decision-making bodies and that their concerns are considered a central component of policies and programmes in the field. In addition, steps have been taken to ensure the advancement of women in the Organization itself.

**Commission on the Status of Women**. The **Commission on the Status of Women**, made up of 45 Member States, examines women's progress towards equality throughout the world, prepares recommendations on promoting women's rights in political, economic, social and educational fields, and addresses women's rights problems requiring immediate attention. It also drafts treaties and other instruments aimed at improving the status of women in law and in practice.

The activities of the Commission have evolved from defining rights to exploring factors that have prevented women from enjoying them. Thus, emphasis has shifted to the underlying social and cultural causes of gender discrimination. The Commission, for example, has elaborated the *Declaration on the Elimination of Violence against Women*, adopted by the General Assembly in 1993. The Declaration includes a clear definition of violence as being physical, sexual and psychological violence occurring in the family or the community and perpetrated or condoned by the state.

The Commission has facilitated international guidelines and law for the advancement of women, most notably the 1979 *Convention on the Elimination of Discrimination against Women* (*see Chapter 3, page 179*) and the 1999 *Protocol* to the Convention (*see page 221, above*)

**Women and development**. Through its operational bodies, the United Nations works to further the empowerment of women, particularly in regard to overall development efforts (*see Chapter 3, page 178*). In addition to the work done by the United Nations Secretariat, in

# Women's Conferences

United Nations conferences, combined with the energy of national women's movements, have galvanized understanding, interest and action concerning the advancement of women around the world.

Three world conferences — Mexico City, 1975; Copenhagen, 1980; and Nairobi, 1985 — greatly enhanced international awareness of the concerns of women and created invaluable links between national women's movements and the international community.

At the Fourth World Conference on Women (Beijing, 1995), representatives of 189 governments adopted the Beijing Declaration and Platform for Action, aimed at removing obstacles to women's participation in all spheres of public and private life. The Platform identifies 12 critical areas of concern:

- The persistent and increasing burden of poverty on women;
- Unequal access to and inadequate educational opportunities;
- Inequalities in health status, and unequal access to and inadequate health-care services;
- Violence against women;
- Effects of conflict on women;
- Inequality in women's participation in the definition of economic structures and policies and in the production process itself;
- Inequality in the sharing of power and decision-making;
- Insufficient mechanisms to promote the advancement of women;
- Lack of awareness of, and commitment to, internationally and nationally recognized women's human rights;
- Insufficient mobilization of mass media to promote women's contribution to society;
- Lack of adequate recognition and support for women's contribution to managing natural resources and safeguarding the environment;
- The girl child.

At the special session of the General Assembly in 2000 to follow up on the Conference, countries pledged additional initiatives — such as strengthening legislation against all forms of domestic violence, and enacting laws and policies to eradicate harmful practices such as early and forced marriage and female genital mutilation. Targets were set to ensure free compulsory primary education for both girls and boys, and to improve women's health through wider access to health care and prevention programmes.

---

particular the Division for the Advancement of Women, and the specialized agencies, funds and programmes, there are two entities dedicated exclusively to women: the **United Nations Development Fund for Women (UNIFEM)** and the **International Research and Training Institute for the Advancement of Women (INSTRAW)**.

Both were created to support programmes and projects that improve the quality of life for women (*see Chapter 3, pages 179-181*).

(*On women's rights, see* www.un.org/womenwatch).

## The rights of children

Millions of children die every year from malnutrition and disease. Countless others become victims of war and extreme forms of exploitation and abuse, such as sexual exploitation. The **United Nations Children's Fund (UNICEF)** (*see also Chapter 3, page 181*), the only United Nations agency mandated to advocate for children's rights, is striving to sustain global commitment to the *Convention on the Rights of the Child* (*see page 221, above*), which embodies universal ethical principles and international legal standards of behaviour towards children.

The General Assembly in 2000 adopted two *Optional Protocols* to the Convention: one prohibits the recruitment of children under 18 into armed forces or their participation in hostilities; the other strengthens prohibitions and penalties concerning the sale of children, child prostitution and child pornography.

The **Committee on the Rights of the Child**, established under the Convention, meets regularly to monitor the progress made by states parties in fulfilling their obligations. The Committee makes suggestions and recommendations to governments and to the General Assembly on the ways children's rights under the Convention may be met.

Regarding the problem of child labour, the goals of the United Nations are to protect working children from exploitation and hazardous conditions that endanger their physical and mental development, to ensure children's access to at least minimum levels of education, nutrition and health care, and, in the long term, to achieve the progressive elimination of child labour.

- The International Programme on the Elimination of Child Labour, an initiative of the **International Labour Organization (ILO)**, involves technical cooperation, as well as awareness raising and mobilization. Direct interventions focus on child labour prevention; search for alternatives, such as decent employment for parents of child workers; and rehabilitation, education and vocational training for children.
- UNICEF supports programmes providing education, counselling and care to children working in very hazardous conditions — as sex slaves or as domestic workers — and vigorously advocates against the violation of their rights;

- The General Assembly has urged governments to take action on the problem of street children, who are increasingly involved in and affected by crime, drug abuse, violence and prostitution.
- The Subcommission on the Promotion and Protection of Human Rights has called for steps to halt the recruitment or conscription of children into armed forces. The Secretary-General's **Special Representative for Children and Armed Conflict** (*see Chapter 5, page 250*) works to enhance child protection during conflicts.
- The Commission on Human Rights has appointed a **Special Rapporteur on the Sale of Children, Child Prostitution and Child Pornography**.

## The rights of minorities

A well-defined interest has emerged in issues affecting minorities as ethnic, racial and religious tensions have escalated, threatening the economic, social and political fabric of countries. Meeting the aspirations of national, ethnic, religious and linguistic groups and ensuring the rights of persons belonging to minorities acknowledges the equality of all individuals, furthers their participation in society and helps to reduce social tensions.

The United Nations has from its inception placed minority rights high on its human rights agenda. The protection of the human rights of members of minorities is guaranteed in the principle of non-discrimination, which is basic to all United Nations human rights law, and specifically in the International Covenant on Civil and Political Rights.

The adoption in 1992 by the General Assembly of the *Declaration on the Rights of Persons Belonging to National or Ethnic, Religious and Linguistic Minorities* gave a new impetus to United Nations work, and in 1995 the Commission on Human Rights approved the establishment by its Subcommission of a **Working Group on Minorities**. The Working Group recommends practical measures for the better promotion and protection of the rights of persons belonging to minorities.

## Indigenous peoples

The United Nations has increasingly taken up the cause of indigenous people, who are considered one of the world's most disadvantaged groups. Indigenous peoples are also called "first peoples", tribal peoples, aboriginals and autochthons. There are at least 5,000 indigenous groups, made up of 300 million people, living in over 70 countries on five continents. Excluded from decision-making processes, many have been marginalized, exploited, forcefully assimilated and subjected to repression, torture and murder when they speak out in defence of their rights. Fearing persecution, they often become refugees and sometimes must hide their identity, abandoning their languages and traditional customs.

In 1982, the Subcommission of the Commission on Human Rights established a **Working Group on Indigenous Populations**. The Group reviews developments pertaining to the rights of indigenous peoples and promotes international standards concerning their rights. The Group prepared a draft *Declaration on the Rights of Indigenous Peoples* for eventual adoption by the General Assembly. The draft is now being considered by the Commission.

In 2000, ECOSOC established the **Permanent Forum on Indigenous Issues** as a subsidiary organ. The 16-expert forum, composed of an equal number of government and indigenous experts, will advise ECOSOC, help to coordinate United Nations activities, and discuss indigenous concerns relating to development, culture, the environment, health and human rights.

The 1992 Earth Summit heard the collective voice of indigenous peoples as they expressed their concerns about the deteriorating state of their lands and the environment. UNDP, UNICEF, IFAD, UNESCO, the World Bank and WHO all have programmes directed at specific indigenous groups working to improve health and literacy and combat environmental degradation of their native lands.

At the conclusion of the International Year of the World's Indigenous People (1993), the Assembly proclaimed the **International Decade of the World's Indigenous People (1995-2004)**, which aims at fostering partnerships to improve the living conditions of indigenous people.

### Persons with disabilities

More than 500 million persons — 8 per cent of the world's population, an estimated 80 per cent of them living in the developing world — suffer from some type of physical, mental or sensory impairment.

Persons with disabilities are often excluded from the mainstream of society. Discrimination takes various forms, ranging from the denial of education opportunities to more subtle forms, such as segregation and isolation through the imposition of physical and social barriers. Society also suffers, since the loss of the enormous potential of persons with disabilities impoverishes humankind. Changing the perception and concept of disability involves both changes in values and increased understanding at all levels of society.

Since its inception, the United Nations has sought to advance the status of persons with disabilities and to improve their lives. United Nations concern for the well-being and rights of persons with disabilities is rooted in its founding principles, which are based on human rights, fundamental freedoms and equality of all human beings.

In the 1970s, the concept of human rights for persons with disabilities gained wider international acceptance. The General Assembly adopted in 1971 the *Declaration on the Rights of Mentally Retarded Persons*, and in 1975 the *Declaration on the Rights of Disabled Persons*, which sets the standards for equal treatment and access to services accelerating their social integration.

The International Year of Disabled Persons (1981) led to the adoption by the General Assembly of the *World Programme of Action Concerning Disabled Persons*, a policy framework for promoting the rights of persons with disabilities. The Programme identifies two goals for international cooperation: equality, and full participation of persons with disabilities in social life and development.

A major outcome of the United Nations Decade of Disabled Persons (1983-1992) was the adoption by the General Assembly in 1993 of the *Standard Rules on the Equalization of Opportunities for Persons with Disabilities*. The Rules serve as an instrument for policy-making and as a basis for technical and economic cooperation.

A new set of standards for the protection of people with mental illness — the *Principles for the protection of persons with mental illness and the improvement of health care* — was adopted by the Assembly in 1991.

The Assembly in 1994 endorsed a long-term strategy to further the implementation of the *World Programme of Action*, with the goal of "a society for all". Accessibility, employment, and social services and social safety nets are the priority policy issues set forth by the Assembly in 1997.

**United Nations activities**. A growing body of data suggests the need to address disability issues in the context of national development, within the broad human rights framework. The United Nations works with governments, NGOs, academic institutions and professional societies to promote awareness and build national capacities for broad human rights approaches to persons with disabilities.

The growing public support for disability action has highlighted the need to build national capacities for improved information services, outreach and institutional mechanisms to promote equalization of opportunities. The United Nations has been increasingly involved in helping countries strengthen their national capacities to promote disability action in their overall development plans (*for further information, see* www.un.org/esa/socdev/disabled).

## Migrant workers

With increasing movement of people across international frontiers in search of work, a new human rights convention was approved to curb discrimination against migrant workers. In 1990, following 10 years of negotiations, the *International Convention on the Protection of the Rights of All Migrant Workers and Members of Their Families* was adopted by the General Assembly.

- The Convention covers the rights of both documented and undocumented migrant workers and their families;
- Makes it illegal to expel migrant workers on a collective basis or to destroy their identity documents, work permits or passports;
- Entitles migrant workers to receive the same remuneration, social benefits and medical care as nationals; to join or take part in trade unions; and, upon ending their employment, to transfer earnings, savings and personal belongings;
- Grants children of migrant workers the right to registration of birth and nationality and of access to education.

As of 2000, the Convention had not yet acquired the necessary number of ratifications (20) to enter into force.

## Administration of justice

The United Nations has taken many steps to strengthen the protection of human rights in the judicial process. When individuals are under investigation by state authorities, when they are arrested, detained, charged, tried or imprisoned, there is always the need to ensure that the application of the law shows due regard for human rights protection.

The United Nations has worked to develop standards and codes to serve as models for national legislation, covering matters such as the treatment of prisoners, the protection of detained juveniles, the use of firearms by police, the conduct of law-enforcement officials, the role of lawyers and prosecutors, and the independence of the judiciary. Many of these standards have been developed through the United Nations Commission on Crime Prevention and Criminal Justice and the Centre for International Crime Prevention (*see Chapter 3, pages 189-190*).

The OHCHR has a programme of technical assistance focusing on human rights training for legislators, judges, lawyers, law enforcement officers, prison officials and the military.

## Future priorities

Despite the work of the United Nations, there continue to be massive and widespread violations of human rights. Five decades after the Universal Declaration of Human Rights was adopted, violations across the broad spectrum of human rights continue to dominate news from around the world. At least part of this can be attributed to the heightened awareness of human rights and the stepped-up monitoring of problem areas, particularly child abuse, violence against women, and abuses that until only recently were considered acceptable behaviour by traditional standards.

Indeed, measures to promote and protect human rights are stronger than ever, and increasingly linked to the fight for social justice, economic development and democracy. In his reform programme for the United Nations, Secretary-General Kofi Annan declared that human rights would be the cross-cutting theme in the multifaceted work of the Organization, thus highlighting the central role their promotion and protection would play in all its policies and programmes. Human rights are increasingly becoming part of the daily operations of the United Nations in the field. The vigorous action of the High Commissioner for Human Rights, and steps taken to enhance cooperation and coordination among United Nations partners, are expressions of the concrete efforts under way to strengthen the ability of the United Nations system to fight for human rights.

*(For further information, see* www.unhchr.ch*).*

# PART TWO

## Chapter 5

## Humanitarian Action

# HUMANITARIAN ACTION

Since it first coordinated humanitarian relief operations in Europe following the devastation and massive displacement of people in the Second World War, the United Nations has been relied on by the international community to respond to natural and man-made disasters that are beyond the capacity of national authorities alone. Today, the Organization is a major provider of emergency relief and longer-term assistance, a catalyst for action by governments and relief agencies, and an advocate on behalf of people struck by emergencies.

In the last decade, civil wars have become a central cause of emergency situations. In 1999 alone, millions were uprooted from their homes by war — 1.2 million in Angola, 850,000 in Kosovo, 750,000 in Ethiopia and Eritrea, 550,000 in East Timor, 200,000 in Chechnya and countless more in other conflicts around the world.

Natural disasters — floods, droughts, storms and earthquakes — killed more than 50,000 people and caused economic losses exceeding $90 billion in 1998, the latest year for which information is available. The figure for that year alone exceeds the disaster costs for the entire 1980s. More than 90 per cent of all disaster victims live in developing countries — a striking indicator of the degree to which poverty, population pressures and environmental degradation exacerbate suffering and destruction.

Confronted with renewed conflict and the escalating human and financial costs of natural disasters, the United Nations has been engaged on two fronts. On one hand it has sought to bring immediate relief to the victims, primarily through its operational agencies; on the other hand, it has sought more effective strategies to prevent emergencies from arising in the first place.

When disaster strikes, the United Nations and its agencies rush to deliver humanitarian assistance. In 2000 alone, the Office for the Coordination of Humanitarian Affairs launched 16 inter-agency appeals that raised more than $1.4 billion to assist 35 million people in 16 countries and regions. The Office of the United Nations High Commissioner for Refugees has been providing international protection and assistance to over 22 million people annually — refugees as well as a growing number of internally displaced persons. The World Food Programme has regularly delivered one third of the world's emergency food assistance, saving millions of lives.

*Disaster prevention* seeks to reduce the vulnerability of societies to disaster, and to address their man-made causes. Early warning is especially important for short-term prevention, and United Nations agencies are increasing their capacity in this area: the Food and Agriculture Organization monitors impending famines, while the World Meteorological Organization carries out tropical cyclone forecasting and drought monitoring. Preparedness is equally vital, and the United Nations Development Programme assists disaster-prone countries in developing contingency planning and other preparedness measures.

*Conflict prevention* (*see Chapter 2, page 70*) involves strategies such as preventive diplomacy, preventive disarmament and human rights promotion. Recent crises have illustrated dramatically the link between war and human rights abuses and refugee flows. Longer-term prevention strategies address the root causes of conflict in a comprehensive manner. They foster security, economic growth, good governance and respect for human rights—which remain the best protection against disaster, whether natural or, as is increasingly the case, man-made.

## Coordinating humanitarian action

The past decade has seen an upsurge in the number and intensity of civil wars. These have caused large-scale humanitarian crises— with extensive loss of life, massive displacements of people, and widespread damage to societies— in complicated political and military environments. To address these "complex emergencies", the United Nations has upgraded its capacity to respond quickly and effectively.

The General Assembly in 1991 established the **Inter-Agency Standing Committee** to coordinate the international response to humanitarian crises. The **United Nations Emergency Relief Coordinator** is the Organization's focal point for this endeavour, acting as the system's principal policy adviser, coordinator and advocate on issues pertaining to humanitarian emergencies. The Emergency Relief Coordinator heads the **Office for the Coordination of Humanitarian Affairs (OCHA)**, which coordinates United Nations assistance in humanitarian crises that go beyond the capacity and mandate of any single agency.

Many actors — governments, non-governmental organizations (NGOs), United Nations agencies — seek to respond simultaneously to complex emergencies. OCHA works with them to ensure that there is a coherent framework within which everyone can contribute promptly and effectively to the overall effort.

When an emergency strikes, OCHA coordinates the international response. It consults with the United Nations Country Team in the

## Responding to emergencies

Responding to emergencies and disasters requires rapid deployment of resources — human, financial and logistical. OCHA has developed mechanisms so that quick, appropriate responses are made to the needs on the ground.

A 24-hour Disaster Response System provides round-the-clock readiness for disasters: it monitors field situations to identify natural disasters, environmental emergencies and industrial accidents to help coordinate the actions of the international community.

United Nations Disaster Assessment and Coordination Teams permit rapid response to complex emergencies. Made up of specially trained national emergency management experts, as well as OCHA staff, the Teams can be deployed within hours to help the authorities assess the situation and coordinate relief.

When disaster occurs, OCHA coordinates the mobilization and deployment of military and civil protection assets — such as specialized personnel and disaster relief equipment — from countries and international organizations. OCHA maintains a Central Register of Disaster Management Capacities that may be available for international assistance. A warehouse in Pisa, Italy, stocks relief items ready for airlift.

In addition, United Nations Disaster Management Teams, consisting of country-level heads of the United Nations agencies under the leadership of the Resident Coordinator (usually from UNDP), have been established in many disaster-prone developing countries. Such teams make arrangements to coordinate relief activities in anticipation of an emergency.

In collaboration with international agencies and NGOs, the United Nations has helped launch programmes aimed at improving disaster preparedness in more than 70 countries.

---

country concerned and undertakes inter-agency consultations at Headquarters to reach agreement on the priorities for action. OCHA then provides support for the coordination of activities in the affected country.

The Office coordinates field missions by United Nations agencies to assess needs; helps to mobilize resources by launching consolidated inter-agency appeals; organizes donor meetings and follow-up arrangements; monitors the status of contributions in response to the appeals; and issues situation reports to keep donors and others updated on developments. On average, 27 inter-agency appeals are launched each year: they have raised over $12 billion for emergencies since 1992.

OCHA works with its partners in the humanitarian community to build a consensus around policies and to identify specific humanitarian issues arising from operational experience in the field. It tries to ensure that major humanitarian issues are addressed, including those that fall between the mandates of humanitarian organizations — such as the plight of internally displaced persons.

By advocating on humanitarian issues, OCHA gives voice to the silent victims of crises and ensures that the views and concerns of the humanitarian community are reflected in overall efforts towards recovery and peace-building. OCHA promotes greater respect for humanitarian norms and principles, and draws attention to specific issues, such as the access to affected populations, the humanitarian impact of sanctions, anti-personnel landmines and the unchecked proliferation of small arms.

OCHA's **Central Emergency Revolving Fund** is a cash-flow mechanism facilitating an immediate response to an emergency. It is used to help humanitarian agencies with cash-flow problems before donor contributions are available. The borrowing agency must reimburse the amount loaned within one year. Since 1992, the Fund has been used more than 50 times, with a total of over $127 million disbursed.

OCHA manages ReliefWeb, the world's foremost humanitarian web site, which provides the latest information on emergencies around the world *(see* www.reliefweb.int*)*.

## Providing assistance and protection

Four United Nations entities — UNHCR, WFP, UNICEF and UNDP— have primary roles in providing protection and assistance in humanitarian crises.

Children and women constitute the majority of refugees and displaced persons. In acute emergencies, the **United Nations Children's Fund (UNICEF)** works alongside other relief agencies to help re-establish basic services such as water and sanitation, set up schools, and provide immunization services, medicines and other supplies to uprooted populations.

UNICEF also consistently urges governments and warring parties to act more effectively to protect children. Its programmes in conflict zones have included the negotiation of ceasefires to facilitate the provision of services such as child immunization. To this end, UNICEF has pioneered the concept of "children as zones of peace" and created "days of tranquillity" and "corridors of peace" in war-affected regions. Special programmes assist traumatized children and help to reunite unaccompanied children with parents or extended families. In 1999, UNICEF provided humanitarian assistance in 39 countries.

The **United Nations Development Programme (UNDP)** is the agency responsible for coordinating activities for natural disaster mitigation, prevention and preparedness. When emergencies occur, UNDP Resident Coordinators coordinate relief and rehabilitation efforts at the national level. Often governments call on UNDP to help design rehabilitation programmes and to direct donor aid.

## Protecting children in war

In over 30 countries, more than 300,000 young persons under 18 are ruthlessly exploited as soldiers — some as young as seven or eight, girls as well as boys. Two million children have been killed in war and civil strife during the past decade, and 6 million have been maimed or disabled. Many others, orphaned by war or separated from their parents, have been traumatized by the struggle for survival. To tackle this tragedy:

- The Security Council has called for stronger efforts to end the use of children as soldiers. Peacekeeping operations, as part of their mandate, include the protection of children, and two new peacekeeping missions, in Sierra Leone and the Democratic Republic of the Congo, include civilian specialists in child protection.

- The Secretary-General's **Special Representative for Children and Armed Conflict**, Mr. Olara Otunnu, has been working since 1997 to increase global awareness of the impact of conflict on children, and to mobilize the political support of governments and civil society to strengthen child protection. He has been advocating key protective actions, such as placing the welfare of children on peace agendas and putting children's needs at the centre of recovery programmes after a conflict. Travelling to war zones, he has urged warring parties to adhere to a commitment to the security of children; not to target civilian sites such as schools and hospitals; and stop recruiting children under 18.

- UNICEF has long been working with governments and rebel movements to demobilize child soldiers, reunite them with their families and foster their social reintegration.

- The General Assembly in 2000 adopted a Draft Optional Protocol to the Convention on the Rights of the Child, under which states parties agree to raise the age limit for both compulsory recruitment and participation in combat from 15 to 18. In their Millennium Declaration, world leaders urged ratification and full implementation of the Convention and Protocol.

To ensure that relief programmes pave the way for development, UNDP and humanitarian agencies work together to integrate a concern for long-term development in their relief operations. UNDP supports programmes for the demobilization of former combatants, comprehensive mine action, the return and reintegration of refugees and internally displaced persons, and the restoration of the institutions of governance.

To ensure that the resources provided will have the greatest possible impact, each project is carried out in consultation with local and national government officials. This community-based approach has helped provide urgent but lasting relief for hundreds of thousands of victims of war or civil upheaval. Today, many conflict-scarred communities have improved their living standards thanks to training programmes, credit schemes and infrastructure projects.

## Protecting the protectors

Attacks against United Nations personnel and other humanitarian workers have increased dramatically in the last few years, with scores of staff members killed, taken hostage or detained while working in conflict areas.

Between 1992 and 2000, 198 civilian staff lost their lives in the line of duty and 228 were taken hostage or kidnapped while serving in United Nations operations worldwide. In 1999 alone, 16 civilians lost their lives; in the same year, 292 violent incidents were reported, including armed robbery, assault and rape.

Condemning such attacks, the Security Council has stressed that the responsibility for the safety of United Nations staff rests with host countries and warring parties. The 1994 Convention on the Safety of United Nations and Associated Personnel obliges the governments of countries where the United Nations is at work to safeguard its staff, and to take preventive measures against murders and abductions. United Nations officials hope to classify attacks against United Nations and humanitarian personnel as war crimes prosecutable by the International Criminal Court. In 2000, the General Assembly authorized increased resources enabling the Organization to take immediate steps to strengthen its security management system.

---

On the **Office of the United Nations High Commissioner for Refugees (UNHCR)**, see *Protection and assistance to refugees*, below.

In emergencies, the **World Food Programme (WFP)** provides fast, efficient, self-sustaining relief to millions of people who are victims of natural or man-made disasters, including refugees and the internally displaced. Such crises consume most of WFP's resources. A decade ago, two out of three tons of the food aid provided by WFP was used to help people become self-reliant. Today, the picture is reversed, with 80 per cent of WFP resources going to victims of man-made disaster.

In 1999, WFP assisted 29 million internally displaced people, refugees and returnees, and 41 million victims of natural disaster. The agency is responsible for mobilizing food and funds for transport for all large-scale refugee-feeding operations managed by UNHCR.

WFP is increasingly involved in projects using food aid to support demobilization of ex-combatants and demining of war zones. After war or disaster strikes, WFP moves in with reconstruction and rehabilitation projects aimed at repairing the damaged infrastructure.

The majority of those affected by disasters live in rural areas. The **Food and Agriculture Organization of the United Nations (FAO)** is the lead agency in providing early warning of impending food crises and assessing food supply problems throughout the world.

FAO's Global Information and Early Warning System provides regular and updated information on the global food situation. It also carries out assessments of the food situation in food-insecure countries due to man-made or natural disasters.

Based on assessments made in collaboration with WFP, emergency operations for food aid are prepared and jointly approved by FAO and WFP. FAO provides agricultural inputs for rehabilitating food production and gives technical advice in agricultural emergencies. Its Special Relief Operations Service provides considerable support to disaster-stricken farmers.

The assistance programmes of the **World Health Organization (WHO)** focus on assessing the health needs of those affected by emergencies and disaster, providing health information and assisting in coordination and planning. WHO carries out emergency programmes in areas such as nutritional and epidemiological surveillance, control of epidemics (including HIV/AIDS), immunizations, management of essential drugs and medical supplies, reproductive health and mental health. WHO makes special efforts to eradicate polio and to control malaria in countries affected by emergencies.

## International protection and assistance to refugees

Throughout 1999, the **Office of the United Nations High Commissioner for Refugees (UNHCR)** (*see also Chapter 1, page 40*) provided international protection and assistance to some 22 million people who had fled war or persecution. Of these, some 17 million were refugees and returnees, and some 4.6 million were internally displaced persons. Internal conflicts have become the main cause of refugee crises.

UNHCR has been the lead humanitarian agency during the conflicts in the Balkans, which produced the largest refugee flows in Europe since the Second World War (*see Chapter 2, page 104*). It was the lead agency in addressing the massive exoduses out of Kosovo and East Timor in 1999. It has also been assisting refugees, displaced people and returnees in Africa's Great Lakes region and other parts of the continent, and in south-west Asia.

Refugees are defined as those who have fled their countries because of a well-founded fear of persecution for reasons of their race, religion, nationality, political opinion or membership in a particular social group, and who cannot or do not want to return.

# Refugees in their own country

Internally displaced persons (IDPs) are people who have been forced to flee their homes to escape war, generalized violence, human rights violations or natural and man-made disasters, and who have not crossed an international border. Civil wars have created large groups of internally displaced all over the world. Today, there are an estimated 20 to 25 million internally displaced — more than the number of refugees.

Primary responsibility for internally displaced people lies first and foremost with national governments. But at times governments are unable — or unwilling — to meet their responsibilities.

Refugees usually find in a second country a place of safety, food and shelter. They are protected by a well-defined body of international laws and conventions, and are assisted by UNHCR and other organizations. The internally displaced often face far more insecure conditions. They may be trapped in an ongoing internal conflict, at the mercy of warring parties that make the provision of relief hazardous and sometimes impossible. The government, which may view them as "enemies of the state", retains ultimate control over their fate. There are no specific international conventions to cover them and, until recently, donors have been reluctant to intervene in internal conflicts to help them.

The needs of internally displaced persons are similar to those of refugees: they need immediate protection and assistance, as well as long-term solutions, such as return or resettlement.

Effective coordination is particularly important in assisting the internally displaced, since there is no single international lead agency. Work in this area is carried out jointly by the International Committee of the Red Cross, UNHCR, OCHA, the Secretary-General's Representative for Internally Displaced Persons and the Office of the United Nations High Commissioner for Human Rights.

The Secretary-General's Representative, Mr. Francis M. Deng, has issued guiding principles on the internally displaced, which define who they are, outline a large body of  international law protecting a person's basic rights, and set out the responsibility of states. The principles have been accepted by more and more states.

UNHCR has been called to assist an estimated 4.6 million internally displaced in various regions. Increasingly — in the former Yugoslavia, East Timor, Colombia and Chechnya — UNHCR has decided to assist all uprooted people on the basis of humanitarian needs, rather than refugee status.

Notwithstanding these efforts, many internally displaced remain without humanitarian assistance or protection, underlining the selective, uneven, and in many cases inadequate response of national authorities and the international community, and the need to find more effective ways to help the internally displaced.

The legal status of refugees is defined in two international treaties, the 1951 *Convention relating to the Status of Refugees* and its 1967 *Protocol*, which spell out their rights and obligations. As of December 2000, 137 states were parties to one or both treaties.

UNHCR's most important function is international protection — trying to ensure respect for refugees' basic human rights, including their ability to seek asylum, and ensure that no one is returned involuntarily to a country where he or she has reason to fear persecution. Other types of assistance include:

- help during major emergencies involving the movement of large numbers of refugees;
- regular programmes in such fields as education, health and shelter;
- assistance to promote the self-sufficiency of refugees and their integration in host countries;
- voluntary repatriation;
- resettlement in third countries for refugees who cannot return to their homes and who face protection problems in the country where they first sought asylum.

Although UNHCR's mandate is to protect and assist refugees, it has been called upon more and more to come to the aid of a wider range of people living in refugee-like situations. They include people displaced within their own countries; former refugees who may need UNHCR monitoring and assistance once they have returned home; stateless people; and people who receive temporary protection outside their home countries, but who do not receive the full legal status of refugees. Today, refugees comprise just over half of the people of concern to UNHCR.

Asylum seekers are persons who have left their countries of origin and have applied for recognition as refugees in other countries, and whose applications are still pending. UNHCR is currently assisting 1.2 million people in this category. The largest groups of asylum seekers are living in industrialized countries.

Most refugees want to return home as soon as circumstances permit, and UNHCR is currently assisting 2.6 million returnees. One of the most successful repatriation operations was the return of over 1.7 million refugees to Mozambique following a peaceful settlement of the civil war in 1993 (*see Chapter 2, page 83*). In 1999, the largest repatriation movements assisted by UNHCR were to Kosovo (751,400), Afghanistan (252,700), East Timor (127,500) and Liberia (94,900).

# People in flight

## Number of people of concern to UNHCR*

Total:       22.2 million

By region:
| | |
|---|---|
| Africa | 6.2 million |
| Asia | 7.3 million (Afghanistan, 2.6 million) |
| Europe | 7.3 million (former Yugoslavia, 2.9 million) |
| Latin America and Caribbean | 0.1 million |
| North America | 1.2 million |
| Oceania | 0.08 million |

Some 3.7 million Palestinians, who are assisted by UNRWA, are not included. However, Palestinians outside the UNRWA area of operations, such as those in Iraq or Libya, are of concern to UNHCR.

*Includes refugees, asylum seekers, returnees, displaced people and others of concern as of 1 January 2000. Source: UNHCR

However, the sudden return of large numbers of people can quickly overwhelm fragile economic and social infrastructures. To ensure that returnees can rebuild their lives after they go back home, UNHCR works with a range of organizations to facilitate reintegration. This requires emergency assistance for those in need, development programmes for the areas that have been devastated and job-creation schemes.

The links between peace, stability, security, respect for human rights and sustainable development are increasingly seen as crucial in the search for durable solutions to the refugee problem.

## Palestine refugees

The **United Nations Relief and Works Agency for Palestine Refugees in the Near East (UNRWA)** has been providing education, health, relief and social services to Palestine refugees since 1950 (*see Chapter 1, page 43*). The General Assembly created UNRWA to provide emergency relief to some 750,000 Palestine refugees who had lost their homes and livelihoods as a result of the 1948 Arab-Israeli conflict (*see Chapter 2, page 95*). By 2000, UNRWA was providing essential services to more than 3.7 million registered Palestine refugees in Jordan, Lebanon, the Syrian Arab Republic, and the West Bank and Gaza Strip.

UNRWA's humanitarian role has been reinforced by recurrent conflicts in the Middle East, such as the civil war in Lebanon and the Palestinian uprising (*intifada*) *(see Chapter 2, pages 97-98)*.

Education is UNRWA's largest area of activity, accounting for half of its regular budget and two-thirds of its staff. Its 647 elementary and junior secondary schools accommodated more than 468,000 pupils in the 1999/2000 school year, while the eight UNRWA vocational training centres had over 4,600 trainees.

The Agency's network of 122 health centres handled 7.1 million patient visits in 1999. Environmental health services were provided to the 1.2 million refugees living in 59 refugee camps.

Some 205,000 people received special hardship assistance in 1999, which sought to ensure minimum standards of nutrition and shelter and to promote self-reliance through poverty-alleviation programmes. The income-generation programme in the West Bank and Gaza Strip has provided more than 27,000 loans worth $41 million to small businesses and micro-enterprises, achieving a repayment rate approaching 100 per cent in the Gaza Strip.

UNRWA cooperates closely with the Palestinian Authority. After the 1993 accords between Israel and the Palestine Liberation Organization and the establishment of the Palestinian Authority in the West Bank and Gaza Strip (*see Chapter 2, page 98*), UNRWA started its *Peace Implementation Programme* to ensure that the benefits of the peace process were realized at the local level. The Programme has helped to upgrade infrastructure, create employment and improve socio-economic conditions in refugee communities throughout its area of operations. By the end of 1999, the Programme had received more than $181 million in contributions and pledges. The European Gaza Hospital, an initiative of the European Union and UNRWA, opened in 2000.

The international community considers UNRWA a stabilizing factor in the Middle East. The refugees themselves look upon UNRWA's programmes as a symbol of the international community's commitment to a solution of the Palestine refugee issue.

# PART TWO

## Chapter 6

# INTERNATIONAL LAW

Among the United Nations most pervasive achievements has been the development of a body of international law — conventions, treaties and standards — that play a central role in promoting economic and social development, as well as international peace and security. Many of the treaties brought about by the United Nations form the basis of the law governing relations among nations. While the United Nations work in this area does not always receive attention, it has a daily impact on the lives of people everywhere.

The United Nations Charter specifically calls on the Organization to help in the settlement of international disputes by peaceful means, including arbitration and judicial settlement (Art. 33), and to encourage the progressive development of international law and its codification (Art. 13). Over the years, the United Nations has sponsored over 500 multilateral agreements, which address a broad range of common concerns among states and are legally binding for the countries that ratify them.

In many areas, the United Nations legal work has been pioneering. It has been in the forefront of tackling problems as they take on an international dimension, providing the legal framework for protecting the environment, regulating migrant labour, curbing drug trafficking and combating terrorism, to mention a few.

This work continues today, with the United Nations providing input into the trend towards a greater centrality of international law in governing interaction across a wider spectrum of issues, such as human rights law and international humanitarian law.

## Judicial settlement of disputes

The primary United Nations organ for the settlement of disputes is the **International Court of Justice** (*see also Chapter 1, pages 13-14*). Since its founding in 1946, states have submitted 119 cases to it, and international organizations have requested 23 advisory opinions. Most cases have been dealt with by the full Court, but since 1981 four cases have been referred to special chambers at the request of the parties.

The World Court, as it is popularly known, has made scores of judgments on international disputes involving economic rights, rights of passage, the non-use of force, non-interference in the internal affairs of states, diplomatic relations, hostage-taking, the right of asylum and nationality. Countries bring such disputes before the Court in search of an impartial solution to their differences. By achieving a peaceful settlement on questions such as land frontiers, maritime boundaries and territorial sovereignty, the Court has often helped to prevent the escalation of disputes (*see also the Court's site at* www.icj-cij.org).

In a typical case of territorial rights, the Court in 1999 settled a sensitive frontier dispute between Botswana and Namibia, with a ruling both countries accepted. In 1994, after Nigerian forces clashed with Cameroonian police, Cameroon instituted proceedings against Nigeria in a sovereignty dispute over the oil-rich Bakassi peninsula, and then over the whole land and sea boundary. The case is still pending before the Court. In 1992, the Court settled a dispute between El Salvador and Honduras that had been in existence for nearly a century and had led to a short but bloody war in 1969. Another dispute was jointly referred to the Court by the Libyan Arab Jamahiriya and Chad. The Court ruled in 1994 that the division of territory was defined by a 1955 treaty between Libya and France; Libya then withdrew its forces from an area along its southern border with Chad.

Various cases have been referred to the Court against the background of conflict or political upheaval. In 1980, the United States brought a case arising from the seizure of its embassy in Tehran and the detention of its staff. The Court held that Iran must release the hostages, hand back the embassy and make reparation. However, before the Court could set the amount of reparation, the case was withdrawn following an agreement between the two countries. In 1989, Iran asked the Court to condemn the shooting down of an Iranian airliner by a United States warship, and to find the United States responsible to pay Iran compensation. The case was closed in 1996 following a compensation settlement.

In 1986, in a case brought by Nicaragua against the United States over the latter's support for Nicaragua's "contras", the Court found that the United States, by supporting the "contras" and laying mines outside Nicaraguan ports — acts that the Court held the United States could not justify on the basis of collective self-defence — had violated its international legal obligations not to intervene in the affairs of another state, not to use force against another state and not to infringe the sovereignty of another state. Accordingly, the Court decided that the United States had to make reparations. However, in 1991, before the amount of the reparation had been determined, Nicaragua requested that the case be dismissed.

In 1992, Libya brought two cases — one against the United Kingdom and one against the United States — concerning the interpretation or application of the Convention for the Suppression of Unlawful Acts against the Safety of Civil Aviation, arising out of the crash, in 1988, of Pan American flight 103 at Lockerbie, Scotland. The cases are still pending before the Court.

In 1993, Bosnia and Herzegovina brought a case against the Federal Republic of Yugoslavia concerning the application of the Convention on the Prevention and Punishment of the Crime of Genocide. The Court called upon the parties to prevent further commission of the crime of genocide and further aggravation of the dispute. In 1996, the Court rejected the objections to its jurisdiction raised by Yugoslavia; the case is still pending before the Court.

The Court in 1996 rejected objections by the United States to its jurisdiction in a case concerning the destruction of Iranian oil platforms by United States warships, and found that it had jurisdiction to consider some of Iran's claims.

States have often submitted questions of economic rights. For instance, a Chamber of the Court in 1989 rejected a claim for compensation put forward by the United States against Italy for the requisition of an Italian company owned by United States corporations. In 1995, in the context of a dispute over fisheries jurisdiction between Canada and the European Union, Spain instituted a case against Canada after the seizing on the high seas by Canada of a Spanish fishing trawler.

A recent case involving claims of environmental protection was brought by Hungary and Slovakia concerning a dispute over the validity of a 1997 treaty that they had concluded on the building of a barrage system on the Danube River. In 1997, the Court found both states in breach of their legal obligations, and called on them to carry out that treaty.

The Court's advisory opinions have dealt with, among other things, admission to United Nations membership, reparation for injuries suffered in the service of the United Nations, the territorial status of Western Sahara, and the expenses of certain peacekeeping operations. Two opinions, rendered in 1996 on the request of the General Assembly and the World Health Organization, concerned the legality of the threat or use of nuclear weapons (*see Chapter 2, page 112*)

In a 1971 advisory opinion requested by the Security Council, the Court stated that the continued presence of South Africa in Namibia was illegal and that South Africa was under obligation to withdraw its administration and end its occupation — clearing the way for the independence of Namibia (*see Chapter 7, page 280*).

## Development and codification of international law

The **International Law Commission** was established by the General Assembly in 1947 to promote the progressive development of international law and its codification. The Commission, which meets annually, is composed of 34 members elected by the General Assembly for five-year terms. Collectively, the members represent the world's principal legal systems, and serve as experts in their individual capacity, not as representatives of their governments. The work of the Commission covers a wide range of topics of international law regulating relations among states.

Most of the Commission's work involves the preparation of drafts on topics of international law. Some topics are chosen by the Commission, others are referred to it by the General Assembly. When the Commission completes work on a topic, the General Assembly usually convenes an international conference of plenipotentiaries to incorporate the draft into a convention, which is then opened to states to become parties, meaning that countries formally agree to be bound by its provisions. Some of these conventions form the very foundation of the law governing relations among states. For example:

- The *Convention on the Non-navigational Uses of International Watercourses*, adopted by the General Assembly in 1997, which regulates the equitable and reasonable utilization of watercourses shared by two or more countries;
- The *Convention on the Law of Treaties between States and International Organizations or between International Organizations*, adopted at a conference in Vienna in 1986;
- The *Convention on the Succession of States in Respect of State Property, Archives and Debts*, adopted at a conference in Vienna in 1983;
- The *Convention on the Prevention and Punishment of Crimes against Internationally Protected Persons, including Diplomatic Agents*, adopted by the General Assembly in 1973;
- The *Convention on the Law of Treaties*, adopted at a conference in Vienna in 1969;
- The *Conventions on Diplomatic Relations* (1961) and *on Consular Relations* (1963), adopted at conferences held in Vienna.

The Commission in 1999 adopted a draft declaration aimed at preventing people from becoming stateless in such situations as separation of a territory or dissolution of a state. The Commission is currently addressing such issues as the prevention of transboundary damage from hazardous activities; state responsibility; unilateral acts of states; the right to diplomatic protection; reservations to treaties; and jurisdictional immunities of states and their property. (*See also the Commission's website:* www.un.org/law/ilc/index.htm).

## International trade law

The **United Nations Commission on International Trade Law (UNCITRAL)** facilitates world trade by developing conventions, model laws, rules and legal guides designed to harmonize international trade law. Established by the General Assembly in 1966, the 36-nation body brings together representatives of the world's geographic regions and principal economic and legal systems.

UNCITRAL has become the core legal body of the United Nations system in the field of international trade law. The International Trade Law Branch of the United Nations Office of Legal Affairs serves as its secretariat.

Over its 32-year history, the Commission has developed widely accepted texts that are viewed as landmarks in various fields of law. These include the 1980 *United Nations Convention on Contracts for the International Sale of Goods*, the 1985 *UNCITRAL Model Law on International Commercial Arbitration*, the 1976 *UNCITRAL Arbitration Rules*, the 1980 *UNCITRAL Conciliation Rules*, the 1994 *UNCITRAL Model Law on Procurement of Goods, Construction and Services*, the 1996 *UNCITRAL Notes on Organizing Arbitral Proceedings* and the 1996 *Model Law on Electronic Commerce.*

Other notable texts include: the 1974 *Convention on the Limitation Period in the International Sale of Goods*; the 1978 *United Nations Convention on the Carriage of Goods by Sea* (*Hamburg Rules*); the 1988 *United Nations Convention on International Bills of Exchange and International Promissory Notes*; the 1988 *UNCITRAL Legal Guide on Drawing Up International Contracts for the Construction of Industrial Works*; the 1991 *United Nations Convention on the Liability of Operators of Transport Terminals in International Trade*; the 1992 *UNCITRAL Legal Guide on International Countertrade Transactions*; and the 1995 *United Nations Convention on Independent Guarantees and Standby Letters of Credit.*

In 1997, the Commission adopted the *UNCITRAL Model Law on Cross-Border Insolvency*, intended to assist states to improve their national insolvency legislation, so as to cope with the growing number of bankruptcies involving enterprises operating in more than one country.

Current work includes the preparation of a legislative guide on privately financed infrastructure projects, which will provide guidance to states preparing or updating legislation relevant to those projects; the preparation of uniform rules for electronic signatures; compilation and publication of Case Law on UNCITRAL Texts (CLOUT); and a draft convention on assignment in receivables financing, which will facilitate the availability of credit at lower cost.

## Environmental law

The United Nations has pioneered the development of international environmental law, brokering major treaties that have advanced environmental protection everywhere (*see also Chapter 3, pages 193-211*). The United Nations Environment Programme (UNEP) administers many of these treaties.

- The *International Convention to Combat Desertification in Those Countries Experiencing Serious Drought and/or Desertification, Particularly in Africa* (1994) seeks to promote international cooperation in taking action to combat desertification and mitigate the effects of drought.
- The *Convention on Biological Diversity* (1992) seeks to conserve biological diversity, promote the sustainable use of its components, and encourage equitable sharing of the benefits arising from the utilization of genetic resources. Its *Cartagena Protocol on Biosafety* (2000) makes it compulsory to clearly label exports of agricultural commodities that may contain genetically modified organisms, and allows governments to state whether or not they are willing to accept such imports.
- The *Framework Convention on Climate Change* (1992) and its *Kyoto Protocol* (1997) obligate states parties to reduce emissions of greenhouse gases causing global warming and related atmospheric problems.
- The *Basel Convention on the Control of Transboundary Movement of Hazardous Wastes and their Disposal* (1989) obligates states parties to reduce shipping and dumping of dangerous wastes across borders, to minimize the amount and toxicity generated by hazardous waste, and to ensure their environmentally sound management as close as possible to the source of generation. States parties in 1999 adopted a *Protocol* on liability and compensation resulting from cross-border movement of hazardous wastes.

- The *Vienna Convention for the Protection of the Ozone Layer* (1985), the *Montreal Protocol* (1987) and its *Amendments* seek to reduce damage to the ozone layer in the atmosphere, which shields life from the sun's harmful ultraviolet radiations.
- The 1979 *Convention on Long-range Transboundary Air Pollution* (*Acid Rain Convention*) and its *Protocols*, negotiated under the auspices of the United Nations Economic Commission for Europe (ECE), provide for the control and reduction of air pollution in Europe and North America.
- The *Rotterdam Convention on the Prior Informed Consent Procedure for Certain Hazardous Chemicals and Pesticides in International Trade* (1998) obligates exporters of a hazardous chemical or pesticide to provide to the importing country information on the substance's potential health and environmental dangers.

The 1971 *Convention on Wetlands of International Importance Especially as Waterfowl Habitat* obligates states parties to use wisely all wetlands under their jurisdiction. The 1972 *Convention Concerning the Protection of the World Cultural and Natural Heritage* obligates states parties to protect unique natural and cultural areas. Both were promoted by the United Nations Educational, Scientific and Cultural Organization (UNESCO).

The International Maritime Organization (IMO) has promoted conventions that have helped to reduce marine pollution (*see page 204*).

## Law of the sea

The *United Nations Convention on the Law of the Sea* is considered one of the most comprehensive instruments of international law. This landmark treaty provides the framework for all aspects of ocean sovereignty, jurisdiction, use, and state rights, as well as obligations. It embodies in one instrument the codification of traditional rules for the uses of the oceans, as well as the development of new rules governing emerging concerns. It is a unique instrument, often referred to as a constitution for the oceans.

It is now universally accepted that any action in the area of ocean affairs and the law of the sea must be in conformity with the provisions of the Convention. This legal legitimacy is based on the near universal acceptance of the Convention — more than 130 states parties, numerous others in the process of ratification or accession, and nearly all, but a handful of states, which recognize and adhere to the Convention and its provisions.

The Convention covers all aspects of ocean space and its uses — navigation and overflight, resource exploration and exploitation, conservation and pollution, fishing and shipping. Its 320 articles and 9 annexes constitute a guide for behaviour by states in the world's oceans, defining maritime zones, laying down rules for delineating sea boundaries, assigning legal rights, duties and responsibilities, and providing machinery for the settlement of disputes.

## Impact of the Convention

States have consistently, through national and international legislation and through related decision-making, asserted the authority of the Convention as the pre-eminent international legal instrument in the field. Thus far, its major impact has been on the near universal acceptance of 12 nautical miles as the limit of the territorial sea, as well as coastal states' jurisdiction over the resources of an "exclusive economic zone" up to the limit of 200 nautical miles, and over the resources of the continental shelf extending beyond the limits of the zone. It has also brought stability in the area of navigation, either through the acceptance of the notion of innocent passage through the territorial sea, or transit passage through narrow straits used for international navigation.

The universal acceptance of the Convention was facilitated in 1994 with the adoption by the General Assembly of the *Agreement Relating to the Implementation of Part XI of the Convention*. The Agreement removed certain obstacles that had prevented mainly industrialized countries from signing on to it.

The Convention has been recognized for its impact on aspects affecting coastal state control over marine scientific research, prevention of pollution and access by landlocked states to and from the sea. Moreover, it is now recognized as the framework and foundation for any future instruments that seek to further define rights and obligations in the oceans — a fact that has been, for instance, reflected in the adoption of the 1995 *Agreement on Straddling Fish Stocks and Highly Migratory Fish Stocks* (*see Chapter 3, page 204*).

## Bodies established under the Convention

The Convention established three specific organs to deal with various aspects of the law of the sea.

The **International Seabed Authority** is the organization through which states parties organize and control activities relating to the deep seabed's mineral resources in the international seabed area, beyond the limits of national jurisdiction. Established in 1994, it is located in Kingston, Jamaica. The Authority has approved plans of work for exploration for a certain type of deep seabed minerals, which would be awarded in a contractual form to states or entities when the so-called "mining code" regulating exploration and exploitation has been approved.

The **International Tribunal for the Law of the Sea**, operational since 1996, is a forum for settling disputes arising out of the interpretation or application of the Convention. Made up of 21 judges elected by the states parties, it is located in the German seaport of Hamburg.

The **Commission on the Limits of the Continental Shelf** makes recommendations to states that claim a shelf extending beyond 200 miles from their coast. Based at United Nations Headquarters, it started its sessions in 1997. Its 21 members, elected by the states parties, serve in their personal capacity.

## Meeting of states parties

Although the Convention does not provide for regular meetings of a conference of states parties, the annual meeting of states parties, which is convened by the Secretary-General, has acted as a forum where issues of concern have been discussed. This is in addition to its assigned administrative functions, such as election of members of the Tribunal and the Commission, as well as other budgetary and administrative matters.

Oversight function of matters relating to ocean affairs and the law of the sea has been carried out by the General Assembly. But in 2000, the Assembly established an open-ended informal consultative process to facilitate its own annual review of developments. The consultative process, convened annually, is to make suggestions to the Assembly on particular issues, with an emphasis on identifying areas where coordination and cooperation among governments and agencies should be enhanced.

## International humanitarian law

International humanitarian law encompasses the principles and rules regulating the means and methods of warfare as well as the humanitarian protection of the civilian population, of sick and wounded combatants and of prisoners of war. Major instruments in this field include the 1949 *Geneva Conventions for the Protection of War Victims* and the two 1977 *Additional Protocols*, concluded under the auspices of the International Committee of the Red Cross.

In the last few years, the United Nations has taken a leading role in efforts to advance international humanitarian law. The Security

Council has become increasingly involved in protecting civilians in armed conflict, promoting human rights and protecting children in wars. The Council has also established two International Criminal Tribunals, for the Former Yugoslavia and for Rwanda, which have been contributing to humanitarian law. So have the preparations for the International Criminal Court, which have highlighted the need to put an end to impunity for perpetrators of genocide, war crimes and crimes against humanity.

The General Assembly, as a political forum of the United Nations, has contributed to elaborating a number of instruments. Among them are the 1948 *Convention on the Prevention and Punishment of the Crime of Genocide*, the 1968 *Convention on the Non-Applicability of Statutory Limitations to War Crimes and Crimes Against Humanity*, the 1980 *Convention on Prohibition and Restrictions on the Use of Certain Conventional Weapons which may be deemed to be Excessively Injurious or to have Indiscriminate Effects* and its four *Protocols*, and the *Principles of International Cooperation in the Detection, Arrest, Extradition and Punishment of Persons Guilty of War Crimes and Crimes Against Humanity*, which the Assembly adopted in 1973.

## International tribunals

Mass violations of international humanitarian law in the former Yugoslavia and in Rwanda (*see Chapter 2, pages 104 and 84*) led the Security Council to establish two international tribunals to prosecute persons responsible for such violation. Both tribunals were established under Chapter VII of the Charter, which deals with enforcement measures, and are subsidiary organs of the Security Council.

- The **International Criminal Tribunal for the Former Yugoslavia**, established in 1993, is composed of four chambers (three Trial Chambers and an Appeals Chamber), a Prosecutor and the Registry. Under its Statute, it can prosecute four kinds of offences: grave breaches of the Geneva Conventions; violations of the laws or customs of war; genocide; and crimes against humanity. The Tribunal is located in The Hague, the Netherlands.
- The **International Criminal Tribunal for Rwanda**, established in 1994, is composed of three Trial Chambers, a Prosecutor and the Registry. In 1998, the Tribunal handed down the first-ever conviction of genocide by an international court. The Tribunal is located in Arusha, Tanzania; the Office of the Prosecutor is in Kigali, Rwanda.

The Tribunals have a common Appeals Chamber and a common Prosecutor. They are engaged in a number of trial proceedings, and have indicted more than 120 alleged war criminals (*see also Chapter 1, page 35*).

In 2000, the Council started the process of establishing a similar court in Sierra Leone (*see Chapter 2, page 90*).

## International Criminal Court (ICC)

The idea of a permanent international court to prosecute crimes against humanity was first considered at the United Nations in the context of the adoption of the Genocide Convention of 1948. For many years, differences of opinions forestalled further developments. In 1992, the General Assembly directed the International Law Commission to prepare a draft Statute for the Court. The massacres in Cambodia, former Yugoslavia and Rwanda (*see Chapter 2*) made the need for it even more urgent.

The *Rome Statute of the International Criminal Court* was adopted at a plenipotentiary conference held in Rome in 1998; 120 countries voted in favour, 7 against and 21 abstained. It needs to be ratified by at least 60 countries before taking effect. By December 2000, 27 countries had ratified it.

The Statute calls for the establishment of a permanent International Criminal Court with power to investigate and bring to justice individuals who commit the most serious crimes of international concern, including genocide, crimes against humanity and war crimes. The Court will also have jurisdiction over the crime of aggression, once a provision is adopted defining it and setting out the conditions under which the Court shall exercise jurisdiction.

The Court is to be a permanent judicial body, with jurisdiction only over crimes committed by individuals. Precedence is given to national courts: states parties are required to utilize their own tribunals in the first instance, and the Court may intervene only when national courts are unable or unwilling to act. States parties, the Security Council and the Court's own Prosecutor will be authorized to bring cases before it. The Security Council will have the authority to halt any prosecution it deems improper.

The Court will have 18 judges, elected by the states parties for a term limited to nine years. No two judges can be from the same country. The judges will elect the President, while the Prosecutor will be elected by secret ballot by the states parties. The Court will be located at The Hague, the Netherlands. (*For more information see:* www.un.org/icc)

# International terrorism

The United Nations has consistently addressed the problem of terrorism, taking both legal and political steps.

In the legal sphere, the United Nations and its specialized agencies — such as the International Civil Aviation Organization (ICAO), the International Maritime Organization (IMO) and the International Atomic Energy Agency (IAEA) — have developed a network of international agreements that constitute the basic legal instruments against terrorism. These are the:

- *Convention on Offences and Certain Other Acts Committed on Board Aircraft* (adopted in Tokyo in 1963);
- Convention for the Suppression of Unlawful Seizure of Aircraft (The Hague, 1970);
- *Convention for the Suppression of Unlawful Acts against the Safety of Civil Aviation* (Montreal, 1971);
- *Convention on the Prevention and Punishment of Crimes against Internationally Protected Persons, including Diplomatic Agents* (New York, 1973);
- *Convention on the Physical Protection of Nuclear Material* (Vienna, 1980);
- *Protocol for the Suppression of Unlawful Acts of Violence at Airports Serving International Civil Aviation* (Montreal, 1988);
- *Convention for the Suppression of Unlawful Acts against the Safety of Maritime Navigation* (Rome, 1988);
- *Protocol for the Suppression of Unlawful Acts against the Safety of Fixed Platforms located on the Continental Shelf* (Rome, 1988); and
- *Convention on the Marking of Plastic Explosives for the Purpose of Detection* (Montreal, 1991).

The General Assembly has brought about four conventions:

- *Convention against the Taking of Hostages* (1979), in which states parties agree to make the taking of hostages punishable by appropriate penalties. They also agree to prohibit certain activities within their territories, to exchange information, and to enable any criminal or extradition proceedings to take place. If a state party does not extradite an alleged offender, it must submit the case to its own authorities for prosecution. By December 2000, the Convention had 94 states parties.
- The *Convention on the Safety of United Nations and Associated Personnel* (1994), requested by the Assembly in 1993 following

many instances of attacks against United Nations personnel in the field which resulted in injury and death. By December 2000, it had 49 states parties.

- The *International Convention for the Suppression of Terrorist Bombings* (1997). It is aimed at denying "safe havens" to persons wanted for terrorist bombings by obligating each state party to prosecute such persons if it does not extradite them to another state that has issued an extradition request. It will enter into force when ratified by 22 states. By December 2000, 17 states had ratified it.
- The *International Convention for the Suppression of the Financing of Terrorism* (1999) obligates states parties either to prosecute or to extradite persons accused of funding terrorist activities, and requires banks to enact measures to identify suspicious transactions. It will enter into force when ratified by 22 states. By December 2000, two states had ratified it.

A committee established by the Assembly in 1996 is elaborating a convention for the suppression of acts of nuclear terrorism.

In the political sphere, the General Assembly adopted in 1994 the *Declaration on Measures to Eliminate International Terrorism*, and in 1996 the *Declaration to supplement the 1994 Declaration*, which condemned all acts and practices of terrorism as criminal and unjustifiable, wherever and by whomever committed. The Assembly urged states to take measures at the national and international level to eliminate international terrorism.

## Other legal questions

The General Assembly has adopted legal instruments on various other questions. Among them are the *International Convention against the Recruitment, Use, Financing and Training of Mercenaries* (1989), the *Body of Principles for the Protection of All Persons under Any Form of Detention or Imprisonment* (1988) and the *Declaration on the Enhancement of the Effectiveness of the Principle of Refraining from the Threat or Use of Force in International Relations* (1987).

The Assembly has adopted numerous international instruments on the recommendation of the **Special Committee on the Charter of the United Nations and on the Strengthening of the Role of the Organization**, established by the Assembly in 1974. These include the *United Nations Model Rules for the Conciliation of Disputes between States* (1995); the *Declaration on the Enhancement of Cooperation between the United Nations and Regional Arrangements or Agencies in the Maintenance of International Peace and Security*

(1994); the *Declaration on Fact-finding by the United Nations in the Field of the Maintenance of International Peace and Security* (1991); the *Declaration on the Prevention and Removal of Disputes and Situations which May Threaten International Peace and Security and on the Role of the United Nations in this Field* (1988); and the *Declaration on the Peaceful Settlement of International Disputes* (1982).

Under the Charter (article 102), Member States should register with the United Nations the international agreements they enter into. The United Nations **Office of Legal Affairs** (*see Chapter 1, page 25*) is responsible for the registration, deposit and publication of treaties and conventions. It publishes the *United Nations Treaty Series*, which contains the text of more than 34,000 treaties and related action. It also issues the volume *Multilateral Treaties Deposited with the Secretary-General*, which includes more than 500 major treaties deposited by Member States (*see* http://untreaty.un.org).

(*On amendments to the United Nations Charter, see Chapter 1, page 5.*)

# PART TWO

## Chapter 7

## Decolonization

# DECOLONIZATION

More than 80 nations whose peoples were under colonial rule have joined the United Nations as sovereign independent states since the world Organization was founded in 1945. Many other Territories have achieved self-determination through political association with other independent states or through integration with other states. The United Nations has played a crucial role in that historic change by encouraging the aspirations of dependent peoples and by setting goals and standards to accelerate their attainment of independence. The Organization has also supervised elections leading to independence — in Togoland (1956 and 1968), Western Samoa (1961), Namibia (1989) and most recently a popular consultation in East Timor (*see pages 280 and 283, below*).

The decolonization efforts of the United Nations derive from the Charter principle of "equal rights and self-determination of peoples", as well as from three specific chapters in the Charter — XI, XII and XIII — devoted to the interests of dependent peoples. Since 1960, the United Nations has also been guided by the General Assembly's *Declaration on the Granting of Independence to Colonial Countries and Peoples* (*see page 277, below*), also known as the Declaration on decolonization, by which Member States proclaimed the necessity of bringing colonialism to a speedy end. The Organization has also been guided by General Assembly resolution 1541 (XV) of 1960, which defined the three options offering full self-government for Non-Self-Governing Territories (*see page 279, below*).

Despite the great progress made against colonialism, some 1.3 million people still live under colonial rule, and the United Nations continues its efforts to help achieve self-determination or independence in the remaining Non-Self-Governing Territories. To this end, the General Assembly in 2000 declared 2001-2010 as the second International Decade for the Eradication of Colonialism.

## International Trusteeship System

Under Chapter XII of the Charter, the United Nations established the International Trusteeship System for the supervision of Trust Territories placed under it by individual agreements with the states administering them.

The System applied to: (i) Territories held under Mandates established by the League of Nations after the First World War; (ii) Territories detached from "enemy states" as a result of the Second World War; and (iii) Territories voluntarily placed under the System by states responsible for their administration. The goal of the System was to promote the political, economic and social advancement of the Territories and their development towards self-government and self-determination.

The **Trusteeship Council** (*see Chapter 1, page 13*) was established under Chapter XIII of the Charter to supervise the administration of Trust Territories and to ensure that governments responsible for their administration took adequate steps to prepare them for achieving the Charter goals.

In the early years of the United Nations, 11 Territories were placed under the Trusteeship System (*see Part Three, page 306*). All Territories have either become independent states, or voluntarily associated themselves with a state.

The last Territory to do so was the Trust Territory of the Pacific Islands (Palau), administered by the United States. The Security Council in 1994 terminated the United Nations Trusteeship Agreement for that Territory, after it chose free association with the United States in a 1993 plebiscite. Palau became independent in 1994, and joined the United Nations the same year.

With no Territories left on its agenda, the Trusteeship System had completed its historic task.

## Non-Self-Governing Territories

The Charter also addresses the issue of other Non-Self-Governing Territories not brought into the Trusteeship System.

Chapter XI of the Charter — the Declaration regarding Non-Self-Governing Territories — provides that Member States administering Territories which have not attained self-government recognize "that the interests of the inhabitants of these Territories is paramount" and accept as a "sacred trust" the obligation to promote their well-being.

To this end, administering Powers, in addition to ensuring the political, economic, social and educational advancement of the peoples, undertake to assist them in developing self-government and democratic political institutions. Administering Powers have an obligation to transmit regularly to the Secretary-General information on the economic, social and educational conditions in the Territories under their administration.

In 1946, eight Member States — Australia, Belgium, Denmark, France, the Netherlands, New Zealand, the United Kingdom and the United States — enumerated the Territories under their administration that they considered to be non-self-governing. In all, 72 Territories were enumerated, of which eight became independent before 1959.

Transmission of information by the administering Power was discontinued for 21 others for various reasons. In some cases, such as Puerto Rico, Greenland, Alaska and Hawaii, the General Assembly accepted the cessation of information; in others, the decision was taken unilaterally by the administering Power.

In 1963, the Assembly approved a revised list of 64 Territories to which the 1960 Declaration on decolonization applied. The list included the two remaining Trust Territories at that time (Nauru and the Trust Territory of the Pacific Islands); the Non-Self-Governing Territories for which information was transmitted under Chapter XI of the Charter (article 73e), including four administered by Spain; Namibia (then referred to as South West Africa); and those Territories about which no information had been transmitted, but which the Assembly had deemed to be Non-Self-Governing — namely the Territories under Portuguese administration and Southern Rhodesia (now Zimbabwe). The list was expanded in 1965 to include French Somaliland (now Djibouti) and Oman. The Comoro Islands were included in 1972 and New Caledonia in 1986.

From 1960 to 1990, 53 Territories attained self-government. As of 2000, there were 17 Non-Self-Governing Territories (*see table on the following page*). The current administering Powers are France, New Zealand, the United Kingdom and the United States.

## Declaration on the Granting of Independence to Colonial Countries and Peoples

The demands of the peoples of the Territories to achieve self-determination, and the international community's perception that Charter principles were being too slowly applied, led the General Assembly to proclaim, on 14 December 1960, the *Declaration on the Granting of Independence to Colonial Countries and Peoples* (*resolution 1514 (XV)*).

The Declaration states that subjecting peoples to alien subjugation, domination and exploitation constitutes a denial of fundamental human rights, is contrary to the Charter, and is an impediment to the promotion of world peace and cooperation. It adds that "immediate steps shall be taken, in Trust and Non-Self-Governing Territories or

# Territories to which the Declaration on the Granting of Independence to Colonial Countries and Peoples continues to apply (as of 2000)

| TERRITORY | ADMINISTERING AUTHORITY |
|---|---|
| **Africa:** | |
| Western Sahara | Spain[1] |
| | |
| **Asia and the Pacific:** | |
| American Samoa | United States |
| East Timor[2] | |
| Guam | United States |
| New Caledonia[3] | France |
| Pitcairn | United Kingdom |
| Tokelau | New Zealand |
| | |
| **Atlantic Ocean, Caribbean and Mediterranean:** | |
| Anguilla | United Kingdom |
| Bermuda | United Kingdom |
| British Virgin Islands | United Kingdom |
| Cayman Islands | United Kingdom |
| Falkland Islands (Malvinas) | United Kingdom |
| Gibraltar | United Kingdom |
| Montserrat | United Kingdom |
| St. Helena | United Kingdom |
| Turks and Caicos Islands | United Kingdom |
| United States Virgin Islands | United States |

[1] On 26 February 1976, Spain informed the Secretary-General that as of that date it had terminated its presence in the Territory of the Sahara and deemed it necessary to place on record that Spain considered itself thenceforth exempt from any international responsibility in connection with its administration, in view of the cessation of its participation in the temporary administration established for the Territory. In 1990, the General Assembly reaffirmed that the question of Western Sahara was a question of decolonization that remained to be completed by the people of Western Sahara.

[2] Formerly administered by Portugal, and under Indonesian control between 1975 and 1999, East Timor is now administered by the United Nations Transitional Administration in East Timor, established by Security Council resolution 1272 (1999) and endowed with overall responsibility for administering the Territory until it achieves independence.

[3] On 2 December 1986, the General Assembly determined that New Caledonia was a Non-Self-Governing Territory.

all other Territories which have not yet attained independence, to transfer all powers to the peoples of those Territories, without any conditions or reservations, in accordance with their freely expressed will and desire, without any distinction as to race, creed or colour in order to enable them to enjoy complete independence and freedom".

On 15 December 1960, the Assembly approved resolution 1541 (XV), defining the three legitimate political status options offering full self-government — free association with an independent state, integration into an independent state, or independence. (*For the list of Territories that have become integrated or associated with independent states, see Part Three, page 305*).

The Assembly, in 1961, established a 17-member Special Committee — enlarged to 24 members in 1962 — to examine the application of the Declaration, and to make recommendations on its implementation. Commonly referred to as the **Special Committee of 24 on Decolonization**, its full title is the **Special Committee on the Situation with Regard to the Implementation of the Declaration on the Granting of Independence to Colonial Countries and Peoples.**

The Committee meets annually, hears appointed and elected representatives of the Territories and petitioners, dispatches visiting missions to the Territories, and organizes seminars on the political, social, economic and educational situations in the Territories.

In the years following the adoption of the Declaration, some 60 former colonial Territories, inhabited by more than 80 million people, attained self-determination through independence and joined the United Nations as sovereign Members (*see Part Three, pages 303-304*).

In considering the Non-Self-Governing Territories, the General Assembly has each year reaffirmed that the continuation of colonialism in any form and manifestation is incompatible with the Charter, the Universal Declaration of Human Rights and the Declaration on decolonization.

The Assembly has called upon the administering Powers to take all necessary steps to enable the peoples of the Non-Self-Governing Territories to exercise fully their right to self-determination and independence. It has called upon the administering Powers to complete the withdrawal of the remaining military bases from the Territories, and to ensure that no activity of foreign economic and other interests hinders the implementation of the Declaration.

In this respect, New Zealand has extended the Committee continuos cooperation regarding Tokelau, and Portugal regarding East Timor. France began cooperating with the Committee in 1999, following the signing of an agreement on the future of New Caledonia.

Two administering Powers in recent years have not participated in the work of the Committee. The United States has maintained that it remains conscious of its role as an administering Power and will continue to meet its responsibilities under the Charter. The United Kingdom has stated that while most of the Territories under its administration chose independence, a small number have preferred to remain associated with it.

To mark the thirtieth anniversary of the Declaration in 1990, the Assembly in 1988 declared 1990-2000 as the International Decade for the Eradication of Colonialism. In 2000, the General Assembly voted to declare the period 2001-2010 as the **Second International Decade for the Eradication of Colonialism**.

In respect to certain territories, such as Western Sahara, the Assembly has entrusted the Secretary-General with specific tasks to facilitate the process of decolonization, in accordance with the Charter and the objectives of the Declaration (*see below*).

## Namibia

The United Nations helped bring about the independence of Namibia in 1990 — a case history that reveals the complexity of the efforts required to ensure a peaceful transition.

Formerly known as South West Africa, Namibia was an African Territory once held under the League of Nations Mandate System. The General Assembly in 1946 asked South Africa to administer the Territory under the Trusteeship System. South Africa refused, and in 1949 informed the United Nations that it would no longer transmit information on the Territory, maintaining that the Mandate had ended with the demise of the League.

In 1950 the International Court of Justice held that South Africa continued to have international obligations towards the Territory and that the United Nations should supervise its administration — an opinion South Africa rejected.

The General Assembly in 1966, stating that South Africa had not fulfilled its obligations, terminated that Mandate and placed the Territory under the responsibility of the United Nations. To administer the Territory until independence, the Assembly in 1967 established the United Nations Council for South West Africa. It was renamed the Council for Namibia in 1968, when the Assembly proclaimed that the Territory would be known as Namibia, in accordance with the wishes of its people.

The Security Council in 1969 termed the presence of South Africa illegal and called for its withdrawal. The International Court of Justice stated in 1971 that South Africa was obligated to withdraw. But South Africa remained, imposing apartheid laws and continuing to exploit Namibia's resources.

In 1976, the Security Council demanded that South Africa accept elections for the Territory under United Nations supervision. The General Assembly stated that independence talks must involve the South West Africa People's Organization (SWAPO) — the sole representative of the Namibian people.

In 1978, Canada, France, the Federal Republic of Germany, the United Kingdom and the United States submitted to the Security Council a settlement proposal. This provided for elections for a Constituent Assembly under United Nations auspices. The Council endorsed the Secretary-General's recommendations for implementing the proposal, asked him to appoint a Special Representative for Namibia, and established the United Nations Transition Assistance Group (UNTAG).

Years of negotiations by the Secretary-General and his Special Representative, as well as United States mediation, led to the 1988 agreements to achieve peace in southern Africa, under which South Africa agreed to cooperate with the Secretary-General to ensure Namibia's independence through elections.

The operation that led to Namibia's independence started in April 1989. UNTAG's civilian staff supervised and controlled the entire electoral process, conducted by the Namibian authorities. UNTAG's military staff monitored the ceasefire between SWAPO and South Africa and the demobilization of all military forces. Its police officers ensured a smooth electoral process and monitored the local police.

The elections for the Constituent Assembly, held in November, were won by SWAPO. The Secretary-General's Special Representative, Martti Ahtisaari, declared the elections "free and fair".

After the elections, South Africa withdrew its remaining troops. The Constituent Assembly drafted a new Constitution, approved in February 1990, and elected SWAPO leader Sam Nujoma as President for a five-year term. In March, Namibia became independent, with the Secretary-General administering the oath of office to Namibia's first President. In April, the country joined the United Nations.

## Western Sahara

The United Nations has been dealing since 1963 with an ongoing dispute on Western Sahara — a Territory on the north-west coast of Africa bordering with Morocco, Mauritania and Algeria.

Western Sahara became a Spanish colony in 1884. In 1963, both Morocco and Mauritania laid claim to it. The International Court of Justice, in a 1975 opinion requested by the General Assembly, rejected the claims of territorial sovereignty by Morocco or Mauritania.

The United Nations has been seeking a settlement in Western Sahara since the withdrawal of Spain in 1976 (*see footnote on page 278*) and the ensuing fighting between Morocco, which had "reintegrated" the Territory, and the Popular Front for the Liberation of Saguia el-Hamra and Río de Oro (Frente POLISARIO), supported by Algeria.

The Organization of African Unity (OAU) called in 1979 for a referendum allowing the people of the Territory to exercise their right to self-determination. Morocco agreed in 1981 to a ceasefire and to an internationally supervised referendum, while making it clear that it would not negotiate directly with POLISARIO. By 1982, 26 OAU member States had recognized the "Saharawi Arab Democratic Republic (SADR)" proclaimed by POLISARIO in 1976. When POLISARIO was seated at the 1984 OAU summit, Morocco withdrew from the OAU.

The General Assembly reaffirmed in 1983 and 1984 that the people of the Territory had yet to exercise their right to self-determination and independence, and that the parties should negotiate a ceasefire allowing for a referendum.

A joint good offices mission by the Secretary-General and the OAU Chairman led to their 1988 settlement proposal providing for a ceasefire and a referendum to choose between independence and integration with Morocco — a proposal both parties accepted.

The Security Council in 1990 approved the Secretary-General's proposal that, during a transitional period, a Special Representative of the Secretary-General would be responsible for all matters relating to the referendum, assisted by the **United Nations Mission for the Referendum in Western Sahara (MINURSO)**. All Western Saharans aged 18 and over counted in the 1974 Spanish census would have the right to vote, whether living in the Territory or outside. An Identification Commission would update the census and identify voters. Refugees living outside the Territory would be identified with the assistance of the Office of the United Nations High Commissioner for Refugees.

In 1991, the Security Council established MINURSO and the Secretary-General called for a ceasefire to come into effect on 6 September. In view of continued sporadic fighting, the Council dispatched 228 MINURSO military observers to verify the end of hostilities.

While both parties reiterated their confidence in the United Nations and their commitment to the plan, they continued to have different views, in particular on the criteria for voter eligibility.

The Secretary-General had set out such criteria in a 1991 report to the Security Council. Morocco accepted them, while considering them unduly restrictive. POLISARIO stated that it had been originally agreed that the sole basis of the electorate would be the list of Saharans counted in the 1974 census, and that the criteria would unduly expand the electorate beyond the persons included in the census, with the possible inclusion of persons who were not Saharans from the Territory.

In 1994, the Security Council asked the Identification Commission to start the identification and registration of voters, on the basis of a compromise proposed by the Secretary-General and accepted by both parties. In 1999, the Commission issued a provisional list of nearly 85,000 people eligible to vote; those deemed non-eligible could appeal the decision. But disagreements remained, especially on the eligibility of Saharans living in Morocco.

In spite of the mediation of the Secretary-General, his Special Representative and his Personal Envoy, former United States Secretary of State James A. Baker III, disagreements have continued. Pending issues have included repatriating refugees, completing the identification of voters, issuing a second provisional voter list, and dealing with the appeal process, which involves three tribal groups whom Morocco considers Saharans and POLISARIO Moroccan.

## East Timor

A major United Nations operation is overseeing the transition of East Timor towards independence — after the East Timorese people voted in favour of such a transition in a popular consultation conducted by the United Nations in 1999.

The island of Timor lies to the north of Australia, in the south-central part of the chain of islands forming the Republic of Indonesia. The western part of the island was a Dutch colony and became part of Indonesia when the country attained independence. East Timor was a Portuguese colony.

The General Assembly in 1960 placed East Timor on the list of Non-Self-Governing Territories. In 1974, recognizing the right to self-determination and independence of its colonies, Portugal sought to establish a provisional government and a popular assembly, which would determine the status of East Timor.

But civil war broke out in 1975 between the newly formed political parties. Portugal withdrew, stating that it was unable to control the situation (*see footnote on page 278*). One East Timorese side declared independence as a separate country, while another proclaimed independence and integration with Indonesia. In December, Indonesian troops landed in East Timor, and a "provisional government" was formed. Portugal broke off relations with Indonesia and brought the matter before the Security Council.

The Council and the General Assembly called on Indonesia to withdraw its forces and urged all states to respect East Timor's territorial integrity, as well as the rights of its people to self-determination in accordance with the Declaration on decolonization.

The "provisional government" in 1976 held elections for an assembly, which when convened called for integration with Indonesia. Indonesia issued a law for the integration of the Territory, and the pro-independence movement started armed resistance and an international campaign of opposition. Portugal maintained that the East Timorese had not exercised their right to self-determination; Indonesia maintained that the decolonization process in East Timor was complete and that its people had chosen self-government through integration with Indonesia. The United Nations did not recognize either the legitimacy of the assembly or the Indonesian annexation, and continued to recognize Portugal as the legal administering Power.

At the request of the General Assembly, the Secretary-General in 1983 started talks with Indonesia and Portugal to promote a just and comprehensive settlement. His good offices, and those of his Personal Representative, appointed in 1997, culminated in the May 1999 agreements, which paved the way for a popular consultation giving the East Timorese people a choice between an autonomous status with Indonesia or a transition to independence under the aegis of the United Nations.

On the basis of the agreements, the **United Nations Mission in East Timor (UNAMET)** organized and conducted voter registration and the 30 August ballot, at which 78.5 per cent of the 450,000 registered voters rejected the proposed autonomy within Indonesia. When the results were announced, militias opposing independence unleashed a campaign of systematic destruction and violence, killing many and forcing more than 200,000 East Timorese to flee their homes, mostly to West Timor. The United Nations had to evacuate most of its personnel, but 86 international staff remained in the headquarters compound in Dili, the capital, together with some 1,000 East Timorese who had taken refuge there.

After intensive talks, which included a high-level mission sent by the Security Council to Jakarta and Dili, Indonesia accepted the deployment of a United Nations-authorized multinational force to restore peace and security. Acting under Chapter VII of the Charter, the Security Council in September 1999, authorized the dispatch of the International Force in East Timor (INTERFET), which helped to restore order.

In October, the Council established a large operation, the **United Nations Transitional Administration in East Timor (UNTAET)**, with full executive and legislative authority during the country's transition to independence. Mr. Sergio Vieira de Mello was appointed head of UNTAET and Special Representative of the Secretary-General in East Timor. In February 2000, the military component of UNTAET took over from INTERFET the task of maintaining peace and security.

The Administration's mandate includes providing security and maintaining law and order, assisted by its military component made up of some 8,800 troops and 1,600 civilian police. In line with its mandate, UNTAET has established a civil administration throughout the Territory, and is helping to develop social services, assist in reconstruction, and build East Timor's capacity towards nationhood.

# PART THREE

**Appendices**

# UNITED NATIONS MEMBER STATES

(as of July 2002)

| Member State | Date of Admission | Scale of Assessments for 2002 (per cent) | Population (est.) |
|---|---|---|---|
| Afghanistan | 19 November 1946 | 0.007 | 22,474,000 |
| Albania | 14 December 1955 | 0.003 | 3,145,000 |
| Algeria | 8 October 1962 | 0.071 | 30,835,000 |
| Andorra | 28 July 1993 | 0.004 | 90,000 |
| Angola | 1 December 1976 | 0.002 | 13,527,000 |
| Antigua and Barbuda | 11 November 1981 | 0.002 | 77,000 |
| Argentina | 24 October 1945 | 1.159 | 36,224,000 |
| Armenia | 2 March 1992 | 0.002 | 3,458,000 |
| Australia | 1 November 1945 | 1.640 | 19,485,000 |
| Austria | 14 December 1955 | 0.954 | 8,066,000 |
| Azerbaijan | 2 March 1992 | 0.004 | 8,114,000 |
| Bahamas | 18 September 1973 | 0.012 | 308,000 |
| Bahrain | 21 September 1971 | 0.018 | 655,000 |
| Bangladesh | 17 September 1974 | 0.010 | 140,369,000 |
| Barbados | 9 December 1966 | 0.009 | 268,000 |
| Belarus[a] | 24 October 1945 | 0.019 | 9,973,000 |
| Belgium | 27 December 1945 | 1.138 | 10,264,000 |
| Belize | 25 September 1981 | 0.001 | 231,000 |
| Benin | 20 September 1960 | 0.002 | 6,417,000 |
| Bhutan | 21 September 1971 | 0.001 | 2,141,000 |
| Bolivia | 14 November 1945 | 0.008 | 8,274,000 |
| Bosnia and Herzegovina | 22 May 1992 | 0.004 | 4,067,000 |
| Botswana | 17 October 1966 | 0.010 | 1,695,000 |
| Brazil | 24 October 1945 | 2.093 | 172,386,000 |
| Brunei Darussalam | 21 September 1984 | 0.033 | 344,000 |
| Bulgaria | 14 December 1955 | 0.013 | 7,867,000 |
| Burkina Faso | 20 September 1960 | 0.002 | 11,856,000 |
| Burundi | 18 September 1962 | 0.001 | 6,502,000 |
| Cambodia | 14 December 1955 | 0.002 | 13,311,000 |
| Cameroon | 20 September 1960 | 0.009 | 15,203,000 |
| Canada | 9 November 1945 | 2.579 | 31,082,000 |
| Cape Verde | 16 September 1975 | 0.001 | 437,000 |
| Central African Republic | 20 September 1960 | 0.001 | 3,782,000 |
| Chad | 20 September 1960 | 0.001 | 8,322,000 |
| Chile | 24 October 1945 | 0.187 | 15,402,000 |
| China | 24 October 1945 | 1.545 | 1,284,972,000 |
| Colombia | 5 November 1945 | 0.171 | 42,803,000 |
| Comoros | 12 November 1975 | 0.001 | 727,000 |
| Congo | 20 September 1960 | 0.001 | 3,110,000 |
| Costa Rica | 2 November 1945 | 0.020 | 3,873,000 |
| Côte d'Ivoire | 20 September 1960 | 0.009 | 16,939,000 |

| Member State | Date of Admission | Scale of Assessments for 2002 (per cent) | Population (est.) |
|---|---|---|---|
| Croatia | 22 May 1992 | 0.039 | 4,655,000 |
| Cuba | 24 October 1945 | 0.030 | 11,230,000 |
| Cyprus | 20 September 1960 | 0.038 | 690,000 |
| Czech Republic | 19 January 1993 | 0.172 | 10,287,000 |
| Democratic People's Republic of Korea | 17 September 1991 | 0.009 | 22,428,000 |
| Democratic Republic of the Congo[b] | 20 September 1960 | 0.004 | 52,522,000 |
| Denmark | 24 October 1945 | 0.755 | 5,333,000 |
| Djibouti | 20 September 1977 | 0.001 | 644,000 |
| Dominica | 18 December 1978 | 0.001 | 72,000 |
| Dominican Republic | 24 October 1945 | 0.023 | 8,528,000 |
| Ecuador | 21 December 1945 | 0.025 | 12,879,000 |
| Egypt[c] | 24 October 1945 | 0.081 | 67,886,000 |
| El Salvador | 24 October 1945 | 0.018 | 6,400,000 |
| Equatorial Guinea | 12 November 1968 | 0.001 | 470,000 |
| Eritrea | 28 May 1993 | 0.001 | 3,816,000 |
| Estonia | 17 September 1991 | 0.010 | 1,377,000 |
| Ethiopia | 13 November 1945 | 0.004 | 65,374,000 |
| Federated States of Micronesia | 17 September 1991 | 0.001 | 126,000 |
| Fiji | 13 October 1970 | 0.004 | 823,000 |
| Finland | 14 December 1955 | 0.526 | 5,188,000 |
| France | 24 October 1945 | 6.516 | 59,191,000 |
| Gabon | 20 September 1960 | 0.014 | 1,237,000 |
| Gambia | 21 September 1965 | 0.001 | 1,420,000 |
| Georgia | 31 July 1992 | 0.005 | 5,239,000 |
| Germany | 18 September 1973 | 9.845 | 82,357,000 |
| Ghana | 8 March 1957 | 0.005 | 19,734,000 |
| Greece | 25 October 1945 | 0.543 | 10,020,000 |
| Grenada | 17 September 1974 | 0.001 | 101,000 |
| Guatemala | 21 November 1945 | 0.027 | 11,683,000 |
| Guinea | 12 December 1958 | 0.003 | 8,274,000 |
| Guinea-Bissau | 17 September 1974 | 0.001 | 1,227,000 |
| Guyana | 20 September 1966 | 0.001 | 763,000 |
| Haiti | 24 October 1945 | 0.002 | 8,132,000 |
| Honduras | 17 December 1945 | 0.004 | 6,575,000 |
| Hungary | 14 December 1955 | 0.121 | 9,917,000 |
| Iceland | 19 November 1946 | 0.033 | 281,000 |
| India | 30 October 1945 | 0.344 | 1,017,544,000 |
| Indonesia[d] | 28 September 1950 | 0.201 | 214,840,000 |
| Iran (Islamic Republic of) | 24 October 1945 | 0.236 | 64,530,000 |
| Iraq | 21 December 1945 | 0.102 | 23,584,000 |
| Ireland | 14 December 1955 | 0.297 | 3,839,000 |
| Israel | 11 May 1949 | 0.418 | 6,445,000 |
| Italy | 14 December 1955 | 5.104 | 57,948,000 |
| Jamaica | 18 September 1962 | 0.004 | 2,598,000 |

| Member State | Date of Admission | Scale of Assessments for 2002 (per cent) | Population (est.) |
|---|---|---|---|
| Japan | 18 December 1956 | 19.669 | 127,130,000 |
| Jordan | 14 December 1955 | 0.008 | 5,051,000 |
| Kazakhstan | 2 March 1992 | 0.029 | 14,831,000 |
| Kenya | 16 December 1963 | 0.008 | 31,293,000 |
| Kiribati | 14 September 1999 | 0.001 | 84,000 |
| Kuwait | 14 May 1963 | 0.148 | 1,971,000 |
| Kyrgyzstan | 2 March 1992 | 0.001 | 4,955,000 |
| Lao People's Democratic Republic | 14 December 1955 | 0.001 | 5,403,000 |
| Latvia | 17 September 1991 | 0.010 | 2,359,000 |
| Lebanon | 24 October 1945 | 0.012 | 3,556,000 |
| Lesotho | 17 October 1966 | 0.001 | 2,189,000 |
| Liberia | 2 November 1945 | 0.001 | 3,108,000 |
| Libyan Arab Jamahiriya | 14 December 1955 | 0.067 | 5,408,000 |
| Liechtenstein | 18 September 1990 | 0.006 | 33,000 |
| Lithuania | 17 September 1991 | 0.017 | 3,488,000 |
| Luxembourg | 24 October 1945 | 0.080 | 441,000 |
| Madagascar | 20 September 1960 | 0.003 | 16,437,000 |
| Malawi | 1 December 1964 | 0.002 | 11,140,000 |
| Malaysia[e] | 17 September 1957 | 0.237 | 22,633,000 |
| Maldives | 21 September 1965 | 0.001 | 276,000 |
| Mali | 28 September 1960 | 0.002 | 10,400,000 |
| Malta | 1 December 1964 | 0.015 | 395,000 |
| Marshall Islands | 17 September 1991 | 0.001 | 57,000 |
| Mauritania | 27 October 1961 | 0.001 | 2,747,000 |
| Mauritius | 24 April 1968 | 0.011 | 1,200,000 |
| Mexico | 7 November 1945 | 1.095 | 101,754,000 |
| Monaco | 28 May 1993 | 0.004 | 34,000 |
| Mongolia | 27 October 1961 | 0.001 | 2,425,000 |
| Morocco | 12 November 1956 | 0.045 | 29,170,000 |
| Mozambique | 16 September 1975 | 0.001 | 17,656,000 |
| Myanmar | 19 April 1948 | 0.010 | 48,364,000 |
| Namibia | 23 April 1990 | 0.007 | 1,788,000 |
| Nauru | 14 September 1999 | 0.001 | 13,000 |
| Nepal | 14 December 1955 | 0.004 | 23,593,000 |
| Netherlands | 10 December 1945 | 1.751 | 16,044,000 |
| New Zealand | 24 October 1945 | 0.243 | 3,850,000 |
| Nicaragua | 24 October 1945 | 0.001 | 5,205,000 |
| Niger | 20 September 1960 | 0.001 | 11,227,000 |
| Nigeria | 7 October 1960 | 0.056 | 116,929,000 |
| Norway | 27 November 1945 | 0.652 | 4,513,000 |
| Oman | 7 October 1971 | 0.062 | 2,478,000 |
| Pakistan | 30 September 1947 | 0.061 | 144,971,000 |
| Palau | 15 December 1994 | 0.001 | 20,000 |
| Panama | 13 November 1945 | 0.018 | 2,897,000 |
| Papua New Guinea | 10 October 1975 | 0.006 | 4,920,000 |
| Paraguay | 24 October 1945 | 0.016 | 5,636,000 |

| Member State | Date of Admission | Scale of Assessments for 2002 (per cent) | Population (est.) |
|---|---|---|---|
| Peru | 31 October 1945 | 0.119 | 26,347,000 |
| Philippines | 24 October 1945 | 0.101 | 77,131,000 |
| Poland | 24 October 1945 | 0.319 | 38,641,000 |
| Portugal | 14 December 1955 | 0.466 | 10,024,000 |
| Qatar | 21 September 1971 | 0.034 | 598,000 |
| Republic of Korea | 17 September 1991 | 1.866 | 47,343,000 |
| Republic of Moldova | 2 March 1992 | 0.002 | 4,285,000 |
| Romania | 14 December 1955 | 0.059 | 22,408,000 |
| Russian Federation[f] | 24 October 1945 | 1.200 | 144,400,000 |
| Rwanda | 18 September 1962 | 0.001 | 7,949,000 |
| Saint Kitts and Nevis | 23 September 1983 | 0.001 | 46,000 |
| Saint Lucia | 18 September 1979 | 0.002 | 157,000 |
| Saint Vincent and the Grenadines | 16 September 1980 | 0.001 | 109,000 |
| Samoa | 15 December 1976 | 0.001 | 159,000 |
| San Marino | 2 March 1992 | 0.002 | 27,000 |
| Sao Tome and Principe | 16 September 1975 | 0.001 | 140,000 |
| Saudi Arabia | 24 October 1945 | 0.559 | 21,028,000 |
| Senegal | 28 September 1960 | 0.005 | 9,803,000 |
| Seychelles | 21 September 1976 | 0.002 | 81,000 |
| Sierra Leone | 27 September 1961 | 0.001 | 4,587,000 |
| Singapore | 21 September 1965 | 0.396 | 4,131,000 |
| Slovakia | 19 January 1993 | 0.043 | 5,404,000 |
| Slovenia | 22 May 1992 | 0.081 | 1,985,000 |
| Solomon Islands | 19 September 1978 | 0.001 | 463,000 |
| Somalia | 20 September 1960 | 0.001 | 9,157,000 |
| South Africa | 7 November 1945 | 0.411 | 44,328,000 |
| Spain | 14 December 1955 | 2.539 | 40,266,000 |
| Sri Lanka | 14 December 1955 | 0.016 | 16,865,000 |
| Sudan | 12 November 1956 | 0.006 | 31,809,000 |
| Suriname | 4 December 1975 | 0.002 | 419,000 |
| Swaziland | 24 September 1968 | 0.002 | 938,000 |
| Sweden | 19 November 1946 | 1.035 | 8,833,000 |
| Switzerland | 10 September 2002 | * | 7,231,000 |
| Syrian Arab Republic[g] | 24 October 1945 | 0.081 | 16,720,000 |
| Tajikistan | 2 March 1992 | 0.001 | 6,293,000 |
| Thailand | 16 December 1946 | 0.254 | 62,914,000 |
| The former Yugoslav Republic of Macedonia[h] | 8 April 1993 | 0.006 | 2,044,000 |
| Timor-Leste | 27 September 2002 | * | 750,000 |
| Togo | 20 September 1960 | 0.001 | 4,657,000 |
| Tonga | 14 September 1999 | 0.001 | 99,000 |
| Trinidad and Tobago | 18 September 1962 | 0.016 | 1,300,000 |
| Tunisia | 12 November 1956 | 0.031 | 9,673,000 |
| Turkey | 24 October 1945 | 0.444 | 68,610,000 |
| Turkmenistan | 2 March 1992 | 0.003 | 4,835,000 |
| Tuvalu | 5 September 2000 | 0.001 | 10,000 |

| Member State | Date of Admission | Scale of Assessments for 2002 (per cent) | Population (est.) |
|---|---|---|---|
| Uganda | 25 October 1962 | 0.005 | 22,788,000 |
| Ukraine | 24 October 1945 | 0.053 | 49,112,000 |
| United Arab Emirates | 9 December 1971 | 0.204 | 2,654,000 |
| United Kingdom | 24 October 1945 | 5.579 | 59,542,000 |
| United Republic of Tanzania[i] | 14 December 1961 | 0.004 | 35,965,000 |
| United States of America | 24 October 1945 | 22.000 | 284,797,000 |
| Uruguay | 18 December 1945 | 0.081 | 3,361,000 |
| Uzbekistan | 2 March 1992 | 0.011 | 25,068,000 |
| Vanuatu | 15 September 1981 | 0.001 | 202,000 |
| Venezuela | 15 November 1945 | 0.210 | 24,632,000 |
| Viet Nam | 20 September 1977 | 0.013 | 79,175,000 |
| Yemen | 30 September 1947 | 0.007 | 19,114,000 |
| Yugoslavia | 24 October 1945 | 0.020 | 10,651,000 |
| Zambia | 1 December 1964 | 0.002 | 10,649,000 |
| Zimbabwe | 25 August 1980 | 0.008 | 12,960,000 |

States which are not Members of the United Nations but which participate in certain of its activities, shall be called upon to contribute towards the expenses of the Organization on the basis of the following percentage rates:

| | |
|---|---|
| Holy See | 0.001 |

---

*To be determined.

[a]On 19 September 1991, Byelorussia informed the United Nations that it had changed its name to Belarus.

[b]The Republic of Zaire informed the United Nations that, effective 17 May 1997, it had changed its name to Democratic Republic of the Congo.

[c]Egypt and Syria were original Members of the United Nations from 24 October 1945. Following a plebiscite on 21 February 1958, the United Arab Republic was established by a union of Egypt and Syria and continued as a single Member. On 13 October 1961, Syria, having resumed its status as an independent State, resumed its separate membership in the United Nations. On 2 September 1971, the United Arab Republic changed its name to the Arab Republic of Egypt.

[d]By letter of 20 January 1965, Indonesia announced its decision to withdraw from the United Nations "at this stage and under the present circumstances". By telegram of 19 September 1966, it announced its decision "to resume full cooperation with the United Nations and to resume participation in its activities". On 28 September 1966, the General Assembly took note of this decision and the President invited representatives of Indonesia to take seats in the Assembly.

[e]The Federation of Malaya joined the United Nations on 17 September 1957. On 16 September 1963, its name was changed to Malaysia, following the admission to the new federation of Singapore, Sabah (North Borneo) and Sarawak. Singapore became an independent State on 9 August 1965 and a United Nations Member on 21 September 1965.

[f]The Union of Soviet Socialist Republics was an original Member of the United Nations from 24 October 1945. In a letter dated 24 December 1991, Boris Yeltsin, the President of the Russian Federation, informed the Secretary-General that the membership of the Soviet Union in the Security Council and all other United Nations organs was being continued by the Russian Federation with the support of the 11 member countries of the Commonwealth of Independent States.

[g]Egypt and Syria were original Members of the United Nations from 24 October 1945. Following a plebiscite on 21 January 1958, the United Arab Republic was established by a union of Egypt and Syria and continued as a single Member. On 13 October 1961, Syria, having resumed its status as an independent State, resumed its separate membership in the United Nations.

[h]The General Assembly decided on 8 April 1993 to admit to United Nations membership the States being provisionally referred to for all purposes within the United Nations as "the former Yugoslav Republic of Macedonia" pending settlement of the difference that had arisen over its name.

[i]Tanganyika was a United Nations Member from 14 December 1961 and Zanzibar was a Member from 16 December 1963. Following the ratification on 26 April 1964 of Articles of Union between Tanganyika and Zanzibar, the United Republic of Tanganyika and Zanzibar continued as a single Member, changing its name to the United Republic of Tanzania on 1 November 1964.

## GROWTH IN UNITED NATIONS MEMBERSHIP, 1945-2002

| Year | Number | Member States |
|------|--------|---------------|
| 1945 | Original 51 | Argentina, Australia, Belgium, Bolivia. Brazil, Belarus, Canada, Chile, China, Colombia, Costa Rica, Cuba, Czechoslovakia, Denmark, Dominican Republic, Ecuador, Egypt, El Salvador, Ethiopia, France, Greece, Guatemala, Haiti, Honduras, India, Iran, Iraq, Lebanon, Liberia, Luxembourg, Mexico, Netherlands, New Zealand, Nicaragua, Norway, Panama, Paraguay, Peru, Philippines, Poland, Russian Federation, Saudi Arabia, South Africa, Syrian Arab Republic, Turkey, Ukraine, United Kingdom of Great Britain and Northern Ireland, United States of America, Uruguay, Venezuela, Yugoslavia |
| 1946 | 55 | Afghanistan, Iceland, Sweden, Thailand |
| 1947 | 57 | Pakistan, Yemen[1] |
| 1948 | 58 | Myanmar |
| 1949 | 59 | Israel |
| 1950 | 60 | Indonesia |
| 1955 | 76 | Albania, Austria, Bulgaria, Cambodia, Finland, Hungary, Ireland, Italy, Jordan, Lao People's Democratic Republic, Libyan Arab Jamahiriya, Nepal, Portugal, Romania, Spain, Sri Lanka |
| 1956 | 80 | Japan, Morocco, Sudan, Tunisia |
| 1957 | 82 | Ghana, Malaysia |
| 1958 | 82[2] | Guinea |
| 1960 | 99 | Benin, Burkina Faso, Cameroon, Central African Republic, Chad, Congo, Côte d'Ivoire, Cyprus, Gabon, Madagascar, Mali, Niger, Nigeria, Senegal, Somalia, Togo, Democratic Republic of the Congo |
| 1961 | 104[3] | Mauritania, Mongolia, Sierra Leone, United Republic of Tanzania |
| 1962 | 110 | Algeria, Burundi, Jamaica, Rwanda, Trinidad and Tobago, Uganda |
| 1963 | 112 | Kenya, Kuwait |
| 1964 | 115 | Malawi, Malta, Zambia |
| 1965 | 117[4] | Gambia, Maldives, Singapore |
| 1966 | 122[5] | Barbados, Botswana, Guyana, Lesotho |
| 1967 | 123 | Democratic Yemen1 |
| 1968 | 126 | Equatorial Guinea, Mauritius, Swaziland |
| 1970 | 127 | Fiji |

| Year | Number | Member States |
|---|---|---|
| 1971 | 132 | Bahrain, Bhutan, Oman, Qatar, United Arab Emirates |
| 1973 | 135 | Bahamas, German Democratic Republic, Germany, Federal Republic of[6] |
| 1974 | 138 | Bangladesh, Grenada, Guinea-Bissau |
| 1975 | 144 | Cape Verde, Comoros, Mozambique, Papua New Guinea, Sao Tome and Principe, Suriname |
| 1976 | 147 | Angola, Samoa, Seychelles |
| 1977 | 149 | Djibouti, Viet Nam |
| 1978 | 151 | Dominica, Solomon Islands |
| 1979 | 152 | Saint Lucia |
| 1980 | 154 | Saint Vincent and the Grenadines, Zimbabwe |
| 1981 | 157 | Antigua and Barbuda, Belize, Vanuatu |
| 1983 | 158 | Saint Kitts and Nevis |
| 1984 | 159 | Brunei Darussalam |
| 1990 | 159[1,6] | Liechtenstein, Namibia |
| 1991 | 166 | Democratic Peopleís Republic of Korea, Estonia, Federated States of Micronesia, Latvia, Lithuania, Marshall Islands, Republic of Korea |
| 1992 | 179 | Armenia, Azerbaijan, Bosnia and Herzegovina,[7] Croatia,[7] Georgia, Kazakhstan, Kyrgyzstan, Moldova, San Marino, Slovenia,[7] Tajikistan, Turkmenistan, Uzbekistan |
| 1993 | 184[8] | Andorra, Czech Republic, Eritrea, Monaco, Slovak Republic, The former Yugoslav Republic of Macedonia[7] |
| 1994 | 185 | Palau |
| 1999 | 188 | Kiribati, Nauru, Tonga |
| 2000 | 189 | Tuvalu, Yugoslavia[7] |
| 2002 | 191 | Switzerland, Timor-Leste |

[1]Yemen was admitted to membership in the United Nations on 30 September 1947 and Democratic Yemen on 14 December 1967. On 22 May 1990, the two countries merged and have since been represented as one Member with the name íYemenî.
[2]The total remains the same because from 21 January 1958 Syria and Egypt continued as a single member (United Arab Republic)
[3]Syria resumed its status as an independent State.
[4]Indonesia withdrew as of 20 January 1965.
[5]Indonesia resumed its membership as of 28 September 1966.
[6]The Federal Republic of Germany and the German Democratic Republic were admitted to membership in the United Nations on 18 September 1973. Through the accession of the German Democratic Republic to the Federal Republic of Germany, effective from 3 October 1990, the two German States have united to form one sovereign State.
[7]The Socialist Federal Republic of Yugoslavia was an original Member of the United Nations, the Charter having been signed on its behalf on 26 June 1945 and ratified 19 October 1945, until its dissolution following the establishment

and subsequent admission as new members of Bosnia and Herzegovina, the Republic of Croatia, the Republic of Slovenia, The former Yugoslav Republic of Macedonia, and the Federal Republic of Yugoslavia. The Republic of Bosnia and Herzegovina, the Republic of Croatia and the Republic of Slovenia were admitted as Members of the United Nations on 22 May 1992. On 8 April 1993, the General Assembly decided to admit as a Member of the United Nations the state being provisionally referred to for all purposes within the United Nations as "The former Yugoslav Republic of Macedonia" pending settlement of the difference that had arisen over its name. The Federal Republic of Yugoslavia was admitted as a Member of the United Nations on 1 November 2000.

[8]Czechoslovakia was an original Member of the United Nations from 24 October 1945. In a letter dated 10 December 1992, its Permanent Representative informed the Secretary-General that the Czech and Slovak Federal Republic would cease to exist on 31 December 1992 and that the Czech Republic and the Slovak Republic, as successor States, would apply for membership in the United Nations. Following the receipt of such applications, the Security Council, on 8 January 1993, recommended to the General Assembly that the Czech Republic and the Slovak Republic be admitted to United Nations membership. They were thus admitted on 19 January 1993 as Member States.

# PEACEKEEPING OPERATIONS: PAST AND PRESENT

**(As of December 2000)**

**\*UNTSO**
United Nations Truce Supervision Organization (Jerusalem)
June 1948

**\*UNMOGIP**
United Nations Military Observer Group in India and Pakistan
January 1949

**UNEF I**
First United Nations Emergency Force (Gaza)
November 1956 June 1967

**UNOGIL**
United Nations Observation Group in Lebanon
June December 1958

**ONUC**
United Nations Operation in the Congo
July 1960 June 1964

**UNSF**
United Nations Security Force in West New Guinea (West Irian)
October 1962 April 1963

**UNYOM**
United Nations Yemen Observation Mission
July 1963 September 1964

**\*UNFICYP**
United Nations Peacekeeping Force in Cyprus
March 1964

**DOMREP**
Mission of the Representative of the Secretary-General in the Dominican Republic
May 1965 October 1966

**UNIPOM**
United Nations India-Pakistan Observation Mission
September 1965 March 1966

**UNEF II**
Second United Nations Emergency Force (Suez Canal and later Sinai peninsula)
October 1973 July 1979

**\*UNDOF**
United Nations Disengagement Observer Force (Syrian Golan Heights)
June 1974

**\*UNIFIL**
United Nations Interim Force in Lebanon
March 1978

**UNGOMAP**
United Nations Good Offices Mission in Afghanistan and Pakistan
May 1988 March 1990

**UNIIMOG**
United Nations Iran-Iraq Military Observer Group
August 1988 February 1991

**UNAVEM I**
United Nations Angola Verification Mission I
January 1989 June 1991

**UNTAG**
United Nations Transition Assistance Group (Namibia and Angola)
April 1989 March 1990

**ONUCA**
United Nations Observer Group in Central America
November 1989 January 1992

**\*UNIKOM**
United Nations Iraq-Kuwait Observation Mission
April 1991

**UNAVEM II**
United Nations Angola Verification Mission II
June 1991 February 1995

**ONUSAL**
United Nations Observer Mission in El Salvador
July 1991 April 1995

**\*MINURSO**
United Nations Mission for the Referendum in Western Sahara
April 1991

**UNAMIC**
United Nations Advance Mission in Cambodia
October 1991 March 1992

**UNPROFOR**
United Nations Protection Force (former Yugoslavia)
March 1992 December 1995

**UNTAC**
United Nations Transitional Authority in Cambodia
March 1992 September 1993

**UNOSOM I**
United Nations Operation in Somalia I
April 1992 March 1993

**ONUMOZ**
United Nations Operation in Mozambique
December 1992 December 1994

**UNOSOM II**
United Nations Operation in Somalia II
March 1993 March 1995

**UNOMUR**
United Nations Observer Mission Uganda-Rwanda
June 1993 September 1994

**\*UNOMIG**
United Nations Observer Mission in Georgia
August 1993

**UNOMIL**
United Nations Observer Mission in Liberia
September 1993 September 1997

**UNMIH**
United Nations Mission in Haiti
September 1993 June 1996

**UNAMIR**
United Nations Assistance Mission for Rwanda
October 1993 March 1996

**UNASOG**
United Nations Aouzou Strip Observer Group (Chad/Lybia)
May June 1994

**UNMOT**
United Nations Mission of Observers in Tajikistan
December 1994 May 2000

**UNAVEM III**
United Nations Angola Verification Mission III
February 1995 June 1997

**UNCRO**
United Nations Confidence Restoration Operation in Croatia
March 1995 January 1996

**UNPREDEP**
United Nations Preventive Deployment Force (former Yugoslav Republic of Macedonia)
March 1995 February 1999

**\*UNMIBH**
United Nations Mission in Bosnia and Herzegovina
December 1995

**UNTAES**
United Nations Transitional Administration for Eastern Slavonia, Baranja and Western Sirmium (Croatia)
January 1996 January 1998

**\*UNMOP**
United Nations Mission of Observers in Prevlaka (Croatia)
January 1996

**UNSMIH**
United Nations Support Mission in Haiti
July 1996 July 1997

**MINUGUA**
United Nations Verification Mission in Guatemala
January May 1997

**MONUA**
United Nations Observer Mission in Angola
July 1997 February 1999

**UNTMIH**
United Nations Transition Mission in Haiti
August-November 1997

**MIPONUH**
United Nations Civilian Police Mission in Haiti
December 1997 March 2000

**UNPSG**
United Nations Civilian Police Support Group (Croatia)
January-October 1998

**MINURCA**
United Nations Mission in the Central African Republic
April 1998 February 2000

**UNOMSIL**
United Nations Observer Mission in Sierra Leone
July 1998 October 1999

**\*UNMIK**
United Nations Interim Administration Mission in Kosovo
June 1999

**\*UNAMSIL**
United Nations Mission in Sierra Leone
October 1999

**\*UNTAET**
United Nations Transitional Administration in East Timor
October 1999

**\*MONUC**
United Nations Observer Mission in the Democratic Republic of the Congo
December 1999

**\*UNMEE**
United Nations Mission in Ethiopia and Eritrea
July 2000-

---

\*Current operation, as of December 2000.

# DECOLONIZATION

Trust and Non-Self-Governing Territories that have achieved independence since the adoption of the 1960 Declaration*

**State or entity**                    **Date of admission to the United Nations**

## Africa

| State or entity | Date of admission to the United Nations |
|---|---|
| Algeria | 8 October 1962 |
| Angola | 1 December 1976 |
| Botswana | 17 October 1966 |
| Burundi | 18 September 1962 |
| Cape Verde | 16 September 1975 |
| Comoros | 12 November 1975 |
| Djibouti | 20 September 1977 |
| Equatorial Guinea | 12 November 1968 |
| Gambia | 21 September 1965 |
| Guinea-Bissau | 17 September 1974 |
| Kenya | 16 December 1963 |
| Lesotho | 17 October 1966 |
| Malawi | 1 December 1964 |
| Mauritius | 24 April 1968 |
| Mozambique | 16 September 1975 |
| Namibia | 23 April 1990 |
| Rwanda | 18 September 1962 |
| Sao Tome and Principe | 26 September 1975 |
| Seychelles | 21 September 1976 |
| Sierra Leone | 27 September 1961 |
| Swaziland | 24 September 1968 |
| Uganda | 25 October 1962 |
| United Republic of Tanzania[1] | 14 December 1961 |
| Zambia | 1 December 1964 |
| Zimbabwe | 18 April 1980 |

## Asia

| State or entity | Date of admission to the United Nations |
|---|---|
| Brunei Darussalam | 21 September 1984 |
| Democratic Yemen | 14 December 1967 |
| Oman | 7 October 1971 |
| Singapore | 21 September 1965 |

---

* *Declaration on the Granting of Independence to Colonial Countries and Peoples,* adopted by the General Assembly on 14 December 1960.

| State or entity | Date of admission to the United Nations |
|---|---|

## Caribbean

| | |
|---|---|
| Antigua and Barbuda | 11 November 1981 |
| Bahamas | 18 September 1973 |
| Barbados | 9 December 1966 |
| Belize | 25 September 1981 |
| Dominica | 18 December 1978 |
| Grenada | 17 December 1974 |
| Guyana | 20 September 1966 |
| Jamaica | 18 September 1962 |
| Saint Christopher and Nevis | 23 September 1983 |
| Saint Lucia | 18 September 1979 |
| Saint Vincent and the Grenadines | 16 September 1980 |
| Suriname[2] | 4 December 1975 |
| Trinidad and Tobago | 18 September 1962 |

## Europe

| | |
|---|---|
| Malta | 1 December 1964 |

## Pacific

| | |
|---|---|
| Federated States of Micronesia | 17 September 1991 |
| Fiji | 13 October 1970 |
| Kiribati | 14 September 1999 |
| Marshall Islands | 17 September 1991 |
| Nauru | 14 September 1999 |
| Papua New Guinea | 10 October 1975 |
| Palau | 15 December 1994 |
| Samoa | 15 December 1976 |
| Solomon Islands | 19 September 1978 |
| Tuvalu | 5 September 2000 |
| Vanuatu | 15 September 1981 |

[1] The former Trust Territory of Tanganyika, which became independent in December 1961, and the former Protectorate of Zanzibar, which achieved independence in December 1963, united into a single state in April 1964.

[2] By resolution 945(X), the General Assembly accepted the cessation of the transmission of information regarding Suriname following constitutional changes in the relationship between the Netherlands, Suriname and the Netherlands Antilles.

# DECOLONIZATION

Dependent Territories that have become integrated
or associated with independent states since
the adoption of the 1960 Declaration*

| Territory | Remarks |
| --- | --- |
| Cameroons under British administration | The northern part of the Trust Territory joined the Federation of Nigeria on 1 June 1961 and the southern part joined the Republic of Cameroon on 1 October 1961 |
| Cook Islands | Fully self-governing in free association with New Zealand since August 1965 |
| Ifni | Returned to Morocco in June 1969 |
| Niue | Fully self-governing in free association with New Zealand since August 1974 |
| North Borneo | North Borneo and Sarawak joined the Federation of Malaya in 1963 to form the Federation of Malaysia |
| São Joao Batistade de Ajuda | Nationally united with Dahomey (now Benin) in August 1961 |
| Sarawak | Sarawak and North Borneo joined the Federation of Malaya in 1963 to form the Federation of Malaysia |
| West New Guinea (West Irian) | United with Indonesia in 1963 |
| Cocos (Keeling) Islands | Integrated with Australia in 1984 |

---

* *Declaration on the Granting of Independence to Colonial Countries and Peoples*, adopted by the General Assembly on 14 December 1960.

# DECOLONIZATION

Trust Territories that have achieved self-determination

**Togoland** (under British administration)
> United with the Gold Coast (Colony and Protectorate), a Non-Self-Governing Territory administered by the United Kingdom, in 1957 to form Ghana

**Somaliland** (under Italian administration)
> United with British Somaliland Protectorate in 1960 to form Somalia

**Togoland** (under French administration)
> Became independent as Togo in 1960

**Cameroons** (under French administration)
> Became independent as Cameroon in 1960

**Cameroons** (under British administration)
> The northern part of the Trust Territory joined the Federation of Nigeria on 1 June 1961 and the southern part joined the Republic of Cameroon on 1 October 1961

**Tanganyika** (under British administration)
> Became independent in 1961 (in 1964, Tanganyika and the former Protectorate of Zanzibar, which had become independent in 1963, united as a single state under the name of the United Republic of Tanzania)

**Ruanda-Urundi** (under Belgian administration)
> Voted to divide into the two sovereign states of Rwanda and Burundi in 1962

**Western Samoa** (under New Zealand administration)
> Became independent as Samoa in 1962

**Nauru** (administered by Australia on behalf of Australia, New Zealand and the United Kingdom)
> Became independent in 1968

**New Guinea** (administered by Australia)
> United with the Non-Self-Governing Territory of Papua, also administered by Australia, to become the independent state of Papua New Guinea in 1975

**Trust Territory of the Pacific Islands:**
**(a) Federated States of Micronesia**
>    Became fully self-governing in free Association with the United States
>    in 1990
**(b) Republic of the Marshall Islands**
>    Became fully self-governing in free Association with the United States
>    in 1990
**(c) Commonwealth of the Northern Mariana Islands**
>    Became fully self-governing as a Commonwealth of the United States in
>    1990
**(d) Palau**
>    Became fully self-governing in free Association with the United States
>    in 1994

# BUDGET OF THE UNITED NATIONS

For the 2000-2001 biennium, the appropriation for the regular budget of the United Nations (i.e. excluding the bulk of Offices and Programmes, as well as the Specialized Agencies and other associated bodies), as initially approved in 1999, totalled $2,535,689,200, divided into 13 main categories of expenditures, as follows (in United States dollars):

| | | |
|---|---|---:|
| 1. | Overall policy-making, direction and coordination | 473,645,300 |
| 2. | Political affairs | 231,586,300 |
| 3. | International justice and law | 55,386,800 |
| 4. | International cooperation for development | 268,767,900 |
| 5. | Regional cooperation for development | 347,230,400 |
| 6. | Human rights and humanitarian affairs | 123,613,100 |
| 7. | Public information | 143,605,500 |
| 8. | Common support services | 441,857,400 |
| 9. | Internal oversight | 19,220,600 |
| 10. | Jointly financed activities and special expenses | 60,845,500 |
| 11. | Capital expenditures | 42,617,400 |
| 12. | Staff assessment* | 314,248,000 |
| 13. | Development account | 13,065,000 |

*To equalize the net pay of all United Nations staff members, whatever their national tax obligations, the Organization deducts from their salaries a sum of money designated as "staff assessment". The rate of withholding is roughly equivalent to the amount paid by United States citizens for federal, state and local taxes calculated at the standard rate. The money collected by the United Nations from the staff assessment is then credited towards the United Nations membership "dues" of the staff member's home country.

Most Governments excuse nationals who are United Nations employees from further taxation. The United States is the main exception; its citizens who work for the Secretariat must pay the same income taxes as all other United States citizens. To enable them to pay their taxes, the United Nations refunds to United States employees that part of their staff assessment which is equal to what the national revenue authorities require for taxes. The citizen then pays that amount to those authorities. In this way, United States nationals are not required to pay taxes twice.

The regular programme budget to which these assessments apply covers expenses relating to substantive programmes, programme support and administrative activities of the Organization both at Headquarters and around the globe.

The main source of funds for the regular budget is the contributions of Member States, who are assessed on a scale specified by the Assembly on the recommendation of the 18-member Committee on Contributions. The fundamental criterion on which the scale of assessments is based is the real capacity of Member States to pay. The Assembly has fixed a maximum of 22 per cent of the budget for any one contributor and a minimum of 0.001 per cent. (For scale of assessments of Member States, see pages 289-293.)

Initial income estimates for the biennium 2000-2001, other than assessments on Member States, totalled $361,298,900.

| | | |
|---|---|---|
| 1. | Income from staff assessment* | 318,911,500 |
| 2. | General income | 37,178,000 |
| 3. | Services to the public | 5,209,400 |

———————

* See footnote on page 308.

# UNITED NATIONS SPECIAL OBSERVANCES

## INTERNATIONAL DECADES AND YEARS

| | |
|---|---|
| 1993-2002 | Second Industrial Development Decade for Africa |
| 1993-2002 | Asian and Pacific Decade of Disabled Persons |
| 1993-2003 | Third Decade to Combat Racism and Racial Discrimination |
| 1994-2004 | International Decade of the World's Indigenous People |
| 1995-2004 | United Nations Decade for Human Rights Education |
| 1997-2006 | United Nations Decade for the Eradication of Poverty |
| 2001-2010 | Second International Decade for the Eradication of Colonialism |
| 2001-2010 | International Decade for a Culture of Peace and Non-violence for the Children of the World |
| 2001 | International Year of Volunteers |
| 2001 | United Nations Year of Dialogue among Civilizations |
| 2001 | International Year of Mobilization against Racism, Racial Discrimination, Xenophobia and Related Intolerance |
| 2002 | International Year of Mountains |
| 2002 | International Year of Ecotourism |
| 2003 | International Year of Freshwater |
| 2005 | International Year of Microcredit |

## ANNUAL DAYS AND WEEKS

| | |
|---|---|
| 8 March | United Nations Day for Women's Rights and International Peace |
| 21 March | International Day for the Elimination of Racial Discrimination |
| Beginning 21 March | Week of Solidarity with the Peoples Struggling against Racism and Racial Discrimination |
| 22 March | World Day for Water |
| 3 May | World Press Freedom Day |
| 15 May | International Day of Families |
| 22 May | International Day for Biological Diversity |
| Beginning 25 May | Week of Solidarity with the Peoples of Non-Self-Governing Territories |
| 4 June | International Day of Innocent Children Victims of Aggression |
| 5 June | World Environment Day |
| 17 June | World Day to Combat Desertification and Drought |
| 20 June | World Refugee Day |
| 26 June | International Day against Drug Abuse and Illicit Trafficking |

| | |
|---|---|
| 26 June | International Day in Support of Victims of Torture |
| First Saturday of July | International Day of Cooperatives |
| 11 July | World Population Day |
| 9 August | International Day of the World's Indigenous People |
| 12 August | International Youth Day |
| 16 September | International Day for the Preservation of the Ozone Layer |
| September | International Day of Peace |

(Opening day of the regular annual session of the General Assembly)

| | |
|---|---|
| 1 October | International Day of Older Persons |
| First Monday of October | World Habitat Day |
| Second Wednesday of October | International Day for Natural Disaster Reduction |
| 4-10 October | World Space Week |
| 16 October | World Food Day |
| 17 October | International Day for the Eradication of Poverty |
| 24 October | United Nations Day |
| 24-30 October | Disarmament Week |
| 16 November | International Day for Tolerance |
| 20 November | Africa Industrialization Day |
| 21 November | World Television Day |
| 25 November | International Day for the Elimination of Violence against Women |
| 29 November | International Day of Solidarity with the Palestinian People |
| 1 December | World AIDS Day |
| 2 December | International Day for the Abolition of Slavery |
| 3 December | International Day of Disabled Persons |
| 10 December | Human Rights Day |
| 18 December | International Migrants Day |

## OTHER INTERNATIONAL DAYS

Other international days observed throughout the United Nations system include:

| | |
|---|---|
| 21 February | International Mother Language Day |
| 23 March | World Meteorological Day |
| 7 April | World Health Day |
| 23 April | World Book and Copyright Day |
| 17 May | World Telecommunication Day |
| 31 May | World No-Tobacco Day |
| 23 August | International Day for the Remembrance of the Slave Trade and its Abolition |
| 8 September | International Literacy Day |
| Last week in September | World Maritime Day |
| 5 October | World Teachers' Day |
| 9 October | World Post Day |

| | |
|---|---|
| 10 October | World Mental Health Day |
| 24 October | World Development Information Day |
| 20 November, Varies | Universal Children's Day |
| 5 December | International Volunteer Day for Economic and Social Development |
| 7 December | International Civil Aviation Day |

# UNITED NATIONS INFORMATION CENTRES, SERVICES AND OFFICES

## AFRICA

### Accra

United Nations Information Centre, Gamel Abdul Nassar/Liberia Roads (P.O. Box 2339), Accra, Ghana
Telephone: (233 21) 665 511/244 051
Fax: (233 21) 665 578/668 427(FAO)
E-mail: unicar@ncs.com.gh
Services to: Ghana, Sierra Leone

### Addis Ababa

United Nations Information Service, Africa Hall, Economic Commission for Africa (P.O. Box 3001), Addis Ababa, Ethiopia
Telephone: (251 1) 515 826, (251 1) 517 200
Fax: (251 1) 510 365 (ECA) or (251 1) 514 416
E-mail: ecainfo@un.org
Services to: Ethiopia, Economic Commission for Africa

### Algiers

United Nations Information Centre, 9A, rue Emile Payen, Hydra (Boite postale 823), Algiers, Algeria
Telephone: (213 2) 69 12 12
Fax: (213 2) 69 23 55
E-mail: unic.dz@undp.org        (Internet: www.unic.org.dz)
Services to: Algeria

### Antananarivo

United Nations Information Centre, 22 rue Rainitovo, Antananarivo, Madagascar
Telephone: (261 20) 22 241 15
Fax: (261 20) 22 333 15
E-mail: erick.rabe@undp.org        (Internet:www.onu.dts.mg)
Services to: Madagascar

### Brazzaville

United Nations Information Centre, Avenue Foch, Case Ortf 15 (P.O. Box 13210 or 1018), Brazzaville, Congo
Telephone: (242) 81 44 47/81 46 81
Fax: (242) 81 27 44
Services to: Congo

### Bujumbura

United Nations Information Centre, 117, Avenue de la Révolution (P.O. Box 2160), Bujumbura, Burundi
Telephone: (257) 225 018/228 569

Fax: (257) 241 798
E-mail:unicbuj@cbinf.com
Services to: Burundi

## Cairo

United Nations Information Centre, 1, Osoris St. Garden City (P.O. Box 262),
Cairo, Egypt
Telephone: (20 2) 531 5593
Fax: (20 2) 3553705
E-mail: unic.eg@undp.org    (Internet: www.un.org.eg/unic)
Services to: Egypt, Saudi Arabia

## Dakar

United Nations Information Centre, 12, Avenue Leopold S. Senghor, Immeuble
UNESCO, (P.O. Box 154) Dakar, Senegal
Telephone: (221) 823 30 70, 823 40 66
Fax: (221) 822 26 79
E-mail: loum@sonatel.senet.net
Services to: Senegal, Cape Verde, Gambia, Guinea-Bissau, Côte d'Ivoire,
Mauritania, Guinea

## Dar es Salaam

United Nations Information Centre, Marogoro Road/Sokoine Drive, Old Boma
Building, Ground Floor (P.O. Box 9224), Dar es Salaam
Telephone: (255 51) 112923, 119510
Fax: (255 51) 113272 (UNDP)
E-mail: unic.urt@raha.com
Services to: United Republic of Tanzania

## Harare

United Nations Information Centre, Sanders House, 2nd Floor, cnr. First
Street/Jason Moyo Avenue
(P.O. Box 4408), Harare, Zimbabwe
Telephone: (263 4) 777 060, 777 047
Fax: (263 4) 750 476
E-mail: unic@samara.co.zw    (Internet: www.samara.co.zw/unic)
Services to: Zimbabwe

## Khartoum

United Nations Information Centre, United Nations Compound, Gamma'a Ave
(P.O. Box 1992), Khartoum, Republic of the Sudan
Telephone: (249 11) 773 772
Fax: (249 11) 773 772, 773 128, 783 764
E-mail: fo.sdn@un.org
Services to: Sudan, Somalia

## Kinshasa

United Nations Information Centre, Bâtiment Deuxième République, Boulevard du 30 Juin (P.O. Box 7248), Kinshasa, Democratic Republic of the Congo
Telephone: (243 12) 33431, 33424, 33425 ext. 213/203
Fax: (871) 150 3261
E-mail : amisi.ramzahi@undp.org
Services to: Democratic Republic of the Congo

## Lagos

United Nations Information Centre, 17 Kingsway Road, Ikoyi (P.O. Box 1068), Lagos, Nigeria
Telephone: (234 1) 269 4886
Fax: (234 1) 269 1934
E-mail: uniclag@unic.org.ng
Services to: Nigeria

## Lomé

United Nations Information Centre, 107 Boulevard du 13 Janvier (P.O. Box 911) Lomé, Togo
Telephone: (228) 212 306
Fax: (228) 212 306 (same as telephone no.)
E-mail: cinu@rdd.tg
Services to: Benin, Togo

## Lusaka

United Nations Information Centre, P.O. Box 32905, Lusaka 10101, Republic of Zambia
Telephone: (260 1) 228 487, 228 488,
Fax: (260 1) 222 958
E-mail: unic@zamnet.zm
Services to: Zambia, Botswana, Malawi, Swaziland

## Maseru

United Nations Information Centre, UN Road, UN House (P.O. Box 301), Maseru 100, Lesotho
Telephone: (266) 312 496
Fax: (266) 310 042 (UNDP)
E-mail: fo.les@undp.org
Services to: Lesotho

## Monrovia

United Nations Information Centre, Dubar Building, Virginia, Liberia
Telephone: (231) 226 194/195/211
Fax: (231) 326 210
Services to: Liberia

## Nairobi

United Nations Information Centre, United Nations Office, Gigiri (P.O. Box 30552), Nairobi, Kenya
Telephone: (254 2) 623292/3, 623677, 623798
Fax: (254 2) 624349
E-mail: irene.mwakes@unep.org
Services to: Kenya, Seychelles, Uganda

## Ouagadougou

United Nations Information Centre, Avenue Georges Konseiga, Secteur No. 4 (P.O. Box 135), Ouagadougou 01, Burkina Faso
Telephone: (226) 30 60 76/33 65 03
Fax: (226) 31 13 22
E-mail: cinu.oui@fasonet.bf
Services to: Burkina Faso, Chad, Mali, Niger

## Pretoria

United Nations Information Centre, Metro Park Building, 351 Schoeman Street (P.O. Box 12677), Tramshed 0126, Pretoria, South Africa
Telephone: (27 12) 338 5077, 338 5078
Fax: (27 12) 320 1122
E-mail: unic@un.org.za
Services to: South Africa

## Rabat

United Nations Information Centre, Angle Charia Ibnouzaid, Et Zankat Roundanat, No. 6, (P.O. Box 601), Rabat, Morocco
Telephone: (212 77) 686 33/632 04
Fax: (212 77) 683 77
E-mail: cinu@fusion.net.ma     (Internet: www.cinu.org.ma)
Services to: Morocco

## Tripoli

United Nations Information Centre, Muzzafar Al Aftas St., Hay El-Andalous (2) (P.O. Box 286), Tripoli, Libyan Arab Jamahiriya
Telephone: (218 21) 477 0251; 477 7885
Fax: (218 21) 477 7343
E-mail: fo.lby@undp.org
Services to: Libyan Arab Jamahiriya

## Tunis

United Nations Information Centre, 61 Boulevard Bab-Benat (P.O. Box 863), Tunis, Tunisia
Telephone: (216 1) 560 203
Fax: (216 1) 568 811
E-mail: cinfo.tunis@un.intl.tn     (Internet: www.unic-tunis.intl.tn)
Services to: Tunisia

## Windhoek

United Nations Information Centre, 372 Paratus Building, Independence Avenue (Private Bag 13351), Windhoek, Namibia
Telephone: (264) 61 233034/5
Fax: (264) 61 233036
E-mail: unic@un.na
Services to: Namibia

## Yaoundé

United Nations Information Centre, Immeuble Kamdem, rue Joseph Clère (P.O. Box 836), Yaoundé, Republic of Cameroon
Telephone: (237) 23 51 73
Fax: (237) 22 08 26
E-mail: unic@camnet.cm
Services to: Cameroon, Gabon, Central African Republic

## THE AMERICAS

### Asunción

United Nations Information Centre, Estrella 345, Edificio City B 3er. Piso, Asunción, Paraguay
Telephone: (595 21) 451 816
Fax: (595 21) 449 611
E-mail: unic@undp.org.py
Services to: Paraguay

### Buenos Aires

United Nations Information Centre, Junín 1940, 1er piso, 1113 Buenos Aires, Argentina
Telephone: (54 11) 4801 0155/4803 7671
Fax: (54 11) 4804 7545
E-mail: unicbue@vianetworks.net.ar     (Internet: www.unic.org.ar)
Services to: Argentina, Uruguay

### La Paz

United Nations Information Centre, Av. Mariscal Santa Cruz No. 1350 (P.O. Box 9072), La Paz, Bolivia
Telephone: (591 2) 358 590/358 591 through 595
Fax: (591 2) 391 368 (UNDP)
E-mail: unicbol@eos.pnud.bo
Services to: Bolivia

### Lima

United Nations Information Centre, Lord Cochrane 130, San Isidro (L-27) (P.O. Box 14 0199), Lima, Perú
Telephone: (511) 441 8745, 422 4149, 422 0879
Fax: (511) 441 8735
E-mail: uniclima@chavin.rcp.net.pe
Services to: Peru

## Managua

United Nations Information Centre, Palacio de la Cultura
(P.O. Box 3260), Managua, Nicaragua
Telephone: (505 2) 66 42 53,
Fax: (505 2) 22 23 62
E-mail: cedoc@sdnnic.org.ni
Services to: Nicaragua

## Mexico City

United Nations Information Centre, Presidente Masaryk 29-6o. piso, 11570
México, D.F.
Telephone: (52 5) 250 1364, 250 1555
Fax: (52 5) 203 8638
E-mail: dpi-mexico@un.org      (Internet: www.cinu.org.mx)
Services to: Mexico, Cuba, Dominican Republic

## Panama City

United Nations Information Centre, Calle Gerardo Ortega y Ave. Samuel Lewis,
Banco Central Hispano Building, 1st floor (P.O. Box 6-9083 El Dorado), Panamá,
Republic of Panama
Telephone: (507) 223 0557/269 6280
Fax: (507) 223 2198
E-mail: cinup@sinfo.net      (Internet: www.onu.org.pa/cinup)
Services to: Panama

## Port of Spain

United Nations Information Centre, Bretton Hall, 2nd Floor, 16 Victoria Avenue
(P.O. Box 130), Port of Spain, Trinidad, West Indies
Telephone: (1 868) 623 4813, 623 8438
Fax: (1 868) 623 4332
E-mail: unicpos@opus.co.tt
Services to: Trinidad and Tobago, Antigua and Barbuda, Bahamas, Barba-
dos, Belize, Dominica, Saint Kitts and Nevis, Grenada, Guyana, Jamaica,
Saint Lucia, Netherlands Antilles, Saint Vincent and the Grenadines, Suriname

## Rio de Janeiro

United Nations Information Centre, Palácio Itamaraty, Av. Marechal Floriano
196, 20080-002 Rio de Janeiro, RJ Brazil
Telephone: (55 21) 253 2211
Fax: (55 21) 233 5753
E-mail: nacoes.unidas@openlink.com.br
Services to: Brazil

# San Salvador

United Nations Information Centre (temporarily inactive)
Edificio Escalón, 2o. Piso, Paseo General Escalón y 87 Avenida Norte, Colonia
Escalón (P.O. Box 2157), San Salvador, El Salvador
Telephone: (503) 279 1925 (UNDP)
Fax: (503) 279 1929 (UNDP)
Services to: El Salvador

# Santa Fé de Bogotá

United Nations Information Centre, Calle 100 No. 8A-55, Of. 815 (P.O. Box
058964), Santa Fé de Bogotá 2, Colombia
Telephone: (57 1) 257 6044/7576/7916/6065
Fax: (57 1) 257 7936
E-mail: uniccol@mbox.unicc.org        (Internet: www.onucolombia.org)
Services to: Colombia, Ecuador, Venezuela

# Santiago

United Nations Information Service, Edificio Naciones Unidas, Comisión
Económica para América Latina y el Caribe, Avenida Dag Hammarskjöld, Casilla
179-D, Santiago, Chile
Telephone: (56 2) 210 2000, 210 2371, 210 2202
Fax: (56 2) 208 1947/208 0252 (ECLAC)
E-mail: dpisantiago@eclac.cl        (Internet: www.eclac.org/prensa)
Services to: Chile, Economic Commission for Latin America and the Carib-
bean

# Washington, D.C.

United Nations Information Centre, 1775 K Street, N.W., Suite 400, Washington,
D.C. 20006, United States
Telephone: (202) 331 8670
Fax: (202) 331 9191, 331 9155
E-mail: dpi-washington@un.org        (Internet: www.unicwash.org)
Services to: United States of America

# ASIA AND THE PACIFIC

# Bangkok

United Nations Information Service, United Nations Economic and Social Com-
mission for Asia and the Pacific (ESCAP), United Nations Building, Rajdamnern
Avenue Bangkok 10200, Thailand
Telephone: (66 2) 288 1866, 288 1861
Fax: (66 2) 288 1052
E-mail: unisbkk.unescap@un.org        (Internet: www.unescap.org.unis)
Services to: Thailand, Cambodia, Lao People's Democratic Republic, Ma-
laysia, Singapore, Socialist Republic of Viet Nam, Hong Kong, ESCAP

## Beirut

United Nations Information Service, Riad El Solh Square (P.O. Box No.11-8575), Beirut, Lebanon
Telephone: (961 1) 981 301/311/401
Fax: (961 1) 981 516
E-mail: nfriji@escwa.org.lb    (Internet: www.escwa.org.lb/unis)
Services to: Jordan, Lebanon, Kuwait, Syrian Arab Republic, Economic and Social Commission for Western Asia

## Colombo

United Nations Information Centre, 202-204 Bauddhaloka Mawatha (P.O. Box 1505), Colombo 7, Sri Lanka
Telephone: (94 1) 580 691
Fax: (94 1) 581 116 (UNDP)
E-mail: anusha.atukorale@undp.org
Services to: Sri Lanka

## Dhaka

United Nations Information Centre, IDB Bhaban (14$^{th}$ floor) Begum Rokeya Sharani, Sher-e-Bangla Nagar, (P.O. Box 3658), Dhaka 1000, Bangladesh
Telephone: (880 2) 8117 868/8117 898
Fax: (880 2) 812 343
E-mail: unicdha@citechco.net
Services to: Bangladesh

## Islamabad

United Nations Information Centre, House No. 26, 88th Street, G-6/3 (P.O. Box 1107), Islamabad, Pakistan
Telephone: (92 51) 270 610/812 012/213 553, (92 51) 823 976
Fax: (92 51) 271 856
E-mail: unic@paknet2ptc.pk    (Internet: www.un.org.pk/unic)
Services to: Pakistan

## Jakarta

United Nations Information Centre, Gedung Dewan Pers, 5th Floor, 32-34 Jalan Kebon Sirih, Jakarta, Indonesia
Telephone: (62 21) 380 0292/385 4550
Fax: (62 21) 380 0274
E-mail: unicjak@rad.net.id
Services to: Indonesia

## Kabul

United Nations Information Centre (temporarily inactive)
Shah Mahmoud Ghazi Watt (P.O. Box 5), Kabul, Afghanistan
Telephone: 24437/22684
Services to: Afghanistan

## Kathmandu

United Nations Information Centre, (P.O. Box 107) Pulchowk, Patan, Kathmandu, Nepal
Telephone: (977 1) 524 366
Fax: (977 1) 543 723
E-mail: registry.np@undp.org
Services to: Nepal

## Manama

United Nations Information Centre, Villa 131, Road 2803, Segaya (P.O. Box 26004), Manama 328, Bahrain
Telephone: (973) 231 046
Fax: (973) 270 749
E-mail: unic@balteco.com.bh
Services to: Bahrain, Qatar, United Arab Emirates

## Manila

United Nations Information Centre, NEDA Building, 106 Amorsolo Street, Legaspi Village, Makati City (P.O. Box 7285 ADC (DAPO) Pasay City), Metro Manila, Philippines
Telephone: (63 2) 892 0611 through 25, Exts. 255 258, 893 3882; 892 4445/4483
Fax: (63 2) 816 3011, 817 8539
E-mail: unic-mla@philonline.com.ph
Services to: Philippines, Papua New Guinea, Solomon Islands

## New Delhi

United Nations Information Centre, 55 Lodi Estate, New Delhi-110003, India
Telephone: (91 11) 462 34 39 and 462 88 77
Fax: (91 11) 462 0293
E-mail: feodor@giasdl01.vsnl.net.in      (Internet: www.unic.org.in)
Services to: India, Bhutan

## Sana'a

United Nations Information Centre, Handhal Street, 4, Al-Boniya Area (P.O. Box 237), Sana'a, Republic of Yemen
Telephone: (967 1) 274 000/041
Fax: (967 1) 274 043
E-mail: unicyem@y.net.ye
Services to: Yemen

## Sydney

United Nations Information Centre, 46-48 York Street, 5th Floor (GPO Box 4045), Sydney, NSW, 2001 Australia
Telephone: (61 2) 9262-5111
Fax: (61 2) 9262 5886
E-mail: unsyd@ozemail.com.au
Services to: Australia, Fiji, Kiribati, Nauru, New Zealand, Tonga, Tuvalu, Vanuatu, Western Samoa

## Tehran

United Nations Information Centre, 185 Ghaem Magham Farahani Ave, Tehran 15868 (P.O. Box 15875-4557, Tehran), Islamic Republic of Iran
Telephone: (98 21) 873 1534
Fax: (98 21) 204 4523
E-mail: iali@unic.un.org.ir    (Internet: http://195.146.36.16/unic_Tehran/unic.htm)
Services to: Iran

## Tokyo

United Nations Information Centre, UNU Building, 8th Floor, 53-70, Jingumae 5-chome, Shibuya-ku, Tokyo 150, Japan
Telephone: (81 3) 5467 4451/4454
Fax: (81 3) 5467 4455
E-mail: unictok@blue.ocn.ne.jp    (Internet: www.unic.or.jp)
Services to: Japan

## Yangon

United Nations Information Centre, 6 Natmauk Road (P.O. Box 230), Yangon, Myanmar
Telephone: (95 1) 292 619, 292 622
Fax: (95 1) 544 531
E-mail: unic.myanmar@undp.org
Services to: Myanmar

# EUROPE

## Ankara

United Nations Information Centre, 197 Atatürk Bulvari, Ankara, Turkey
Telephone: (90 312) 426 8113
Fax: (90 312) 468 9719
E-mail: unic@un.org.tr    (Internet: www.un.org.tr/unic.html)
Services to: Turkey

## Athens

United Nations Information Centre, 36 Amalias Avenue GR-10558 Athens, Greece
Telephone: (30 1) 523 0640
Fax:(30 1) 523 3639
E-mail: unicgre@mbow.unicc.org    (Internet: www.unic.gr)
Services to: Greece, Cyprus, Israel

## Bonn

United Nations Information Centre, Haus Carstanjen, Martin-Luther-King-Strasse 8, D-53175 Bonn, Germany
Telephone: (49 228) 815 277
Fax: (49 228) 815 2777
E-mail: unic@uno.de    (Internet: www.uno.de)
Services to: Germany

## Brussels

United Nations Information Centre and Liaison Office with the European Community, 14 rue Montoyer, UN House, 1000 Brussels, Belgium
Telephone: (32 2) 289 2895/2890
Fax: (32 2) 502 4061
E-mail: unicbel@be.psinet.com    (Internet: www.uno.be)
Services to: Belgium, Luxembourg, the Netherlands

## Bucharest

United Nations Information Centre, 16 Aurel Vlaicu (P.O.Box 1-701), Bucharest, Romania
Telephone: (40 1) 211 32 42, 211 88 28, 211 35 06
Fax: (40 1) 211 35 06
E-mail: cristina.ion@undp.ro
Services to: Romania

## Copenhagen

United Nations Information Centre, Centre Midtermolen 3, DK-2100 Copenhagen, Denmark
Telephone: (45) 35 46 73 00
Fax: (45) 35 46 73 01
E-mail: unic@un.dk    (Internet: www.un.dk)
Services to: Denmark, Finland, Iceland, Norway, Sweden

## Geneva

United Nations Information Service, UN Office at Geneva, Palais des Nations, 1211 Geneva 10, Switzerland
Telephone: (41 22) 917 2300; 917 2302; 917 2325
Fax: (41 22) 917 0030, 917 0073
E-mail: presse_geneve@unog.ch    (Internet: www.unog.ch/unis/unis1.htm)
Services to: Switzerland, Bulgaria

## Lisbon

United Nations Information Centre, Rua Latino Coelho, 1, Edificio Aviz, Bloco A-1, 10°, 1050-132 Lisboa, Portugal
Telephone: (351) 21 319 0790
Fax: (351) 21 352 0559
E-mail: lisbon@ccmail.unicc.org    (Internet: www.onuportugal.pt)
Services to: Portugal

## London

United Nations Information Centre, Millbank Tower (21st floor), 21-24 Millbank, London SW1P 4QH, United Kingdom
Telephone: (44 171) 630 1981
Fax: (44 171) 976 6478
E-mail: info@uniclondon.org    (Internet: www.unitednations.org.uk)
Services to: United Kingdom, Ireland

## Madrid

United Nations Information Centre, Avenida General Perón, 32-1 (P.O. Box 3400), 28020 Madrid, Spain
Telephone: (34 91) 555 8087/555 8142
Fax: (34 91) 597 1231
E-mail: unicspa@mbox.unicc.org     (Internet: www.onu.org)
Services to: Spain

## Moscow

United Nations Information Centre, 4/16 Glazovsky Per, Moscow 121002, Russian Federation
Telephone: (7 095) 241 2894, (7 095) 241 2537
Fax: (7 095) 230 2138
E-mail: dpi_moscow@unic.ru     (Internet: www.unic.ru)
Services to: Russian Federation

## Paris

United Nations Information Centre, 1 rue Miollis, 75732, Paris Cedex 15, France
Telephone: (33 1) 45 68 10 00
Fax: (33 1) 43 06 46 78
E-mail: unic.paris@unesco.org     (Internet: www.onu.fr)
Services to: France

## Prague

United Nations Information Centre, Panska 5, 11000 Prague 1, Czech Republic
Telephone: (420 2) 24 21 10 49
Fax: (420 2) 24 22 54 25
E-mail: unicprg@terminal.cz     (Internet: www.unicprague.cz)
Services to: Czech Republic

## Rome

United Nations Information Centre, Palazzetto Venezia, Piazza San Marco 50, 00186 Rome, Italy
Telephone: (39 6) 678 9907
Fax: (39 06) 679 3337
E-mail: onuitalia@onuitalia.it     (Internet: www.onuitalia.it)
Services to: Italy, Holy See, Malta, San Marino

## Vienna

United Nations Information Service, Vienna International Centre, Wagramer Strasse 5, A-1220 Vienna (UN Office at Vienna, P.O. Box 500, A-1400 Vienna), Austria
Telephone: (43 1) 26060 4666
Fax: (43 1) 26060 5899
E-mail: UNIS@unis.un.or.at     (Internet: www.unis.unvienna.org)
Services to: Austria, Hungary, Slovakia

## Warsaw

United Nations Information Centre, Al. Niepodleglosci 186, 00-608 Warszawa
(P.O. Box 1, 02-514 Warsaw 12), Poland
Telephone: (48 22) 25 57 84
Fax: (48 22) 825 49 58
E-mail: registry.pl@undp.org      (Internet: www.unic.un.org.pl)
Services to: Poland

# OFFICES IN THE COMMONWEALTH OF
# INDEPENDENT STATES AND ERITREA

## Almaty

United Nations Office, c/o KIMEP, 4 Abai Avenue, 480100 Almaty, Kazakhstan
Telephone: (7 3272) 642 618/480/271
Fax: (7 3272) 642 608
E-mail: vp@un.almaty.kz
Services to: Kazakhstan

## Asmara

United Nations Office, Andinet Street, Zone 4 Admin. 07
Airport Road, (near Expo), Asmara, Eritrea
Telephone: (291 1) 18 11 43/18 21 66
Fax: (291 1) 18 10 81
E-mail: fo.eri@undp.org
Services to: Eritrea

## Baku

United Nations Office, 3 UN 50$^{th}$ Anniversary, Baku 1, Baku, Azerbaijan
Telephone: (99412) 98 98 88/98 16 28/98 16 89
Fax: (99412) 98 32 35
E-mail: office@un.azeri.com
Services to: Azerbaijan

## Kiev

United Nations Office, 1 Klovsky Uzviz, 1, Kiev 252021, Ukraine
Telephone: (380 44) 253 93 63
Fax: (380 44) 293 26 07
E-mail: registry@un.kiev.ua      (Internet: www.un.kiev.ua)
Services to: Ukraine

## Minsk

United Nations Office, 17 Kirov Street, 6th Floor 220000 Minsk, Belarus
Telephone: (375 172) 27 48 76, 27 81 49, 27 45 27
Fax: (375 172) 26 03 40
E-mail: victor.radivinovski@undp.org      (Internet: www.un.minsk.by)
Services to: Belarus

## Tashkent

United Nations Office, 4 Taras Shevchenko St., Tashkent 700029, Uzbekistan
Telephone: (998 71) 133 0977/139 4835
Fax: (998 71) 120 6291/133 6965
E-mail: fouzb@fouzb.undp.org      (Internet: www.undp.uz)
Services to: Uzbekistan

## Tbilisi

United Nations Office, Eristavi St. 9, Tbilisi 380079, Republic of Georgia
Telephone: (995 32) 99 85 58; 25 11 26/28/29/31
Fax: (1 995 32) 2502 71 or 72
E-mail: fo.geo@undp.org.ge
Services to: Georgia

## Yerevan

United Nations Office, 14 Karl Libknekht Street, 1st floor, 375001 Yerevan, Armenia
Telephone: (374 2) 151 647
Fax: (374 2) 151 647
E-mail: dpiarm@arminco.com      (Internet: www.undpi.am)
Services to: Armenia

# FOR FURTHER READING

This selection of United Nations publications and products can be obtained from the Organization, some at no charge and other as sales items. The letters in parentheses at the end of each entry refer to where the publications can be obtained (*see Where to Order, page 330*).

## Periodicals

**UN Chronicle.** UN/DPI. E/F. Annual subscription $20 (a)
Quarterly magazine providing coverage of the work of the UN and its agencies.

**Africa Recovery.** UN/DPI. E/F. Annual subscription: $20 (a)
Quarterly magazine covering issues of economic and social reform in Africa and international cooperation for development.

**Development Update.** UN/DPI. Free
Bi-monthly newsletter with updates on the development activities of the UN system.

## General

**Charter of the United Nations.** UN/DPI. DPI/511. ISBN 92-1-002025-1. E/A/C/F/R/S. $3

**Yearbook of the United Nations.** E. $150 (a)
The most comprehensive reference book on all aspects of the work of the UN system. Published annually, it provides a detailed account of UN activities in a given calendar year.

**Discovering the United Nations.** UN/DPI. DPI/2006. E. $5 (a)
Written especially for children, this booklet teaches about the UN through questions and answers, activity proposals and quizzes.

**Understanding the United Nations. The Official Guidebook.** UN/DPI. 80 pp. Sales No. E.97.I.8. ISBN: 92-1-100536-1. E. $14.95 (a)
A photographic tour of the UN daily working, at Headquarters and all over the world.

**Image and Reality: Questions and Answers about the United Nations.** UN/DPI. 1999. 50 pp. DPI/2003. Sales No. E.99.I.7. ISBN: 92-1-100801-8. E/C/F/S. $5 (a)
Provides simple answers to some of the most frequently asked questions about the UN.

**"We the Peoples." The Role of the United Nations in the 21st Century,** by Secretary-General Kofi Annan. 2000. 80pp. Sales No. 00.I.16. ISBN: 9211008441. E/F. $10.00 (a)
Examines the challenges facing the world community and outlines a vision for the UN in the new century.

**The United Nations in Our Daily Lives**. 1998. 116 pp. Sales No. E.98.I.11. ISBN: 92-1-1-100654-6. E/F. $5.00 (a)

In a story format designed for a general audience, illustrates the many ways in which the UN is a part of everyone's life and how much we rely on its programmes.

## Annual reports

**Report of the Secretary-General on the Work of the Organization**, UN/DPI. E/A/C/F/R/S (a)

Outlines the activities of the United Nations system in the previous 12 months.

**World Economic and Social Survey: Trends and Policies in the World Economy.** United Nations. E/F/S. $55 (a)

Authoritative and reliable, it offers unique insight and commentary on current trends and policies in the world economy. Issued by the UN Department of Economic and Social Affairs.

**Trade and Development Report.** UN Conference on Trade and Development. E/F. $45 (a)

It makes compelling reading for those seeking answers to some of the most pressing policy challenges in today's rapidly changing global economy.

**World Investment Report.** UN Conference on Trade and Development. E. $49 (a)

The most up-to-date and comprehensive source of information as well as analysis regarding foreign direct investment.

**The Least Developed Countries Report.** UN Conference on Trade and Development. E/F. $45 (a)

The most comprehensive and authoritative source of socio-economic analysis and data on the world's 48 least developed countries.

**Human Development Report.** UN Development Programme. E/F/S/A/R. $22.95 (also available in CD-ROM: $29.95) (a)

A comprehensive guide to global human development: it contains thought-provoking analyses of major issues, updated Human Development Indicators that compare the relative levels of human development of over 175 countries, and agendas to help transform development priorities.

**UNDP Poverty Report.** UN Development Programme. E/F/S. $15 (a)

Reviews the world situation and documents efforts to overcome global poverty.

**The State of the World's Children.** UNICEF. E/F/S/A and other languages. $12.95. Free summary available from UNICEF (a)

Draws international attention to the challenges facing children and presses for action to promote their well-being.

**The Progress of Nations.** UNICEF. E/F/S. $6.95 (a)

The nations of the world ranked according to their achievements in child health, nutrition, education, water and sanitation, and progress for women.

**The State of the World Population.** UN Population Fund. E/F/S/A and other languages. $12.50 (a)
Annual report on population issues and their impact on world development.

**World Health Report.** World Health Organization. Geneva. E/F/S/A/C/R. (b)
Takes an expert look at health trends, assesses the global situation and predicts how health conditions, diseases, and the tools for managing them will evolve.

**World Development Report.** World Bank/Oxford University Press. $25.95. E/F/S. (c)
Produced by the World Bank, it focuses on major development issues facing policy-makers worldwide. Includes selected World Development Indicators.

**World Economic Outlook.** International Monetary Fund. E/F/S/A. (D)
Global economic survey published twice a year (May and October).

## Peace and security

**The Blue Helmets.** UN/DPI. 1996. 820 pages. DPI/1800. Sales No. E.96.I.14. ISBN: 92-1-100611-2. E/F. $29.95 (a)
A review of UN peacekeeping, with a comprehensive account of peacekeeping operations from their inception in 1948 up to early 1996.

**UN Peacekeeping: 50 Years (1948-1998).** UN/DPI. 1998. 88 pages. DPI/2004. E/F/S.
An overview of five decades of peacekeeping operations.

**United Nations Disarmament Yearbook.** E. $55 (a)
Annual publication reviewing the main developments and negotiations during the year in all areas of disarmament

## Economic and Social

**The World's Women 2000: Trends and Statistics.** 2000. 200 pp. Sales No. E. 00.XVII.14. ISBN: 92-1-161428-7. $16.95. (a)
A unique compilation of the latest data documenting progress for women worldwide in six areas: health, human rights and political decision-making, and families.

**Global Environment Outlook 2000.** UNEP/Earthscan Publications Ltd. 432 pp. Sales No: E. 00.III.D.96. ISBN: 1853835889. $35.00 (a)
The UN Environment Programme's comprehensive review and analysis of environmental conditions around the world.

**Agenda 21: The UN Programme of Action from Rio.** UN/DPI. 1992. 294 pages. DPI/1344. Sales No. E.93.I.11. ISBN: 92-1-100509-4. E/F/S. $25. (a)
The complete text of the recommendations adopted at the 1992 Earth Summit in Rio de Janeiro, which set out a comprehensive blueprint for achieving sustainable development.

**The World Conferences - Developing Priorities for the 21st Century.** UN/DPI. 1997. 112 pp. Sales No. E.97.I.5. ISBN: 92-1-100631-7. E/F/S. $12.00 (a)

Provides a broad perspective on the recommendations and current actions flowing from the conferences on Children, Human Rights, Social Development, Crime, Environment, Women, Population, Food, Human Settlements, Small Islands, Trade and Natural Disasters.

**World Labour Report 2000. Income security and social protection in a changing world.** International Labour Office. 2000. 321 pp. ISBN: 92-2-110831-7. E/F/S. $34.95. (e)

Examines the changing context in which women and men are trying to achieve income security for themselves and their families.

## Human Rights

**Human Rights Today: a United Nations Priority.** UN/DPI. 1998. 74 pp. Sales E.98.I.22. ISBN: 92-1-100796-6. E/F/S.

Outlines United Nations action in the field to ensure rights for all, and provides a blueprint of the work of the various intergovernmental human rights bodies.

**Human Rights: A Compilation of International Instruments.** 950 pp. Sales No. 94.XIV.1. ISBN: 92-1-154099-2. E/F/S. $55. (a)

This two-volume set constitutes a comprehensive catalogue of the existing human rights instruments adopted at both universal and regional levels.

## WHERE TO ORDER

(a)    For North America, Latin America and the Caribbean and Asia and the Pacific: United Nations Publications, Room DC2-853, 2 UN Plaza, New York, NY 10017, USA. Telephone: (212) 963 8302, Toll Free 1 800 253 9646 (North America only). Fax: (212) 963 3489. E-mail: publications@un.org. Internet: www.un.org/publications.

For Europe, Africa and the Middle East: United Nations Publications, Sales Office and Bookshop, CH-1211, Geneva 10, Switzerland. Telephone: (41 22) 917 2614, Fax: (41 22) 917 0027, E-mail: unpubli@unog.ch. Internet: www.un.org/publications.

(b)    World Health Organization (WHO):

Distribution and Sales, 20 Avenue Appia, CH 1211 Geneva 27, Switzerland.

Tel.: (41 22) 791 2476. Fax: (41 22) 791 4857. E-mail: publications@who.ch

In the USA: WHO Publications, 49 Sheridan Ave., Albany, NY 12210. Tel: (518) 436 9686, E-mail: QCORP@compuserve.com.

(c)    World Bank:

The World Bank, P.O. Box 960, Herndon, VA 20172-0960, USA. Tel. (703) 661 1580 or (800) 645 7247. Fax (703) 661 1501. E-mail: books@worldbank.org

(d)    International Monetary Fund (IMF)

Publication Services, Catalog Orders, 700 19th Street, NW, Washington, D.C. 20431, U.S.A. Tel.: (202) 623 7430. Fax: (202) 623 7201. E-mail: pubweb@imf.org

**(e)**   International Labour Office (ILO):
ILO Publications, 4 route des Morillons, CH-1211 Geneva 22, Switzerland.
Tel.: (41 22) 799 7301. Fax: (41 22) 798 6358.
E-mail: pubvente@ilo.org

*United Nations Bookshops*

United Nations, Concourse Level, First Ave. & 42nd St., New York, NY 10017. Tel.: (212) 963 7680, 1 800 553 3210 (US and Canada), Fax: (212) 963 4910, E-mail: bookshop@un.org

United Nations, Palais des Nations, Door 40 and Door 6, CH-1211 Geneva 10, Switzerland, Tel.: (41 22) 917 2613/14, Fax: (41 22) 917 0027, E-mail: unipubli@unog.ch

Immunization, 166, 168, 182
IMO, 56–57, 149–150, 204–205
technical cooperation, 150
Indigenous people
human rights, 237–238
International Decade, 238
International Year, 238
Permanent Forum, 238
Industrial development, 60–61, 145–146
Inequality among countries, 128, 130–131, 157–158, 160
Informatics, 192–193
Information centres, services and offices, 30, 225, 313–326
INFOTERRA, 198
Inmarsat, 150
INSTRAW, 47, 180–181, 235
Intellectual property, 59–60, 153–154
conventions, 154
Inter-Agency Committee on Women and Gender Equality, 179
Inter-Agency Standing Committee, 246, 248
Intergovernmental Oceanographic Commission, 191
Intergovernmental Panel on Climate Change (IPCC), 200, 207
International Atomic Energy Agency. See IAEA
International Bank for Reconstruction and Development (IBRD). See World Bank
International Centre for Settlement of Investment Disputes (ICSID), 55
International Centre for Theoretical Physics, 211
International Civil Aviation Organization, 56, 148–149
International Civilian Mission in Haiti (MICIVIH), 94–95
International Civilian Support Mission in Haiti, 94–95
International Court of Justice. See ICJ
International Criminal Court, 269

International Criminal Tribunal for Rwanda (ICTR), 36, 268–269
International Criminal Tribunal for the former Yugoslavia (ICTY), 36, 268
International days, decades, weeks and years. See under subjects
International Development Association (IDA), 53–54, 135, 162–163
International Finance Corporation (IFC), 54, 135, 138–139
International Fund for Agricultural Development. See IFAD
International Labour Conference, 49, 230
International Labour Organization. See ILO
International law, 25–26
codification, 262–263
International Law Commission, 262–263
International Maritime Academy, 57
International Maritime Law Institute, 57
International Maritime Organization. See IMO
International Monetary Fund. See IMF
International Narcotics Control Board, 187–188
International Peace Conference, 3
International Register of Potentially Toxic Chemicals (IRPTC), 199
International Research and Training Institute for the Advancement of Women, 47, 180–181, 235
International Seabed Authority, 266–267
International security, 67–109
International Telecommunication Union, 3, 57–58, 151–152
International Trade Centre UNCTAD/WTO, 37, 142
International Tribunal for the Law of the Sea, 267

International Trusteeship System, 275–276
Internet, 151, 154, 177, 193
Intervention, 71
Iraq
  humanitarian assistance, 31, 101–102
  peacekeeping operations, 99–102
ITC, 37, 142
ITU, 3, 57–58, 151–152

## J

Jammu and Kashmir, 98–99
Joint UN Programme on HIV/AIDS (UNAIDS), 134, 167

## K

Kuwait
  peacekeeping operations, 99–102

## L

Labour, 49–50, 146–148, 230–231
  conventions, 231
  rights, 230–231
Landlocked developing countries, 131
Landmines, 110, 117–118
  1997 Ottawa Convention, 110, 118
  clearance, 117
Law of the sea, 265–267
League of Nations, 3
Least developed countries, 129, 131
Lebanon
  peacekeeping operations, 96–97
Legal Committee (6th Committee), 8
Legal Counsel, 26
Lifelong education, 173
Loans, 52–56
  for development, 135–138, 160, 162, 164

## M

Marine environment, 198–199, 204–205, 211
  conventions, 198
Maternal health, 165
Meteorology, 58–59, 156, 201, 205–208
Middle East
  peace process, 97–98
  peacekeeping operations, 95–98
Migrant workers
  1990 Convention, 221, 240
Millennium Declaration, 128, 160, 167, 173
  targets, 161
Minorities
  human rights, 222, 237
Money laundering, 190
Multilateral Investment Guarantee Agency (MIGA), 54, 136, 138–139

## N

Namibia, 280–281
Natural resources, 195, 208–210
New technologies, 151, 180, 193
Nobel Peace Prize, 41, 43, 50
Non-governmental organizations, 12
Non-self-governing territories, 276–280
Nuclear safety, 113–114, 210–211
Nuclear weapons, 112–116
  1968 Non-Proliferation Treaty (NPT), 110, 113
  1996 Comprehensive Test-Ban Treaty (CTBT), 62, 110, 113
  safeguards, 113–114
  treaties and agreements, 110–111, 113–114
  verification, 114
Nuclear-weapon-free zones, 114